I LIKE IKE

SCHOLASTIC

ENCYCLOPEDIA
✦✦✦ OF THE ✦✦✦
PRESIDENTS
And Their Times

DAVID RUBEL

WITH A FOREWORD
BY JAMES M. McPHERSON

SCHOLASTIC

For Julia

Design: Jon Glick/mouse+tiger design
Maps: Jon Glick

Photo Researchers: Diane Hamilton, Nora E. Malek, Brooke Palmer, Erika Rubel, Julia Rubel
Proofreader: Laura Jorstad

We would like to thank Allan Shrem and Lee Schogel of the World Collectible Center for kindly allowing us access to their collection of presidential campaign memorabilia.

Copyright © 1994 by Scholastic Inc.
Updated 1997, 2001, 2005, 2009.

PHOTO CREDITS
All images are from the Library of Congress, the National Archives, and Agincourt Press, except: Guilford Court House National Military Park: 21 (bottom); Levi Strauss: 67 (top); Utah Division of State History: 81 (bottom); American Heritage Center, University of Wyoming: 86 (bottom); Arizona Historical Society/Tucson: 94 (bottom); Kansas State Historical Society: 102 (bottom); Hogan Jazz Archive: 111 (bottom); World Collectible Center: 140 (top), 164 (bottom), 185 (bottom), 204 (bottom); National Archives of Canada: 155 (bottom); Soviet Life: 169 (bottom); National Aeronautics and Space Administration: 174 (bottom), 181 (bottom), 197 (bottom); Veterans of Foreign Wars of the United States: 187 (bottom); Con Edison: 191 (top); Dori Jacobson/Sophia Smith Collection/Smith College: 191 (bottom); Apple Computer, Inc.: 195 (bottom); National Safe Kids Campaign: 199 (top); Earth Times: 201 (bottom); South African Department of Foreign Affairs: 203 (top); Magic Johnson Foundation: 203 (bottom); Oklahoma City National Memorial: 207; Centers for Disease Control and Prevention: 210 (top); National Human Genome Research Institute: 210 (bottom); AP/Wide World Photos: 213 (bottom), 217 (bottom), 218, 219, 221 (bottom); White House Historical Association: 227 (bottom); Rutherford Hayes Presidential Center: 230; Joyce C. Naltchayan/The White House: 235.

Library of Congress Cataloging-in-Publication Data available.

ISBN-13: 978-0-545-10149-3
ISBN-10: 0-545-10149-2

10 9 8 7 6 5 4 3 2 1   09 10 11 12 13

Printed in the U.S.A.   56
First printing, January 2009

TABLE OF CONTENTS

FOREWORD
by James M. McPherson

Suppose you woke up one morning and didn't remember who you were. You couldn't recognize your mother and father. Nothing in your house seemed familiar. You couldn't remember what you did yesterday, or the day before, or any other time. You would be suffering from a condition called amnesia—the total loss of memory. You wouldn't know anything about your own history. With such a condition, you would have to start all over again to learn how to get along in the world.

The same problem of amnesia would be the condition of a society that didn't know its own history. People would remember nothing about their past or how their country got to be the way it is today. Nobody would have a clue how to get along and how to make things work. That is why it is important to study history. We need to know the past so that we can understand where we are, *who* we are, in the present. We also need to know the past so that we can prepare for the future.

When we study American history, we often focus on the achievements of important people in all walks of life: inventors, civil rights leaders, artists and musicians, military commanders, sports heroes, and so on. Above all, we focus on the forty-three people who have been president of the United States since George Washington was first elected to that office in 1789. The president is the most important official in our national government. Congress makes the laws and the Supreme Court interprets them, but it is the president who enforces the laws and appoints other government officials, including the justices of the Supreme Court. The president is also the commander in chief of the armed forces, a key position in times of war. Thirteen of the forty-three presidents have led the country during major wars in our history.

This book tells the stories of these forty-three presidents. (Because Grover Cleveland was elected for two separate terms, he is counted twice to make a total of forty-four presidential administrations.) Important events happened during all of their administrations. Not all of the events were political. There were key inventions like the electric lightbulb, the automobile, the phonograph and movies, radio and television, the airplane, and the computer that have changed the way we live. World wars

with enormous loss of life took place. Baseball, football, and other sports developed and grew in popularity. Terrible disasters like the sinking of the *Titanic* and the terrorist attacks on the World Trade Center and the Pentagon took place. Improvements in medicine and public health made it possible for Americans to live longer and better lives. Slavery was abolished. Minority groups and women earned equal constitutional rights and began to move toward equal opportunities. The United States experienced a transformation from a country on the margins of the North Atlantic to the most powerful nation in the world.

This attractive, readable, and informative book describes all of these events and much more. It provides colorful biographies of all the presidents and tells what happened during each of their terms in office. You will also learn the answers to many interesting questions. Who was the first president to live in the White House? How did the White House get its name? Where did the nickname *Uncle Sam* for the U.S. government come from? Who was the first president to be photographed? To ride a train? To fly in an airplane? To wear a beard? Who was the only president who never married? The only one to get married in the White House? Which president was the first to have a telephone in the White House? To have electric lights? Which president first invited children to an Easter egg roll on the White House lawn? Which president started the tradition of throwing out the first ball to start the major league baseball season? Which president was the first to hold a press conference? To speak on the radio? To appear on television? Who was the first president who had been a Boy Scout? Which president first appointed a woman as a Supreme Court justice?

Some of the answers may surprise you. Some will surprise your parents and maybe even your teachers. This book is packed full of fascinating stories. Some of them are stranger than fiction. But they are all true. You will spend many wonderful hours reading this book—and you will never be bored. Best of all, you will never suffer from historical amnesia. When you wake up on future mornings, you will know what country you are living in and how it got to be the way it is. You will also be better prepared to take your place in the world as you grow up.

HOW TO USE THIS BOOK

This book tells the story of the United States through its presidents. It is organized by year, with one page for each year that there has been a president. The year is marked on the top outside corner of each page. The book begins in 1789 and ends for now in 2009. The pages for each president correspond to the years of his presidency. However, not every event described is placed on the same page as the year in which it happened; the one-page-per-year format is just a useful way to give a sense of time as it passes.

The outside column of each page describes the political history of the presidency—the laws that were passed, the wars that were fought, the treaties that were signed, and so on. Meanwhile, the inside column is devoted to the story of ordinary Americans. Words and pictures describe developments in the arts, medicine, and science, as well as trends in daily life.

HOW TO LOOK UP . . .

★**A PRESIDENT**—Look up the president's name in the Table of Contents and turn to the page listed.

★**WHO WAS PRESIDENT DURING A PARTICULAR YEAR**—Find the page corresponding to that year. At the bottom of the page, you will find the president's name and his years in office.

★**PRESIDENTIAL ELECTION RESULTS**—A chart listing the results of every presidential election begins on page 222.

★**IMPORTANT EVENTS AND PEOPLE**—Look up the subject in the index at the back of the book. The index will list the numbers of the pages on which that event or person is discussed.

WORDS IN RED mean that a subject is discussed in greater detail elsewhere in the book. To find out where, look up the subject in the index. The most detailed entry will also be marked in red.

★ **STATISTICS ABOUT EACH PRESIDENT** The birth date, birthplace, death date, political party, vice president, first lady, children, and nickname of each president are listed on the first page of that president's term.

★ **MANIFEST DESTINY MAPS** These show the growth of the United States. The first time each state appears, it is highlighted in red and labeled with the year of its admission. States already admitted to the Union are shown in pink. Territories not yet admitted are shown in green.

★ **PRESIDENTIAL CAMPAIGNS** To find out about a particular campaign, turn to the page corresponding to the year of the campaign in which you are interested.

BORN: FEBRUARY 22, 1732

BIRTHPLACE: POPE'S CREEK, VA.

DIED: DECEMBER 14, 1799

PARTY: FEDERALIST

VICE PRESIDENT: JOHN ADAMS

FIRST LADY: MARTHA DANDRIDGE CUSTIS

STEPCHILDREN: JOHN PARKE CUSTIS, MARTHA PARKE CUSTIS

NICKNAME: FATHER OF HIS COUNTRY

THE FIRST PRESIDENT TO APPEAR ON A POSTAGE STAMP.

GEORGE WASHINGTON

1st President
★
1789 to 1797

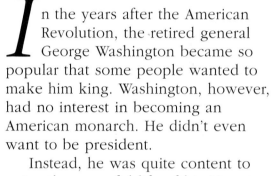

I n the years after the American Revolution, the retired general George Washington became so popular that some people wanted to make him king. Washington, however, had no interest in becoming an American monarch. He didn't even want to be president.

Instead, he was quite content to enjoy the peaceful life of his Mount Vernon, Virginia, estate. But the new nation that he had helped to create needed him.

When the American colonies declared their independence from Great Britain in 1776, their first task was to win the Revolutionary War. But they also had to create a new form of government. Great Britain was ruled by a king, but most Americans wanted to be governed by leaders elected by the people.

The first plan for such a government was set forth in 1777 in the Articles of Confederation. This plan included some features that linked the states together,

BILL OF RIGHTS BECOMES PART OF U.S. CONSTITUTION

RICHMOND, December 15, 1791— Today, the Virginia state legislature ratified the first ten amendments to the U.S. Constitution. This raised the number of states ratifying the amendments to the three-quarters required by the Constitution.

The framers of the Constitution had divided the new central government into three branches so that each branch could check and balance the others. However, they had done little to protect the individual rights of the citizens. Critics of the Constitution had vowed to fight its ratification unless individual liberties were also spelled out clearly.

The first ten amendments, known as the Bill of Rights, guar-antee to all citizens the freedoms of speech, religion, and assembly. They also protect citizens from having to testify against themselves and from having their homes searched without cause.

Most Americans trust George Washington, but they have been worried about giving too much power to any one person. History contains many examples of modest people being corrupted by power. The Bill of Rights is intended to protect the rights of every citizen no matter who becomes president.

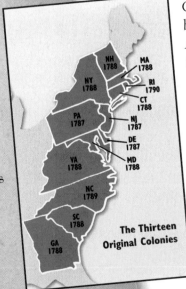

NH 1788
MA 1788
NY 1788
RI 1790
CT 1788
PA 1787
NJ 1787
DE 1787
VA 1788
MD 1788
NC 1789
SC 1788
GA 1788

The Thirteen Original Colonies

but it lacked a strong central government that could compel action. Individual states still passed their own laws, issued their own money, and levied their own taxes.

The powerlessness of the federal government under the Articles of Confederation became obvious in 1786 when a revolt erupted in Massachusetts. Farmers there rebelled because many were being jailed for not paying their debts. The federal government could neither put down the uprising nor force other states to help.

THE CONSTITUTIONAL CONVENTION

Because the Articles of Confederation weren't working, a national meeting was convened to develop a new plan. Delegates from the states gathered in Philadelphia on May 25, 1787. George Washington presided over this conference, which became known as the Constitutional Convention.

The Constitution that thirty-nine of the delegates signed in September 1787 set up a new government with three distinct branches. The legislative branch included two chambers, the House of Representatives and the Senate. The judicial branch would be headed by the Supreme Court. Finally, the executive branch would be led by the president.

CHOOSING THE FIRST PRESIDENT

Presidents have never been elected by the direct vote of the people. Instead, each state chooses a number of electors equal to its representation in Congress. These electors then vote for the president. Until 1832, electors were typically chosen by state legislatures. After that, electors were chosen directly by the people, except in South Carolina.

When the Electoral College met for the first time in January 1789, George

THE EARLY YEARS

IN 1753, GEORGE WASHINGTON was working as a surveyor in Virginia and also serving as a major in the colonial militia. In October 1753, the royal governor of Virginia sent the twenty-one-year-old Washington on a mission to demand that French troops leave land in the Ohio Valley claimed by Great Britain. When the French refused to leave, the French and Indian War began.

Because of the military experience he gained during this war, Washington was chosen in June 1775 to lead the new Continental Army. He suffered many more defeats than victories during the Revolutionary War but never lost badly enough to lose the war entirely. Instead, his real task was to keep the army together, and he did.

★MYTHS ABOUT GEORGE WASHINGTON

There are many stories that people tell about George Washington. One is that he lost all his teeth and had to wear wooden ones. In fact, he did wear false teeth, but they weren't made out of wood. Instead, he had sets made from gold, lead, and ivory. One set was even made from hippopotamus teeth.

Another myth about Washington was that, as a boy, he chopped down his father's cherry tree. When asked to tell the truth, Washington supposedly replied, "I cannot tell a lie. I did it." This is certainly not a true story. Rather, it was invented by Parson Mason Weems for his book *The Life and Memorable Actions of George Washington,* first published in 1800. Weems's intention was to create inspiring legends for the new country.

★ CHIEF RED JACKET

One of the most pressing problems facing Washington was trouble on the nation's western frontier. Because white farmers were so eager to occupy the rich farmland in the nation's interior, they often settled illegally on native land. The Chickasaws, Cherokees, Creeks, and Seminoles eventually decided to fight back.

In 1792, Washington met with the Seneca chief Red Jacket, to whom he gave a silver medal as a token of respect. Red Jacket believed that all the Indian tribes would inevitably have to make peace with the powerful whites. At the same time, he worked hard to protect the Senecas' customs, religion, and language.

★ THE COTTON GIN

Before Eli Whitney invented the cotton gin in 1793, the farmers and slaves who cleaned cotton had to pick the seeds out by hand. Whitney's invention saved a tremendous amount of work, because it picked the seeds out mechanically. One person operating a cotton gin could clean as much cotton as fifty people working the old way.

This new technology enabled farmers in the South to expand their plantings by thousands of acres. Cotton soon became so important to the region that southerners began calling it King Cotton.

★ THE FIRST LADY

When George Washington became president, his wife, Martha, was wary of living a public life. As time went on, however, she grew fond of her role as first lady. She hosted state dinners every week, and on Friday afternoons, she and Abigail Adams, the vice president's wife, held casual receptions for anyone who might want to attend. The informality of these receptions was supposed to show that the new government was not above the people. But visitors to the president's house still wore fine clothes and called Martha "Lady Washington."

Washington was the clear choice of the electors. But the retired general was still reluctant to serve, a fact that probably helped him win.

Americans were still worried about one man having too much power. If there had to be a president, most people thought it should be someone who didn't want the job. When the vote for president was finally taken, Washington was the unanimous choice.

HAMILTON AND JEFFERSON One of the president's first tasks was to appoint people to head each of the four executive departments: Foreign Affairs (later called State), War, Treasury, and Justice. For the first secretary of the treasury, Washington chose Alexander Hamilton. Along with James Madison and John Jay, Hamilton had written the *Federalist* papers, a series of published essays that had urged ratification of the Constitution.

Hamilton's political rival, Thomas Jefferson, became the first secretary of state. Unlike Hamilton, who favored a strong federal government, Jefferson feared that the central government might grow too strong. Recently, as a diplomat in France, he had seen how the French ruling classes lived in luxury, while poor people dressed in rags and begged in the street. He blamed these problems on France's powerful central government.

Jefferson was worried that a strong central government in the United States might oppress people, too. Meanwhile, Hamilton worried that a weak central government would accomplish nothing. Usually President Washington sided with Hamilton.

At first, Washington asked each of his four department heads to meet with him separately. But this took up a lot of time and was not very effective. Eventually, the president came up with a better way.

1792

In late 1791, he instructed the secretaries to meet with him as a single group. This group became known as the cabinet.

PAYING THE STATES' DEBTS

One of the most important issues facing the cabinet during Washington's first term was the public debt owed by the states. During the Revolutionary War, most states had borrowed money from foreign and American investors to pay their soldiers. This money eventually had to be paid back. Early in 1790, Hamilton came up with a plan. He proposed that the new federal government pay off the states' debts.

Hamilton had two reasons for suggesting this. The first was that he wanted to establish the federal government's credit. The best way to do this was to prove that it could pay off a debt. Paying off the states' debts would encourage citizens and foreign governments to lend more money to the federal government in the future.

The second reason was to bring the states closer together in the new Union. If the debts became the responsibility of the federal government, the states would have to work together to pay them off.

IMPLIED POWERS

The problem with paying off the states' debts was that the Constitution had not granted the federal government the power to do this. On the other hand, it had not withheld this power, either. Hamilton argued that by not forbidding it, the Constitution implied the existence of such a power. Hamilton's theory has been called the doctrine of implied powers.

Jefferson thought that Hamilton's argument was dangerous. He believed that the more power the government

CAMPAIGN ★ 1792

WHEN THE ELECTORAL COLLEGE MET in 1789 and again in 1792, each elector voted for two people. The person getting the most votes became president, as long as the winner received a majority of the electoral votes. In both elections, the winner was George Washington. In 1789 and again in 1792, not a single elector cast a vote against him. Washington was the only president ever to be elected unanimously.

The person with the second highest electoral vote became vice president. In both the 1789 and 1792 elections, John Adams received the second highest total. Therefore, he served as Washington's vice president.

Under the Constitution, the vice president has much less responsibility and power. His role is to break tied votes in the Senate and to take over the presidency should the president resign or die. Adams called the job the "most insignificant office that ever the invention of man contrived or his imagination conceived."

Buttons were made to honor Washington's first inauguration on April 30, 1789. One design consisted of his initials and the words "Long Live the President." Another featured an eagle. Although these buttons played no role in the campaign, they are considered forerunners of the campaign buttons that candidates use today.

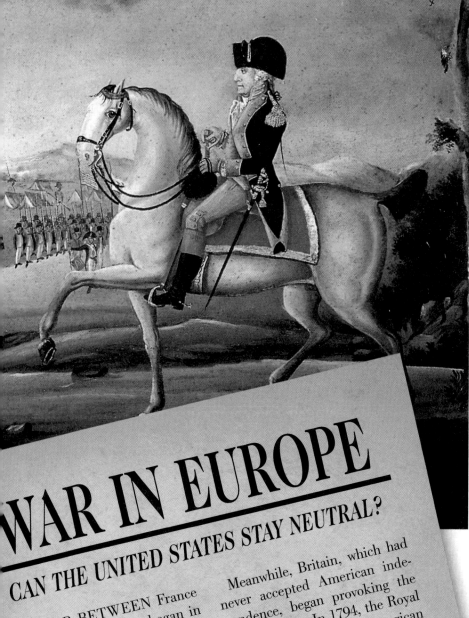

took, the less freedom the people would have. In response to Hamilton, he argued that unless the Constitution explicitly granted the power to do something, that thing couldn't be done. Hamilton and Jefferson's debate has continued throughout the history of the United States.

THE FIRST NATIONAL BANK Part of Hamilton's plan included the establishment of a national bank to hold federal deposits and issue paper money. Many people, especially farmers, conducted business by trading goods. When they used money, it was in the form of gold and silver coins. Because America had only small stores of these precious metals, most people used coins that had been minted in other countries. Everything from English pounds to Russian kopecks passed from hand to hand.

The proposal of a national bank met with a great deal of opposition, especially from Jefferson, who feared any concentration of governmental power. In exchange for Jefferson's acceptance of the national bank, which Congress approved in 1791, Hamilton agreed to move the nation's capital so that it would be closer to Jefferson's home state of Virginia.

The first capital was New York City. With a population of some thirty-three thousand people, New York City was also the largest city in the country. Its streets were jammed daily with residents and country folk who had come to sell their goods. Farmers' wagons

WAR IN EUROPE

CAN THE UNITED STATES STAY NEUTRAL?

THE WAR BETWEEN France and Great Britain that began in 1793 had an immediate effect on the United States. Both Britain and France still controlled territory in North America, and the naval battles they fought off the West Indies constantly disrupted U.S. shipping.

During the Revolutionary War, the Continental Congress had signed a treaty with King Louis XVI of France. In exchange for his military aid, the Americans promised to defend the French West Indies against British attack. In 1793, the French government asked America for help. But the United States refused, believing the treaty no longer applied because Louis XVI had been overthrown and executed.

Meanwhile, Britain, which had never accepted American independence, began provoking the United States. In 1794, the Royal Navy began boarding American ships that were suspected of carrying British deserters. During these raids, the British kidnapped not only former British sailors, but also innocent Americans. The practice was called impressment.

clattering along cobblestone streets made a terrible racket.

Besides Jefferson, other members of the government thought it would be wise to move the capital from New York to another location outside the control of any one state. For the new capital, George Washington chose a site on the Potomac River between Maryland and Virginia. Each of these states then agreed to donate some land for the creation of a new District of Columbia, within which the new capital city of Washington would be built. In the meantime, Philadelphia became the temporary capital.

THE PROCLAMATION OF NEUTRALITY

The first major test of Washington's foreign policy came during his second term in office. Soon after the French Revolution began in 1789, France declared war on Great Britain. The French had provided a great deal of aid to the Americans during the American Revolution, and now they asked for similar help in return. Jefferson was inclined to say yes. But many officials, including Hamilton, argued against aid to France. Almost every American agreed on one point, however. No one wanted to get involved in the actual fighting.

In April 1793, knowing that it would be best to stay out of a European war, Washington issued the Proclamation of Neutrality, which advised the states to remain friendly with both sides. He also warned Americans not to smuggle weapons or other contraband that might drag the United States into the war.

Jefferson generally supported Washington's policies with regard to France and Great Britain. But he grew increasingly tired of fighting with Hamilton. Finally, in late 1793, he resigned as secretary of state.

★ THE SLAVE TRADE

The slave trade between Africa and North America began in the 1600s. By the 1790s, there were about seven hundred thousand slaves in the United States. Although the northern states all outlawed slavery between 1777 and 1804, the

South became even more dependent on slave labor after the invention of the cotton gin, which led to more cotton planting.

Some slaves were taught skills, such as how to read and write. A few even managed to earn enough money to buy their freedom. But most slaves were beaten into obedience. Many slaveholders persuaded themselves that Africans were less than human. Therefore, they believed it was acceptable to treat African slaves brutally, as though they were animals.

★ THE FRENCH REVOLUTION

By 1789, the French government was almost bankrupt. Peasants in the countryside and poor people in the cities were on the verge of rioting for food. Only the aristocracy of titled landowners remained rich.

In May 1789, the government convened an emergency meeting of the Estates-General, a special parliament made up of delegates from the clergy, the aristocracy, and the common people. Both the clergy and the aristocracy wanted to protect their privileges. But the representatives of the common people wanted to eliminate all of these advantages.

Alarmed by the people's demands, King Louis XVI sent twenty thousand soldiers to Versailles, where the Estates-General was meeting. News of this troop movement enraged Parisians, who responded by attacking the Bastille prison and capturing the weapons stored there. The storming of the Bastille on July 14, 1789, is considered the beginning of the French Revolution.

★ FAMILY FARMS

Farming was the most important industry in the United States until the twentieth century. George Washington called it "the most healthy, the most useful, and the most noble employment of man." In Washington's time, most farms were small and self-sufficient, producing only a tiny surplus of crops that could be traded for manufactured goods. Women played a particularly important role on these small farms.

Girls worked with their mothers on family farms to make everything from beeswax for candles to yarn for clothing. What little extra they made, they traded at the local country store for items they couldn't make themselves, such as printed cloth and sugar.

★**PAINTING IN AMERICA** The most promising art students in America were usually sent to Europe for their training. The two most famous American painters of this time, Benjamin West and John Singleton Copley, both settled in London, where they followed the fashion of painting scenes from history.

In America, the most popular paintings were portraits. Most American artists painted little else until the 1840s, when the introduction of photography reduced the demand for them. The leading portrait painters of the time were Gilbert Stuart and Charles Willson Peale. Both men painted George Washington, who was known to be a patient subject. The most famous of these works is an unfinished portrait of Washington begun by Stuart in 1794. An etching based on this portrait appears on the dollar bill.

★**ROYAL GIFT** Despite his achievements as a general and president, George Washington saw himself primarily as a farmer. Throughout his life, he remained interested in the breeding of animals. His specialty was breeding mules.

A mule is the offspring of a male donkey and a female horse. Washington was always trying to improve the strength of his mules.

Learning of Washington's passion, the king of Spain sent him an excellent donkey as a gift. Washington named the donkey Royal Gift and used him to breed many fine mules. He occasionally mated Royal Gift with female donkeys and sent the offspring all over the country to raise the quality of the breeding stock nationwide.

THE WHISKEY REBELLION Although Washington worked hard to keep the United States out of the European war, he was not reluctant to use military force at home. An important example of this was the Whiskey Rebellion.

In March 1791, Congress enacted a tax on whiskey. This tax outraged farmers, who often made whiskey from their extra corn. (Otherwise, the corn would spoil.) As a result, some people on the western frontier used whiskey as money.

In July 1794, when federal agents tried to collect the whiskey tax in western Pennsylvania, farmers there rebelled. Then, when the governor of the state failed to punish the farmers and collect the tax himself, the problem became a national one.

Because the Whiskey Rebellion represented a direct challenge to the authority of the federal government, Washington decided to raise a volunteer army and enforce the law himself.

In fact, the Whiskey Rebellion never posed a serious military threat. Most of the rebels turned and ran when they saw Washington's army coming. Yet the incident was an important test of the new national government. In putting down the Whiskey Rebellion, Washington proved that the federal government had the power to enforce its laws.

Meanwhile, Washington's policy of neutrality was being tested by the British, who began stopping and searching U.S. ships that they thought were carrying supplies to the French. The British also began encouraging Indians to attack settlers on the nation's northwest frontier.

In order to avoid war, the U.S. minister to Great Britain, John Jay, negotiated a new treaty with the British. In exchange for Britain's promise to withdraw its troops from the Northwest Territory, the United States agreed to allow the

inspection of its ships on the high seas. Many people criticized Jay's Treaty for bargaining away the nation's neutrality rights. But the treaty did postpone a war that America was not prepared to fight. Washington signed the treaty and managed to get it ratified by the Senate.

THE NORTHWEST TERRITORY Disputes between settlers and native peoples on the nation's frontier were a constant problem for Washington. At first, he tried to solve the problem militarily. In 1791, in fact, he had sent Gen. Arthur St. Clair into the Northwest Territory to build a fort there.

Washington specifically warned St. Clair to watch out for surprise attacks, but St. Clair didn't listen. Instead, his two-thousand-man army was ambushed by Indians on November 4, 1791, on the site of present-day Fort Wayne, Indiana. The Americans suffered more than nine hundred casualties.

When Washington found out, he was furious. Another president might have tried to cover up the embarrassing blunder, but Washington immediately informed Congress and sent another general, "Mad" Anthony Wayne, to replace St. Clair.

Wayne was more careful. Before confronting the Indians, he spent time training his men in Indian tactics. Then, on August 20, 1794, he won a decisive victory at the Battle of Fallen Timbers. Later, during the summer of 1795, Wayne spent six weeks negotiating a peace treaty with delegates from the Great Lakes, Mississippi, and Ohio River tribes.

George Washington's famous Farewell Address, announcing his retirement, was published on September 19, 1796. In it, he warned the nation against becoming permanently allied with foreign powers.

CAMPAIGN ★ 1796

AS MOST PEOPLE EXPECTED, Vice Pres. John Adams ran for president in 1796. Like Washington and Alexander Hamilton, Adams was a member of the Federalist party, which supported a strong central government and life terms for senators.

Adams's opponent, former secretary of state Thomas Jefferson, had very different political ideas. Jefferson led a new party called the Democratic-Republicans, which favored more power for the states and limited terms for public office.

Out of personal respect for George Washington, the Democratic-Republicans had been relatively quiet during his two terms in office. Now that Washington was retiring, however, they were ready for a fight.

During the American Revolution, Adams and Jefferson had been friends and colleagues. But the rough campaign of 1796, the first to have two opposing candidates, turned them into enemies. The Democratic-Republicans claimed that Adams wanted to become an American king, while the Federalists condemned Jefferson as a demagogue—that is, someone who manipulates popular fears for his or her own political ends.

It was probably Washington's endorsement that won the election for Adams. Jefferson came in second, however, and became Adams's vice president. This was the only time in American history that the president and vice president were members of different political parties. In 1804, the Twelfth Amendment to the Constitution changed the way the president and vice president were chosen so that it wouldn't happen again.

FULL OF LOVE FOR THEE AND THINE

JOHN ADAMS

BORN: OCTOBER 30, 1735

BIRTHPLACE: BRAINTREE, MASS.

DIED: JULY 4, 1826

PARTY: FEDERALIST

VICE PRESIDENT: THOMAS JEFFERSON

FIRST LADY: ABIGAIL SMITH

CHILDREN: ABIGAIL, JOHN QUINCY, SUSANNA, CHARLES, THOMAS

NICKNAME: DUKE OF BRAINTREE

THE FIRST PRESIDENT TO LIVE IN THE WHITE HOUSE.

JOHN ADAMS

2nd President

★

1797 to 1801

John Adams

The most critical problem facing John Adams when he took office was French raiding of American shipping. U.S. neutrality in the war between Great Britain and France had led to a boom in Atlantic trade. Both warring nations badly wanted supplies from the United States, but neither was willing to let the other receive any goods.

In 1794, the United States had signed Jay's Treaty with Great Britain. In retaliation, the French government had begun encouraging pirates to attack U.S. merchant ships headed for Great Britain. As the number of plundered U.S. ships neared three hundred, Americans began demanding war with France. There was even a wild rumor that the French might be planning an invasion.

Remembering the warning against foreign entanglements delivered by Washington in his Farewell Address, Adams held back.

ALIEN AND SEDITION ACTS PASSED BY CONGRESS

IN 1798, as the United States moved closer to war with France, John Adams signed into law the Alien and Sedition Acts to protect America's national security.

There were four acts in all: The Alien Act and the Alien Enemies Act gave the president the power, especially during wartime, to deport or imprison foreigners whom he considered dangerous. The Naturalization Act made it harder for immigrants to become U.S. citizens.

Even more significant was the Sedition Act, which outlawed criticism of the U.S. government. Jefferson saw these new laws as a way for the Federalists to control their political rivals. Because the Democratic-Republicans had a lot of support among recent immigrants, Jefferson was worried that the Naturalization Act would take away these votes. The Sedition Act also limited the freedom of the Democratic-Republicans to complain about the policies of the government.

In opposing these new laws, Jefferson became the first person to apply the Constitution to an actual dispute. He argued that the Sedition Act was unconstitutional because it violated the freedom of speech guaranteed by the First Amendment.

The Growth of the U.S. 1791-1797

VT 1791

KY 1792

TN 1796

1798

Instead of fighting, he sent a delegation of three diplomats to negotiate with French foreign minister Charles Talleyrand. Unwilling to greet the U.S. mission personally, Talleyrand sent three of his aides to meet the Americans. (These men were later referred to as X, Y, and Z by Adams, who did not wish to reveal their names.)

However, before the Frenchmen would even talk to the Americans, they demanded a bribe of $250,000. This demand outraged Adams, who was famous for strictly following the law.

WAR FEVER AT HOME   When news of the XYZ Affair reached the United States, the nation caught war fever. A popular slogan was "Millions for defense, but not one cent for tribute." *Tribute* meant the payment of bribes in order to stop the attacks on U.S. shipping.

Even so, Adams would not declare war. The United States was not yet able to fight at sea, and it would take some time to build a capable navy. In the meantime, Adams persuaded Congress to end U.S. trade with France. He also made arrangements for the powerful British navy to protect transatlantic shipping.

It was in this wartime atmosphere of 1798 that Adams obtained passage of the Alien and Sedition Acts. These laws made it hard for the Democratic-Republicans to organize opposition to the government. Jefferson's earlier, unpopular support for the French Revolution also hindered the Democratic-Republicans in their efforts to reverse Adams's policies.

Jefferson publicly accused Adams of signing these laws in order to frustrate his political foes. In this, he was at least partially correct. Over the next year, no fewer than ten Democratic-Republican newspaper editors were jailed under the Sedition Act.

THE EARLY YEARS   JOHN ADAMS GREW UP ON A FARM in Braintree (now Quincy), Massachusetts, where he liked to spend his time hunting in the woods and playing a variety of games. Adams particularly liked flying kites, shooting marbles, and making toy boats.

After graduating from Harvard, he became a lawyer in Boston. His most famous case was argued in 1770, when he successfully defended the nine British soldiers accused in the Boston Massacre. In that prerevolutionary incident, a resentful mob of Bostonians menaced a squad of frightened redcoats. The soldiers shot and killed five colonists despite orders not to fire.

From 1774 until 1777, Adams served as a delegate from Massachusetts to the Continental Congress in Philadelphia. There, he nominated George Washington to be commander-in-chief of the new Continental Army. He also helped Thomas Jefferson compose the Declaration of Independence.

★**THE FIRST LADY**   For long periods of time during the American Revolution and afterward, John Adams lived away from his Massachusetts home in Philadelphia, New York, France, and England. While he was away, his wife, Abigail, had to manage the family farm and raise their five children. Many of the nation's founders, including Thomas Jefferson, suffered financially because of the time they spent away from their homes. But Abigail Adams's shrewd handling of her husband's financial affairs kept the family prosperous.

Although she was the wife of one president and the mother of another, Abigail herself felt disappointed at the lack of opportunities she had as a woman. She regretted especially that the women of her time were denied the same education that men received. In letters she wrote to her husband, Abigail urged him to "remember the ladies" who had served the country so well during the Revolution.

★ BLACK CHURCHES

Around 1800, churches began to play an important role in the lives of many African Americans in the North. Unable to attend most schools and unwelcome in politics, many black people turned to churches because they offered opportunities for education and community organizing.

In the South, however, slaves were often prevented from attending church services. Their white owners worried that allowing them to gather in large groups would be dangerous. They were also concerned that slaves might become literate through reading the Bible and therefore become discontented as well.

★ JOHNNY APPLESEED

Sometime about 1800, twenty-six-year-old John Chapman began collecting apple seeds from cider presses in western Pennsylvania. He used these seeds to grow small plants, which he intended to sell to pioneer families on the western frontier.

At the time, homesteaders were busily settling the Ohio River Valley. During his travels, Chapman sold or gave away thousands of his apple seedlings to these people.

Although John Chapman was a real person, his exploits inspired the myth of Johnny Appleseed. Stories were told of a cheerful, generous vagabond who had bare feet, an upside-down pan for a hat, and a coffee sack for a shirt. In addition to planting apple trees, Johnny Appleseed was famous for his gentleness with animals, his love of nature, and his peaceful relationship with the Indians.

★ RETIREMENT

Although the end to his presidency was quite rocky, Adams enjoyed a peaceful retirement at his home in Massachusetts. He spent most of his time there reading literature in his library. Even after his eyesight began to fail, his eighteen grandchildren and great-grandchildren took turns reading aloud to him. As time went on, he even renewed his friendship with Jefferson.

At the age of eighty-nine, Adams proudly watched his son John Quincy win election as the sixth president of the United States. Two years later, he was invited to participate in Boston's celebration of the fiftieth anniversary of the Declaration of Independence. But Adams never made it, dying quietly during the early evening on July 4, 1826. His last words were "Jefferson still survives."

Although Adams had no way of knowing this, Jefferson had died a few hours earlier at his Monticello estate in Virginia.

To protest the Alien and Sedition Acts, Jefferson and James Madison wrote the Kentucky and Virginia Resolves, which argued that the new laws were void because they were unconstitutional. Jefferson and Madison even went so far as to insist that states had the right to reject some federal laws. This argument would become much more important in the years leading up to the Civil War.

THE QUASI-WAR

From the spring of 1798 through 1800, despite the official state of peace between the two nations, U.S. frigates battled the French navy. Adams hesitated to declare war because he hoped the fighting would soon stop. He thought the French were too busy in Europe to continue bothering with North America.

In September 1800, a second mission to Talleyrand negotiated an end to what had become known as the Quasi-War, because it was never declared. France agreed to recognize the neutrality of U.S. shipping. In exchange, Adams agreed to resume trade with France.

This treaty particularly benefited shipbuilders and merchants in port cities along the Atlantic coast. But the new trade policy had little impact on citizens in the interior, most of whom were either farmers or artisans, such as potters and blacksmiths.

Farmers typically taught their sons at home or sent them to country schools during the few months they weren't needed on the farm. Their daughters, like the children of free blacks, received even less education, if any at all. In contrast, the white men who ran the government were wealthy and quite well educated. One reason that Jefferson opposed life terms for senators was that he feared the creation of a professional class of politicians, who would be completely removed from the people.

Soon after concluding the treaty with France in the fall of 1800, John Adams and his family moved to the nation's new capital in Washington. Although ten years had passed since architects and engineers had begun work on the city, it was still rough, muddy, and sparsely populated. The president's house wasn't finished yet, and the wing in which the Adamses lived was uncomfortable and drafty. They stayed there less than a year, but during that time, the damp, poorly heated house and wild, lonely city had a harmful effect on Abigail Adams's health.

Although John Adams was widely popular during the Quasi-War, he lost most of that popularity during his last year in office. People came to believe that his government was too isolated and that it ignored their wishes. Voters also agreed with Thomas Jefferson that the Alien and Sedition Acts limited their personal freedom. Even the Federalists, led by Alexander Hamilton, turned against Adams because of his refusal to declare war on France.

THE MIDNIGHT APPOINTMENTS

Adams was not surprised when he lost the 1800 election to Jefferson. Still, the president was a stubborn, embittered man. He was determined that the policies of his administration should continue. To ensure this, he appointed a large number of judges during his final days in office. Because these appointments came so late in his term, they were known as the Midnight Appointments.

Adams's plan was to fill the courts with Federalists who would frustrate the will of Jefferson and the Democratic-Republicans. Jefferson's refusal to honor these last-minute appointments led to the landmark Supreme Court case *Marbury v. Madison*.

CAMPAIGN ★ 1800

THE CAMPAIGN OF 1800 WAS A REPLAY of the election of 1796 between Adams and Jefferson. Although neither candidate made public appearances or statements, the contest was a bitter one.

In the tradition of early American etiquette, both men pretended that they didn't want to be president. But this false modesty never stopped their supporters from openly insulting the opposing candidate at every opportunity. The Federalists, who were still in power, even used the Sedition Act to prosecute the Democratic-Republican press.

When the Electoral College met, Jefferson and Aaron Burr each received seventy-three electoral votes, defeating the Federalist ticket of John Adams and Charles Pinckney. It had been understood during the campaign that Jefferson would serve as president and Burr as vice president. After the election, however, Burr refused to step aside, and because of the tied vote, the final decision was left up to the House of Representatives. After thirty-five separate votes, the House remained deadlocked.

Jefferson's old rival, Alexander Hamilton, faced a dilemma. He had enough influence with Federalist members of Congress to break the deadlock, but which candidate should he support? Hamilton disliked Jefferson personally, but he didn't trust Burr at all.

In the end, Hamilton decided that his country was more important than his personal feelings. Therefore, on February 17, 1801, on the thirty-sixth ballot, he persuaded

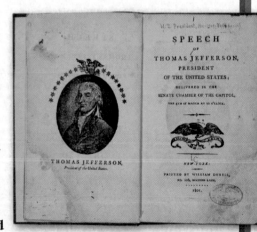

several congressmen not to vote at all. This swung the election to Jefferson, who became the third president of the United States.

THOMAS JEFFERSON
3rd President
★
1801 to 1809

BORN: APRIL 13, 1743

BIRTHPLACE: GOOCHLAND COUNTY, VA.

DIED: JULY 4, 1826

PARTY: DEMOCRATIC-REPUBLICAN

VICE PRESIDENTS: AARON BURR, GEORGE CLINTON

FIRST LADY: MARTHA WAYLES SKELTON

CHILDREN: MARTHA, JANE, (UNNAMED SON), MARY, LUCY, AND LUCY JEFFERSON; BEVERLY, MADISON, AND ESTON HEMINGS

NICKNAME: RED FOX

JEFFERSON'S GRANDSON WAS THE FIRST BABY BORN IN THE WHITE HOUSE.

John Adams did not remain in Washington to see Jefferson's inauguration on March 4, 1801. Bitter at his loss, Adams quietly left town at dawn rather than stay to watch Jefferson take his oath of office. As a result, the transfer of power was not gracious, but it was nevertheless the first time in American history that political control passed peacefully from one party to another.

After the viciousness of the 1800 campaign, Jefferson tried to calm the nation by stressing unity and toleration in his inaugural address. To prove that he meant what he said, the new president quickly asked Congress to repeal the Alien and Sedition Acts, and people jailed under these laws were soon freed.

The election of 1800 has often been called the Revolution of 1800 because that year the Democratic-Republicans took control of both houses

JEFFERSON BUYS FRENCH LAND

THE UNITED STATES got the biggest bargain in history when Robert Livingston and James Monroe negotiated the massive Louisiana Purchase during the spring of 1803.

The Louisiana Territory, which covered 828,000 square miles and stretched from the Mississippi River to the Rocky Mountains, was first explored by the Spanish in the 1600s. The French later colonized the area, founding New Orleans at the mouth of the Mississippi River in 1718.

Throughout the 1700s, control of the area passed back and forth between the French and the Spanish. Between 1800 and 1802, Napoléon's victories in Europe forced the Spanish to give the territory back to France. Spain had allowed U.S. ships to travel freely up and down the Mississippi, but Jefferson feared the French might revoke this important privilege.

It was the job of Jefferson's envoys to secure this right of free passage and, if possible, to buy New Orleans. But when the two American diplomats arrived, French foreign minister Charles Talleyrand surprised them by offering to sell the entire Louisiana Territory. Was the United States interested?

Livingston and Monroe were flabbergasted. Although the purchase went well beyond their instructions, the two men soon agreed to a price of fifteen million dollars for the land, or about four cents an acre.

The Louisiana Purchase

of Congress as well as the executive branch of government.

The Democratic-Republicans were able to win the presidency as well as comfortable majorities in both the House and the Senate because the campaign had shown the clear differences between the two parties. The Federalists believed in strong laws to protect business and property. They also warned that a Democratic-Republican government would lead to mob rule, as the French Revolution had.

But the country was tired of such fearful politics. Unlike most Federalists, Jefferson was more of a philosopher than a politician. He was more concerned with the principles of democracy and individual freedom than he was with the details of government.

In keeping with his Democratic-Republican ideals, Jefferson concentrated on making the federal government smaller and less involved in the daily lives of the people. He reduced the size of the military, recalled more than half of the American diplomats in Europe, and ordered a careful review of all government spending. In time, these measures reduced the national debt by about one-half.

THE BARBARY PIRATES Jefferson's first crisis as president came in foreign affairs. The Barbary pirates were vicious buccaneers who operated out of the North African states of Morocco, Algiers, Tunis, and Tripoli. They attacked merchant ships and kidnapped sailors, imprisoning and often torturing them.

For years, the United States had been paying tribute to the leaders of the Barbary states. In exchange for these payments, the Barbary pirates had agreed not to attack U.S. ships. By 1801, the United States had paid nearly two million dollars in tribute.

THE EARLY YEARS BEGINNING IN 1762, THOMAS JEFFERSON **studied law under George Wythe, who also taught future Supreme Court chief justice John Marshall. Jefferson's apprenticeship ended in April 1767, when he was admitted to the bar in Virginia.**

Jefferson served in the Virginia House of Burgesses from 1769 until 1774, and in the Continental Congress after that. Only thirty-three years old, Jefferson was the youngest delegate to the congress in Philadelphia, but he was nevertheless given the task of writing the Declaration of Independence.

The Continental Congress spent days debating Jefferson's work, dissecting every word and phrase. In the end, several changes were made. For instance, a passage attacking slavery was deleted. The document was finally approved on July 4, 1776.

★ **MONTICELLO** Jefferson was known as a Renaissance man because he had an extraordinary range of interests. One was architecture. When the government held a competition to design the president's new home, Jefferson submitted a design anonymously. He didn't win.

Jefferson did design his own house, named Monticello, outside Charlottesville, Virginia. The first section of the house, built between 1770 and 1775, was modeled on the Italian villas designed by Andrea Palladio in the sixteenth century. Palladio's villas were in turn based on classical Roman buildings.

★ **THE CLERMONT** In August 1807, people on the banks of the Hudson River in New York City saw a very strange sight. A ship, smoking as though on fire, was steadily moving up the river against the current. Even more peculiar were its sails, which were rolled up and therefore useless. Only later did people learn that the *Clermont* was a steamship.

Its builder, engineer Robert Fulton, had been working on the ship's design for more than five years. Although the *Clermont* wasn't the very first steamship, it was the first to succeed commercially. Fulton's boat began carrying passengers and freight in September 1807. Within two months, it turned a profit for its owners.

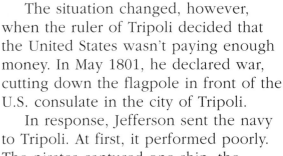

★ BENJAMIN BANNEKER

Benjamin Banneker was one of the country's first important black scholars. From an early age, Banneker had a talent for mathematics and science. He was almost entirely self-taught. He learned astronomy by charting the movement of the planets in the night sky. He learned mathematics from borrowed textbooks.

In 1790, President Washington appointed Banneker to the District of Columbia Commission so that Banneker could help survey the proposed site of the new capital city. Meanwhile, between 1791 and 1802, Banneker published a popular annual almanac, sending a copy of the first one to Jefferson, who was then secretary of state. Banneker included with the almanac a note asking Jefferson to use his influence to make life better for the country's blacks.

★ TRIANGULAR TRADE

For more than a century, the businessmen who brought slaves to North America followed the same triangular route. They carried rum from distilleries in New England to West Africa, where they traded the rum for slaves. The slaves were usually members of tribes who had been captured during a war or kidnapped from their villages.

These slaves were kept shackled in the holds of ships all the way back across the Atlantic. Eventually, they were traded in the West Indies for molasses, which was then carried to New England for use in making rum. Meanwhile, slave traders in the West Indies shipped most of the new slaves off to buyers in North and South America.

Although there was not nearly enough support in the country to outlaw slavery altogether, Jefferson did manage, before leaving office, to persuade Congress to ban the slave trade. A new law that went into effect on January 1, 1808, ended the importation of slaves into the United States. Sadly, tens of thousands of slaves continued to be smuggled into the country illegally.

The situation changed, however, when the ruler of Tripoli decided that the United States wasn't paying enough money. In May 1801, he declared war, cutting down the flagpole in front of the U.S. consulate in the city of Tripoli.

In response, Jefferson sent the navy to Tripoli. At first, it performed poorly. The pirates captured one ship, the *Philadelphia,* in October 1803 and turned its guns against the remaining U.S. ships. Only a daring raid by Lt. Stephen Decatur saved the day by destroying the ship and preventing its guns from being used any longer against the Americans.

In April 1805, the U.S. fleet captured Derna, one of Tripoli's main seaports. The loss of Derna forced the ruler of Tripoli to sign a peace treaty ending the payment of tribute forever. Even so, pirates from the other Barbary states continued to disrupt U.S. shipping in the Mediterranean for another ten years.

THE LOUISIANA PURCHASE

Another foreign matter also occupied the president's attention. Napoléon's military victories in Europe had recently forced Spain to turn over much of its North American territory to France, including the port of New Orleans. Jefferson feared that France might now try to deny Americans the right to travel up and down the Mississippi River, which would badly hurt trade on the western frontier.

The people settling the Mississippi River country at this time were mostly poor farming families. The only land these people could afford was on the untamed western frontier.

Families would usually travel west on foot, carrying their belongings on their backs. If they were lucky enough, they might have a milk cow that could help them with the hauling. Once they found a place to settle, they would build a

crude log cabin. The roof, usually made of sod or thatch, often leaked. The final job would be to chop down trees and turn the surrounding forest into fields that could be planted.

Believing farmers were the key to a stable and productive nation, Jefferson wanted to be sure that farmers on the western frontier could always ship their goods to market down the Mississippi River. Therefore, when Napoléon offered the entire Louisiana Territory for sale, Jefferson was both shocked and excited. The problem was that nothing in the Constitution gave him the power to buy land.

Throughout Jefferson's long career in government, he had argued consistently against Hamilton's doctrine of implied powers. In theory, Jefferson believed that larger government meant less freedom for the people. Therefore, the best government was small, simple, and frugal.

Although the president had to compromise his thinking to make the Louisiana Purchase, in the end the offer was too good to pass up. Besides adding huge tracts of land to the young nation, the Louisiana Purchase guaranteed free passage along the Mississippi River forever. The irony for Jefferson was that the purchase also ensured the need for a strong central government to manage the huge new country.

MARBURY V. MADISON
Back in the capital, Jefferson's ongoing battles with the Federalists led to an important Supreme Court decision. After the election of 1800 (but before the Democratic-Republicans came to power), the Federalist Congress had hastily passed the Judiciary Act of 1801, creating a number of new federal judgeships.

CAMPAIGN ★ 1804

THE ELECTION OF 1800 HAD POINTED OUT **a serious flaw in the way that the president and vice president were chosen. When Jefferson and Burr both received the same number of electoral votes, the stalemate had nearly caused a constitutional crisis. Had it not been for Alexander Hamilton's involvement, the House of Representatives might have remained deadlocked indefinitely.**

To remedy this oversight, the Twelfth Amendment was passed and ratified in time for the 1804 election. It changed the rules of the Electoral College so that the electors now voted separately for president and vice president.

Jefferson was once again the presidential candidate of the Democratic-Republicans. But Burr, the disloyal vice president, was dropped from the ticket and replaced by New York governor George Clinton.

The Federalists weren't much of a factor in this election. Their candidate, Charles Pinckney of South Carolina, had run on the same ticket with John Adams in 1800. He was an experienced and qualified statesman, but Jefferson was a popular president and won easily.

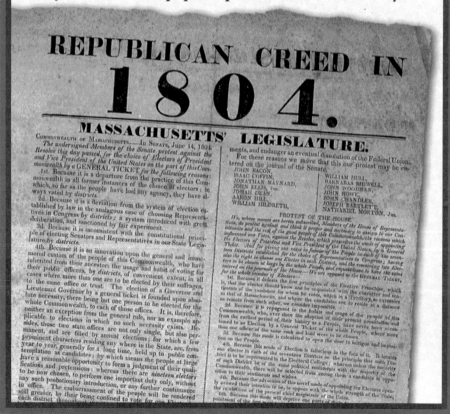

This portrait of Jefferson was painted by Caleb Boyle, probably in 1801.

1805

LEOPARD ATTACKS CHESAPEAKE

FOUR SAILORS IMPRESSED AS THREE DIE

OFF THE VIRGINIA COAST, June 22, 1807—The British warship *Leopard* fired today on the American frigate *Chesapeake*. The British commander had demanded that the U.S. captain allow his ship to be boarded. When the *Chesapeake*'s captain refused, the *Leopard* opened fire, killing three sailors and wounding eighteen.

After the *Leopard* disabled the *Chesapeake*, the captain of the *Leopard* sent over a boarding party, which impressed four sailors from the *Chesapeake*'s crew. One man was indeed a deserter from the Royal Navy, but the others were U.S. citizens. President Jefferson expressed his outrage at the continuation of the British policy of impressment, under which the Royal Navy has stopped U.S. ships on the high seas and carried away the high seas by force.

As a result of the *Leopard*'s actions, state legislatures all over the country are now demanding war with Great Britain.

Adams had filled these positions at the last minute with Federalists whom he believed would frustrate Jefferson's policies. Because these Midnight Appointments were made so late, there wasn't even time to deliver the official commission to one of the new judges, William Marbury. After Jefferson took office, his secretary of state, James Madison, refused to deliver Marbury's commission, so Marbury sued.

The case went all the way to the Supreme Court. In his 1803 decision, Chief Justice John Marshall declared that a section of the Judiciary Act of 1789 was unconstitutional. This decision established the important principle of judicial review. Marshall's ruling demonstrated that the Supreme Court could void an act of Congress if the law in question violated any part of the Constitution.

THE BURR CONSPIRACY

In his second inaugural address, Jefferson spoke of the successes of his administration and looked to the future. He announced plans to build new roads to the western lands and canals in the East to connect that region's major waterways. Canals promoted trade by making it easier to transport goods.

What Jefferson didn't know was that his second term would be marred by a dangerous conspiracy. A crisis abroad also contributed to the turmoil that forced him to postpone these plans.

Aaron Burr was a jealous and bitter man. After losing the fight for the presidency in 1800, he became desperate to get even with Jefferson.

While Jefferson ran for reelection in 1804, Burr ran for governor in New York. In order to obtain the support of the Essex Junto, a powerful group of New England Federalists, Burr had to promise that, if he became governor, New York would secede from the Union and join Massachusetts in a new Federalist country.

THE BURR-HAMILTON DUEL Alexander Hamilton was shocked to learn of this plan. Because he couldn't stand the thought of his home state leaving the Union, he began working against Burr. When Burr learned of this, he became enraged and challenged Hamilton to a duel. On July 11, 1804, Burr shot and killed Hamilton.

Charged with Hamilton's murder, Burr fled south. But when the charges were later dropped, he returned to Washington and presided over the Senate until the end of his vice-presidential term in 1805.

Although Burr lost the election in New York, he still pursued treasonous activities. He met with the British minister to the United States, asking him for half a million dollars and the help of the Royal Navy in taking over the Louisiana Territory. When the British ignored him, Burr went to Louisiana anyway, where he tried to incite a rebellion by himself.

Jefferson was told of Burr's plans by Gen. James Wilkinson, the military governor of the Louisiana Territory. Burr had recently approached Wilkinson with the idea of establishing a new empire.

In 1807, Burr was arrested for treason. Chief Justice John Marshall presided at his trial. In the end, Burr was acquitted because, according to Marshall's strict interpretation of the Constitution, Burr's plotting hadn't broken any laws.

★ RELIGIOUS FREEDOM

Of all his many accomplishments, Jefferson was the most proud of the law guaranteeing religious freedom that he helped enact in his home state of Virginia. This law, finalized in 1786, stated that Virginians were free to attend churches of their own choice, or no church at all.

Some people attacked Jefferson for being an atheist, or someone who doesn't believe in any god. In fact, Jefferson did believe in a single Creator, and he also admired the teachings of Jesus. Yet what he really cherished was religious tolerance. "It does me no injury," he once wrote, "for my neighbor to say there are twenty gods, or no god. It neither picks my pocket nor breaks my leg."

★ LEWIS AND CLARK

One of the most important members of the Lewis and Clark expedition was a sixteen-year-old Shoshone girl named Sacajawea. Along with her French-Canadian trapper husband, she joined the Corps of Discovery in 1804, while Meriwether Lewis (left) and William Clark were wintering in the Dakotas.

As Lewis and Clark continued their trip westward, they encountered a number of different Indian tribes. Sacajawea's ability to communicate with these native peoples proved invaluable in persuading them that the expedition's intentions were peaceful.

★THE SHAKERS

Cooperative religious communities in the United States date back to colonial times. One of the first was founded by Ann Lee, who came to America in 1774 to escape persecution in England. Her followers were a radical sect of the Quakers known as the Shaking Quakers, or simply the Shakers. They valued hard work, thrift, simplicity, and devotion to God. They also believed in equality of the sexes.

By the 1830s, there were more than six thousand Shakers living in approximately twenty communities, most in upstate New York and Massachusetts. Because Shakers did not believe in having children, their communities could survive only by recruiting new members.

★NOAH WEBSTER

In 1800, Noah Webster began work on a comprehensive dictionary of the English language. A famous dictionary of English had already been published by the British scholar Samuel Johnson in 1755. But Webster understood that the English language was written and spoken differently in the United States than it was in England.

In 1806, and again in 1807, Webster published small dictionaries as he kept working on the larger project, which eventually became his life's work. The complete dictionary was finally published in 1828. This 1828 dictionary contained more than seventy thousand words, or twelve thousand more words than even Johnson's contained.

★AUDUBON'S BIRDS

The tales of early-nineteenth-century explorers such as Lewis and Clark helped popularize natural history in the United States. One man who became excited by ornithology, or the study of birds, was a failed storekeeper named John James Audubon. After giving up his business on the Kentucky frontier, Audubon became the most famous painter of animals in the world.

Audubon's specialty was birds. His four-volume *Birds of America,* published between 1827 and 1838, included 435 full-color illustrations. Audubon's drawings made him a sensation in London, where he would often amuse himself by walking around town dressed as an American frontiersman. For show, he would put on a fringed leather jacket and slick down his hair with bear grease.

Although he was found innocent, Burr was completely discredited. After the trial, he left for Europe, where he tried to interest the French in conquering Canada. He finally returned to New York in 1812 under a false name and practiced law there until his death in 1836.

THE LEWIS AND CLARK EXPEDITION

Even before he approved the Louisiana Purchase, President Jefferson, an amateur naturalist, sent an expedition to explore the Louisiana Territory. He asked his personal secretary, Meriwether Lewis, to lead the expedition.

With Jefferson's permission, Lewis wrote to William Clark, a veteran soldier, asking him to become coleader of the expedition. A month later, Lewis received Clark's reply. Although Clark wrote that he believed the Corps of Discovery would encounter many great difficulties along the way, he also told Lewis that he was eager to try.

On May 14, 1804, Lewis and Clark left St. Louis accompanied by thirty soldiers and ten civilians, including experts in botany, zoology, sign language, and navigation. Later, they took on a fur trapper and his Shoshone wife, Sacajawea, to help them communicate with the potentially hostile Indians they knew they would encounter.

The explorers sailed up the Missouri River into what is now North Dakota. They lived on rations of salt pork and biscuits as well as wild game and fish. On November 7, 1805, the expedition reached the Pacific Ocean.

Because the Indian tribes there were in contact with trading ships, Lewis and Clark hoped to catch a ride back east to Washington. They waited for months in the hope that a ship might arrive. Eventually, they decided to make the return journey by land, arriving back in St. Louis on September 23, 1806.

1808

Both Lewis and Clark made maps and kept journals of their trip across the continent. The journals in particular provided an enormous amount of new scientific information about the country's interior.

Lewis and Clark's diaries included notes about the terrain and peoples they encountered. The two explorers also brought back specimens of the hundreds of new plants and animals they found along the way. They even presented Jefferson with a prairie dog, which lived out the rest of its life at the White House.

THE EMBARGO ACT

It was near the end of his second term in office that Jefferson faced his most dangerous foreign crisis. The trouble began in June 1807, when the British warship *Leopard* fired on the American frigate *Chesapeake*. Despite the public's demand for war, Jefferson wanted to remain reasonable. He told his minister to Great Britain to demand an apology.

When the British refused, Jefferson convinced Congress to authorize an embargo, not just against Britain but against all of Europe. He believed that withholding U.S. goods would force both France and Britain to respect U.S. neutrality. He signed the resulting Embargo Act in December 1807.

But the embargo was a disaster, hurting Americans much more than it did the British or the French. Without European buyers, many U.S. crops simply rotted away in storage. Meanwhile, thousands of people in the shipping business, including sailors and shipbuilders, lost their jobs. A year later, Congress passed a bill repealing the embargo, which Jefferson reluctantly signed on March 1, 1809, three days before leaving office.

CAMPAIGN ★ 1808

IN 1808, JAMES MADISON RAN FOR PRESIDENT as the Democratic-Republican candidate. Physically, he didn't look much like a president—or rather, he didn't look the way most people thought a president should look.

Madison was just five feet, four inches tall, and he weighed barely one hundred pounds. His nose was scarred from frostbite. But Jefferson thought that his secretary of state would make an excellent president, and that was good enough for the rest of the party. The Democratic-Republicans soon nicknamed their candidate the Great Little Madison.

Of course, Madison didn't have much opposition. The retirement of John Adams and the death of Alexander Hamilton had so devastated the Federalist party that it wasn't even able to nominate a candidate formally. Instead, Federalists loosely supported the same ticket of Charles Pinckney and Rufus King that the party had run in 1804. Although Federalist New England went for Pinckney, Madison carried the rest of the country easily.

Between the presidencies of John Adams and his son John Quincy Adams, the Democratic-Republicans held the White House for six consecutive terms, covering twenty-four years. This string of presidents is sometimes referred to as the Jefferson Dynasty, because both Madison and his successor, James Monroe, considered themselves to be pupils of Jefferson. The period is also called the Virginia Monarchy, because all three men came from Virginia.

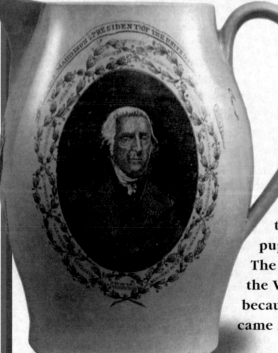

JAMES MADISON
4th President
★
1809 to 1817

James Madison

BORN: MARCH 16, 1751

BIRTHPLACE: PORT CONWAY, VA.

DIED: JUNE 28, 1836

PARTY: DEMOCRATIC-REPUBLICAN

VICE PRESIDENTS: GEORGE CLINTON, ELBRIDGE GERRY

FIRST LADY: DOLLEY DANDRIDGE PAYNE TODD

CHILDREN: NONE

NICKNAME: FATHER OF THE CONSTITUTION

THE FIRST PRESIDENT TO WEAR TROUSERS REGULARLY (INSTEAD OF KNEE BREECHES).

James Madison inherited a country in crisis. The Embargo Act had just been repealed, but its deadening effect on the U.S. economy was still being felt throughout the country. To make matters worse, neither France nor Britain was any closer to respecting U.S. neutrality on the high seas.

Jefferson's solution hadn't worked, and it was now up to his handpicked successor, Madison, to deal with the problem. The Embargo Act had proven that exports were crucial to the U.S. economy, and the only way to export goods to Europe was by ship. Madison's task was to find a way to protect U.S. shipping without reducing trade.

WAR HAWKS RISE TO POWER

FRONTIER CONGRESSMEN TAKE OVER WASHINGTON

THE MIDTERM ELECTIONS of 1810 brought a new generation of politicians to Washington. Angry with the slow pace of government, voters across the country turned out nearly half the members of Congress and replaced them with young men whose ideas were very different from those of their stately elders.

These men took advantage of the public outrage at Britain's harassment of U.S. shipping and campaigned for war. As a result, they were nicknamed War Hawks. Thirty-four-year-old Henry Clay of Kentucky and John C. Calhoun of South Carolina, who was five years younger, were the leaders of this group. Both men had been raised on the frontier, and their behavior reflected their upbringing. Clay and Calhoun were both rambunctious, with little of the Old World gentility that had characterized the Founding Fathers.

In addition to demanding war with Britain, the War Hawks wanted to expand the country northward by invading Canada and southward by conquering Florida and taking whatever Indian lands were available.

A DEAL WITH NAPOLÉON

Madison didn't have many options, but neither was he particularly bold. Instead, he was a shy man by nature with a quiet speaking voice, and he liked to think matters through a number of times before coming to a decision. His treasury secretary once said that Madison was "slow in taking his ground, but firm when the storm rises."

Madison tried a variety of strategies. The first was to enforce the Non-Intercourse Act of 1809, which had been passed during Jefferson's final days in office. This law represented a new approach to the embargo. It lifted the trade restrictions on all nations except Britain and France and promised to lift the restrictions on these two nations as well if they promised to respect the neutrality of U.S. shipping.

Unfortunately, the Non-Intercourse Act didn't work either. Britain and France paid no attention, and trade continued to suffer. So Madison tried a different approach. In 1810, he signed into law Macon's Bill Number Two, which offered a different sort of deal: If either Britain or France agreed to respect U.S. neutrality, the United States would cut off trade with the other nation. Napoléon was the first to accept this deal on behalf of France, so Madison reimposed the trade embargo on Britain.

INDIAN RELATIONS

Meanwhile, relations between Indians and white settlers were heating up along the western frontier. Ever since the Battle of Fallen Timbers in 1794, white settlers had been pushing Indians out of the Ohio River Valley and farther into the nation's interior.

Thomas Jefferson had wanted to integrate native peoples into white society by teaching them how to farm in the European fashion and how to

JAMES MADISON WAS RAISED IN A HOUSE built by his grandfather within view of Virginia's Blue Ridge Mountains. As Madison grew up, there were two great traumas in his life. The first was a local smallpox epidemic. The second was the French and Indian War.

THE EARLY YEARS

When British general Edward Braddock was defeated by the French and their Indian allies in 1755, many Virginians feared an Indian invasion. That never happened, but the threat of one turned Madison against Indians for the rest of his life.

After serving in the Virginia House of Delegates and the Continental Congress, Madison became in 1787 a delegate to the Constitutional Convention in Philadelphia. Because of his work there, he would later be called the Father of the Constitution.

★ THE FIRST LADY

Known for her charm and intelligence, Dolley Madison stands out as one of the nation's most extraordinary first ladies. During the War of 1812, she also proved that she could be remarkably cool in a crisis.

In August 1814, the first lady was planning a dinner party for forty guests when the British closed in on Washington. The president was already safely out of town, and now his wife was told to flee. But before she left, she packed up the Declaration of Independence, the national seal, a portrait of George Washington, and her pet parrot, sending them all ahead of her to safety.

★ BEAU BRUMMELL

The clothes worn by fashionable American men during the first half of the nineteenth century were examples of the Regency style that was popular in Great Britain. This style was named after its chief patron, George, the prince regent, who later became King George IV.

At the time, the most fashionable man in the world was Beau Brummell. It usually took Brummell an entire morning to dress in his long jacket, tight breeches, and elaborately ruffled scarf. His look featured country clothes that had been sharpened up for city wear. Meanwhile, fashionable women followed the French style of long, high-waisted dresses with richly embroidered hems.

1811

★ TOM MOLINEAUX

One of the most popular sports during the early nineteenth century was boxing. The best boxer in the country was a freed slave from Virginia named Tom Molineaux. While still in his twenties, Molineaux moved to New York, where he fought in amateur matches. In 1809, at the age of twenty-five, he sailed to England to box professionally.

In December 1810, Molineaux became the first American to fight an English champion. He lost to Tom Cribb in the fortieth round. The rematch, which Molineaux also lost, drew a record crowd of forty thousand people.

Other popular sports at this time included horse racing, tenpin bowling, rowing, and gouging, which was a frontier sport. The point of gouging was to pluck out an opponent's eyeball. In the Ohio River Valley, people grew their thumbnails especially long for this purpose.

★ UNCLE SAM

During the War of 1812, a merchant in Troy, New York, named Samuel Wilson supplied barrels of beef to the U.S. Army. He stamped these barrels "U.S." to show that they were government property. Because Wilson was commonly known as Uncle Sam, and because the barrels were stamped with these initials, people began referring to the U.S. government as Uncle Sam.

Cartoonists began using the symbolic figure of Uncle Sam in the early 1830s. The British humor magazine *Punch* developed the most familiar caricature: a bearded man with a top hat and striped pants. Political cartoonist Thomas Nast used Uncle Sam extensively during the 1870s. But the most famous Uncle Sam ever drawn was created by James Montgomery Flagg, whose well-known World War I recruiting poster was captioned "I Want You for U.S. Army."

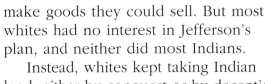

make goods they could sell. But most whites had no interest in Jefferson's plan, and neither did most Indians.

Instead, whites kept taking Indian land, either by conquest or by deception. Treaties were made and broken. Promises were made and not kept. In this way, by 1810, settlers had seized one hundred million acres of fertile Indian land.

TECUMSEH'S CONFEDERACY

When the Shawnee chief Tecumseh saw what was happening, he tried to stop the land grabs. His strategy was to form an alliance of all the frontier tribes from the Canadian border down to Florida.

Tecumseh was intelligent enough to understand that white settlers were using alcohol to cheat Indians out of their land and control them. He realized that to fight the settlers, the Indians would have to stop drinking the rum and whiskey the settlers offered them.

On November 7, 1811, while Tecumseh was away in the south trying to enlist the Creeks in his confederacy, white soldiers marched on his village. In the ensuing battle of Tippecanoe Creek, Gen. William Henry Harrison, who would later become president himself, beat off a dawn attack and won a decisive victory.

Tecumseh vowed to seek revenge and got his chance during the War of 1812. But the result turned out to be another Harrison victory, and Tecumseh was killed in that battle, fighting alongside the British in Canada.

THE WAR HAWKS

A cautious man, Madison moved slowly with regard to the British. But the rest of the country had little patience for his seemingly endless waiting. During the midterm elections of 1810, voters replaced nearly half the

members of Congress with much younger politicians who promised to end the nation's ongoing humiliation. These new congressmen were known as War Hawks because they promised, if elected, to declare war on Great Britain.

Despite the great pressure brought by the election of so many War Hawks, Madison held firm for more than a year. In June 1812, however, he finally gave in and asked Congress for a declaration of war. He had few other options left.

THE WAR OF 1812 Everyone knew the reasons for war: the impressment of U.S. sailors, the lack of respect for U.S. neutrality, and the continuing British agitation of Indian tribes along the western frontier. Nevertheless, the declaration didn't come easily. Congress debated it for seventeen days before finally approving the resolution in a rather close vote.

By far the most vocal opposition to "Mr. Madison's War" came from Federalist New England. Despite the aggressive enthusiasm whipped up by the War Hawks, merchants in New England wanted nothing to do with a war against their biggest customer, Great Britain.

To protest Madison's decision, most New Englanders began boycotting the war and refusing to allow their state militias to join in the fighting. Some New England merchants even flirted with treason as they became fabulously wealthy selling supplies to both sides.

As Madison soon discovered, however, New England's opposition to the war was just the beginning of his troubles. As he had always known, the War of 1812 turned out to be much more difficult to win than it had been to declare.

CAMPAIGN ★ 1812

THE CAMPAIGN OF 1812 WAS THE FIRST ever held in wartime. Although the War Hawks had been very successful in 1810, by the fall of 1812 opposition to the war, now that it had come, was strong and growing, especially in New England.

Madison ran for reelection against former New York City mayor DeWitt Clinton. Although Clinton was also a Democratic-Republican, he was running for president independent of his party, which was backing Madison. Clinton did, however, have the support of the New England Federalists, who again chose not to nominate a candidate. (Clinton also happened to be the nephew of Madison's first vice president, George Clinton, who died in April 1812.)

The campaign was most notable for Clinton's outrageous habit of promising different things to different people. To people who supported the war, he promised to continue the fight. To people such as the Federalists, who opposed the war, he made speeches blaming the entire mess on Madison and promised to negotiate an immediate peace.

The lack of enthusiasm in the country for Madison's policies gave Clinton a chance, but the president's strong support in the South and the West was enough to see him through. Clinton won four New England states in addition to Delaware, New York, New Jersey, and five of Maryland's eleven votes. But Madison took the rest, winning 128 electoral votes to Clinton's 89.

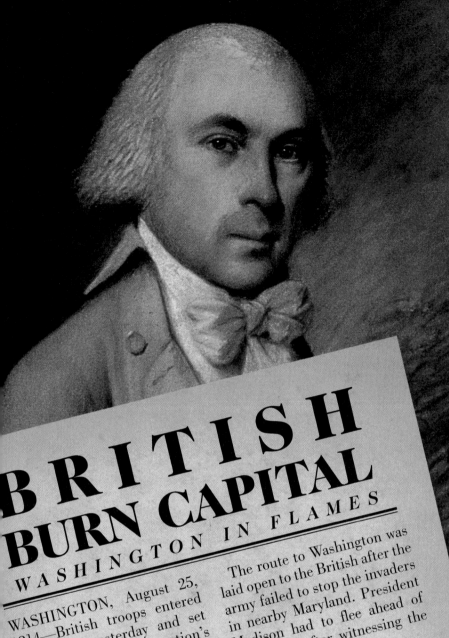

A portrait of Madison by James Sharples, painted about 1796.

1813

Things went wrong from the start. For example, when the president called for fifty thousand army volunteers, only five thousand signed up. To make up the difference, the army began enlisting African Americans, both free blacks and slaves. Many slaves fought in the army, hoping to win their freedom. But they were generally returned to slavery after the war.

THE INVASION OF CANADA Unwilling to challenge the powerful British navy at sea, Madison instead decided to focus on a land campaign against British Canada. The most obvious invasion routes passed through New York and New England, but none of these states would permit a federal attack across its border because they opposed the war.

As a result, the first invasion of Canada was launched from Detroit in July 1812. Madison unwisely chose an aging Revolutionary War veteran, William Hull, to lead the expedition. General Hull crossed the border, but fearing Indian attacks, he quickly withdrew back to Detroit, which he later surrendered to the lesser army of British general Isaac Brock without even firing a shot. For his cowardice, Hull was later court-martialed.

BRITISH BURN CAPITAL
WASHINGTON IN FLAMES

WASHINGTON, August 25, 1814—British troops entered the capital yesterday and set fire to many of the nation's important public buildings. The first that the British burned was the Capitol, which was still under construction. Then the British marched to the president's house and set that on fire as well. As night fell, the British rested in empty boardinghouses and watched the city burn.

This morning, British soldiers prepared to destroy the rest of the town, but a storm came up suddenly. The storm accomplished what the American army had been unable to do: It forced the British to retreat.

The route to Washington was laid open to the British after the army failed to stop the invaders in nearby Maryland. President Madison had to flee ahead of his troops after witnessing the brief battle.

By the time that British troops reached the undefended capital, most of the government officials and residents had left. Only a few women remained behind, packing their belongings. The president's wife, Dolley, stayed behind long enough to save some of the government's valuable papers.

THE TAKING OF THE CITY OF WASHINGTON IN AMERICA

From this poor start, things got even worse when General Brock marched his troops to the Niagara River and began making preparations to invade New York. To prevent this, on October 13, 1812, a small federal regiment under Capt. James E. Wool attacked Brock's camp on the Canadian side of the river.

At first, the battle went well for the Americans. Brock was killed, and the British scattered. Wool clearly had the upper hand. But as he waited anxiously for reinforcements, the British regrouped, and his edge slipped away.

Just before all hope was lost, New York state militiamen did arrive on the New York side of the river. But they stopped there and wouldn't cross over to help their countrymen. Their orders were clear: Defend New York, but do not cross the river into Canada. Instead, they watched from the New York side as the British massacred Wool's regiment.

THE BURNING OF WASHINGTON

As James Madison took the oath of office at his second inauguration in March 1813, the country was in the midst of its greatest crisis since the Revolution. The plan to invade Canada had failed, and now the British were on the offensive.

The Americans enjoyed a bit of success in the Northwest, where Capt. Oliver Hazard Perry won control of Lake Erie in September 1813 and a month later Gen. William Henry Harrison won the battle of the Thames River (during which Tecumseh was killed). But the British were meanwhile preparing a devastating counterpunch, which they unleashed at the end of 1813.

That December, British forces crossed the Canadian border and burned Buffalo, New York. Eight months later, they swept past weak U.S. defenses in the Chesapeake Bay and marched on Washington, burning the capital on August 24, 1814.

★ FRANCIS SCOTT KEY

When the British attacked Baltimore during the War of 1812, they had as a prisoner aboard one of their ships an influential Washington lawyer named Francis Scott Key. From this excellent vantage point, Key was able to witness the British bombardment of Fort McHenry during the night of September 13–14, 1814.

The British kept up the attack throughout the night. The flashes from their cannon made the scene seem like a nightmare. Then, suddenly, the firing stopped. At dawn, Key strained to see whether the U.S. flag was still flying above the fort. His joy at seeing the Stars and Stripes inspired him to write "The Star-Spangled Banner." The song became the official national anthem in 1931. It was the only piece of poetry that Key ever wrote.

★ THE WHITE HOUSE

When the British invaded Washington, they burned the president's house. After the fire, only the walls of the residence remained, and these were blackened by smoke.

To cover up the smoke damage, workers painted the outside walls of the reconstructed building white. The result was so eye-catching that people began referring to the president's house as the White House. In 1901, the name of the building was officially changed at the request of Pres. Theodore Roosevelt.

★ GERRYMANDERING

Elbridge Gerry was Madison's second vice president and, before that, governor of Massachusetts. During his term as governor, Gerry supported the creation of a strange-looking voting district, the point of which was to maximize his party's influence. Because the district's shape reminded some people of a salamander, they began using the term *gerrymander* to describe this practice of drawing district lines to favor one political party over another.

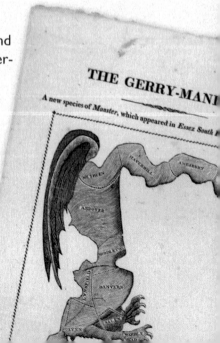

THE GERRY-MANI

A new species of *Monster*, which appeared in *Essex South P...*

★FRANCIS CABOT LOWELL

In the fall of 1810, a wealthy American merchant named Francis Cabot Lowell sailed from Boston to England. He said that he was taking a vacation, but he actually wanted to study the workings of English textile factories.

Upon returning to Massachusetts, Lowell hired an engineer named Paul Moody to help him build his own textile factory. The machinery that Lowell couldn't buy, he had Moody make.

In 1814, Lowell opened the first fully mechanized cloth-making factory in the United States. He offered good wages and set up clean quarters for his workers, which made work at his factory attractive to local farm girls. Lowell's factory also served an example to other business owners of how profitable manufacturing could be. In this way, Lowell helped change the focus of the New England economy from shipping to manufacturing.

★MEDICINE

American medical education during the early nineteenth century was not very good. The treatments the doctors used were based more on folk remedies than on science. Sometimes, doctors would apply leeches to a patient to suck out a disease. Plants and herbs were also popular medicines, especially in rural areas.

Although many women practiced herbal medicine, most doctors were men. These men kept offices in their homes, but more often they made house calls. When necessary, they even moved in with a patient until he or she was cured.

Many Indian tribes also used herbs to treat diseases, but western Algonquins practiced a different kind of therapy. Their medicine men belonged to the Midewiwin, or Grand Medicine Society. When someone in the tribe became ill, the members of this society would seek a vision, during which spirits would instruct them in ways to cure the patient.

PEACE TALKS

In the meantime, the British had informed Madison in January 1814 that they were prepared to discuss terms for peace. Madison had accepted the offer immediately and sent a delegation to meet with the British at a neutral site, the town of Ghent in Belgium.

The British believed that they could dictate the terms of the peace. After all, they were winning the war. As far as they were concerned, the Americans should be the ones making concessions.

Therefore, the British began by presenting a list of demands: They wanted the Americans to stop fishing in the waters off Newfoundland. They also wanted the Canadian border moved to provide access to the Mississippi River. Finally, they wanted to create a territory in the Ohio River Valley between the United States and Canada to be inhabited by their Indian allies.

John Quincy Adams, son of former president John Adams, was among the U.S. peace commissioners sent to Ghent. Although an experienced diplomat, Adams was shocked by these demands. He advised his fellow commissioners to return home immediately. But Henry Clay wasn't yet ready to leave.

Clay had much less diplomatic experience than Adams, but he was a good deal shrewder. He decided that the British were bluffing and that they would be willing to accept much less in exchange for peace. The Napoleonic Wars in Europe were winding down, and Great Britain had better things to do than continue fighting a war an ocean away. Clay convinced the rest of the U.S. delegation to stay and press for better terms. The British held firm for several months but eventually began to reduce their demands.

When the Treaty of Ghent was finally signed in December 1814,

THE TREATY OF GHENT

it included none of the original demands. In fact, all it did was end the fighting and restore the status quo ante bellum, which means the state of things as they existed before the war.

Neither side gained or lost any territory, and other matters were left unresolved—such as the neutrality rights of U.S. shipping. But the Treaty of Ghent did have a lasting effect in that it paved the way for closer relations between the two countries. After the war, Britain showed a great deal more respect to the United States than it had ever shown before.

THE BATTLE OF NEW ORLEANS

Of course, while the Treaty of Ghent was still being negotiated, the war went on. Ironically, the last battle was fought on January 8, 1815, two weeks after the signing of the treaty in Ghent. The battle of New Orleans took place anyway because Ghent was a continent away, and in 1815 it took much longer than two weeks for news to travel across the Atlantic. Neither side in New Orleans knew that the war had ended.

The British army had arrived at New Orleans in late December to find the U.S. positions below the city well guarded. After several cautious attempts to breach the American fortifications, eight thousand British soldiers launched an all-out attack on January 8.

Gen. Andrew Jackson, who led the U.S. troops, fought a brilliant defensive battle. By the end of the bloody day, the British had lost more than two thousand men. Of their four generals, one was dead, one was dying, and another was disabled. The Americans lost only twenty-one men, and Jackson became a national hero.

CAMPAIGN ★ 1816

ONCE HE BECAME THE CANDIDATE of the Democratic-Republican party in 1816, Secretary of State James Monroe was practically guaranteed the presidency. Secretary of War William Crawford had a strong following in Congress that might have posed a threat, but Crawford never mounted a serious challenge because he was unwilling to risk what promised to be a powerful place in the new cabinet.

In many ways, Monroe was Madison's natural successor. As secretary of state, he had occupied the same office for Madison that Madison had filled for Jefferson. Indeed, Jefferson had also served as secretary of state during the Washington administration. Moreover, Monroe was widely admired for his warm, generous personality.

Meanwhile, the Federalists failed yet again to nominate a candidate. At the Hartford Convention, a meeting of Federalists held in December 1814, delegates from Connecticut, Massachusetts, and Rhode Island had gathered to discuss seceding from the Union and starting their own country. Although this never occurred, most Americans began thinking of the Federalists as unpatriotic and possibly treasonous. The failure of the Hartford Convention in 1815 thus eliminated what little influence the Federalists still had in the country.

The best the Federalists could do was support Rufus King of New York, who had run for vice president in 1804 and again in 1808. A dedicated public servant, King had once been George Washington's minister to Great Britain. But King, the last of the Federalists, was no match for Monroe. The only states that King carried were Connecticut, Delaware, and Massachusetts.

BORN: APRIL 28, 1758

BIRTHPLACE: WESTMORELAND COUNTY, VA.

DIED: JULY 4, 1831

PARTY: DEMOCRATIC-REPUBLICAN

VICE PRESIDENT: DANIEL D. TOMPKINS

FIRST LADY: ELIZABETH KORTRIGHT

CHILDREN: ELIZA, (UNNAMED SON), MARIA

NICKNAME: LAST OF THE COCKED HATS

THE LAST PRESIDENT TO HAVE
SERVED AS AN OFFICER IN THE
REVOLUTIONARY WAR.

1817

JAMES MONROE
5th President
★
1817 to 1825

James Monroe

The British burned the president's house so thoroughly during the War of 1812 that years passed before it was habitable again. Even as James Monroe took the oath of office in March 1817, there remained work to be done. So, rather than live in temporary housing as the Madisons had, Monroe decided to take a grand tour of the country until the work on the president's house was completed. He wanted to have a close-up look at the country he would be governing.

Beginning his trip in Washington, Monroe traveled north as far as Portland, Maine. From there, he turned west to Detroit and then southeast back toward Washington. The triangular trip took fifteen weeks and gave Monroe a better knowledge of the country than any president before him, with the possible exception of George Washington.

MARSHALL ISSUES LANDMARK RULINGS

THE YEAR 1819 was a remarkable one for the Supreme Court and its chief justice, John Marshall. The Court's rulings in two landmark cases that year changed forever the balance of power in the federal government.

The first case, *Dartmouth College v. Woodward*, involved the charter of Dartmouth College, which the state of New Hampshire had recently tried to change. Dartmouth's charter was originally granted in 1769, when New Hampshire was still a British colony.

However, as Marshall himself pointed out in his decision, the case was really about contracts. The chief justice explained that Dartmouth's charter was actually a contract that no one side had the power to change by itself. The

Court's ruling thus made it clear that business contracts would be respected in the United States.

In the other case, *McCulloch v. Maryland*, Marshall ruled that the state of Maryland could not tax the Second Bank of the United States because the national bank was a federal institution.

Marshall's ruling emphasized that states could not restrict the federal government's constitutional powers. *McCulloch v. Maryland* also established the constitutionality of the bank itself, thus endorsing Alexander Hamilton's theory of implied powers.

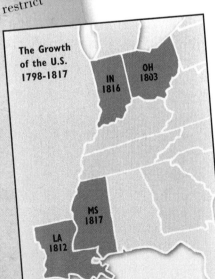

The Growth of the U.S. 1798-1817

OH 1803

IN 1816

MS 1817

LA 1812

THE ERA OF GOOD FEELINGS

Everywhere he went, the triumphant Monroe was greeted with cheers by large crowds lining the roadways. Even in the heart of New England, Federalists applauded the Democratic-Republican president, and one Boston newspaper was moved to describe Monroe's joyful reception as the beginning of an "era of good feelings" for the country.

New England, which had detested James Madison, was quicker to accept Monroe because the region's economy had changed a great deal in the years during and after the War of 1812. Before the war, New England had depended almost exclusively on its trade with Great Britain. When the war cut that trade off, New Englanders had to find other ways to make their livings.

NEW ENGLAND FACTORIES

Pioneering industrialists such as Francis Cabot Lowell opened factories that helped shift the economic focus of New England from shipping to manufacturing. As a result, the region and the country became much more self-sufficient.

Factories such as Lowell's were decent places to work, unlike the grim, dirty factories of industrial England. Although the workforce of young men and women typically put in twelve- and fourteen-hour days, they made good wages and were given clean, pleasant quarters in which to live. The evening lectures that some factories offered their workers provided the only schooling most factory girls ever got.

On the other hand, work at factories owned by less charitable people could be harsh and cruel, and eventually the conditions at most factories sank to that level. Greedy owners would

THE EARLY YEARS

JAMES MONROE'S FATHER DIED when he was about sixteen years old. The system of inheritance at that time was called primogeniture. Under this system, a man's oldest son inherited all of his family's property. Because James was the firstborn son of five children, he inherited everything.

About the same time, Monroe enrolled at the College of William and Mary in Williamsburg, Virginia. His mind wasn't on his studies, however. Instead, like most students at William and Mary, he was caught up in the patriotic fever sweeping the colonies. In March 1776, unable to resist any longer, he dropped out of college and enlisted in the Continental Army.

★ JOHN JACOB ASTOR AND THE FUR TRADE

The fur trade with the Indians was for many years an important part of the North American economy. In colonial times, the most important fur trading centers were in the Great Lakes and the Ohio River Valley.

John Jacob Astor was the poor son of a German butcher. Astor came to this country at the age of twenty, just after the Revolutionary War. His first employer was a fur trader in New York City. Astor quickly learned the business and soon made a small fortune, buying furs upstate and selling them in London.

Beaver furs were especially valuable because hats made from them were very fashionable in Europe. In fact, so many beavers were trapped and killed that they were soon in danger of extinction. With his fur trade profits, Astor invested in New York City real estate. Eventually, he became the richest man in the country.

★ WEDDING AT THE WHITE HOUSE

In 1818, James Monroe hired Samuel L. Gouverneur as a private secretary. Soon thereafter, the young man fell in love with Monroe's daughter Maria. After a two-year courtship, the couple decided to marry. The date was set for March 9, 1820.

The wedding was the first ever held in the White House. The ceremony was a small, private affair. Only forty-two guests were invited. Everyone else had to wait until the reception five days later to congratulate the new couple.

★ LITERATURE IN AMERICA

The outpouring of patriotism encouraged by the Era of Good Feelings helped create America's first national literature. The most important writers of this period were James Fenimore Cooper and Washington Irving.

Cooper published several stories about the frontier, known collectively as the Leatherstocking tales, in which he portrayed Indians as "noble savages." His most famous book, *The Last of the Mohicans* (1826), helped popularize the American wilderness.

Irving specialized in short stories. His best-known works include "The Legend of Sleepy Hollow," featuring schoolmaster Ichabod Crane, and "Rip Van Winkle." Irving was also the first American author to win fame in Europe.

★ THE MASON AND DIXON LINE

Every American knew that there existed a clear political division between the free North and the slave South. On most maps of the country, this division was generally represented by the Mason and Dixon Line.

Between 1765 and 1768, two Englishmen named Charles Mason and Jeremiah Dixon surveyed the 233-mile-long border between the royal land grants of Pennsylvania and Maryland. This border had been set by the king of England at latitude 39°43'.

In the years leading up to the Civil War, however, the Mason and Dixon Line came to symbolize much more than simply the border between two states. In the minds of most Americans, it was more importantly the line between freedom and slavery.

employ entire families to work side by side on the factory floor. Even the youngest children were used to carry supplies to boys and girls old enough to work the machinery.

Even worse, instead of paying cash wages, many factory owners provided their workers only with run-down houses and credit at the company store, where the workers had to shop because they had no cash. And because the company store charged high prices, the workers were always in debt.

As long as the workers owed money, they couldn't leave their jobs. And the longer they stayed, the deeper in debt they became. Eventually, they became slaves to the factory owners.

THE AMERICAN SYSTEM

Meanwhile, former War Hawks Henry Clay and John C. Calhoun championed a series of projects designed to improve and update the country's infrastructure—that is, its roads, bridges, and canals. The bills that they introduced in Congress were part of an ambitious plan devised by Clay called the American System.

One of these bills imposed a tariff, or tax, on manufactured goods being imported into the country. This tariff made European goods more expensive to buy and thus encouraged Americans to purchase locally manufactured items. Also, the money raised by the tariff would be used to build roads and canals in the western territories.

Monroe agreed that Calhoun's public works projects were good for the nation. But, like Madison before him, he worried that funding internal improvements was not constitutional. A Jeffersonian at heart, Monroe feared that this sort of construction went well beyond the powers granted to the federal government by the Constitution.

THE CUMBERLAND ROAD

When Congress passed a bill in 1822 to fund an extension of the Cumberland Road, Monroe vetoed the bill because he believed that road building was the responsibility of the states. It was the only bill that Monroe vetoed in his eight years as president.

During Monroe's administration, the country grew at an amazingly fast rate. Much of this was due to westward expansion that took place along the route of the Cumberland Road. Beginning outside Baltimore, the Cumberland Road eventually extended through Pennsylvania, Virginia, Ohio, and Indiana before ending in Illinois. The road made it much easier for people to settle the Northwest Territory.

The first section of the road—from Cumberland, Maryland, to Wheeling in western Virginia—was built between 1811 and 1818. Before the road was extended, settlers reaching Wheeling often boarded steamships there to travel farther west along the Ohio River.

Although roads were popular because they were less expensive to build, transportation of goods by canal was actually faster and cheaper. On the day that Monroe took office, the United States had only a hundred miles of canal. By the end of his second term, however, that number had jumped to one thousand miles. These additional canal miles made it much easier for surplus western beef and corn to be sold in New England, where manufacturing was quickly displacing agriculture.

THE GROWTH OF REGIONALISM

Between 1816 and 1821, six new states joined the Union, making a total of twenty-four. Although

---

CAMPAIGN ★ 1820

THE ERA OF GOOD FEELINGS MADE James Monroe one of the most popular presidents in the history of the United States. His first term was considered a great success. The peace continued, and profitable new businesses were started every day. Relations with Britain were the best they had ever been, and the Missouri Compromise had resolved the controversy between free and slave states, at least for the time being. As a result, nobody seriously wanted to replace a president who had delivered so much peace and prosperity.

Because both Jefferson and Madison had served two terms in office, it was expected that Monroe would run again. And because the Democratic-Republicans were so sure that he would be reelected, they didn't even bother to nominate him formally. What little remained of the Federalist party didn't offer any opposition. As a result, the presidential race in 1820 was essentially an election without a campaign.

When the Electoral College finally met in December 1820, Monroe won all the electoral votes but one. The single exception was cast by New Hampshire governor William Plumer. It has been reported that Plumer voted against Monroe so that George Washington would remain the only president ever elected unanimously. According to Plumer's son, however, the New Hampshire governor simply hated Monroe.

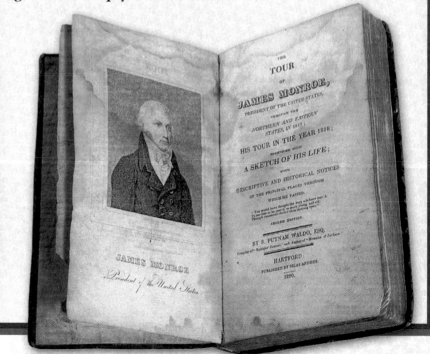

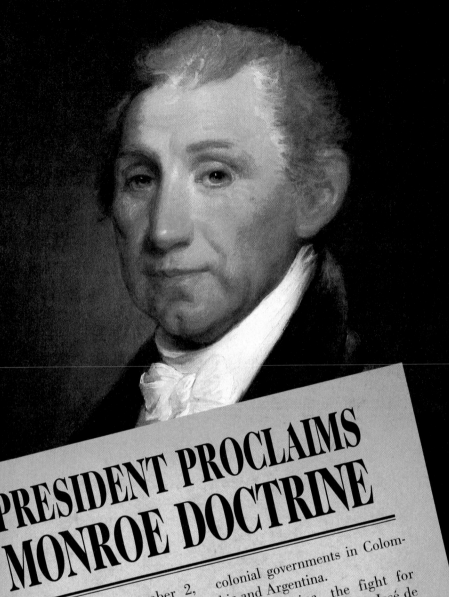

they were generally welcomed, the admission of these new states in the South and West unsettled some Americans in the North. The reason was that new regions of the country would, of course, have concerns of their own. Therefore, the concerns of people living in the original thirteen states would necessarily matter less.

For example, northern factory owners wanted higher tariffs on imported manufactured goods. They also wanted raw materials to remain cheap. Western farmers wanted exactly the opposite. They liked to get high prices for the raw materials they grew and pay low prices for the factory goods they bought. In the South, plantation owners were concerned about slave labor, any shortage of which would hurt their ability to produce cotton at a competitive price.

SLAVERY IN THE NEW STATES Each of these three regions worried about the balance of power in Congress, but the North and South were especially concerned about the issue of slavery. Many northerners wanted to abolish this brutal institution, which the South was equally determined to keep.

Both sides knew that the key votes on slavery would be cast in the West. If the new western states were admitted as slave states, then slavery would most likely continue into the future. If they were admitted as free states, then slavery would probably pass away, even in the South. Either way, the balance of power would soon shift decisively.

PRESIDENT PROCLAIMS MONROE DOCTRINE

WASHINGTON, December 2, 1823—President Monroe used the opportunity of his annual message to Congress today to announce a bold new foreign policy. In his speech, written by Secretary of State John Quincy Adams, the president warned European nations against trying to establish (or reestablish) any more colonies in the Americas. Monroe also made it clear that his new doctrine does not apply to colonies already in existence.

The speech was prompted by fears that some European powers might be planning to help Spain recapture its lost colonies in South America. Highly publicized wars of independence have recently overthrown the Spanish colonial governments in Colombia and Argentina.

In Argentina, the fight for independence was led by José de San Martin. In Colombia, Simón Bolívar led the successful revolution against Spanish rule. Both men have since served as models for other leaders in Central and South America who believe in the principle of self-rule.

The nation's founders had chosen to pass over the issue of slavery because it was simply too controversial. Had they attempted to resolve the issue one way or the other, the Constitution would never have been ratified. Instead, the fate of the slaves was left to the future.

In the thirty years since the Constitutional Convention, the cotton gin had made the South even more dependent on slave labor. To ensure that slavery would continue, southerners now began demanding its extension to the new western states.

THE MISSOURI COMPROMISE

The issue came to a turning point in 1819, when settlers in Missouri applied for statehood. The question on everyone's mind was: Would Missouri be admitted as a slave state or as a free state? In Washington, Congress debated whether or not the federal government had the power to ban slavery in the new states.

Southerners argued that banning slavery in Missouri would deprive slaveholders of their property—that is, their slaves. Many northerners, however, couldn't bear the thought of slavery spreading to one state after another. Unable to move forward, Congress adjourned until its next session without reaching a decision.

When Congress met again in 1820, there was a new wrinkle in the debate. Now the territory of Maine wanted to join the Union as well. Being so far north, Maine would certainly be admitted as a free state.

On that basis, a compromise was reached. Maine and Missouri would be admitted together, Maine as a free state and Missouri as a slave state. That way, the number of slave states and free states would remain equal. There would be twelve of each.

★ THE DISCOVERY OF SOUTH PASS

In mid-February 1824, a group of fur trappers found and crossed a wide gap in the Rocky Mountains in present-day Wyoming. Because it took place during the middle of the winter, the crossing was difficult. The snow was knee-deep, and the mountain men had nothing to drink, except for the snow they melted by the heat of their hands.

The route they discovered, later called South Pass, turned out to be the easiest way through these difficult mountains. In the 1840s, South Pass became the principal gateway to the West, and it was used by thousands of settlers following the Oregon Trail.

★ THE CHEROKEE ALPHABET

About 1809, when the Cherokee silversmith Sequoyah was in his forties, he began to work on a writing system for his tribe. The Cherokees had a spoken language but not a written one. Sequoyah believed that the increased knowledge a written language would bring might help his people remain independent of the whites.

At first, he tried using pictographs, as the ancient Egyptians had done. When these didn't work, he began adapting letters from the English, Greek, and Hebrew alphabets to represent the sounds of the spoken Cherokee language. By 1821, he had created the first Cherokee alphabet.

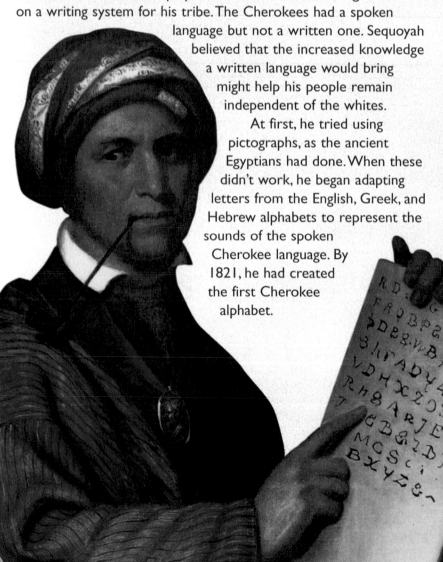

★ EDUCATION

Emma Willard was a pioneer in women's education. In 1819, she presented New York State with a plan to improve the way young women were schooled. When the state legislature rejected her plan, she founded the Troy Female Seminary instead.

The seminary, located in upstate New York, was the first college-level school for women in the United States. Few people thought that women needed or could use advanced education. Other colleges, for example, admitted only men. But Willard would not accept any such limitations, and the Troy Female Seminary proved that she was right.

★ THE AMERICAN COLONIZATION SOCIETY

In 1817, a Presbyterian minister in New Jersey named Robert Finley founded the American Colonization Society. Its goal was to end the practice of slavery. But Finley's opposition to slavery didn't mean that he wanted blacks and whites to live together. Instead, his group thought the best solution was to resettle freed black slaves in Africa.

The American Colonization Society founded Monrovia on the west coast of Africa in 1822. This colony, which became an independent republic in 1848, was supposed to be a new homeland for the freed slaves. Its name was soon changed to Liberia, but its capital kept the name Monrovia to honor President Monroe.

The problem was that most American blacks had no interest in moving to Africa, because very few had been born there. Instead, they wanted to prosper in America, which had become their home.

★ MEDICAL SCIENCE

During the early nineteenth century, the science of medicine progressed slowly. Doctors could only guess at some of the ways in which the human body worked. The X-ray machine hadn't been invented yet, so there was no way to look inside living human bodies.

In 1822, however, a remarkable accident gave army surgeon William Beaumont an unusual opportunity. One of his patients, a French-Canadian trapper named Alexis St. Martin, had accidentally shot himself in the stomach, and the shotgun blast had left a permanent hole in St. Martin's belly.

Through this hole, Beaumont was able to observe the process of digestion as it took place inside St. Martin. After performing a variety of experiments on the cooperative trapper, Beaumont even published a book on the subject. His studies added much to contemporary knowledge of the digestive system.

What made the deal work, however, was that southerners also agreed to a northern demand that slavery be banned in the rest of the Louisiana Territory north of latitude 36°30'.

Monroe seriously considered vetoing the Missouri Compromise. He didn't believe that the federal government had the power to tell a state whether or not it could permit slavery. That was up to the citizens of each state to decide. But Monroe also suspected that a veto would likely lead to civil war. After three days of contemplation and consultation with his advisers, Monroe signed the Missouri Compromise on March 6, 1820.

THE INVASION OF FLORIDA

During Monroe's time in office, there was little trouble along the western frontier. But the president did face a problem in Georgia, where Seminoles and white settlers began killing one another in large numbers. Seminole raiding parties, which included runaway slaves, burned the farms of whites whom they believed were stealing their land.

Most of the Seminoles lived in Florida, which was still a colony of Spain. They made their villages in swampy, jungle-like wetlands that also attracted fugitive slaves because there were so many easy places to hide. Both the Seminoles and the Creeks liked to help escaped slaves because they shared the slaves' hatred of whites. In some villages, the blacks and Indians intermarried and raised families together.

In 1817, Monroe sent Andrew Jackson, the country's most capable general, to punish the raiders. Jackson's hatred of Indians was well known, and when forty of his men were killed in an ambush, he used the attack as an excuse to invade Florida. Jackson burned Seminole villages and hanged many tribal leaders. Then he

captured the Spanish stronghold of Pensacola, which gave him control of northern Florida.

Although Jackson didn't specifically disobey his orders, his decision to invade Florida proved embarrassing to the Monroe administration. The Spanish minister to the United States demanded that Jackson be punished. But Secretary of State John Quincy Adams defended Jackson, and he used Jackson's military presence as a negotiating tool with Spain.

Meeting with the Spanish minister, Adams demanded that Spain either control the Seminoles and fugitive slaves or else transfer control of the territory immediately to the United States. With General Jackson's army already in place, Spain decided to sell. For five million dollars, the United States bought all of Spain's land east of the Mississippi River, as well as its claim to territory in Oregon.

THE MONROE DOCTRINE

Now that the United States controlled so much of North America, John Quincy Adams suggested to President Monroe that he warn the nations of Europe against any further colonization of the Western Hemisphere. On December 2, 1823, the president delivered a speech to Congress outlining what soon became known as the Monroe Doctrine.

Neither an executive order nor a law, the Monroe Doctrine was a statement of policy that has guided U.S. actions ever since. Historians have compared its importance to that of George Washington's Farewell Address and John Hay's future Open Door policy with regard to China. For the first time, the United States recognized that it had important national interests outside its geographic borders.

CAMPAIGN ★ 1824

WITH THE PASSING AWAY OF THE FEDERALISTS, there was now just one party left. The next president would surely be a Democratic-Republican. But different party members wanted the job, and in the end, the election became a four-way race among regional candidates.

Treasury Secretary William Crawford of Georgia was the early front-runner, but he suffered a stroke during the campaign that undermined his candidacy. Secretary of State John Quincy Adams had the solid backing of New England, while Speaker of the House Henry Clay enjoyed a great deal of support in the West. Of all the contenders, however, only war hero Andrew Jackson of Tennessee could count on votes from every region of the country.

The election of 1824 was also noteworthy because it marked the first time that the popular vote was considered important enough to be counted. In fact, most of the electors in 1824 were chosen by the direct vote of the people—instead of by state legislatures, as they had been previously. The right to vote, however, was still restricted to adult white males.

Jackson won more electoral votes than anyone else. But he didn't win a majority, so the election was thrown into the House of Representatives. With Clay's support, Adams was able to win a narrow victory on the first ballot. Adams then made Clay his secretary of state.

BORN: JULY 11, 1767

BIRTHPLACE: BRAINTREE, MASS.

DIED: FEBRUARY 23, 1848

PARTY: DEMOCRATIC-REPUBLICAN

VICE PRESIDENT: JOHN C. CALHOUN

FIRST LADY: LOUISA CATHERINE JOHNSON

CHILDREN: GEORGE, JOHN, CHARLES, LOUISA

NICKNAME: OLD MAN ELOQUENT

THE ONLY PRESIDENT TO NAME A
SON GEORGE WASHINGTON.

1825

JOHN QUINCY ADAMS
6th President
★
1825 to 1829

J. Q. Adams

THE RAILROAD IS HERE!
WORK BEGINS ON THE B&O LINE

BALTIMORE, July 4, 1828— Work began today on the United States' first steam-powered railroad, the Baltimore & Ohio. The first B&O line will connect Baltimore and Ellicott's Mills, Maryland, thirteen miles away.

The ceremonial first stone was laid by Charles Carroll, the last surviving signer of the Declaration of Independence, at a formal ceremony held this afternoon.

The work is expected to take about two years. After that, B&O executives plan to extend the railroad to Wheeling in western Virginia within the next twenty-five years.

The Baltimore & Ohio Railroad was chartered last year to

help Baltimore compete with other cities for the profitable western trade. The Erie Canal, which opened in 1825, has funneled a great deal of this trade through New York City. Baltimore's merchants are hoping that the B&O line will do as much for their city.

After the House of Representatives chose John Quincy Adams to be the sixth president in February 1825, Adams's friends gave him some advice. They told him to fire all of Monroe's appointees and name his own people to federal office.

Adams's advisers were worried because many holdovers from the Monroe administration had backed Andrew Jackson during the 1824 presidential campaign.

Now that Jackson had lost the race in the House, his supporters were very angry. They believed that Adams had made a corrupt bargain with Henry Clay to steal the election, and many vowed revenge. They made plans to block Adams at every turn until Jackson could claim the presidency in 1828.

As it turned out, the advice that Adams got was good, but he refused to take it because he didn't think it would be right or fair for him to reward

37

his own followers with powerful political appointments. Instead, the Adams administration remained filled with people who did not wish the new president well.

THE AMERICAN SYSTEM

Once in office, John Quincy Adams became the first president to champion the government's role in making internal improvements for the benefit of trade. Both Madison and Monroe had vetoed government-financed road and canal construction projects because they believed them to be unconstitutional. Adams, however, wanted the government to take an active role in expanding commerce.

The president was a strong supporter of the American System, developed by Secretary of State Clay while Clay was still in the House of Representatives. The point of the American System was to create a self-sufficient national economy. Clay believed that fostering a factory base in the North would create important new markets for cotton grown in the South and grain and beef raised in the West. In exchange, people in the South and West would buy goods manufactured in the North.

Specifically, Clay proposed high tariffs on imported goods, funding for internal improvements, and the strengthening of the national bank. The tariffs would protect New England's young factory economy, barely a decade old, from having to compete with cheap European goods. Meanwhile, new roads and canals would make it easier for farmers to bring their crops to market. Finally, a stronger national bank would produce the sort of stable national credit system necessary for internal trade to flourish.

The congressmen who fought the American System did so for a number of reasons. Some were merely trying to

THE EARLY YEARS

*B*ECAUSE JOHN ADAMS WAS ONE of the country's most important diplomats, his eldest son, John Quincy, spent much of his childhood abroad. John Quincy was only ten years old when he traveled to Europe for the first time in 1778. Just three years later, he was sent to Russia with Francis Dana, another American diplomat. Dana wanted John Quincy along because the boy spoke French fluently. (At the time, French was the official language of diplomacy.)

In 1797, while in London, Adams met his future wife, Louisa Johnson. Although her father was American, she had been born and raised in London, which made her the only foreign-born woman to become first lady.

★FREEDOM'S JOURNAL

Founded in 1827, *Freedom's Journal* was the first antislavery newspaper ever published by African Americans. A New York City pastor named Samuel E. Cornish edited the paper, along with John Brown Russwurm. After Russwurm relocated to Liberia in 1829, Cornish continued to publish the newspaper under the name *Rights of All*.

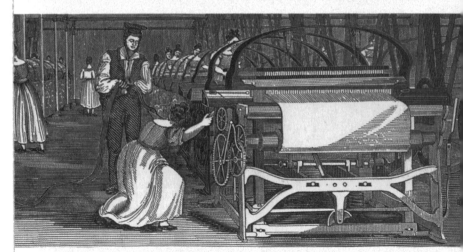

★FACTORY GIRLS

Most early American manufacturers, particularly those in New England, relied on young, unmarried women for their workforce. Farmers' daughters were actively recruited to work in clothing mills, and many jumped at the opportunity to help support their families and make some extra money for themselves.

These factory girls usually worked twelve-hour days. Their pay was about $2.50 a week, which was more than a woman could earn doing any other kind of work.

★PHOTOGRAPHY

John Quincy Adams was the first president to be photographed. Early photographs were called daguerreotypes after French inventor Louis Daguerre, who had perfected the process. Daguerre captured his images on copper plates coated with silver iodide, which he exposed to light and then to mercury vapor. The earliest daguerreotypes had to be exposed in sunlight for twenty minutes, or the pictures wouldn't come out.

★AFTER THE PRESIDENCY

After John Quincy Adams lost the 1828 election to Andrew Jackson, most people expected him to retire. Instead, in 1830, the sixty-three-year-old Adams ran for a seat in the House of Representatives and won. He thus became the first president to serve in Congress after leaving the White House.

Adams was often in the minority on issues such as the national bank, which he favored, and the annexation of Texas, which he opposed. He had a great success in 1844, however, when he helped win repeal of a congressional rule suppressing all petitions against slavery. Initially, only a few congressmen opposed this "gag" rule, first passed in 1836. But over the next eight years, Adams led a tireless crusade that eventually succeeded in repealing the measure.

In February 1848, John Quincy Adams suffered a stroke on the floor of the House. The eighty-year-old former president was carried to a nearby chamber. He died there two days later because doctors considered it too dangerous to move him.

make Adams look bad so that Jackson would win election in 1828. Others worried that the federal government was becoming too powerful.

Although elected as a Democratic-Republican, Adams didn't share the strict constructionist views of the Virginia Monarchy. He believed, as Alexander Hamilton had, that the federal government's powers were not limited to those specified in the Constitution. In fact, the country's rapid growth in recent years had forced the federal government to exercise more power than ever before.

This development worried many Americans who believed, as Thomas Jefferson had, that a strong national government was dangerous because it meant less freedom for the states. Southerners were particularly concerned, because they didn't want the federal government to become any more involved in the slavery issue.

Because of the opposition that Adams faced within Congress, he was able to win passage of only two public works bills. The first extended the Cumberland Road into Ohio. The second funded the construction of a new canal between the Ohio River and the Chesapeake Bay.

THE PANAMA CONGRESS

In 1826, the new Latin American republics that had formerly been Spanish colonies held a congress to promote friendship within the region. They also wanted to discuss the possibility of a unified policy toward Spain. Simón Bolívar of Colombia, who organized the event, chose Panama as the meeting place.

Mexican and Colombian ministers asked Secretary of State Clay to send two U.S. delegates. Both Clay and Adams were delighted. Although neither was sure that democratic governments could survive in Latin America, both were eager to offer U.S. friendship and trade.

1828

In Congress, however, opposition to the mission was strong. Southerners, in particular, objected because the new Latin American republics had outlawed slavery. With the help of Jacksonians in Congress, these southerners were able to delay the mission—by withholding funds and blocking confirmation of the delegates—until the Panama Congress was over.

THE TARIFF OF ABOMINATIONS Throughout his presidency, in accordance with the principles of Clay's American System, Adams pressed for higher tariffs on imported manufactured goods. Finally, during his last year in office, Congress passed a tariff bill. But it wasn't the bill that Adams had proposed.

In an attempt to embarrass the president, the Jacksonians in Congress had amended Adams's plan so that it raised tariffs on imported raw materials as well. The Jacksonians were sure that New England congressmen, who otherwise supported Adams, would never vote for such a bill because it would raise the prices New England factories paid for their raw materials.

They were wrong. The Tariff of 1828 passed and was signed into law by the president. It soon became known as the Tariff of Abominations because it was so hated. The new tariff rates dramatically raised prices on all sorts of goods, which made the public furious.

Although the new law didn't embarrass Adams personally, the foul mood it created in the country eliminated whatever small chance he had of winning reelection. On the other hand, whatever good the tariff fracas did Andrew Jackson, it also passed on to him a crisis in the making.

CAMPAIGN ★ 1828

ANDREW JACKSON STARTED HIS SECOND CAMPAIGN for president soon after he lost his first. Throughout Adams's term in office, the shadow of Jackson dogged the president.

As the election of 1828 neared, the Democratic-Republican party split into two camps. The Jacksonians called themselves Democrats. The Adams forces called themselves National Republicans.

Because the candidates took similar stands on many issues, the election turned on a series of personal attacks. Adams was hammered for allegedly making a "corrupt bargain" with Clay to win the 1824 election. Meanwhile, the National Republicans printed handbills decorated with a line of coffins that accused Jackson of executing soldiers for minor offenses during the War of 1812.

Adams's supporters also portrayed Jackson as a crude, uneducated man, always ready for a brawl.

Wealthy eastern businessmen found these traits repulsive, but ordinary voters on the frontier loved them. In contrast, they considered the highly educated Adams distant and unappealing.

Andrew Jackson's nickname was Old Hickory, because he was supposed to be as tough as hickory wood. His supporters made use of this image and publicized his campaign by erecting hickory poles all over the country. They also sponsored local picnics, parades, and barbecues. These efforts made Jackson's campaign the first grassroots effort ever in U.S. presidential history.

Later, Jackson claimed that his election in 1828 was a victory for the common man. In any case, it certainly was a victory. Adams carried his base in the Northeast and nothing else.

1829

BORN: MARCH 15, 1767

BIRTHPLACE: WAXHAW, S.C.

DIED: JUNE 8, 1845

PARTY: DEMOCRAT

VICE PRESIDENTS: JOHN C. CALHOUN,
MARTIN VAN BUREN

FIRST LADY: RACHEL DONELSON ROBARDS

CHILDREN: NONE

NICKNAME: OLD HICKORY

THE FIRST PRESIDENT
TO RIDE A TRAIN.

ANDREW JACKSON
7th President
★
1829 to 1837

Andrew Jackson

WEBSTER, HAYNE DEBATE STATES' RIGHTS

WASHINGTON, January 27, 1830—Sen. Daniel Webster of Massachusetts ended his nine-day-long debate today with Sen. Robert Y. Hayne of South Carolina. The subject of their exchange was Hayne's claim that a state had the right to "nullify," or choose not to obey, a federal law.

The debate began when Hayne delivered a speech on January 19 asserting the rights of states to be free of federal interference. Hayne insisted that the Tariff of Abominations was responsible for South Carolina's current economic problems. He argued that no state should have to accept a federal law that harmed its interests.

Beginning yesterday, Webster's response held the attention of both the Senate and the country. According to Webster, no single state has the right to question laws passed by the Congress. Only the Supreme Court, according to Webster, can do that.

The Massachusetts senator closed his penetrating remarks with the words, "Liberty and Union, now and forever, one and inseparable!"

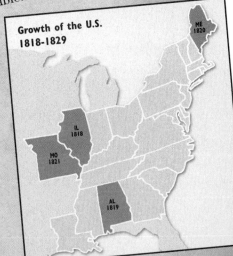

Growth of the U.S. 1818-1829

ndrew Jackson's victory in 1828 marked a new era in American politics, because he was the first common man ever elected president. All six presidents before him had been privileged, landed gentlemen. But Jackson was self-made, a poor orphan who had worked hard to build careers for himself in the law and then the army.

Jackson believed that ordinary Americans—shopkeepers, farmers, pioneers—had enough common sense to make political decisions for themselves. This idea was the cornerstone of Jacksonian democracy, and the people loved him for it.

Whenever possible, Jackson used this popular support to reinforce his political power. He also used the "spoils system." Jackson believed in the phrase, "To the victor belongs the spoils." Therefore, immediately upon taking office, he fired nearly one thousand of the ten thousand people on the federal payroll and replaced them with his own loyal supporters.

41

1830

Because of his strategic use of the spoils system and his frequent direct appeals to the public for support, Jackson is widely considered to have been the first modern president.

He believed that the president spoke with the voice of the people, because the president was the only government official (other than the vice president) elected by all Americans. Not surprisingly, this attitude sometimes brought him into conflict with Congress and the Supreme Court. When that happened, he relied on his popularity to prevail.

AN INAUGURAL MESS

Because Jackson ran as their candidate, the people celebrated his inauguration as no inauguration had been celebrated before. A mob of twenty thousand well-wishers followed Jackson's carriage from the Capitol all the way to the White House. Some of them had traveled hundreds of miles to see Old Hickory sworn into office, and their exuberance now got the better of them.

Many followed Jackson into the White House itself—through the windows as well as the doors. They broke the china, spit tobacco juice on the carpets, and stood on chairs and sofas to get a better view of the goings-on.

Unable to maintain order, Jackson fled the building through a rear window and escaped to a nearby hotel. Eventually, waiters drew the unruly crowd outside by placing tubs of punch on the front lawn.

The damage was costly, but Jackson didn't really mind because the people had been misbehaving out of joy. On the other hand, conservative Washington was scandalized, and this wouldn't be the last time. Soon after Jackson's March 1829 inauguration, another scandal broke. This one involved the new secretary of war, John Eaton.

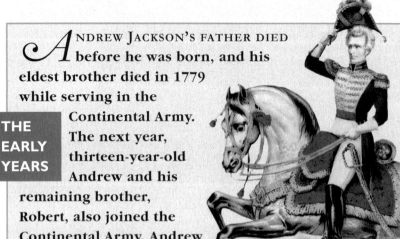

THE EARLY YEARS

ANDREW JACKSON'S FATHER DIED before he was born, and his eldest brother died in 1779 while serving in the Continental Army. The next year, thirteen-year-old Andrew and his remaining brother, Robert, also joined the Continental Army. Andrew served as a colonel's orderly, carrying messages back and forth on horseback.

In April 1781, the brothers were captured and made to march forty miles without food or water to a prisoner-of-war camp. Robert caught smallpox there and died. Andrew's mother died the same year from a disease she caught while caring for wounded soldiers. His mother's death left Andrew alone in the world.

After studying to become a lawyer and serving as Tennessee's first U.S. representative, Jackson headed a volunteer army during the War of 1812. General Jackson won a number of victories against Britain's Indian allies before defeating the British themselves at the battle of New Orleans. Later, Jackson's successful invasion of Florida in 1818 helped John Quincy Adams negotiate the purchase of that colony from Spain.

★ **THE FIRST LADY** When Andrew Jackson wed Rachel Donelson in 1791, she was technically still married to her first husband. Both Donelson and Jackson had believed at the time that a divorce had been granted, but actually the divorce wasn't finalized until 1793. A few months later, Andrew and Rachel wed again, this time legally.

The mistake haunted the couple during the 1828 presidential campaign, when the National Republicans accused Jackson of adultery because he and Rachel had lived together before being legally married. The general tried to shield his wife from the attacks, but Rachel eventually learned that she was being smeared in the national press.

She quickly fell ill, at least in part because of her heartache, and died less than two months after the election. She was buried in the dress that she had bought to wear at her husband's inauguration.

★ TOM THUMB

America's first steam-powered railroad locomotive was built by a wealthy inventor named Peter Cooper. He nicknamed the locomotive Tom Thumb because it was only twenty feet long.

Cooper demonstrated his new invention for the first time in 1830, when the Baltimore & Ohio Railroad opened its first passenger line. The locomotive reached a speed of fifteen miles an hour during its thirteen-mile trip from Baltimore to Ellicott's Mills, proving that train travel was practical even on hilly routes.

On the return trip, Cooper and his passengers came upon a horse. A race was suggested. At first, the horse galloped into the lead. Then Tom Thumb caught up and pulled ahead. It seemed as though the locomotive would win easily, but then the engine broke down suddenly, and the horse won the race.

★ UTOPIAN COMMUNITIES

One response to the horrible conditions in many U.S. factories was the cooperative community. The first of these was founded in 1825 by Robert Owen, who was already famous for pioneering labor reform at his cotton mills in Scotland.

Owen worried about the wide gap that existed between rich and poor people. The community that he founded at New Harmony, Indiana, was supposed to be a utopia, or perfect society, where residents worked together for the good of all. Instead, many lazy and unprincipled people joined the community, because they thought they could get a free ride. New Harmony failed after two years.

★ THE LIBERATOR

In 1831, William Lloyd Garrison began publishing *The Liberator,* which became the most important and hardest hitting of the abolitionist newspapers. Its articles described the horrors of slavery in great detail and helped spark enormous growth in the northern antislavery movement.

While congressmen in Washington debated whether or not slavery should be extended to the new western states, Garrison and his followers demanded that slavery be abolished everywhere, including the South, on moral grounds.

THE PEGGY EATON AFFAIR

During the mid-1820s, while serving in Washington as a senator from Tennessee, Eaton had lived in a boardinghouse run by a woman named Peggy Timberlake, whose husband worked for the navy. When John Timberlake went away on long voyages, Eaton would often escort Mrs. Timberlake to social functions. After her husband died in 1829, Eaton married her.

Rumors circulated around town that the relationship between Eaton and his new wife was "improper." People gossiped that the couple had been involved while John Timberlake was still alive. Led by Floride Calhoun, wife of Vice Pres. John C. Calhoun, the wives of many important government officials shunned Peggy Eaton.

The rules of behavior were very strict during the nineteenth century, especially with regard to women, who were believed to be pure and weak. Peggy Eaton did not fit this image, nor did her background as a barmaid help her win the approval of Washington's high society.

Jackson, however, always stood by her. Her troubles reminded him of the attacks made against his own wife during the last campaign, and he refused to listen to any malicious gossip about her. Instead, he invited her to state dinners and insisted that she be accepted socially by the wives of his cabinet members.

This didn't happen. Instead, most of the cabinet members resigned, and Floride Calhoun left town to avoid socializing with Peggy Eaton. Mrs. Calhoun's departure, of course, did little to help her husband's standing with the president.

In contrast, Secretary of State Martin Van Buren's gracious acceptance of Mrs. Eaton raised his standing with the president just as Vice President Calhoun's was falling.

1832

And during the rest of Calhoun's term, he and the president would grow even farther apart.

THE INDIAN REMOVAL ACT
The most important legislation of Jackson's first term in office was the Indian Removal Act of 1830. For several years, the state of Georgia had been trying to confiscate and sell land belonging to the Cherokee tribe. The Cherokees were among the Five Civilized Tribes that had adopted the ways of white society in order to live peacefully with white people.

To become acceptable to whites, the Cherokees had taken up European-style farming, developed a written language, and even adopted their own constitution. But neither the government of Georgia nor President Jackson had any respect for these efforts.

Old Hickory was well known to be an Indian fighter, not an Indian lover. The Indian Removal Act gave him the power to remove Indians from the South and force them to relocate to unsettled lands west of the Mississippi. During the next few years, Jackson used federal troops to force the Cherokees, Chickasaws, Choctaws, Seminoles, and Creeks to abandon one hundred million acres of land.

The Cherokees asked the Supreme Court for help. They argued that their tribe was legally a foreign nation and thus not subject to the removal law. Chief Justice John Marshall denied their petition but did point out that only the federal government had sovereignty over the Cherokees. Therefore, the state laws of Georgia did not apply to them, and no whites could settle their land without Cherokee permission. Even so, Georgia ignored the decision, and Jackson refused to enforce it, so the forced removals continued.

CAMPAIGN ★ 1832

THE FIRST MAJOR NATIONAL PARTY conventions were held in 1832. Until that time, presidential candidates were generally nominated either by a group of congressmen belonging to the same party or by a state legislature.

In May, the Democratic party met in Baltimore to renominate Jackson. Because of the president's dislike for the vice president (not to mention his wife), John Calhoun was dropped from the ticket and replaced with Martin Van Buren (whom Jackson was clearly grooming as a successor).

To oppose Jackson, the National Republicans nominated Henry Clay, who criticized Jackson for being too tyrannical and abusing the spoils system. National Republican cartoonists followed up on Clay's attacks, caricaturing the president as King Andrew I.

The most important issue of the campaign was the Second Bank of the United States. Clay supported the bank, while Jackson never tried to hide his contempt for it. When Congress passed a bill that summer granting the national bank a new charter, Jackson vetoed the measure. As the temporarily bedridden president told his loyal aide, "The bank, Mr. Van Buren, is trying to kill me, but I will kill it."

Jackson claimed that keeping the bank open favored the interests of the wealthy, while Clay argued that closing it would hurt small borrowers. Clay polled well in the North, but Jackson carried the South and West and won comfortably.

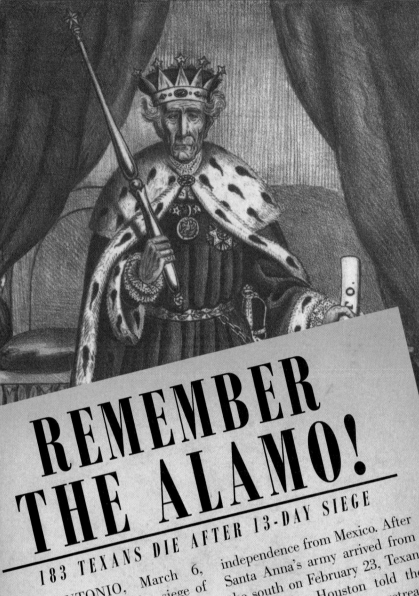

BORN TO COMMAND.

HAD I BEEN CONSULTED

One of the cartoons that caricatured Jackson as King Andrew I.

1833

REMEMBER THE ALAMO!

183 TEXANS DIE AFTER 13-DAY SIEGE

SAN ANTONIO, March 6, 1836—The thirteen-day siege of the Alamo ended today when three thousand Mexican soldiers under Gen. Antonio López de Santa Anna stormed the outer walls of the mission and killed all 183 defenders inside. Only 15 women and children and 1 black slave were spared.

The American dead include James Bowie and William B. Travis, both colonels in the Texas militia, and Davy Crockett, the famous Tennessee frontiersman. Estimates of the Mexican dead and wounded range from one thousand to sixteen hundred men.

The Texans initially captured San Antonio last December, beginning their ongoing war for independence from Mexico. After Santa Anna's army arrived from the south on February 23, Texan general Sam Houston told the defenders of the Alamo to retreat. Writing from inside the Alamo, Travis replied, "I shall never surrender or retreat...VICTORY OR DEATH."

THE NULLIFICATION CONTROVERSY

Although Jackson hated the Tariff of Abominations as much as the public did, Vice President Calhoun hated it even more. As chief executive, Jackson worked with Congress to reduce the tariff rates, but he also took seriously his obligation to enforce the law of the land.

Calhoun believed that the tariff was unconstitutional because it placed a "cruel and unusual" burden on his home state of South Carolina. He argued that states could "nullify," or choose not to obey, federal laws that were not in their own best interests. It was an argument that reminded many of Jefferson and Madison's Kentucky and Virginia Resolves.

The chief congressional spokesman for nullification was South Carolina senator Robert Y. Hayne, who faced off against Daniel Webster of Massachusetts in an important 1830 Senate debate. Afterward, people waited anxiously for Jackson to announce his position on nullification.

In April 1830, at a dinner celebrating Jefferson's birthday, Jackson made the first toast: "Our Union—it must be preserved!" Calhoun's toast was, "The Union—next to our liberty, the most dear." Obviously, Calhoun had not softened his position.

In 1832, Congress finally passed a new law reducing tariff rates, but Calhoun wasn't satisfied. Instead, he resigned as vice president and took a seat in the Senate. Meanwhile, South Carolina decided to nullify both the 1828 and 1832 tariffs.

45

In doing so, state legislators warned that, should Jackson send federal troops to collect the tariffs, South Carolina would secede from the Union.

By the time Congress met again in 1833 following Jackson's reelection, nullification had become the hottest issue in Washington. By nullifying two federal laws, South Carolina had brought into question the same issue of federal superiority that George Washington had settled militarily during the Whiskey Rebellion and John Marshall had addressed legally in the 1819 Supreme Court case *McCulloch v. Maryland*.

Jackson was not about to stand for such behavior and, with the Senate's approval, sent federal troops to the South Carolina border. Meanwhile, Henry Clay shepherded a compromise tariff through Congress. Faced with the choice of invasion or Clay's compromise, South Carolina backed down and began collecting the new tariff fees.

THE SECOND BANK Having thus resolved the nullification crisis, Jackson next turned his attention to the Second Bank of the United States. The future of this national bank, based in Philadelphia but with offices all over the country, had been the most controversial issue of the 1832 campaign.

Jackson had always hated banks, and the Second Bank in particular. Like many westerners, he blamed its conservative policies for tight credit and slow economic growth in the West.

Because the bank's charter expired in 1836, it couldn't stay open beyond that point without an act of Congress. Yet Jackson wanted to close the bank even sooner. So he reached out to the people and asked for their support in destroying the "monster bank."

Jackson also ordered Secretary of the Treasury Louis McLane to withdraw all

★THE BLACK HAWK WAR

While the Cherokees petitioned the Supreme Court to stop the state of Georgia from taking their land, the Sac and Fox tribes in Illinois tried a different approach. They fought. In the end, the Black Hawk War, named after the tribal leader Black Hawk, ended three generations of resistance to white settlement along the northwestern frontier.

In 1832, the Illinois militia, including twenty-three-year-old Capt. Abraham Lincoln, chased Black Hawk's band of warriors and their families from Illinois into Wisconsin. The soldiers caught up with the Indians on the Bad Axe River. Although Black Hawk raised a white flag in surrender, the militiamen attacked anyway, shooting the women and children as well as the men.

★NAT TURNER'S REBELLION

In 1831, Nat Turner began the most important, and bloodiest, slave revolt in U.S. history. A deeply religious man, Turner interpreted a solar eclipse that year as a sign from God that he should free his people.

On the night of August 21, he killed his masters in their sleep. They would be the first of more than fifty whites to die in the uprising. Next, he set off with several dozen other slaves for the seat of Southampton County, Virginia, where he planned to seize weapons and arm his new brigade.

But Turner's band was not nearly strong enough to face the three thousand local militiamen who assembled the next morning. Although Turner himself remained at large for more than two months, he was eventually captured and hanged.

Southern states quickly passed new laws restricting the education of slaves and their ability to travel and gather in groups. Even so, Nat Turner's Rebellion terrified many white southerners, who had wanted to believe that slaves were content and would not revolt.

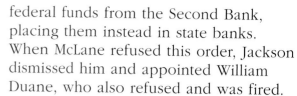

★ **DAVY CROCKETT** Davy Crockett was born into a pioneer family in Tennessee. He grew up living in the wilderness of the western frontier and spent fewer than a hundred days in school. While in his twenties, he made a name for himself as an Indian fighter and "b'ar hunter."

Crockett served off and on in Congress from 1827 until 1835. During that time, he charmed eastern journalists with his many frontier mannerisms. Soon, these men began writing popular books and articles about him, casting Crockett as a frontier folk hero in a raccoon-skin cap. Some even claimed that he could leap the Ohio River and wrestle wildcats. After his death at the Alamo, Crockett lived on in dozens of books, songs, television shows, and movies.

★ **KITCHEN CABINET** Beginning with the administration of George Washington, presidents met regularly with their cabinets to discuss and decide important policy matters. But Andrew Jackson didn't like his cabinet very much, and he liked them even less after the Peggy Eaton affair.

For this reason, he cut down the number of cabinet meetings until finally stopping them altogether. Instead, he discussed politics nearly every night with his closest friends at meetings held in the White House kitchen. These men—including Martin Van Buren, John Eaton, Amos Kendall, and William B. Lewis—came to be known as the Kitchen Cabinet.

★ **AMERICAN COOKING** In colonial America, most cooking in the North was based on British recipes. But the food that Americans ate was also influenced by the availability of local ingredients and by Indian cooking techniques. Pumpkin pie was one popular dish that resulted from a combination of the two cuisines.

This type of cultural exchange also took place in Texas, where local Mexicans taught white settlers how to cook with corn. In the South, cooking was influenced by West Indian and African styles brought over by the slaves. Black-eyed peas, peanuts, okra, and rice were all staples of West African cooking long before they became favorites in the South.

federal funds from the Second Bank, placing them instead in state banks. When McLane refused this order, Jackson dismissed him and appointed William Duane, who also refused and was fired.

After a frustrating search, Jackson finally found someone who would carry out his orders: Attorney General Roger B. Taney, whom Jackson would later send to the Supreme Court. In September 1833, Taney executed the withdrawal of all federal deposits from the Second Bank.

In response to Taney's withdrawal, Second Bank president Nicholas Biddle called in all of his institution's outstanding loans. In part, this was a sensible business decision. If the Second Bank were to close, it would have to settle its affairs.

But Biddle also hoped to pressure Jackson into changing his mind. By calling in so many loans, Biddle tightened credit drastically and brought the country to the brink of a financial panic.

Gradually, the pressure mounted on Jackson. But each time someone complained, the president said, "Go to Nicholas Biddle." In the end, Biddle had to relent. He eased credit, and the near-panic turned into a land boom. The state banks also began lending out their new federal deposits at bargain rates, and this money was used to fuel a new round of land speculation in the West.

TEXAN INDEPENDENCE During his last year in office, Jackson's attention also turned west, to Texas, which was still Mexican territory. While he longed to add Texas to the Union, he also felt bound to honor Mexico's sovereignty and was concerned that the admission of Texas as a slave state would disturb the precarious balance between North and South.

In December 1835, however, white settlers in Texas revolted against the new Mexican government of Antonio López

de Santa Anna, principally because Santa Anna had recently outlawed slavery. Raising an army, they captured the town of San Antonio, alarming Santa Anna and leading to the Mexican siege of the Alamo.

Santa Anna's victory there was short-lived, however. Six weeks later, on April 21, 1836, an army of Texans under the command of Sam Houston won both the battle of San Jacinto and independence for Texas. The Texans' battle cry was "Remember the Alamo!" On July 4, Congress agreed to recognize the new Republic of Texas, taking the first step toward making Texas a part of the Union.

THE SPECIE CIRCULAR

One of Jackson's last actions before leaving office was to issue the Specie Circular. This presidential order of July 1836 declared that paper money could no longer be used to purchase federal land. Instead, buyers would have to use gold or silver coins. (Coins made of precious metals were known as specie.)

Jackson instituted this policy because of the land boom that had been touched off by his successful campaign against the Second Bank. All the new credit being offered by the state banks worried him because it tended to make the economy unstable. Also, he was bothered by the fact that speculators were buying a great deal of public land with devalued paper money.

Of course, such a drastic reversal of policy—from easy credit to no credit— sent land prices tumbling, and the collapse in the land market in turn led to a run of bankruptcies. By the time Jackson left office, businesses all over the country were closing, and with the government still refusing to accept paper money, the panic spread.

CAMPAIGN ★ 1836

OBEYING JACKSON'S ORDERS, the Democratic party nominated Vice Pres. Martin Van Buren as its presidential candidate in 1836. Van Buren's opposition came from the Whig party, which had been formed by Jackson's political enemies in 1834.

Because the Whigs had little in common beyond their hatred of Jackson, the new party was unable to settle on a single candidate. So party members decided to run three regional candidates. They hoped that this strategy would deny Van Buren an electoral majority. If that came about, the election would be thrown into the House of Representatives, where the Whigs had influence.

In the West, the Whigs ran war hero William Henry Harrison. In the North, their candidate was Sen. Daniel Webster. Sen. Hugh Lawson White of Tennessee ran in the South. Of these, only Harrison was regarded as a serious national candidate.

Jackson's endorsement was a mixed blessing for Van Buren. The president was still personally popular, but his controversial policies, especially regarding the Second Bank, posed some problems for the Democrats.

Whenever possible, Van Buren tried to avoid discussing issues, especially slavery. His success depended on a coalition of Democrats from the North and South, and he didn't want to upset any of them.

In the end, he won half the popular vote and a solid electoral majority. But it would be another 152 years before a sitting vice president was again elected president.

M. VAN BUREN, FOR PRESIDENT.

MARTIN VAN BUREN
8th President
★
1837 to 1841

BORN: DECEMBER 5, 1782

BIRTHPLACE: KINDERHOOK, N.Y.

DIED: JULY 24, 1862

PARTY: DEMOCRAT

VICE PRESIDENT: RICHARD M. JOHNSON

FIRST LADY: HANNAH HOES

CHILDREN: ABRAHAM, JOHN, MARTIN JR., SMITH

NICKNAME: LITTLE MAGICIAN

THE FIRST PRESIDENT NOT BORN A BRITISH SUBJECT.

*Just two months after Martin Van Buren took office, the United States was hit by one of the worst financial depressions in the nation's history. The economic crisis that began during the summer of 1837 lasted nearly a decade. These hard times dominated Van Buren's presidency and eventually cost him reelection in 1840.

Van Buren received most of the blame for the crisis, but it was really the fault of Andrew Jackson—whose policies, designed to destroy the Second Bank of the United States, had also severely weakened the national economy.

In order to crush the Second Bank, Jackson had demanded that all federal funds be removed from the national bank and redeposited in state banks. The state banks, however, used this extra money to make many unwise loans, and their loose practices led to a period of inflation during which prices soared.

THOUSANDS OF CHEROKEES DIE ALONG THE TRAIL OF TEARS

DURING 1838 AND 1839, fifteen thousand Cherokees were forced to leave their homeland in Georgia and march west to government reservations in the Indian Territory (now Oklahoma). This journey, during which more than one-fourth of the Cherokees died, has been called the Trail of Tears.

The Cherokees were escorted by federal troops under the command of Gen. Winfield Scott. Along the way, government officials took what little money the Cherokees had. In return, the government provided inadequate supplies for the trip.

Despite shortages of food and many other necessities, General Scott refused to slow the pace of the march. Even the sick and elderly were forced to keep up. This policy caused many deaths.

One observer wrote at the time that "such a denial of justice, and such deafness to screams for mercy, were never heard of in time of peace... since the earth was made."

49

1838

During his last months in office, Jackson had issued the Specie Circular, an executive order intended to curb the inflation and control land speculation in the West. The Specie Circular stated that paper money could no longer be used to purchase government land. Instead, buyers would have to pay for the land with specie.

During the nineteenth century, paper money was valuable only if it was backed by, or could be exchanged for, precious metals such as gold and silver. Coins made from these metals were known as specie. Under this banking system, a one-dollar bill could be exchanged at any time for a dollar's worth of specie.

The Specie Circular forced buyers of land to exchange their paper money for gold or silver. But this created a demand for specie that the banks couldn't meet. Because of the inflation and bad loans the banks had made, there was no longer enough gold and silver to back all the paper money in circulation. So the value of the paper money fell.

THE PANIC OF 1837 The Panic of 1837 began when a number of banks in New York City stopped converting paper money into gold and silver. Loans also became harder to come by. As a result, speculators who were denied credit stopped buying land, and land prices fell sharply.

Nearly one thousand banks around the country failed. When they did, work on the internal improvement projects that the banks had been financing also stopped, throwing many people out of work. In some cities, hungry people rioted for food. Meanwhile, in Washington, Van Buren appeared in expensive, tailored clothes, which hurt his popularity.

At first, Congress did little more than debate the country's problems. But Van

THE EARLY YEARS ALTHOUGH HE LATER BECAME KNOWN for his expensive tastes, Martin Van Buren did not grow up wealthy. His father was a poor farmer and tavern keeper in Kinderhook, New York, a small Dutch village in the Hudson River Valley. The Van Burens spoke Dutch at home, and Little Mat was raised according to European customs.

After school, he often helped his father in the tavern, where famous politicians (including Alexander Hamilton and Aaron Burr) often stopped in on their way to and from the state capital at Albany. Young Martin loved to listen to their arguments, and he quickly developed an interest in politics that would last his entire life. He became such a crafty politician that he was nicknamed the Little Magician.

★ **TRANSCENDENTALISM** During the 1830s, a group of writers including Ralph Waldo Emerson and Henry David Thoreau (shown here in an 1856 daguerreotype) developed the philosophy of transcendentalism. Transcendentalists believed that, because people are basically good, human society can be perfected through experimentation and reform. The most important transcendentalist journal was *The Dial*, founded in 1840 and first edited by Margaret Fuller.

The transcendentalists particularly influenced American literature, but they also were active in social reform movements. Among the causes they championed were women's suffrage, public education, and better working conditions in factories.

★ FRONTIER WOMEN

The first white people to move out west were almost exclusively men. Some were cowboys, and others were miners, but they were all fortune seekers who wandered through the wilderness and rarely put down roots. Not until

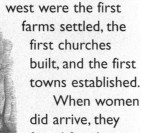

women began moving west were the first farms settled, the first churches built, and the first towns established. When women did arrive, they found freedom on the frontier that they could never have experienced in the established cities of the East. Life in the West was hard, and frontier women had to be tough and capable. But they did receive a certain measure of equality in return.

★ A DANDY PRESIDENT

A small, dapper, and refined man, Van Buren was often criticized for the way that he appeared in public. He wore a coat with a velvet collar and tight-fitting gloves made from very soft leather. He traveled through the muddy and smelly streets of Washington in a luxurious green coach driven by men in fancy uniforms. As a result, people often complained that their president behaved more like a king than a Democrat.

★ THE TELEGRAPH

Portrait painter Samuel F. B. Morse first got the idea for the telegraph in 1832. Five years later, he produced the first working model, which operated by inducing an electric current in a wire. Morse also developed Morse code, which translated letters of the alphabet into groups of long and short pulses. The telegraph provided the first means of communicating instantly over long distances.

To convince the government to fund the development of the telegraph, Morse arranged a demonstration. He had telegraph wire strung between Baltimore and Washington. Then, using equipment set up in the Supreme Court, he transmitted the message "What hath God wrought!" and received an immediate reply. Morse's device was probably more shocking to people in its time than any other invention, including the automobile, the radio, and the computer.

Buren had a plan. He wanted to set up an independent treasury, run by the government, which could protect federal money from irresponsible loans.

A number of congressmen opposed this plan because they didn't want government funds removed from the banks in their home states. It was not until 1840, the last year of Van Buren's term, that Congress finally passed the Independent Treasury Act.

THE TEXAS QUESTION In 1837, the year that Martin Van Buren became president, Washington was still a swampy, malaria-ridden town. Open sewers wound through unpaved streets, while pigs and chickens scurried about. Elsewhere, in busy marketplaces, slaves were bought and sold.

At his inauguration, the new president spoke directly to the issue of slavery, which he had carefully avoided during the 1836 campaign. In his inaugural address, he said that he would fight any attempts to abolish slavery in the South, because southern states had the right to decide the matter for themselves.

What Van Buren now wanted most was for the issue to go away, but it wouldn't. Instead, he was forced to confront slavery again when Texas applied for admission to the Union shortly after winning its independence from Mexico.

If Texas were to be admitted, it would have to be as a slave state. There was no doubt about that, because it was Mexico's attempt to abolish slavery in Texas that had started the rebellion in the first place.

But admitting Texas as a slave state would upset the delicate balance of power between free and slave states that had been preserved by the Missouri Compromise. Therefore, despite Van Buren's strong support for slavery in

1840

general, he decided to oppose the admission of Texas because he feared the political consequences. Specifically, he worried that admitting Texas as a slave state would reopen the entire slavery debate.

The president's stand was unpopular in the South, of course, but it was also attacked by many others who wanted to expand the territory of the country no matter what the cost.

THE CAROLINE AFFAIR Meanwhile, as Congress argued about Texas and the economy, the threat of war returned along the nation's northern border. The trouble began early in 1837, when Canadian rebels attacked Toronto in an effort to end British colonial rule there. When the attempt failed, the rebels retreated to Navy Island in the Niagara River, which separates the United States from Canada.

Americans who supported the Canadian rebels began ferrying supplies to them across the river using the steamship *Caroline*. In response, the British ordered loyal Canadian militia to attack the *Caroline* as it lay anchored off the New York shore. During the successful December raid, the *Caroline* was burned and sent over Niagara Falls. One American was killed, and several were injured.

President Van Buren called the attack an "outrage" and sent troops to the U.S.-Canadian border. Many congressmen urged him to declare war on Britain, but he resisted the pressure and instead declared U.S. neutrality with regard to the Canadian rebellion. Despite this declaration, relations between the British and the Americans remained strained for several years.

CAMPAIGN ★ 1840

THE 1840 ELECTION WAS DOMINATED by the economic depression that followed the Panic of 1837. Many people blamed Van Buren and wanted a change. To oppose the Democratic president, the Whigs again put up William Henry Harrison.

Although Harrison's supporters assured voters that their candidate would end the depression, they didn't say how. Instead, they focused on hoopla. They staged events, advertised widely, and gave out all sorts of souvenirs, such as decorated hairbrushes and tobacco tins. Their strategy made the 1840 election, according to most historians, the first modern presidential campaign.

Harrison's candidacy took on even more momentum when a Democratic newspaper mocked the Whig candidate as a bumpkin who wanted little more than a barrel of hard, or alcoholic, cider and a log cabin in which to drink it. Although Harrison actually lived in a twenty-two-room mansion, the Whigs cleverly saw the opportunity to portray him as a Jacksonian man of the people. To encourage this popular image, they used log cabins for campaign headquarters and served hard cider in cabin-shaped mugs.

They also spread rumors that Van Buren was such a dandy, he ate with a golden spoon and bathed in a tub of cologne. Actually, Harrison was far wealthier than Van Buren.

The campaign was so exciting that an astounding 80 percent of eligible voters cast ballots. Van Buren kept the popular vote respectably close, but he lost the electoral vote by a wide margin, including his home state of New York.

WILLIAM HENRY HARRISON

9th President

★

1841

BORN: FEBRUARY 9, 1773

BIRTHPLACE: CHARLES CITY COUNTY, VA.

DIED: APRIL 4, 1841

PARTY: WHIG

VICE PRESIDENT: JOHN TYLER

FIRST LADY: ANNA TUTHILL SYMMES

CHILDREN: ELIZABETH, JOHN CLEVES, LUCY, WILLIAM HENRY JR., JOHN SCOTT, BENJAMIN, MARY, CARTER, ANNA, JAMES

NICKNAME: OLD TIPPECANOE

THE FIRST PRESIDENT TO DIE IN OFFICE.

In times of crisis, people often turn—sometimes foolishly, sometimes not—to war heroes for leadership. George Washington was such a hero. So was Andrew Jackson.

William Henry Harrison was born on a large Virginia plantation just before the outbreak of the American Revolution. His father, Benjamin Harrison, signed the Declaration of Independence. His first career choice was medicine, but his family's money ran out soon after his father's death in 1791. When that happened, he left medical school and joined the army as a professional soldier.

Harrison saw his first action in the Northwest Territory during the Indian wars of the 1790s. He was commended for his bravery at the Battle of Fallen Timbers in 1794.

While serving as the governor of the Indiana Territory in 1811, he led an army of professional soldiers and militiamen against the village of the Shawnee chief Tecumseh. His ensuing victory at Tippecanoe Creek earned him national fame and the nickname Old Tippecanoe. The Whigs' campaign slogan in 1840 was "Tippecanoe and Tyler, Too."

PNEUMONIA KILLS HARRISON
AFTER ONE MONTH IN OFFICE

WASHINGTON, April 4, 1841—Pres. William Henry Harrison died last night of pneumonia. A messenger has been sent to the home of Vice Pres. John Tyler in Williamsburg, Virginia, to inform him of the news.

Just one month ago, the sixty-eight-year-old president gave the longest inaugural address in history, lasting nearly two hours. He delivered the speech while standing outdoors in a cold wind, wearing neither hat nor overcoat. Later, the president went out walking and got caught in a rainstorm. He came back to the White House drenched. The cold he caught that day later developed into pneumonia.

The president's doctors applied heated suction cups to Harrison's skin, hoping to draw out the disease. When this and other treatments failed, the doctors turned in desperation to traditional Indian cures, including one therapy that involved snakes. None of these worked, and the president died in his bed.

IN MEMORY OF PRESIDENT WM. H. HARRISON, WHO DEPARTED THIS LIFE, APRIL 4, 1841, AGED 68, Deeply lamented by 16 Millions of people.

JOHN TYLER

10th President
★
1841 to 1845

John Tyler

BORN: MARCH 29, 1790

BIRTHPLACE: CHARLES CITY COUNTY, VA.

DIED: JANUARY 18, 1862

PARTY: WHIG

VICE PRESIDENT: NONE

FIRST LADIES: LETITIA CHRISTIAN, JULIA GARDINER

CHILDREN: MARY, ROBERT, JOHN JR., LETITIA, ELIZABETH, ANNE, ALICE, TAZEWELL, DAVID, JOHN ALEXANDER, JULIA, LACHLAN, LYON, ROBERT FITZWALTER, PEARL

NICKNAME: HIS ACCIDENCY

THE FIRST PRESIDENT TO HAVE A VETO OVERRIDDEN.

Because William Henry Harrison was the first president to die in office, his death caused a great deal of confusion. Vice Pres. John Tyler's transition to power should have been simple, but it wasn't.

Tyler didn't even know the president was sick. He was shocked when a government clerk awoke him at his home in Williamsburg, Virginia, with news that Harrison was dead.

Tyler's larger problem was that he had been nominated for vice president simply to balance the Whig ticket. The Whigs needed support in the South, and Tyler was a southerner. He had joined the Whig party because of his hatred for Andrew Jackson and the Democrats. But he had never really accepted the Whigs' nationalist policies. As a result, the Whig party leaders, especially Henry Clay, didn't trust him.

Clay was perhaps the country's leading nationalist, which meant that he wanted

EUROPEAN IMMIGRATION WAVE HITS U.S.

DURING THE 1840s, the United States experienced a massive wave of European immigration. Between 1844 and 1854, nearly three million people made the Atlantic crossing. Of these, 1,300,000 were Irish, and 940,000 were German.

The Irish were escaping a terrible famine in Ireland caused by a series of potato crop failures. Tens of thousands of people starved, but many more fled to the United States.

Because they were too poor to move farther inland, most Irish immigrants settled in the northeastern port cities where they landed. Large Irish neighborhoods quickly grew up in New York, Boston, and Philadelphia.

German immigrants, most of whom arrived with a little more money, generally moved on to the Midwest. Cities such as Milwaukee became magnets for them, as well as for the Scandinavians who followed them to America. By 1860, nearly one-third of the population of Wisconsin was foreign born.

EMIGRANTS LANDING IN NEW YORK.

★ EDGAR ALLAN POE

In 1841, *Graham's Magazine* published a short story by Edgar Allan Poe titled "The Murders in the Rue Morgue." *Graham's* regularly printed works by the best-known American authors—including James Fenimore Cooper, Nathaniel Hawthorne, and Henry Wadsworth Longfellow.

"The Murders in the Rue Morgue" was the first detective story ever written. It exhibited the ghoulish and gruesome style that later made Poe's work famous. His stories, poems, and essays were widely published at the time, but Poe never made much money. In 1843, his best year, he earned just three hundred dollars from his writing.

★ THE OREGON TRAIL

During 1843, "Oregon fever" swept through the Mississippi Valley. A thousand settlers headed west that year to find out whether the Willamette Valley in Oregon was indeed as beautiful and fertile as people said. They followed the two-thousand-mile-long Oregon Trail.

Beginning in Independence, Missouri, the Oregon Trail passed through deserts, over mountains, and across Indian territory. Most families traveled in canvas-covered wagons called prairie schooners because the tops of the wagons often looked liked sails in the wind. (Schooners were popular sailing ships.)

Trains of fifty or so wagons set off each morning at about four o'clock and kept going until dusk, stopping only to graze their animals. Even so, the trip to Oregon usually took six months, because the wagons could make only twelve miles a day over the difficult terrain.

to use the power of the federal government to build a strong, unified country. His current program was a revised version of the American System that he had originally developed during the years after the War of 1812.

During the single month that William Henry Harrison had occupied the White House, it had seemed to many that Henry Clay was actually running the government. On most important matters of policy, Harrison let the senator from Kentucky decide, and this was exactly what Clay wanted.

Tyler, however, was an advocate of states' rights. He believed, as many other southerners did, that a strong federal government threatened individual freedoms, such as the right to own slaves.

Clay and his followers tried to limit Tyler's power by refusing to recognize him as the new president. Instead, they referred to him as "the acting president." Some people even nicknamed Tyler His Accidency (a pun on His Excellency, the form of address used for royalty), but Tyler never doubted that he was the president in all respects that mattered. He made the point by returning, unopened, mail addressed to "Acting President Tyler."

WHIGS IN TURMOIL Tyler's first public clash with Clay came over the national bank. Clay had wanted to bring back a national bank ever since Jackson's undoing of the Second Bank of the United States. Twice he pushed through Congress bills chartering a Third Bank, and twice Tyler angered the Whigs by vetoing them.

To protest Tyler's vetoes, the entire cabinet, with the exception of Secretary of State Daniel Webster, resigned in September 1841. Webster stayed on because he was negotiating an important treaty with Great Britain.

Tyler quickly appointed new cabinet officers who agreed with his policies, but the loss of Whig support had its consequences, and Tyler became the first president to serve without a party.

Although Tyler's domestic policies now met with much greater opposition in Congress, he still had, like all presidents, a great deal of freedom to act when it came to foreign affairs. In his administration's first success, he resolved a border dispute with Canada. The agreement, negotiated by Daniel Webster and Lord Ashburton of Great Britain, granted the United States slightly more than half of the disputed land along the Maine border. In fact, the Webster-Ashburton Treaty fixed the U.S.-Canadian border all the way from the Atlantic Ocean west to the Rocky Mountains.

THE ANNEXATION OF TEXAS

To the south, Tyler took up the matter of Texan statehood, which had been pending since the Van Buren administration. By 1843, most Texans had grown tired of waiting, and their representatives had begun talking with Great Britain about the possibility of remaining independent under British protection.

Around the same time, Tyler began his own secret talks with Texas, which led to a treaty rejected by the Senate in June 1844. This treaty—written by Tyler's new secretary of state, John C. Calhoun—included a section glorifying slavery, which sealed its defeat.

Later in 1844, however, James Knox Polk was elected president because he favored expansion of the nation. Polk's victory persuaded Congress that the public wanted Texas to be annexed. So three days before he left office, Tyler signed a joint resolution of Congress admitting Texas to the Union.

CAMPAIGN ★ 1844

HAVING CAST TYLER OUT OF THEIR PARTY, the Whigs weren't about to nominate him again. Instead, they chose Henry Clay, who had previously run for president in 1824 and again in 1832.

When the Democrats met in May to choose their candidate, former president Martin Van Buren received a majority of the delegate votes on the first ballot. But he never won the two-thirds necessary for nomination, and as support for him waned, the convention turned to James Knox Polk, once the governor of Tennessee. This dark-horse, or long-shot, candidate was so poorly known compared to Clay that the Whigs made "Who Is Polk?" their campaign slogan.

POLK AND DALLAS.

The key issues of the 1844 campaign were western expansion and the spread of slavery. Clay opposed the annexation of Texas, while Polk strongly supported it, as well as the annexation of Oregon as far north as latitude 54°40'. The Democrats' slogan that year was "Fifty-four Forty or Fight!"

Clay's stand on Texas cost him support in the South, where voters thought he was trying to stop the spread of slavery. The Kentuckian hoped that these losses would be offset by a strong showing in the North. But Clay, like Polk, was himself a slaveholder, which third-party abolitionist candidate James G. Birney pointed out often on the campaign trail. Birney didn't win any electoral votes, but he did win enough popular votes in New York to tip the state—and the election—to Polk.

BORN: NOVEMBER 2, 1795

BIRTHPLACE: MECKLENBURG COUNTY, N.C.

DIED: JUNE 15, 1849

PARTY: DEMOCRAT

VICE PRESIDENT: GEORGE M. DALLAS

FIRST LADY: SARAH CHILDRESS

CHILDREN: NONE

NICKNAME: YOUNG HICKORY

THE FIRST PRESIDENT TO HAVE HIS INAUGURATION REPORTED BY TELEGRAPH.

JAMES KNOX POLK
11th President
★
1845 to 1849

During the 1840s, Americans were particularly eager to expand the territory of the United States. An almost unknown expansionist candidate, James Knox Polk, proved the strength of this cause by defeating Henry Clay in the presidential election of 1844. Following the election, Polk focused his attention on fulfilling the nation's "manifest destiny" to rule the North American continent.

The phrase *manifest destiny* was first used by magazine editor John L. O'Sullivan in an 1845 article favoring the annexation of Texas. O'Sullivan used the phrase to refer to the popular belief that it was proper and inevitable for the U.S. government to control all of North America.

GOLD RUSH FEVER
MINERS HURRY TO CALIFORNIA

SAN FRANCISCO, February 28, 1849—The first ship carrying prospectors from the East arrived in port today, thirteen months after James W. Marshall discovered gold at Sutter's Fort.

These miners, nicknamed forty-niners after the year of their arrival, are the first of forty thousand expected to sail to California this year. Just as many are expected to come overland. As President Polk has pointed out, "Nearly the whole of the male population of the country [has] gone to the gold districts."

James Marshall made his discovery in January 1848 while building a sawmill for John Sutter on the American River near Sacramento. By August, when the *New York Herald* first

printed news of his find in the East, there were already four thousand miners living in primitive huts on the hillside above the river.

"My eye was caught by something shining in the bottom of a ditch," Marshall wrote. "I reached my hand down and picked it up; it made my heart thump, for I was certain it was gold."

57

1846

O'Sullivan wrote that it was "our manifest destiny to overspread the continent allotted by Providence for the free development of our yearly multiplying millions."

Like most Americans, Polk agreed that it was the nation's manifest, or obvious, destiny to spread democracy from the Atlantic Ocean to the Pacific. No matter that obstacles such as rivers, mountains, and native peoples stood in the way, because success was inevitable.

Most people believed that the United States was carrying out a divine mission to create one day an "empire for liberty" from Massachusetts all the way to California. Polk often used the idea to justify his actions, especially the taking of new territory. His policy was "the more, the better."

THE OREGON TREATY Because the annexation of Texas had already been completed during the last days of Tyler's term, Polk turned his attention to the acquisition of Oregon. The southern border of Russian lands in Alaska had been set at latitude 54°40'. The northern border of Mexican California was similarly fixed at latitude 42°, also known as the Forty-second Parallel. Between these two borders, from the Rocky Mountains west to the Pacific Ocean, lay the Oregon Territory.

Both the United States and Great Britain had longtime claims to Oregon. At first, Polk refused to negotiate with the British. After all, the Democrats' slogan during the 1844 election had been "Fifty-four Forty or Fight!"

Nevertheless, Polk soon agreed to a compromise. A new boundary was set at the Forty-ninth Parallel, granting to the United States the present-day states of Oregon and Washington. Polk thus became the first president to govern a

THE EARLY YEARS THE OLDEST OF TEN CHILDREN, Jimmy Polk was born on his family's farm in North Carolina. When he was ten years old, the Polks moved to central Tennessee, traveling more than five hundred miles through difficult country in a covered wagon. The family prospered there, eventually coming to own thousands of acres worked by more than fifty slaves.

Jimmy Polk was a sickly child, who did poorly in the rough-and-tumble games favored by boys on the frontier. He was particularly troubled by stones in his gallbladder. When he was seventeen, Polk underwent a dangerous and exceedingly painful operation to remove the stones. The surgeon gave him only liquor to ease the pain. It was not until the time of Polk's presidency that a doctor in Boston first used ether to put a patient to sleep during an operation.

★**AMELIA'S BLOOMERS** Women's clothing during the middle of the nineteenth century could be so confining that it sometimes felt like a cage. Underneath wide hoop skirts and stiff blouses, women wore tightly laced corsets that squeezed their waistlines down to an unnatural twenty inches. These corsets often did permanent damage to the liver and kidneys.

In 1851, a women's rights activist named Amelia Bloomer introduced a new, comfortable style of dress that featured loose-fitting trousers worn underneath a knee-length skirt. The pants quickly became known as bloomers. They were obviously more practical, but they so scandalized the public that women did not begin wearing trousers regularly for another hundred years.

★**THE FIRST LADY** Sarah Childress Polk was an exceptionally popular hostess in Washington because of her charm, liveliness, and intelligence. As first lady, she hosted the first formal Thanksgiving dinner at the White House and, being a devout Presbyterian, banned dancing and liquor at all White House events. For a woman of her time, she was unusually well educated, having attended the exclusive Moravian Female Academy in North Carolina. The president often consulted with her on policy matters.

★ THE SENECA FALLS CONVENTION

Many female leaders of the abolitionist movement also wanted to end the "domestic slavery" of women in the United States. In July 1848, a group of these feminists met in Seneca Falls, New York, where they founded the women's rights movement.

The delegates to the Seneca Falls Convention prepared a list of the specific ways in which women suffered discrimination and also agreed to a number of resolutions for change. One of these pointed out that women deserved the right to vote. Even so, only four western states gave women the right to vote before 1900, the first of these being Wyoming in 1869.

Women's Rights Convention.

A Convention to discuss the social, civil and religious condition and rights of Woman, will be held in the Wesleyan Chapel, at Seneca Falls, N. Y., on Wednesday and Thursday the 19th and 20th of July current, commencing at 10 o'clock A. M.

During the first day, the meeting will be exclusively for Women, which all are earnestly invited to attend. The public generally are invited to be present on the second day, when LUCRETIA MOTT, of Philadelphia, and others both ladies and gentlemen, will address the Convention.

★ FREDERICK DOUGLASS

Frederick Douglass was just twenty years old when he ran away from his master in Maryland. Seven years later, in 1845, he wrote an autobiography that became one of the most important works of the antislavery movement. His *Narrative of the Life of Frederick Douglass, an American Slave* inspired thousands of abolitionists with its detailed description of the horrors of slavery. Later, during the Civil War, Douglass recruited blacks to serve in the Union army and advised Pres. Abraham Lincoln on issues relating to African Americans.

United States that extended all the way from the Atlantic to the Pacific.

After settling this dispute in the Northwest, Polk next turned his expansionist gaze toward the Mexican colonies in the Southwest and California. Soon, he would become the first president to act militarily in support of the cause of manifest destiny.

THE MEXICAN WAR

Even after Texas formally joined the Union in 1845, the United States and Mexico continued to fight over Texas's southern border. Congress insisted that it be the Rio Grande, while the Mexicans refused to recognize any border south of the Nueces River.

At first, Polk tried bargaining. He offered to pay Mexico for the disputed land (and expressed a willingness to buy New Mexico and California as well). When the Mexicans, still angry over the annexation of Texas, refused him, Polk sent troops under Gen. Zachary Taylor to the Rio Grande.

In early May 1846, Mexican troops engaged U.S. soldiers in a skirmish. Eight days later, Polk asked Congress for a declaration of war, because Mexican soldiers had "shed American blood upon the American soil." Two days after that, Polk got what he wanted. The vote was 40–2 in the Senate and 174–14 in the House.

The Mexican War became the central political event of Polk's presidency. His party rallied to him, while the Whigs became divided. Those from the South and West approved of the war, while northern abolitionists believed that the Mexican War was part of a secret plan to expand slavery into the Southwest.

The Mexican army vastly outnumbered U.S. forces in the area, but superior American technology and strategy overcame this disadvantage. For example,

the revolver, invented in 1835 by Samuel Colt, proved to be a powerful weapon in combat.

Although Colt's original firearms business had failed in 1842, the success of his revolver during the Mexican War led to a large government contract. Colt used the money to build the world's largest private armory, where he made significant advances in the use of interchangeable parts.

The Mexican War ended in February 1848 with the signing of the Treaty of Guadalupe Hidalgo. Under its terms, Mexico ceded to the United States more than five hundred thousand square miles of territory, including New Mexico and California. In return, the U.S. paid Mexico fifteen million dollars and agreed to allow Mexicans living on the land to remain there if they so chose. The Mexican Cession was the nation's largest acquisition of land since the Louisiana Purchase.

RETIREMENT During the 1844 campaign, Polk had promised that, if elected, he would serve only one term. Although he was now hugely popular and could easily have won a second four years, he resolved instead to keep his word and announced that he would retire in 1849.

"I feel exceedingly relieved that I am now free from all public cares," he wrote in his diary on the last day of his term. "I am sure I shall be a happier man in my retirement."

Although Polk expected to enjoy a long and peaceful retirement at his home in Nashville, he fell ill during a goodwill tour of the South shortly after leaving office. His condition grew worse until he finally died just three months after witnessing the inauguration of his successor, Zachary Taylor.

CAMPAIGN ★ 1848

WITH POLK'S RETIREMENT, the Democrats turned to Sen. Lewis Cass of Michigan, who had unsuccessfully sought the party's nomination four years earlier. The Whigs drafted Gen. Zachary Taylor, a hero of the Mexican War.

Although the election of William Henry Harrison in 1840 had shown again that generals made popular candidates, Taylor was somewhat reluctant to accept the nomination. He had never run for office before, nor even voted in a presidential election. In the end, however, he agreed to run and also to accept the Whig platform, which stated the party's goals.

The main issue of the campaign was again the extension of slavery. Of particular concern was the Wilmot Proviso, a congressional bill that would have banned slavery in all of the territories acquired as a result of the Mexican War. The Wilmot Proviso twice passed the House only to be defeated in the Senate.

Taylor refused to comment on this bill, but his ownership of more than one hundred slaves made his position appear clear. Cass openly opposed the measure, arguing that the decision should be left up to the citizens of each territory.

Former president Martin Van Buren ran as the candidate of the new antislavery Free Soil party. Although the Free Soilers were not yet willing to abolish slavery, they did oppose its spread and endorsed the Wilmot Proviso.

As James Birney had four years earlier, Van Buren performed well enough in his home state of New York to swing a close election to Taylor, who won with less than half of the popular vote in the first presidential election held in every state on the same day.

BORN: NOVEMBER 24, 1784

BIRTHPLACE: ORANGE COUNTY, VA.

DIED: JULY 9, 1850

PARTY: WHIG

VICE PRESIDENT: MILLARD FILLMORE

FIRST LADY: MARGARET MACKALL SMITH

CHILDREN: ANNE, SARAH KNOX, OCTAVIA, MARGARET, MARY ELIZABETH, RICHARD

NICKNAME: OLD ROUGH AND READY

RODE HIS HORSE SIDESADDLE INTO BATTLE.

ZACHARY TAYLOR

12th President
★
1849 to 1850

Z. Taylor

The most important issue facing Zachary Taylor when he took office was the possible extension of slavery into the territories of the Mexican Cession. Southerners continued to view any limitation on slavery as a threat to their region, while northern abolitionists refused to tolerate the spread of human bondage to any new states.

Taylor had been careful not to reveal his opinion on the issue during the campaign. Instead, he let people assume that, because he owned slaves himself, he must support slavery. These same people were shocked to learn after the election that the new president intended to oppose the extension of slavery into the new territories.

Instead, Taylor proposed to Congress that two-thirds of the Mexican Cession be set aside for huge new states in New Mexico and California and that both of these states be free.

Southerners who had supported Taylor were furious at what seemed to be a change of heart. People in South Carolina were so upset that they again threatened to secede from the Union,

PRESIDENT TAYLOR DIES IN OFFICE

WASHINGTON, July 9, 1850— Pres. Zachary Taylor died this evening in his bedroom at the White House. The cause was a digestive illness. During the last few days, his doctors had tried numerous cures, including the drug opium, but Taylor's condition steadily worsened.

Just before the end, he said, "I am about to die. I expect the summons very soon. I have tried to discharge my duties faithfully. I regret nothing, but I am sorry that I am about to leave my friends."

Taylor began to feel sick five days ago after spending Independence Day at the unfinished Washington Monument, listening to hours of patriotic speeches in the hot July sun.

Returning to the White House, he ate a bowl of cherries and drank a pitcher of cold milk. Later, he developed severe intestinal cramps. His doctors believe that either the milk or the cherries were contaminated with cholera, a stomach disease caused by poor sanitation.

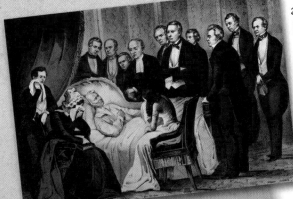

1850

as they had during the nullification controversy of 1833.

There was no simple solution, but now that gold had been found outside Sacramento, statehood for California became a pressing matter. As a result of the Gold Rush, the population of California grew from ten thousand to one hundred thousand in just a few years, as a wilderness suddenly became one of the richest territories in the nation.

Moderates called for a compromise. Otherwise, the fight over slavery could lead to civil war. To avoid this outcome, Sen. Henry Clay proposed a series of resolutions in January 1850 designed to satisfy, if not please, both sides. His plan was later called the Great Compromise.

It called for the admission of California as a free state, leaving the issue of slavery in the rest of the Mexican Cession up to the people who lived there. Most northerners were willing to accept this, but southerners needed a strong inducement if they were going to agree.

THE FUGITIVE SLAVE ACT

The plum that Clay offered them was the Fugitive Slave Act. This notorious bill, the most controversial element of Clay's package, made northerners responsible for returning runaway slaves to their southern masters. (At the time, escaped slaves were allowed to remain free if they could successfully reach the North.)

Abolitionists were outraged by the Fugitive Slave Act because it also gave southerners the right to pursue runaway slaves into the North, kidnap them, and take them back to the South without having to go through any legal processes.

While he lived, President Taylor opposed the Compromise of 1850 and made it known that he planned to veto any bill that made possible the spread of slavery. After his death, however, that decision was passed on to Vice Pres. Millard Fillmore.

THE EARLY YEARS

ZACHARY TAYLOR WAS RAISED in Kentucky while that state was still at the edge of the western frontier, and he grew up under the constant threat of Indian attack. Living in the wilderness, he received only the most basic schooling and remained a poor speller all his life.

At the age of twenty-four, he decided to make a career for himself in the army. During his forty years as an officer, he survived the War of 1812, the Black Hawk War, and the Mexican War. His victory over a much stronger Mexican army at Buena Vista in 1847 made him both a national hero and an attractive candidate for president.

★ POSTAGE DUE

During the nineteenth century, presidential candidates never attended party conventions. Instead, they stayed at home and awaited the results. To notify Taylor of his nomination, the president of the Whig convention sent the general a letter. But he didn't put any postage on the envelope.

Sending mail without postage was a common practice at the time because it forced the recipient to pay the postage due. Taylor, however, received so many postage-due letters from admirers that he told his local post office to stop delivering them. As a result, the first notice of his nomination never arrived. Weeks later, the Whigs realized what had happened and sent another letter, this time with the postage already paid.

★ UNCLE TOM'S CABIN

In 1852, Harriet Beecher Stowe published *Uncle Tom's Cabin*. Ten thousand copies of this antislavery novel were sold in the first week, and three hundred thousand were sold in the first year after its publication.

The book helped to persuade many people that slavery was indeed a terrible institution. It also encouraged disobedience of the Fugitive Slave Act and stiffened opposition to the spread of slavery. But most northerners were still unwilling to abolish slavery in the South, where it was most entrenched.

Many years later, during the height of the Civil War, Pres. Abraham Lincoln invited Mrs. Stowe to the White House. Shaking her hand, he reportedly said, "So this is the little lady who made this big war!"

BORN: JANUARY 7, 1800

BIRTHPLACE: CAYUGA COUNTY, N.Y.

DIED: MARCH 8, 1874

PARTY: WHIG

VICE PRESIDENT: NONE

FIRST LADY: ABIGAIL POWERS

CHILDREN: MILLARD, MARY

NICKNAME: LAST OF THE WHIGS

ESTABLISHED THE FIRST PERMANENT LIBRARY IN THE WHITE HOUSE.

MILLARD FILLMORE

13th President
★
1850 to 1853

Millard Fillmore

Millard Fillmore was chosen as the Whigs' vice-presidential candidate in 1848 because of his loyalty to the party. During the early 1830s, he helped found the Whig party in western New York. Later, as a congressman from the Buffalo area, he tried to prevent the eventual split between Tyler and the congressional Whigs. When the split came, however, he sided with the party.

Although Fillmore had a reputation for being a dull speaker and mediocre leader, he was also known as an honorable man. He never smoked or drank, and he gambled only once in his life. (At the age of fifteen, he entered and won a turkey raffle at a New Year's Day party.)

During the 1848 election campaign, Fillmore was largely ignored. He didn't meet Zachary Taylor until after the election and was excluded from any role in shaping the new cabinet. Taylor might have found Fillmore useful

PERRY OPENS JAPAN TO U.S. TRADE

EDO BAY, Japan, July 8, 1853—Commo. Matthew C. Perry sailed into Edo Bay today with two U.S. Navy warships. Perry's mission is to force Japan, which has been isolated for two centuries, to establish diplomatic and trade relations with the United States.

The Japanese immediately ordered Perry to leave, but the commodore refused. He told the Japanese government that it must appoint a suitable official to receive the diplomatic letters he is carrying. Otherwise, he will deliver them by force.

Perry believes that the Japanese defenses are no match for American naval power. He has long argued that only a strong show of force and a "resolute attitude" can win concessions from the Japanese.

Perry's expedition was first ordered by President Fillmore in March 1852. Since then, it has been publicized around the world.

Officials in the State Department expect that, once Perry compels Japan to accept trade with America, other Western powers will force their way into Japanese ports as well.

in helping to promote his programs in Congress, but the president kept him so far from power that the vice president was even denied the courtesy of making political appointments in his home state. All of that changed, of course, when Taylor died.

THE COMPROMISE OF 1850

As president, Taylor had strongly opposed the Compromise of 1850, especially those parts designed to appease the South. President Fillmore, however, supported the compromise. He thought it was the only way the nation could avoid a civil war.

In September 1850, Fillmore signed the five separate bills that made up the Great Compromise. By far, the most controversial of these was the Fugitive Slave Act.

Many northerners hated this law, which gave slave owners the right to come north, kidnap blacks accused of being runaways, and take them south again without a trial or even a hearing. Abolitionist newspapers wrote often about cases in which free blacks were enslaved by mistaken or unscrupulous slave catchers.

Antislavery activists tried to obstruct the law whenever possible. Some of them offered free legal advice to escaped slaves, and others posted notices warning blacks of the dangers posed by kidnappers.

Fillmore knew all this but thought that supporting the compromise was the only way to prevent secession. He also believed that resolving the crisis might even earn him the 1852 Whig nomination for president. In this, he was wrong. Northern Whigs refused to accept him because he had signed the Fugitive Slave Act, and thus denied the nomination, Fillmore retired.

CAMPAIGN ★ 1852

BEFORE HE WAS MADE THE DEMOCRATIC NOMINEE, Franklin Pierce had no intention of becoming president. The office, he had said, was "utterly repugnant to my tastes and wishes." Having retired from the Senate ten years earlier, he had little interest in returning to Washington, and his wife had even less. Both considered the capital an unpleasant city.

The Democratic convention, which had been deadlocked, made Pierce its compromise choice on the forty-ninth ballot, rejecting four other candidates including Lewis Cass, James Buchanan, and Stephen Douglas. Although Pierce's name was not even mentioned before the thirty-fifth ballot, the party quickly came together behind him. "We Polked you in 1844; we'll Pierce you in 1852," the Democrats warned the Whigs.

Although Millard Fillmore was an incumbent president, he faced an unusually tough battle for the nomination of his party. Because he had signed the Fugitive Slave Act, northern Whigs sided with yet another general, Mexican War hero and antislavery candidate Winfield Scott. Scott was nicknamed Old Fuss and Feathers because he had always insisted that his subordinates strictly follow military regulations.

Although Fillmore received the backing of the southern "cotton" Whigs, the northern "conscience" Whigs were still able to win the nomination for Scott on the fifty-third ballot. But this division within the party proved impossible to overcome during the general election campaign. With the backing of a united Democratic party, Pierce easily won the popular and electoral votes.

FRANKLIN PIERCE
1853

14th President
★
1853 to 1857

BORN: NOVEMBER 23, 1804

BIRTHPLACE: HILLSBOROUGH, N.H.

DIED: OCTOBER 8, 1869

PARTY: DEMOCRAT

VICE PRESIDENT: WILLIAM R. KING

FIRST LADY: JANE MEANS APPLETON

CHILDREN: FRANKLIN JR., FRANK ROBERT, BENJAMIN

NICKNAME: HANDSOME FRANK

ALWAYS INSISTED THAT GRACE BE SAID BEFORE A MEAL.

Franklin Pierce was famous throughout New Hampshire as a brilliant courtroom lawyer. People came from all over to hear his trial speeches. He was such an accomplished speaker, in fact, that he was able to deliver his entire inaugural address from memory.

In this address, Pierce stated his personal belief that owning slaves was a legal right guaranteed by the Constitution. However, he also acknowledged that extremism on both sides, the proslavery South and the antislavery North, was now threatening the Union.

Overall, though, Pierce's tone was mournful. Two months earlier, his only surviving son, Bennie, had been killed in a train accident, and the Pierces never really recovered from this loss.

TUBMAN LEADS PARENTS TO FREEDOM ON UNDERGROUND RAILROAD

DORCHESTER COUNTY, Maryland, June 1857—The runaway slave Harriet Tubman returned to Maryland this month to free her parents, who had remained slaves after their daughter's escape to freedom in 1849. Tubman's trip was one of nineteen she has made to help slaves escape to the North. She has been one of the "conductors" on the Underground Railroad. The "stations" on this railroad are operated by sympathetic whites, many of whom are Quakers. Almost all of the conductors are black, however.

The escaped slaves move from station to station at night, under the cover of darkness. It is estimated that some fifty thousand slaves have traveled to freedom this way. Tubman has personally led as many as three hundred people to safety.

She has been called the Moses of Her People, after the Hebrew leader who led the Jews out of bondage in ancient Egypt. Rewards for Tubman's capture have reached as high as forty thousand dollars.

Two years passed before First Lady Jane Pierce felt well enough again to appear in public, and the White House remained a gloomy place throughout Pierce's term.

As president, Pierce was careful to include influential southerners in his cabinet. As secretary of war, for example, he picked Mississippi's Jefferson Davis, a strongly proslavery senator. In fact, Pierce seemed so beholden to the southern wing of the Democratic party that he was called a doughface. This term referred to northern politicians who were known to have strong southern sympathies.

THE GADSDEN PURCHASE During the Pierce administration, the United States continued to expand. In 1853, U.S. minister to Mexico James Gadsden negotiated the ten-million-dollar purchase of territory in present-day Arizona and New Mexico. This land, totaling 29,644 square miles, was sought because it lay along the path of a proposed transcontinental railroad. With its acquisition, cartographers could for the first time draw U.S. maps that showed the modern outline of the forty-eight continental states.

Pierce also wanted to buy the Spanish island of Cuba, which lay just ninety miles south of Florida. Following the president's wishes, Secretary of State William L. Marcy told U.S. minister to Spain Pierre Soulé to begin negotiating for its purchase. In the meantime, at Marcy's suggestion, Soulé also met in Ostend, Belgium, with the U.S. ministers to Britain and France to plan a negotiating strategy.

The result was the secret Ostend Manifesto of 1854. This document proposed offering Spain up to $120 million for Cuba. If the Spanish refused to sell, however, the ministers recommended taking the island by force.

When the contents of the Ostend Manifesto were subsequently revealed

THE EARLY YEARS FRANKLIN PIERCE GREW UP IN HILLSBOROUGH, New Hampshire, during the War of 1812. As a boy, he loved listening to the stories of battle told by his older brothers, who were then serving in the army. These stories eventually inspired him to become a soldier himself.

When the Mexican War broke out in 1846, Pierce had already served several terms in the House and Senate. Despite this prestigious background, he nevertheless enlisted as a private in the army. Within a year, however, he was made a colonel. And a month after that, he became a brigadier general.

★ **WHALING** Herman Melville's novel *Moby-Dick* tells the story of an epic hunt for a great white whale. When the book was first published in 1851, the U.S. whaling industry was at its height. Whale fat, or blubber, was particularly prized for its many industrial uses.

According to the whalers, most of whom sailed out of ports in southern New England, the most dangerous part of the hunt was the "Nantucket sleigh ride." During this final stage, crewmen in small boats would tie their craft to the struggling whales as one of the mates closed in with a harpoon for the kill.

★ **SLAVE SONGS** Slaves in the South often sang work songs and spirituals to help them get through their long, hard days. (Ironically, slave owners liked to pretend that these slaves sang because they were happy.)

In their songs, slaves combined elements of both African and American music. Some songs like "Nobody Knows the Trouble I've Seen" told the story of the slaves' difficult lives, while others told of happier times ahead. Runaway slaves often sang "Steal Away" and "O Freedom" as they made their way north. The origins of jazz and the blues lie in these moving songs.

★ LEVI'S

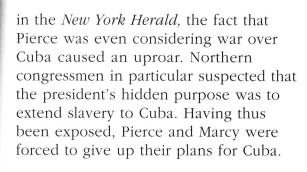

In 1850, a German immigrant named Levi Strauss sailed to San Francisco aboard a ship filled with other fortune seekers. They were just a few of the hundred thousand people drawn to California by the Gold Rush.

Strauss, who planned to open a dry goods store, had brought with him a supply of blue canvas called denim. He intended to sell the material for tents, but when he got to San Francisco, he found that what the miners really needed was sturdy work clothing. So Strauss promptly stitched his denim into the pants that later became famous as blue jeans.

★ RAILROADS

The 1850s were a boom time for railroad building in the United States. Workers laid more than twenty-one thousand miles of track, and new lines opened up the nation's interior, making railroad transportation the country's first billion-dollar industry.

Americans were thrilled by this display of power, speed, and national ingenuity. Writers and poets wrote in awe of the "iron horse" that snorted steam and smoke. "Railroad iron is a magician's rod," wrote Ralph Waldo Emerson. But not everyone appreciated the railroads. "I will not have my eyes put out and my ears spoiled by its smoke and steam and hissing," snarled Henry David Thoreau.

in the *New York Herald,* the fact that Pierce was even considering war over Cuba caused an uproar. Northern congressmen in particular suspected that the president's hidden purpose was to extend slavery to Cuba. Having thus been exposed, Pierce and Marcy were forced to give up their plans for Cuba.

THE KANSAS-NEBRASKA ACT

At the same time, the federal government was considering plans to build the first transcontinental railroad. A senator from Illinois, Stephen Douglas, was working hard to make sure that this railroad took a northerly route through his home state. He knew that wherever the railroad went, business opportunities would follow.

Southerners, of course, wanted the railroad to pass through their region, so Douglas decided to make a deal. If any railroad were going to be built across the Great Plains, a first step would have to be the organization of territories in Kansas and Nebraska. To encourage southerners to go along with this step, Douglas included in his January 1854 Kansas-Nebraska bill a provision that allowed the residents of those territories to decide for themselves whether or not to permit slavery.

Douglas's plan was controversial for many reasons. Most important was that it repealed the Missouri Compromise of 1820, which had outlawed slavery in all Louisiana Purchase lands (including Kansas and Nebraska) north of latitude 36°30'. It was already clear that Nebraskans would vote to prohibit slavery in their territory no matter what, but the outcome of such a vote in Kansas, which bordered on proslavery Missouri, was anybody's guess. Only one thing was certain: The fight would be both hard and bloody.

BLEEDING KANSAS

With Pierce's backing, the Kansas-Nebraska Act passed into law, but it caused much more trouble than it solved. Fanatical abolitionists from New England poured into Kansas, hoping to win control of the territorial government. At the same time, gangs of proslavery thugs from Missouri organized to challenge them.

During March 1855, about four thousand Missourians crossed the border into Kansas and voted illegally. Some forced their way into the polls at gunpoint. Their votes helped elect a proslavery legislature. The territorial governor tried to disqualify many of those who had been elected unfairly, but President Pierce overruled him and let the results of the election stand.

Feeling that they had been cheated, some antislavery settlers responded with violence of their own, and civil war broke out in Kansas. Soon, more than two hundred people would die there.

Nor was slavery-related violence in 1856 limited to Bleeding Kansas. That May, Charles Sumner of Massachusetts was attacked on the floor of the U.S. Senate by Rep. Preston Brooks of South Carolina. Three days earlier, during a debate over Kansas, Sumner had delivered a nasty speech attacking Brooks's cousin, South Carolina senator Andrew P. Butler, and other supporters of slavery. In retaliation, Brooks beat Sumner with a cane until Sumner's head split open. It took the Massachusetts senator three years to recover.

Two days after Sumner's beating, a radical abolitionist named John Brown organized a raid against some proslavery neighbors near Pottawatomie Creek, Kansas. The attack was brutal. Leading a group of seven fanatics, including his four sons, Brown broke into a number of cabins and hacked five men to death.

CAMPAIGN ★ 1856

BY THE TIME the 1856 election came around, the country had lost whatever respect it once had for Franklin Pierce. The public response to his handling of the violence in Kansas had made it clear that he couldn't win reelection, and Pierce himself didn't want to stay around. As a replacement, the Democrats chose James Buchanan, who had been Pierce's minister to Great Britain. Because Buchanan had spent the last three years out of the country, he had avoided many of the controversies that had plagued the Pierce administration.

Buchanan believed that slavery was immoral and even acted against it privately. But he remained acceptable to southern Democrats because, publicly, he opposed any interference with the practice of slavery in the South.

Running against Buchanan was John C. Frémont of California, the first presidential candidate of the new Republican party. The Republicans had come together in 1854 to oppose the spread of slavery into the western territories. Frémont was known as the Pathfinder of the West, because he had led surveying expeditions that helped map the growing nation.

The Republican slogan was "Free Speech, Free Press, Free Soil, Free Men, Frémont, and Victory!" The party warned that compromising with southern slave owners only increased the chances of civil war by prolonging the life of an institution that deserved to be abolished. The Democrats responded that the Republicans were too radical, claiming that a vote for Buchanan was a vote for national stability. Although Frémont carried much of the North, the Democrats' broader national support gave Buchanan a clear-cut victory.

BORN: APRIL 23, 1791

BIRTHPLACE: COVE GAP, PA.

DIED: JUNE 1, 1868

PARTY: DEMOCRAT

VICE PRESIDENT: JOHN C. BRECKINRIDGE

FIRST LADY: NONE

CHILDREN: NONE

NICKNAME: TEN-CENT JIMMY

THE FIRST AND ONLY
BACHELOR PRESIDENT.

JAMES BUCHANAN
15th President
★
1857 to 1861

James Buchanan

SUPREME COURT RULES IN DRED SCOTT CASE

WASHINGTON, March 6, 1857—In a 7–2 decision handed down today, the Supreme Court ruled that the slave Dred Scott cannot sue for his freedom because he is property and not a citizen. Chief Justice Roger B. Taney wrote in his opinion that Scott has "no rights which any white man was bound to respect."

The Court also ruled that the Missouri Compromise of 1820 is unconstitutional because Congress has no power to outlaw slavery in the western territories. Only a state can exclude slavery, the Court ruled.

People in the South are delighted by the decision, while antislavery forces in the North are outraged. "If the people obey this decision, they disobey God," one abolitionist newspaper has written.

Dred Scott is a slave from Missouri who at one time lived with his master's family in Illinois, a free state. Scott's lawyers claimed that by living in a free state, Scott became free as well.

James Buchanan won the election of 1856 by carrying the entire South and a few key northern states as well. Although he was himself a northerner and personally opposed slavery, he won because he favored the interests of the South.

As Buchanan took office in 1857, the most important task facing him was the prevention of civil war. People considered the new president to be one of the most capable and experienced politicians in the country, so there was great anticipation. Everyone wondered what the Buchanan administration would do to resolve the issue of slavery, particularly with regard to its expansion into the western territories.

At his March 4 inauguration, Buchanan stood up to his full six-foot height, spread his broad shoulders apart, and announced that the conflict over slavery had a clear and simple solution.

69

Trained in his youth as a lawyer, the president was famous around the country for his devotion to reason and his passion for the law. Therefore, it came as a surprise to no one when the arguments he made in his inaugural address turned out to be both legal and logical.

Buchanan pointed out that few Americans disputed the constitutionality of slavery in the southern states, where it had always existed. If these states could legally permit slavery within their borders, Buchanan reasoned, how could the federal government deny new states the same privilege? Allowing new territories to decide the slavery issue for themselves was therefore the proper and most reasonable course.

Then, just two days after Buchanan took office, the Supreme Court handed down its decision in the *Dred Scott* case—ruling that slaves, from a legal point of view, were property, not citizens. The Court thus supported Buchanan's argument that ownership of slaves was a constitutional right that the government could neither limit nor deny.

Legally, the matter finally seemed settled, but this viewpoint tragically underestimated the growing opposition to slavery on moral grounds among people who believed that slavery was always wrong and deserved to be outlawed everywhere.

THE KANSAS QUESTION

Meanwhile, the nation's attention returned to Bleeding Kansas, which was now seeking statehood. One of Buchanan's earliest actions had been to appoint Robert Walker of Mississippi as territorial governor there. A loyal southerner, Walker had then put all of his government's weight behind the proslavery forces.

At a convention held in Lecompton in October 1857, delegates approved a proslavery constitution for Kansas. The

THE EARLY YEARS

JAMES BUCHANAN WAS BORN IN A LOG CABIN a few miles outside Mercersburg, Pennsylvania. When he was five years old, his family moved into the town of Mercersburg, where his Irish immigrant father made a living as a merchant and farmer.

Buchanan attended Dickinson College, where he was considered a discipline problem. After his graduation, he became a lawyer. Then, following the death of his fiancée in 1819, he became a politician. Buchanan served in Congress for ten years, first as a Federalist and then as a Jacksonian Democrat. Later, he became James Polk's secretary of state and Franklin Pierce's minister to Great Britain. In 1854, he helped write the Ostend Manifesto.

★ BACHELOR PRESIDENT

Buchanan is the only president never to have married his entire life. Once, when he was twenty-eight years old, he became engaged to Anne Coleman, whose father was one of the wealthiest men in Pennsylvania. They fought, however, and she broke off the engagement. A few months later, she died, possibly a suicide.

Rumors circulated that she had broken off the engagement because she thought Buchanan was only after her money. But Buchanan was doing quite well then as a lawyer and was worth about three hundred thousand dollars.

Buchanan never considered marriage again. During his term as president, his orphaned niece, Harriet Lane (above), served as the official White House hostess.

★ THE MODERN KITCHEN

Throughout her life, Catharine Beecher wrote and lectured about the place of women in American society. She believed strongly that a woman's place was in the home. Along with her famous sister, Harriet Beecher Stowe, she wrote *The American Woman's Home* in 1869.

This manual of household advice described the sisters' design for a new type of kitchen. Their innovations included separate areas for the sink and the stove, as well as two windows for proper ventilation. The Beechers also came up with the idea for built-in cabinets and drawers. Some of their ideas are still used in kitchens today.

★SOJOURNER TRUTH

In 1843, the former slave Isabella Van Wagener changed her name to Sojourner Truth and began traveling around the country. She spoke about the cause of freedom wherever she could, often in churches and on village streets.

Sojourner Truth's passionate and persuasive speeches against slavery and for the rights of women inspired thousands of Americans to give their support to these causes. In 1864, President Lincoln received Sojourner Truth at the White House. She told Lincoln that he was the best president the country ever had but admitted that she had not heard of him before he was nominated. "I had heard of you many times before that," Lincoln told her.

I Sell the Shadow to Support the Substance.

SOJOURNER TRUTH.

★THE PONY EXPRESS
Freight hauler William H. Russell wanted to prove that mail could be carried promptly and profitably across the as-yet-unsettled West. The Pony Express service that he began in April 1860 showed at least that mail could be delivered promptly.

Russell developed a relay system using fast horses and lightweight teenage boys, who rode from station to station along the Pony Express route. The boys changed horses six to eight times each before passing on the mail to the next rider. Using this system, Russell was able to deliver mail from St. Joseph, Missouri, to San Francisco—a distance of nearly two thousand miles—in just ten days. The Pony Express lost a huge amount of money, however, and was put out of business by the completion of the first transcontinental telegraph in October 1861.

PONY EXPRESS!

CHANGE OF TIME!

REDUCED RATES!

10 Days to San Francisco!

LETTERS

WILL BE RECEIVED AT THE

OFFICE, 84 BROADWAY,

NEW YORK,

will be forwarded to connect with the PONY EXPRESS leaving ST. JOSEPH, Missouri,

WEDNESDAY and SATURDAY at 11 P.M.

EXPRESS CHARGES.

Lecompton Constitution was controversial, however, because the Jayhawkers (as antislavery Kansans were known) had boycotted the convention, charging that elections for delegates had been rigged.

Ignoring the boycott, Buchanan backed the Lecompton Constitution and urged Congress to admit Kansas as a slave state. Stephen Douglas led the Senate opposition, insisting that all the people of Kansas be allowed to vote on the constitution before Congress accepted it.

In a statewide referendum held in January 1858, Kansans voted by a wide margin to reject the proslavery Lecompton Constitution. Buchanan didn't give up, persuading Congress to order a second referendum, but again the constitution went down. Finally, in January 1861, Kansas was admitted to the Union as a free state. By that time, however, the nation was on the brink of civil war.

THE LINCOLN-DOUGLAS DEBATES
Meanwhile, Republican Abraham Lincoln decided to challenge Democrat Stephen Douglas in the 1858 Senate race in Illinois. Covered by the national press, the campaign featured seven eloquent debates between the two men. During one of these debates, Lincoln forced Douglas to admit that he believed a territory could outlaw slavery within its borders. This position contradicted the *Dred Scott* decision, which held that owning slaves was a constitutional right.

Douglas's answer helped him defeat Lincoln in Illinois, where slavery was unpopular, but it hurt Douglas in the South. Later, this loss of southern support made it almost impossible for him to win the Democratic nomination for president in 1860.

Lincoln, however, performed so well in his debates with Douglas that, even though he lost the 1858 election, he

nevertheless became a politician of national standing. "A house divided against itself cannot stand," Lincoln said, using a well-known phrase from the Bible to describe the conflict between North and South over slavery.

Events in Kansas had already shown that Americans on both sides were willing to shed blood for their beliefs. Abolitionist John Brown, for instance, developed a plan in 1859 to seize the federal arsenal at Harpers Ferry, Virginia. He intended to use the weapons he captured there to arm slaves he and his small band of raiders would lead in rebellion.

On October 16, Brown and twenty-one of his followers indeed overran the arsenal, but that was as far as they got. The townspeople of Harpers Ferry bottled them up until a force of marines led by Col. Robert E. Lee arrived two days later. The marines stormed the armory, arrested Brown, and put him on trial for treason. He was hanged on December 2.

SECESSION During the last frantic months of his failed presidency, Buchanan tried to remain friendly to the South as he struggled belatedly to preserve the Union. He believed that secession, or withdrawal from the Union, was wrong, but he also feared that resisting the South would lead to highly destructive warfare. In the end, he did little to alter the probably inevitable course of events.

Southern states considered Lincoln's victory in the 1860 presidential election such an outrage that, even before Buchanan left office, seven of them seceded from the Union. They formed the Confederate States of America and in February 1861 elected Jefferson Davis as their president.

CAMPAIGN ★ 1860

THIS YEAR'S PRESIDENTIAL CAMPAIGN was the most fateful in U.S. history. John Brown's October 1859 raid on Harpers Ferry had brought tensions between the North and the South to the breaking point, making the election of 1860 potentially the difference between war and reconciliation.

Meeting in Charleston, South Carolina, the governing Democratic party split over the issue of slavery when front-runner Stephen Douglas refused to include a proslavery plank in the party platform. Two months later, the southern wing of the Democratic party held its own convention, nominating for president Vice Pres. John C. Breckinridge of Kentucky.

Meanwhile, the northern Democrats stuck with Douglas, and the Republicans chose Abraham Lincoln, because of Lincoln's strength in the hotly contested states of Pennsylvania and Indiana. Although the Republicans objected to the expansion of slavery, they were still willing to tolerate it where it already existed. Even so, the prospect of a Republican president so angered many southerners that they threatened to leave the Union if Lincoln were elected. While Lincoln and Douglas competed for votes in the North, Breckinridge competed in the South with John Bell of Tennessee, nominee of the more moderate Constitutional Union party. When all the votes were finally counted, Lincoln won the presidency with nearly two-thirds of the electoral vote but only 40 percent of the popular vote and not a single vote from nine southern states.

BORN: FEBRUARY 12, 1809

BIRTHPLACE: HARDIN COUNTY, KY.

DIED: APRIL 15, 1865

PARTY: REPUBLICAN

VICE PRESIDENTS: HANNIBAL HAMLIN, ANDREW JOHNSON

FIRST LADY: MARY TODD

CHILDREN: ROBERT, EDWARD, WILLIAM, THOMAS

NICKNAME: HONEST ABE

THE FIRST PRESIDENT TO WEAR A BEARD WHILE IN OFFICE.

ABRAHAM LINCOLN
16th President
★
1861 to 1865

Abraham Lincoln

As Lincoln prepared for his March inauguration, events were already overtaking his administration. In the four months since his election, seven states had seceded from the Union to form the Confederate States of America.

Before taking office, Lincoln said that there would be "no bloodshed unless it is forced upon the government." But he also announced that he intended to retain control of all federal property in the South. He made it clear that his primary concern was the preservation of the Union, not the abolition of slavery.

The new president responded to the Confederate attack on Fort Sumter in April 1861 by ordering a naval blockade of all southern ports. The purpose of the blockade was to halt the export of cotton, the South's most important cash crop. The blockade also prevented the agricultural South from importing manufactured goods, such as guns and clothing,

CIVIL WAR!
REBELS TAKE FORT SUMTER

CHARLESTON, South Carolina, April 13, 1861—Maj. Robert Anderson, commander of the federal troops stationed in Charleston Harbor, surrendered Fort Sumter today after a thirty-four-hour bombardment by Confederate artillery. Anderson waited until he was out of ammunition and the fort was in flames before running down the U.S. flag. Remarkably, no one died during the attack, which began at four-thirty yesterday morning.

After taking office a month ago, President Lincoln informed the Confederacy that he intended to resupply Fort Sumter peacefully with food only. This decision placed the burden of whether or not to begin a war on the Confederate authorities. If the rebels attacked a peaceful mission bringing food to Fort Sumter, the responsibility for firing the first shot would be theirs.

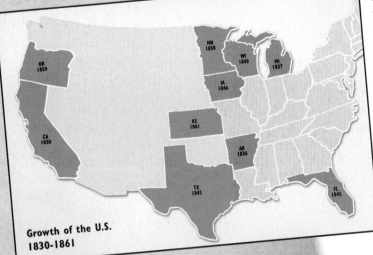

Growth of the U.S. 1830-1861

OR 1859
MN 1858
WI 1848
MI 1837
IA 1846
CA 1850
KS 1861
AR 1836
TX 1845
FL 1845

which it could not easily produce for itself. Meanwhile, the start of the war caused four more wavering states to join the Confederacy.

Because they expected a speedy victory, most northerners backed Lincoln's call for troops enthusiastically. The song "We Are Coming, Father Abraham" was sung at Union army rallies that attracted thousands of recruits. At first, blacks were excluded from the Union army. But as time passed, and the war took unexpected turns for the worse, two hundred thousand blacks were allowed to join the fight.

The Confederacy was no less successful in raising an army. Regional pride was especially strong in the South, and volunteers flocked to enlist in the Rebel army as well.

Fathers and sons went off to battle, while mothers and daughters took over family and business responsibilities. Women also raised money, recruited soldiers, and served as nurses, spies, and scouts. A few even disguised themselves as men and became soldiers.

BULL RUN AND ANTIETAM The first real battle of the Civil War was fought in July 1861 on the banks of a creek called Bull Run in northeastern Virginia, not far from Washington, D.C.

Because the battlefield was so close to the capital, a number of congressmen rode out in carriages to see the defeat of the Confederacy and the end of the rebellion for themselves. Many even brought picnic lunches along with them.

They lost their appetites, however, when Confederate general Thomas J. "Stonewall" Jackson broke the Union attack and sent the Federals scurrying back to Washington. The battle of Bull Run taught the Union that victory would not come so easily.

THE EARLY YEARS

LINCOLN WAS BORN IN A LOG CABIN in Kentucky. The cabin's one room had a dirt floor. When Abe was seven years old, his family moved farther west to Indiana. About Indiana, Lincoln later wrote, "It was a wild region, with many bears and other wild animals still in the woods."

Living on what was then the frontier, Lincoln had barely a year of formal schooling. Unlike his father, however, he did learn to read and write. Among his favorite books was Parson Weems's rather mythological biography of George Washington.

At various times, Lincoln worked as a rail-splitter (turning logs into fence rails), a ferryboat captain, a store clerk, and a postmaster before becoming one of the top trial lawyers in Illinois. He never lost his strong frontier accent, however. Speaking in a high voice, he would pronounce *get* as *git* and *there* as *thar*.

★**THE FIRST LADY** Mary Todd Lincoln was not well liked in Washington. Although she had been charming and witty as a young woman, her mental health, which had always been fragile, was placed under severe stress by her life in the White House.

Because she came from a southern family, four of her brothers had joined the Confederate army at the start of the Civil War. This prompted some congressmen to accuse her of being a Confederate spy. The charge upset her, but it was the death of her twelve-year-old son Willie in 1862 that finally crushed Mary Lincoln. She became noticeably disturbed and went on wild shopping sprees, buying three hundred pairs of gloves in one four-month period. Her husband's assassination sickened her further, and she was eventually committed to an insane asylum.

★**MATHEW BRADY** Mathew Brady was the most famous photographer in the country. He specialized in portraits of famous people, especially presidents. His photographs of Lincoln are among the most memorable images of the nineteenth century.

To document the Civil War, Brady (shown here at Gettysburg in 1863) hired twenty photographers and sent them all over the country, especially to the battlefields. When pictures of the dead at Antietam first appeared at Brady's studio in New York City, *The New York Times* reported that "Mr. Brady has done something to bring home to us the terrible reality and earnestness of war. If he has not brought bodies and laid them on our dooryards and along the streets, he has done something very like it."

★**HOMESTEADING** As early as the Washington administration, federal officials believed that public lands should be sold off to raise funds and encourage settlement. During the 1830s, however, there arose a homesteading movement that advocated giving away the land instead.

In 1862, President Lincoln signed the Homestead Act, which granted 160 acres of public land to anyone willing to farm it for at least five years. During the next forty years, homesteaders claimed more than eighty million acres of public land in the West.

Responding quickly to the defeat at Bull Run, Lincoln made the first of many changes in command, replacing the inept Irvin McDowell with the suave and youthful George B. McClellan.

McClellan was a cautious general. His army was stronger and better equipped than the Confederates. Nevertheless, he moved slowly and avoided confrontation. During the Peninsular Campaign of 1862, which took place on the Virginia peninsula formed by the James and York Rivers beneath the Confederate capital of Richmond, the Rebels boldly outmaneuvered him and beat him on several occasions. Meanwhile, President Lincoln became worried that "delay is killing us."

Later that summer, Robert E. Lee, who was given command of the Confederate army in June, won an impressive victory at the second battle of Bull Run in late August. Following up on that victory, Lee led his troops across the Potomac River into the Union state of Maryland.

One witness called Lee's poorly outfitted invasion force "the dirtiest men I ever saw—a most ragged, lean, and hungry set of wolves." At the subsequent battle of Antietam on September 17, McClellan and Lee fought to a standstill. More than twenty thousand soldiers were killed or wounded that day, the bloodiest in American history. Afterward, Lee retreated back across the Potomac.

THE EMANCIPATION PROCLAMATION Antietam, which could only be loosely called a Union victory, gave President Lincoln the opportunity he needed to announce the Emancipation Proclamation. This executive order freed all the slaves still in areas of rebellion— but not those living in Union slave states, such as Maryland, or in captured southern territory. It also refocused the

1864

government's war aims from the preservation of the Union to the abolition of slavery.

After Antietam, Lincoln dismissed McClellan and replaced him with Ambrose Burnside, who protested his own appointment. Later, Burnside turned out to be right. A month after taking command of the Union army, he suffered a disastrous defeat at Fredericksburg that prompted Lincoln to replace him immediately with Joseph Hooker.

Hooker, too, performed poorly and resigned soon after losing the battle of Chancellorsville in May 1863. Lincoln replaced Hooker with George Meade. Meanwhile, Lee's army was marching north again, this time into Pennsylvania.

Just three days after Meade's promotion—on July 1, 1863—he and Lee met at Gettysburg. For the next seventy-two hours, their armies fought with one another as the outcome of the war hung in the balance. On July 3, the failure of Pickett's Charge against Union-held Cemetery Ridge sealed the Rebel fate. Lee lost more than twenty thousand men, or nearly a third of his army, at Gettysburg, while Union dead and wounded numbered twenty-three thousand.

THE GETTYSBURG ADDRESS On November 19, 1863, Lincoln visited Gettysburg for the dedication of a battlefield cemetery there. The speech he gave that day, which became known as the Gettysburg Address, was just 272 words long.

It didn't mention slavery, the battle, or even the Union army. But its remarkable language captured the reasons why the war was now being fought. After Lincoln finished, the crowd burst into applause.

CAMPAIGN ★ 1864

AS THE 1864 CAMPAIGN GOT UNDER WAY, President Lincoln was in serious political trouble. The end of the Civil War was not yet in sight, and fears about how it would turn out hurt the president's chances for reelection.

Although Lincoln was renominated by the Republicans without opposition, a number of party leaders warned publicly that he could not win the general election.

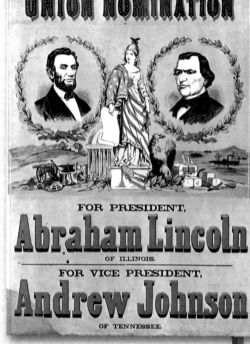

Lincoln actually ran in 1864 as the candidate of the Union party, a name temporarily adopted by Republicans in order to include southern Democrats who had remained loyal to the Union. Emphasizing this political marriage, Lincoln dropped Vice Pres. Hannibal Hamlin from the ticket and replaced him with Andrew Johnson, the military governor of Tennessee and one of the leading spokesmen for the homestead movement.

To oppose Lincoln, the northern Democrats nominated George B. McClellan, whom Lincoln had in 1862 dismissed as commander of the Union army. McClellan blamed Lincoln for the poor performance of Union troops and called for both an immediate cease-fire and a negotiated peace treaty with the South.

During July and August, McClellan appeared to be leading the race, and Lincoln prepared himself for the worst. But Sherman's capture of Atlanta in September demonstrated to the country that the tide of war had turned strongly in the Union's favor. Near the end of the campaign, McClellan tried to back away from his call for peace talks, but his reversal made little difference. The public's renewed confidence in Lincoln carried him to an easy victory in November.

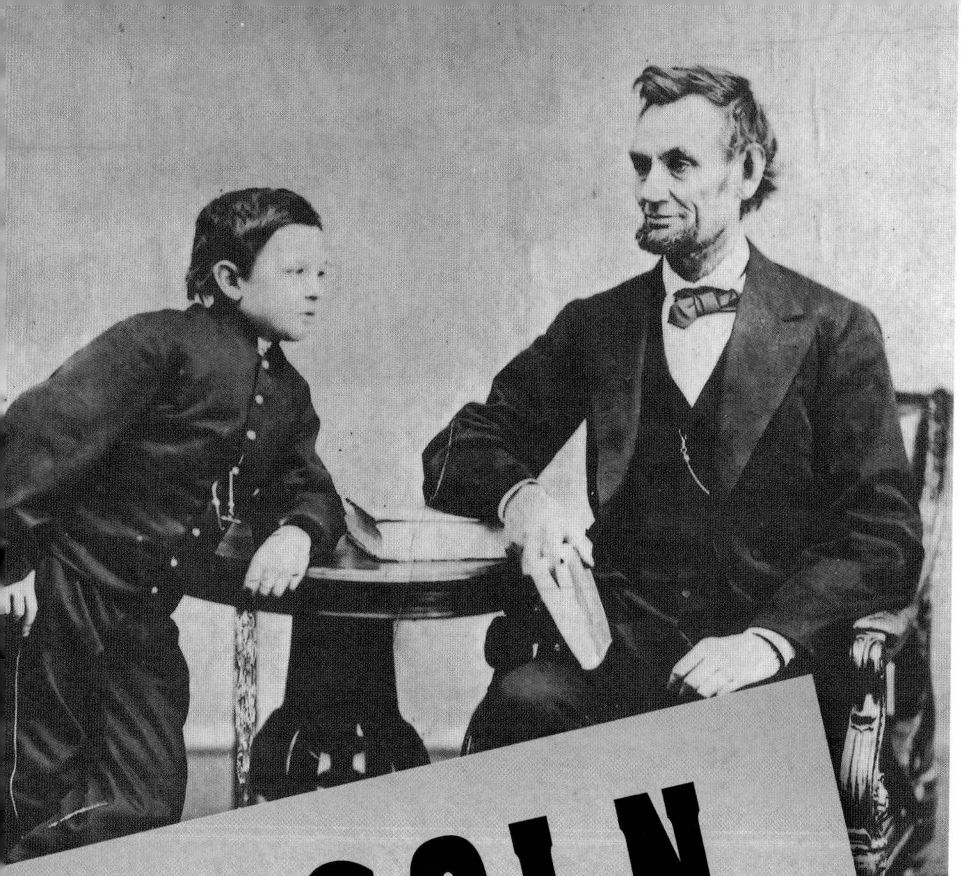

Lincoln in 1865 with his son Thomas, whom the family nicknamed Tad.

In March 1864, Lincoln turned over command of the Union army to Ulysses S. Grant. During 1862 and 1863, Grant had captured important Confederate forts in Tennessee and led Union troops to victory at Vicksburg, Mississippi. Now Lincoln turned Grant's attention to Lee and Richmond. Although Grant's previous campaigns had been costly, bloody ones, Lincoln was willing to tolerate high casualties if they finally brought an end to the war. "I cannot spare this man," Lincoln once said of Grant. "He fights."

SHERMAN'S MARCH TO THE SEA

Meanwhile, Union general William Tecumseh Sherman captured Atlanta in September 1864 and that November began his famously destructive March to the Sea through Georgia. With no Rebel army left that far south to offer any resistance, Sherman's men undermined the South's ability to wage war by systematically smashing railroads, factories, farms, and plantations.

On April 3, 1865, Richmond fell. Six days later, Lee surrendered to Grant at Appomattox Court House, Virginia. Disease, desertion, inadequate resources, and the relentless Union attacks had finally brought the proud Confederacy to its knees.

LINCOLN ASSASSINATED

WASHINGTON, April 15, 1865—President Lincoln died this morning after being shot last night during a performance of the comedy *Our American Cousin* at Ford's Theatre. His assassin, actor John Wilkes Booth, escaped and is still at large.

A fanatical Confederate sympathizer, Booth arrived at the empty theater about 6:00 P.M., when he tampered with the door to the presidential box. He returned during the play's third act and, finding the president unguarded, shot him through the back of the head.

After firing his single-shot Derringer, Booth jumped down to the stage and landed awkwardly, breaking his leg. Although hob-

bled, he was still able to reach his horse in the alley and escape.

The dying president was carried to the bedroom of a nearby boardinghouse. Because of his six-foot, four-inch height, Lincoln was placed diagonally across a bed. When he died just after seven o'clock this morning, Secretary of War Edwin Stanton said, "Now he belongs to the ages."

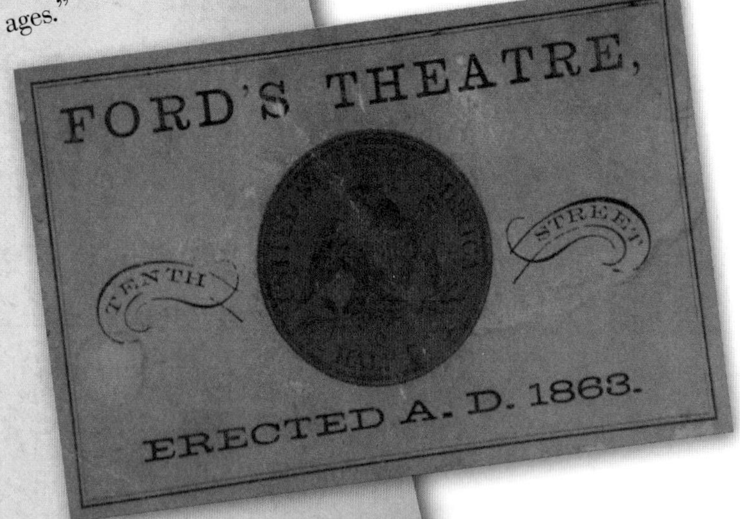

FORD'S THEATRE,

TENTH STREET

ERECTED A. D. 1863.

ANDREW JOHNSON

17th President

★

1865 to 1869

Andrew Johnson

BORN: DECEMBER 29, 1808

BIRTHPLACE: RALEIGH, N.C.

DIED: JULY 31, 1875

PARTY: DEMOCRAT-UNION

VICE PRESIDENT: NONE

FIRST LADY: ELIZA MCCARDLE

CHILDREN: MARTHA, CHARLES, MARY, ROBERT, ANDREW JR.

NICKNAME: TENNESSEE TAILOR

HIS WIFE TAUGHT HIM TO READ AND WRITE.

The news of Abraham Lincoln's assassination shocked every American, none more so than Andrew Johnson. Less than three hours after the president's death, the former tailor's apprentice was sworn into office as Lincoln's successor. At the time, he had been vice president only forty-one days.

Lincoln had won the Civil War for the Union. Now, it was up to Johnson to tackle the equally enormous task of reconstruction. Johnson would have to reunite a nation in which neighbor had fought neighbor, friend had fought friend, and brother had fought brother.

Johnson shared Lincoln's view that the country needed to forgive, forget, and welcome back the rebels. His plan was a simple one: Under the direction of federal governors, the former Confederate states would draft new constitutions abolishing slavery and renouncing secession. After that, they would be free to govern themselves as before. Johnson also proposed that the citizenship of southerners be restored once they had taken a simple oath of allegiance.

JOHNSON ESCAPES CONVICTION IN HIS IMPEACHMENT TRIAL

WASHINGTON, May 16, 1868— The Senate voted today on the first of eleven articles of impeachment brought by the House against Pres. Andrew Johnson. The final count was 35–19, one vote short of the two-thirds majority necessary for conviction.

President Johnson owes his acquittal to seven moderate Republican senators who chose to ignore party loyalty and instead voted with the twelve Democrats.

The House approved the impeachment articles against Johnson on February 24. The principal charges were related to the president's firing of Secretary of War Edwin Stanton. Stanton's dismissal violated the Tenure of Office Act, which had been passed over Johnson's veto.

The House vote of 126–47 made Johnson the first president ever to suffer the indignity of an impeachment. According to the Constitution, a president impeached by the House is then tried before the Senate. If convicted by the Senate, the president is removed from office.

No.

To be taken up at MAIN ENTRANCE

U.S. SENATE

U.S. SENATE

Impeachment of the President

ADMIT THE BEARER

MARCH 13, 1868

Geo. T. Brown
Sergeant-at-Arms.

Philp & Solomons, Wash. D.C.

L IKE ABRAHAM LINCOLN, Andrew Johnson began life as one of the frontier poor. His father, Jacob, died when Andy was just three years old. Growing up without a father meant that he had to work from a very early age.

When he was twelve years old, Andy and his brother were apprenticed to a tailor named Selby and became what were then known as bound boys. They worked for room and board while learning the trade of a tailor. Andrew Johnson received his first schooling while working for Selby, who paid people to read aloud to the apprentices as they sewed.

THE EARLY YEARS

★ SEWARD'S FOLLY

In March 1867, Secretary of State William H. Seward arranged for the United States to purchase Alaska from the Russians. Seward's political rivals thought that he must be crazy to spend $7.2 million for such a huge, frozen, unexplored territory. For many years, while the deal still appeared foolish, people referred to Alaska as Seward's Folly. Then, when miners began finding gold in the Klondike during the 1890s, the shrewdness and foresight of Seward's purchase became clear.

★ KU KLUX KLAN

Dismayed by the loss of the Civil War and made defiant by the humiliations of Reconstruction, many white southerners formed violent vigilante groups to prevent freedmen from voting and electing black candidates to office. The most widespread of these groups was the Ku Klux Klan, founded in 1866 in Pulaski, Tennessee. Its members were mostly Confederate veterans who believed that the white race was superior to all others. Often dressed in white robes and pointed hoods, Klansmen rode through the countryside at night, terrorizing former slaves who tried to own property or vote.

This plan didn't get very far, however, because so-called Radical Republicans in Congress wanted to punish the South for seceding. Also, these congressmen were worried about the Democratic party rising again in the southern states. They still remembered how southern Democrats had dominated the federal government before Lincoln's election in 1860.

THE BLACK CODES The Civil War had ruined the southern economy and brought poverty to every level of southern society. The four million newly liberated slaves, now known as freedmen, were the hardest hit, because they had started with the least.

The Thirteenth Amendment, ratified in December 1865, abolished slavery and liberated all those slaves not already freed by the Emancipation Proclamation. But what were the freedmen to do with their new freedom? Most owned little more than the clothes on their backs. Although Congress established the Freedmen's Bureau to help them find jobs and go to school, southern whites did everything they could to keep the freedmen poor and powerless.

The Black Codes were a series of measures adopted by southern states to deny African Americans their basic rights as citizens, such as the right to vote. Radical Republicans responded by passing the Civil Rights Act of 1866, which spelled out the rights to which all Americans were entitled, regardless of the color of their skin.

Because he was a racist himself, Johnson vetoed the bill. But the Radical Republicans had enough votes in Congress to override this veto, and the bill became law despite the president's opposition.

During the next two years, Congress passed more laws over Johnson's veto,

reorganizing the new southern state governments and forcing them to grant blacks the right to vote. Although extreme racism continued to be a problem throughout the region, African Americans were able to achieve a number of political successes.

In 1870, Hiram R. Revels of Mississippi became the first black elected to the Senate when he won the seat once occupied by former Confederate president Jefferson Davis. All together, between 1869 and the end of Reconstruction in 1877, sixteen blacks were elected to Congress from southern states.

IMPEACHMENT The conflict between Johnson and the Radical Republicans reached a crisis when the president fired Secretary of War Edwin M. Stanton in February 1868. Like the rest of Johnson's cabinet, Stanton had been a holdover from the Lincoln administration. He was also a leader of the Radical Republicans and had been working hard to undermine Johnson's tolerant Reconstruction policies.

The House responded to Johnson's dismissal of Stanton by voting to impeach him for violating the Tenure of Office Act. This law, passed over Johnson's veto in 1867, blocked the president from removing certain government officials without the consent of the Senate.

Johnson hadn't really committed any crime, other than opposing a cabinet member who was determined to control the direction of his administration's Reconstruction program.

Although the president survived his trial in the Senate, his political career seemed over. Denied renomination, he retired to Greenville, Tennessee.

CAMPAIGN ★ 1868

THE UNION PARTY TICKET on which Lincoln and Johnson had run in 1864 didn't survive the Civil War. For the election of 1868, Johnson returned to the Democratic party, and the Republicans took their old name back.

Having only narrowly survived impeachment, the president was given little chance of winning election in his own right. Therefore, at the Democratic convention in July, he faded early as the balloting swung toward former New York governor Horatio Seymour.

At the Republican convention, Civil War hero Ulysses S. Grant was nominated unanimously on the first ballot. Grant seemed to be the perfect choice for president. Voters naturally assumed that the brilliance and daring he had shown on so many southern battlefields would tranfer easily to the political battlefields of Washington. His campaign slogan, "Let Us Have Peace," caught the mood of a country tired of war and the turmoil of Reconstruction.

Reconstruction was, of course, the main issue of the campaign. The Republicans planned to continue the program they had passed over Johnson's vetoes, while the Democrats favored a more lenient approach to reunification with the South.

White southerners supported Horatio Seymour overwhelmingly, but many were not allowed to vote because they had once sworn allegiance to the Confederacy. Their former slaves could vote, however, thanks to Radical Republican laws, and these freedmen voted in huge numbers for Grant. The popular vote was close, but the Republican ticket won the electoral vote by a wide margin.

BORN: APRIL 27, 1822

BIRTHPLACE: POINT PLEASANT, OHIO

DIED: JULY 23, 1885

PARTY: REPUBLICAN

VICE PRESIDENTS: SCHUYLER COLFAX, HENRY WILSON

FIRST LADY: JULIA BOGGS DENT

CHILDREN: FREDERICK, ULYSSES JR., ELLEN, JESSE

NICKNAME: UNCLE SAM

THE ONLY PRESIDENT TO GET A SPEEDING TICKET WHILE DRIVING A HORSE.

ULYSSES S. GRANT

18th President

★

1869 to 1877

1869

From Andrew Johnson, Ulysses S. Grant inherited Reconstruction, an issue that dominated Grant's first term in office. He also inherited a Congress with its own ideas and policies. As a result of laws enacted by the Radical Republicans in Congress, federal troops currently controlled nearly every aspect of life in the South.

Grant understood the desire of the Radical Republicans to ensure justice for the freedmen. But he also believed that the federal government could not force white southerners to accept a way of life that they despised. These conflicting ideas put Grant in a difficult, perhaps impossible, position.

GOLDEN SPIKE
COMPLETES TRANSCONTINENTAL RAILROAD

PROMONTORY POINT, Utah, May 10, 1869—Workers today drove a golden spike that joined the Union Pacific and Central Pacific Railroads, creating the nation's first transcontinental line. The ceremony was attended by a large number of public officials eager to take credit for this remarkable achievement.

Congress first authorized the construction of a transcontinental railroad in 1862. Subsidies and land grants were given to two companies, the Union Pacific and the Central Pacific. The Union Pacific began laying track westward from Omaha, Nebraska, while the Central Pacific worked east from Sacramento, California.

The difficult terrain caused long delays, but the construction crews persevered. The Union Pacific, which laid 1,086 miles of track to reach Promontory Point, used crews made up mostly of Civil War veterans and Irish immigrants. The Central Pacific, which laid 689 miles of track, used primarily Chinese immigrants.

What the voters expected when they elected Grant was a decisive leader, but they didn't get one. Instead, the bold and stern general turned out to be an unsure president. Grant tended to let others make difficult policy decisions for him, and these people quickly took advantage of his gullibility and lack of leadership.

Grant himself was incorruptible, but many of the officials whom he appointed were less than honest. As a result, Grant's administration was rocked early and often by corruption scandals.

THE GILDED AGE
The dishonesty in Washington was no worse than that in the rest of the country. Ruthless people everywhere exploited a society still weakened by the upheaval of the Civil War. Most notorious among these scoundrels were the northerners who went south and used political connections to prey on the defeated Confederacy. These men were called carpetbaggers, because of the carpet-covered suitcases they carried. Their southern accomplices were known as scalawags.

In the North, political machines such as the Tweed Ring in New York City enriched themselves at the taxpayers' expense by controlling large groups of immigrant voters.

At the same time, the country's most successful industrialists were making even more money exploiting workers and consumers alike. These men—including Cornelius Vanderbilt, John D. Rockefeller Sr., and Andrew Carnegie—were called robber barons. Like Boss William Marcy Tweed, they manipulated laws and lawmakers to increase their own wealth and power. Mark Twain called this period of matchless corruption, greed, and splendor the Gilded Age, and the name stuck.

THE EARLY YEARS
GRANT WAS BORN IN THE OHIO COUNTRYSIDE, where his father, Jesse, owned a successful leather-tanning business. Jesse Grant's personality was gruff and combative, but his son was shy and sensitive. Because the boy was particularly good at handling horses, most of his chores involved their care.

When Grant was seventeen, he received an appointment to the U.S. Military Academy at West Point, where he was an average student. Later in his army career, he developed a drinking problem, which forced him to resign in 1854. He tried farming, real estate, and peddling firewood, but little worked. By Christmas 1860, he was so poor that he had to pawn his watch in order to buy presents for his family.

Grant was working at his father's leather goods store in Galena, Illinois, when the Civil War began. Because of the urgent need for experienced officers, Grant was recommissioned as a colonel and then promoted to brigadier general two months later.

★**PROFESSIONAL BASEBALL** On March 15, 1869, Harry Wright and George Ellard organized the first professional baseball team. They called their club the Cincinnati Red Stockings. Baseball had become quite popular during the Civil War, leading Wright and Ellard to believe that they could make a living from the game. The ballplayers whom they hired barnstormed around the country, challenging local amateur clubs to games for which an admission fee was charged. The success of the Red Stockings—they went undefeated during the 1869 season—paved the way for more professional baseball teams and even a professional league.

★ BELL'S TELEPHONE

Speech specialist Alexander Graham Bell first got the idea that sound could be transmitted electrically over telegraph wires during the early 1870s. Working

at night with mechanic Thomas Watson, Bell eventually turned his idea into the telephone, for which he received U.S. Patent Number 174,465 in March 1876.

Although most people considered Bell's invention to be something of a joke, the huge Western Union Telegraph Company saw the telephone's commercial possibilities and backed a rival patent. The fight over Bell's patent rights soon became the most complicated in U.S. legal history. Bell's case was so good, however, that Western Union was forced to settle.

★ U. S. GRANT

Jesse Grant originally named his oldest son Hiram Ulysses Grant, but the younger Grant hated his initials, which spelled H.U.G., so he began signing his name as Ulysses Hiram Grant. Later, when a clerk at West Point mistakenly listed him as Ulysses Simpson Grant, Grant saw no reason to correct the error. His West Point classmates joked that his new initials stood for "Uncle Sam," and Grant was called Sam by his closest friends for the rest of his life. During the Civil War, however, soldiers in his command took to calling him "Unconditional Surrender" Grant because of the harsh terms he forced on his Confederate enemies.

★ SUSAN B. ANTHONY

After the Civil War, Susan B. Anthony became an important leader in the growing women's suffrage movement. Beginning in 1868, she published a newspaper called *Revolution* in New York City. This radical weekly, edited by Elizabeth Cady Stanton, campaigned for many women's issues, including equal pay for equal work and more liberal divorce laws.

When Anthony tried to cast a ballot in the 1872 presidential election, she was arrested, convicted, and fined for voting illegally. When she refused to pay the fine, the matter was dropped. This prevented her from appealing her case to the Supreme Court, which had been her plan.

BLACK FRIDAY

The first scandal involving the Grant administration broke in September 1869, at which time the president had been in office a little over six months. The crisis began when two of the wealthiest robber barons, James Fisk and Jay Gould, tried to corner the gold market. That is, they tried to buy up enough gold to control its supply and thereby raise its price.

Their plan had one problem, which was that the federal government controlled the largest supply of gold in the country. If the scheme were to work, Fisk and Gould would have to keep the government's gold off the market. They paid Grant's brother-in-law, Abel Corbin, to use his influence to do just that.

When Grant realized what was happening, he ordered Treasury Secretary George Boutwell to sell four million dollars' worth of gold from the government's reserves. The sale—which took place on September 24, 1869—ruined Fisk and Gould's plan, but it also sent the price of gold plummeting. When the fall in gold prices triggered a financial panic, Grant's reputation suffered. The day of the gold crash came to be known as Black Friday.

RECONSTRUCTION

Grant tried to shake off the scandal by returning the focus of his administration to Reconstruction. Beginning in 1870, he won passage of a number of bills that gave him the power to enforce civil rights laws in the South. He used the Force Act of 1870 and the Ku Klux Klan Act of 1871 to threaten southern states with federal military action unless they stopped terrorizing the freedmen and denying them the right to vote. In South Carolina, for example, where the Ku Klux Klan was particularly active, Grant declared martial law and ordered mass arrests.

1872

Until the passage of these enforcement laws, the federal government had to rely on local authorities to control the Klan. This system hadn't worked too well, because many local policemen were themselves Klan members. Grant's enforcement of the federal civil rights laws temporarily broke the power of the Klan, but the period of relative safety for African Americans lasted only as long as the federal troops remained in the region.

Then, just as the presidential campaign of 1872 was getting under way, another scandal broke. This one involved the Union Pacific Railroad.

THE CRÉDIT MOBILIER SCANDAL

By 1872, the amount of capital invested in the nation's railroads had reached nearly three billion dollars. This total was in addition to all of the government loans and subsidies that had paid for most of the track work along the first transcontinental line.

In fact, so much federal money was being funneled into railroad construction that major stockholders in the Union Pacific Railroad decided to form a second company, Crédit Mobilier of America, to steal some of it. To make their plan work, they even bribed some congressmen by selling them shares of stock at half the market price.

When the *New York Sun* broke the story of the scandal, Congress appointed a committee to investigate. Among those implicated were Vice Pres. Schuyler Colfax and Rep. James Garfield, the future president. Although investigators found no evidence that Grant had been involved, many people believed that the scandal was a result of his negligence.

Grant's bad fortune continued during his second term when the nation suffered one of worst financial depressions in its history. For several years, the U.S.

CAMPAIGN ★ 1872

GRANT DIDN'T HAVE MUCH TO SHOW for his first term in office. The Radical Republicans still controlled Reconstruction, and little progress had been made on economic issues. Worse still, the corruption scandals had stained his reputation. The Crédit Mobilier scandal, in particular, caused his vice president, Schuyler Colfax, to be dropped from the ticket.

Despite these problems, Grant was renominated without much of a fuss. His opponents within the party, the Liberal Republicans, didn't even bother to show up at the convention hall. Instead, they held their own convention and nominated New York newspaperman Horace Greeley to run against Grant. The disorganized Democrats also supported Greeley's candidacy, because it was their only chance to beat Grant.

Greeley had made a name for himself as the editor of the *New York Tribune*. On the editorial pages of that newspaper, he had promoted the causes of working people and denounced big business. He was also famous for his advice, "Go West, young man, and grow up with the country."

Some people considered Greeley a crackpot because of the many contradictory positions he had taken over the years. For example, Greeley had backed Grant in 1868 but was now critical of him. Greeley wanted to end the corruption, reform the civil service, grant amnesty to former Confederates, and end federal rule in the South.

Because Greeley's campaign never posed much of a threat to Grant, the president's backers were able to persuade voters that Grant was indeed an honest man and that the scandals had not been his fault. The result was a convincing victory for Grant. Meanwhile, Greeley died just a few weeks after the election, even before the electoral vote was counted.

economy had been sickly. The federal government was still paying off its Civil War debt, while railroad construction and the 1871 Chicago Fire had drained private reserves.

THE PANIC OF 1873

When the banking house of Jay Cooke and Company failed in September 1873, the stock market collapsed along with it. The Panic of 1873 lasted five years, put three million people out of work, and forced thousands of small companies out of business.

While the country was still reeling from the depression, Treasury Secretary William Richardson became the focus of the next Grant administration scandal. After taking over for George Boutwell in 1873, Richardson had appointed his friend John D. Sanborn to collect some overdue federal taxes.

Normally, this was a difficult and unrewarding job. But Richardson made an astonishing and illegal deal with Sanborn, allowing Sanborn to keep half of all the money he collected. By the time Congress got around to investigating Sanborn in 1874, he had already pocketed two hundred thousand dollars. In the end, Richardson was forced to resign, and Grant was embarrassed once again.

Grant had scarcely recovered when, in 1875,

CUSTER'S LAST STAND
SEVENTH CAVALRY MASSACRED IN LITTLE BIGHORN BATTLE

MONTANA TERRITORY, June 25, 1876—Gen. George Armstrong Custer and the men under his immediate command were killed today after attacking a huge Indian camp on the banks of the Little Bighorn River.

Seventh Cavalry units under Maj. Marcus Reno and Capt. Frederick Benteen survived by retreating to a line of bluffs above the river.

Custer had been sent on a scouting mission to locate bands of Sioux and Cheyenne who had left their reservations. He disobeyed orders by attacking the village, which held many thousands of Indians, including the chiefs Sitting Bull and Crazy Horse.

During the Civil War, Custer became at twenty-three years old the youngest general in the Union army. Afterward, like many other veterans, he continued his military career fighting Indians in the West. The Sioux called him Son of the Morning Star because of his long blond hair.

85

the next scandal broke. Richardson's replacement as treasury secretary, Benjamin Bristow, had uncovered yet another scheme to cheat the government. This one involved federal officials who, instead of collecting liquor taxes for the government, had been keeping the money and dividing it among themselves and the distillers.

Frustrated by the unending scandals, Grant demanded action. He instructed the federal prosecutors to arrest everyone involved. "Let no guilty man escape," he said. Yet when Grant's own personal secretary, Orville Babcock, was implicated, the president shielded him.

While these Grant appointees were using their positions to get richer, the depression continued. For those who still had jobs, wages declined. In large cities, tens of thousands of homeless people crowded into police stations for shelter. Eventually, the poor demanded a change. In the mid-1870s, thousands of low-salaried and unemployed workers demonstrated in Pittsburgh, New York, Baltimore, and other cities. Often, the police and National Guard broke up these protests with guns and clubs.

THE CIVIL RIGHTS ACT OF 1875

In between scandal investigations, Congress passed the Civil Rights Act of 1875. This was the last major piece of Radical Republican legislation passed during Reconstruction. It guaranteed blacks the civil rights currently being denied them in the South. The new law integrated hotels, theaters, and restaurants. Under its terms, business owners could no longer keep African Americans out or segregate them into back rooms. The act was poorly enforced, however, and eventually declared unconstitutional by the Supreme Court in 1883.

★ **THE BUTCHER OF GALENA** So many of Grant's victories during the Civil War were bloody that soldiers began calling him the Butcher of Galena. (The name referred to his hometown of Galena, Illinois.)

Yet Grant was personally very squeamish. He became physically ill at the sight of blood and refused to eat any meat unless it was cooked until dry. Even the hint of blood in its juices was too much for him.

The responsibility for sending tens of thousands of men to their deaths also sickened the general, who suffered from severe migraine headaches. After especially brutal battles, Grant would often retire to his tent and cry.

★ **MARK TWAIN** Samuel Clemens grew up in Hannibal, Missouri, on the banks of the Mississippi River, where he fell in love with the romance and mystery of river life. He was fascinated by the con men, thieves, and gamblers who populated the paddleboats that traveled to and from New Orleans.

In 1863, Clemens began writing under the pen name Mark Twain. He took the name from a riverman's term referring to a level of water barely safe for navigation. By the time he published *The Adventures of Tom Sawyer* in 1876, Twain was already famous as a humorist and lecturer. In that novel, Tom Sawyer relives many of the adventures that Clemens himself experienced as a child in Hannibal.

★ **MAIL-ORDER CATALOGS** In August 1872, Aaron Montgomery Ward founded the first mail-order company in the United States. His first "catalog" was a single sheet of paper listing approximately 150 items. Ward's main customers were farmers in the countryside who were unable to make regular trips into town. By 1888, when Sears Roebuck began its own catalog, Montgomery Ward's sales had already topped one million dollars a year. Ward was also the originator of the money-back guarantee.

★ BOOKER T. WASHINGTON

Booker T. Washington was the leading African-American spokesman of the late nineteenth century and also one of the country's foremost educators. Born into slavery in Virginia, he was just nine years old when the Civil War ended and he was freed. Dirt-

poor but determined to get an education, he enrolled in 1872 at the Hampton Institute, one of the first schools for blacks in the South. He worked as a janitor there to pay for his expenses.

From an early age, Washington believed that the only way for blacks to gain equality in American society was through education and economic success. In 1881, he took over a small black school in Tuskegee, Alabama, and turned it into the internationally respected Tuskegee Institute.

★ THE GREAT CHICAGO FIRE

On October 8, 1871, the city of Chicago caught fire. For nearly three days, it burned until the blaze was finally brought under control on October 10. Nearly four square miles of homes and stores were destroyed, including the prosperous downtown business district. The Great Fire left ninety thousand people homeless and caused two hundred million dollars' worth of damage. Legend has it that the blaze was started when a cow owned by a Mrs. O'Leary knocked over a lantern in its stall.

The last major Grant administration scandal broke in 1876, when Secretary of War William W. Belknap was discovered to be taking kickbacks from traders at Indian reservations. Cheating the Indians was a long-standing government practice, but rarely did it reach such heights as the president's cabinet. Belknap resigned before a Senate trial could remove him from office. A weary Grant told Congress, "Failures have been errors of judgment, not of intent."

Despite the scandals that marred his time in office, many people still wanted Grant to run for a third term. No president had ever done that before, and Grant wasn't about to become the first. He felt that he had been president for long enough.

The qualities that had served him so well on the battlefield—resolution, independence, and daring—had deserted him as president. He had entered the White House a well-meaning man pledged to peace, honesty, and civil rights. But, as president, he had neither resolved the key issues of Reconstruction nor set high enough standards of behavior for the people he appointed.

AN INDUSTRIAL NATION

In 1803, Thomas Jefferson had looked to the future and seen a nation of farmers. As late as the start of the Civil War, Jefferson's vision still held true. In 1860, the United States was still primarily an agricultural nation. Most Americans were farmers, and farming was the nation's biggest business.

The Civil War changed all that. The need to supply a huge army with clothing, arms, and equipment had shifted the industrial economy of the North into high gear. And when the war ended, the factories just kept going. By the end of Grant's second term, the United States had developed one of the

greatest industrial economies in the world. It dug more coal and iron ore, made more steel, drilled for more oil, laid more railroad track, and built more factories than any other nation on earth.

This enormous change in emphasis had many far-reaching effects. For example, vast numbers of immigrants came to the United States to work in the new factories, and the country's ethnic makeup changed dramatically as a result. From a people of mostly northern European descent, America became a nation of many nationalities— a "melting pot," some called it.

Industrialization also brought about a change in America's identity abroad. Once a distant, backward republic, the United States was now about to become a significant world power.

RETIREMENT Grant left office in 1877. After a trip around the world, he settled in Manhattan, where he invested all of his money in a brokerage firm founded by his son Ulysses Jr. Perhaps not surprisingly, this venture ended in scandal, too. The Grants' partner, Ferdinand Ward, embezzled their money, bankrupting both the company and the Grants. About the same time, the former president learned that he had an advanced case of throat cancer.

Determined to provide for his family before he died, Grant set to work on his memoirs. A month before he died, he moved to Mount McGregor in the Adirondacks. Unable to speak or eat regularly, he sat on the front porch of his cottage, racing to finish his book.

Grant completed the manuscript on July 16, 1885. A week later, he died. The memoirs, published by his friend Mark Twain, sold five hundred thousand copies and restored his family's wealth.

CAMPAIGN ★ 1876

THE 1876 ELECTION WAS BY FAR the most controversial in U.S. history. The Republican candidate, Rutherford B. Hayes of Ohio, was known as a trustworthy, reform-minded administrator. His Democratic opponent, Samuel J. Tilden of New York, was even more famous as a reformer, having helped break up New York City's notorious Tweed Ring. Both men pledged to end the corruption that had plagued the Grant administration.

Because of the backlash against Grant, the revival of the Democratic party's southern wing, and his own sterling national reputation, Tilden was the early favorite. But the Republicans were still the stronger national party, and Hayes's own excellent reputation made the race close. When the popular vote was counted, Tilden appeared to have won the election, but twenty electoral votes remained in doubt.

Tilden needed only one of those electoral votes to win the presidency. But a special election commission made up of ten congressmen and five Supreme Court justices voted 8–7 along party lines to give all the disputed votes to Hayes, who won 185–184.

Southern Democrats, believing that the election had been stolen from them, threatened to secede once again. But Tilden restrained them, and Hayes agreed to the Compromise of 1877.

In order to end the crisis, Hayes promised that, as president, he would withdraw all federal troops from the South, thus ending Reconstruction. He also agreed to rebuild southern railroads and industry that had been destroyed during the Civil War and include at least one southern Democrat in his cabinet. This remarkable backroom bargain brought some calm to U.S. politics, but it also created enormous problems for the new administration.

BORN: OCTOBER 4, 1822

BIRTHPLACE: DELAWARE, OHIO

DIED: JANUARY 17, 1893

PARTY: REPUBLICAN

VICE PRESIDENT: WILLIAM A. WHEELER

FIRST LADY: LUCY WARE WEBB

CHILDREN: SARDIS, JAMES, RUTHERFORD, JOSEPH, GEORGE, FANNY, SCOTT, MANNING

NICKNAME: HIS FRAUDULENCY

THE FIRST PRESIDENT TO USE A TELEPHONE IN THE WHITE HOUSE.

RUTHERFORD BIRCHARD
HAYES
19th President
★
1877 to 1881

R.B. Hayes

Rutherford B. Hayes began his term under trying circumstances. The Compromise of 1877 that had given him the presidency also robbed him of much of the authority that usually came with the job.

Because his victory had been won in the cloakrooms of Congress, rather than at the polls, some newspapermen referred to him as Rutherfraud or His Fraudulency, and out in the country, most people agreed that the election had been rigged. For many years, Hayes had been an honest and decent public servant, but he was never quite able to overcome the bad impression that he made in going along with the compromise.

Southern Democrats, who had been shut out of power since James Buchanan's time, were particularly eager to embarrass Hayes. Ever since the Civil War, Republicans had run "bloody shirt" campaigns against the Democrats. "Waving the bloody shirt" meant reminding voters that the Democrats had been the party of secession and therefore deserved the blame for the bloody war that followed.

EDISON DOES IT AGAIN!
WIZARD OF MENLO PARK INVENTS LIGHTBULB

MENLO PARK, New Jersey, October 21, 1879—Thomas Edison demonstrated his newest invention today at his laboratory here. He calls it the lightbulb.

The entire device consists of a vacuum-sealed glass tube with a filament inside. When electric current is passed through the filament, the filament glows, producing light. Edison's breakthrough came when he found the right material for the filament: scorched cotton thread.

Edison, who invented the phonograph in 1877, first became interested in electric light last year, when he saw an exhibit of electric street lamps. His announcement last fall that he would attempt to develop a cheap and practical form of electric light caused gas company stocks to tumble on Wall Street. It now seems likely that inexpensive electric light will soon replace the gas lamps used in most homes.

As part of the price for accepting Hayes as president, southern Democrats had demanded that the Republicans end Reconstruction immediately. They wanted all the carpetbaggers out of the South, along with the federal troops that had been protecting the freedmen.

Having little choice, Hayes agreed. Therefore, one of his first acts as president was to remove the last federal troops from the South, ending a decade of Radical Republican control in the defeated Confederacy.

Southern whites were overjoyed, but their former slaves were not. The end of Reconstruction meant that political power in the South returned to those people who believed in the superiority of the white race.

By withdrawing the federal troops, Hayes left southern blacks at the mercy of their former masters. Southerners stopped enforcing the federal civil rights laws, and blacks were once again denied their legal right to vote. Furthermore, once the troops left, members of the Ku Klux Klan resumed their nighttime missions of terror and death.

RAILROAD STRIKES Meanwhile, the national economy continued to feel the lasting effects of the Panic of 1873. Railroad companies were in especially bad shape. The cutthroat nature of the business, in which labor was the biggest expense, led to a series of wage cuts for railroad employees. The pay cuts announced in the spring of 1877 were the last straw for many workers.

The first of the railroad strikes arose spontaneously in Baltimore, where firemen on the Baltimore & Ohio line walked out on July 16, 1877. The labor revolt then spread to Pittsburgh, where local militiamen were called out to break

THE EARLY YEARS RUTHERFORD HAYES WAS BORN at his family's home in Delaware, Ohio. The doctor's fee for the delivery was $3.50. Because his father died before he was born, Rutherford was raised by his mother, Sophia, and her bachelor brother, Sardis Birchard.

From his earliest days, Hayes dreamed of holding public office. He did well in school, graduating from Kenyon College and Harvard Law School. In 1852, at the age of thirty, Hayes married Lucy Ware Webb, a fervent abolitionist who persuaded her husband to abandon the Whigs and join the new Republican party. Also, beginning in 1853, Hayes devoted some of his time to defending runaway slaves.

★**LEMONADE LUCY** A devout Methodist, First Lady Lucy Hayes had an immediate impact on life in the White House. Because she was a passionate believer in temperance, she banned all liquor from state functions. Instead, she often served lemonade, causing some of her critics to dub her Lemonade Lucy. Mrs. Hayes is also remembered for leading the president's cabinet in group hymns and for hosting the first White House Easter egg roll, during which children rolled painted Easter eggs up and down the White House lawn.

★**THE INDIAN WARS** The Civil War years were somewhat peaceful for Indian tribes on the Great Plains. Because the U.S. government considered one war to be enough at the time, federal officials negotiated a number of temporary peace treaties with the Sioux and the Cheyennes.

One treaty, signed in 1868, guaranteed the Sioux all rights to the Black Hills of present-day South Dakota, which the tribe considered sacred. Gen. George A. Custer violated this treaty in 1874, when he escorted a survey team into the Black Hills. When the expedition found gold there, a horde of miners descended on the Indian land, provoking the Sioux to war.

Even though the Sioux and Cheyennes were able to defeat Custer and his regiment at the battle of the Little Bighorn, the Indians were no match for the entire U.S. Army. Most were forced back onto reservations, although a few hundred did escape with Sitting Bull to Canada.

★JESSE JAMES AND THE JAMES GANG

Jesse James and his brother Frank were born on a farm near Centerville, Missouri. During the Civil War, they both joined bands of Confederate raiders. These rough outfits preyed on Union supply trains, especially those carrying payrolls. After the war, the James brothers took to robbing banks and civilian trains instead.

The James Gang soon became well known in the East, where stories of western adventure always sold well. Magazines filled their pages with romanticized versions of the brothers' criminal exploits, usually casting Frank and Jesse as heroes who became outlaws because federal lawmen hated all former Confederates.

Barnum & Bailey Greatest Show on Earth
MISS ROSE MEERS THE GREATEST LIVING LADY RIDER
ENTIRELY ORIGINAL IN DRESS, STYLE AND ACTION ENGAGED AT A SALARY OF $100.00 PER DAY.
THE WORLD'S LARGEST, GRANDEST, BEST, AMUSEMENT INSTITUTION.

★P. T. BARNUM

Phineas Taylor Barnum was probably America's greatest showman. His most famous acts were the twenty-five-inch-tall man, Tom Thumb, and singer Jenny Lind, whom Barnum billed as the Swedish Nightingale.

Barnum was already sixty years old when he started his first circus during the early 1870s. In 1881, he teamed up with James A. Bailey. Until then, circuses were one-ring affairs that usually played small towns. The Barnum & Bailey Circus, however, took advantage of Barnum's legendary talent for spectacle. It had three rings, toured major cities, and featured nationally known acts such as the elephant Jumbo. Barnum called it "The Greatest Show on Earth."

up the strike. Instead, the troopers sided with the workers. Eventually, Hayes was forced to use federal troops to restore order. Not until August 2, after hundreds of deaths and thousands of injuries, was service restored on all lines.

CHINESE IMMIGRATION

Hayes also confronted violence born of economic despair in California, where gangs of Irish Americans began attacking Chinese immigrants. The Chinese had come to America to work in California's gold mines and on the railroad crews building new transcontinental lines. At first, they were given only the lowest-paying, most difficult jobs that no other Americans wanted. Even so, many poor Chinese jumped at the chance to work, and by 1877 Chinese immigrants made up nearly 10 percent of the California population.

The trouble began when the gold mines began closing and railroad construction tapered off. These developments forced the Chinese to begin competing with Irish Americans for the same jobs. The Chinese often got the jobs, because they were willing to work for less. This angered the Irish, who believed that they were entitled to the jobs because they had come to America first.

The conflict reached its peak in San Francisco, where Irish gangs beat (and sometimes killed) Chinese Americans on the street. Congress's response was to pass a bill banning Chinese immigration entirely. Hayes thought that this approach would hurt U.S. relations with China, so he vetoed the bill. Instead, he had Secretary of State William Evarts negotiate the Treaty of 1880, which limited Chinese immigration in a manner acceptable to the Chinese government.

The great success of Hayes's term was his "hard money" policy. To help finance the Civil War, the government

1880

had issued paper money called greenbacks. The greenbacks were "soft" or "easy" money, because they weren't backed by gold. That is, they could not be redeemed for gold coins, or specie.

In 1875, Congress had passed the Resumption of Specie Act. This required the government to take the greenbacks out of circulation and resume backing paper money with gold.

Farmers with mortgages and other debtors wanted easy money, because easy money encouraged inflation. With more money in circulation, each dollar was worth less, and their debts became cheaper to pay off. Hayes stood firm, however, and the government resumed specie payments in January 1879.

CIVIL SERVICE REFORM Hayes's other great cause was civil service reform. (Civil servants are the government's civilian workers.) Under the spoils system then in place, civil service jobs typically went to people whose only qualifications for office were favors they had done for the winning candidate.

Because Hayes believed that federal jobs shouldn't be used as political rewards, he issued an executive order in June 1877 barring civil servants from taking part in politics. He also supported the efforts of Interior Secretary Carl Schurz to develop competitive exams for hiring and promotion. But he couldn't persuade Congress to act on such large-scale reforms.

Nevertheless, Hayes did take some action on his own, removing the heads of the post office in St. Louis and the customhouse in New York. These men, Hayes said, had been misusing their public offices for political gain. Ironically, one of them, Chester A. Arthur of New York, soon became president himself.

CAMPAIGN ★ 1880

WHEN HE ACCEPTED THE REPUBLICAN nomination in 1876, Hayes announced that he would serve only one term. Four years later, he hadn't changed his mind, and he retired, leaving the race wide open. The surprise front-runner was former president Grant, who had been persuaded to try for a third term after all. Opposing him for the Republican nomination were Sen. James G. Blaine of Maine and Hayes's treasury secretary, John Sherman of Ohio.

Grant held the lead at the convention for thirty-five ballots but remained about seventy votes short of victory. On the thirty-fourth ballot, Wisconsin delegates cast sixteen votes for a compromise choice, Ohio congressman James Garfield, who had earlier delivered a memorable speech nominating Sherman.

Remaining loyal to Sherman, Garfield jumped up and shouted, "I won't permit it." But two ballots later, the Blaine and Sherman forces drafted him to prevent Grant from getting the nomination.

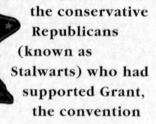

Later, as a gesture to the conservative Republicans (known as Stalwarts) who had supported Grant, the convention chose Chester A. Arthur of New York as Garfield's running mate. To oppose Garfield, the Democrats nominated Winfield S. Hancock, a former Union army general and military governor during Reconstruction.

The election was remarkably close. Garfield won the popular vote by just ten thousand ballots out of nine million cast. But he got those votes where he needed them, especially in New York. During the campaign, he had made a secret deal, known as the Treaty of Fifth Avenue, with New York senator Roscoe Conkling, the leader of the Stalwarts. In exchange for Conkling's support, Garfield agreed to consult Conkling on all federal appointments made in New York. As a result, the state, its thirty-five electoral votes, and the election all went to Garfield.

BORN: NOVEMBER 19, 1831

BIRTHPLACE: ORANGE, OHIO

DIED: SEPTEMBER 19, 1881

PARTY: REPUBLICAN

VICE PRESIDENT: CHESTER A. ARTHUR

FIRST LADY: LUCRETIA RUDOLPH

CHILDREN: ELIZA, HARRY, JAMES, MARY, IRVIN, ABRAM, EDWARD

NICKNAME: PREACHER PRESIDENT

JUGGLED CLUBS TO BUILD UP HIS MUSCLES.

1881

JAMES ABRAM GARFIELD

20th President

★

1881

James A. Garfield.

Most Americans didn't expect much from James A. Garfield. His involvement in the Crédit Mobilier scandal and his campaign deal-making led many to believe that his administration would be just as scandal-ridden as President Grant's had been.

But Garfield proved them wrong. During his first week in office, the new postmaster general found evidence of criminal wrongdoing in the post office. Instead of covering this up, Garfield ordered a full investigation.

The new president also decided to take on Roscoe Conkling, the boss of the Republican party's corrupt Stalwart faction. Although Garfield had once promised Conkling a say in filling federal jobs in New York, he now ignored Conkling's wishes and made these civil service appointments based on merit alone.

During the long weeks that followed the shooting of the president, while he struggled for his life, his popularity rose nearly every day. On a number of occasions, it seemed as though he would get better. But the poor state of medical science at the time eventually killed the president.

PRESIDENT GARFIELD DIES TEN WEEKS AFTER SHOOTING

ELBERON, New Jersey, September 19, 1881—Pres. James Garfield died tonight, ten weeks after being shot by mentally ill office-seeker Charles Guiteau. Guiteau shot Garfield on July 2 as the president walked through a Washington railroad station.

Guiteau was an obscure New York Stalwart who joined his local party in supporting Garfield. After the election, he unreasonably expected an important federal job as a reward. When Garfield's subordinates refused him, Guiteau decided that the president had to die.

Immediately after the shooting, Garfield was carried back to the White House and treated there. But once his condition sta-

bilized, he was taken by train to the New Jersey coast to escape the heat of the Washington summer. The track along the route was lined with straw to make the journey easier.

The immediate cause of Garfield's death appears to have been blood poisoning brought on by the doctors who have been treating him. They often failed to wash their hands and used unsterile instruments while examining him.

CHESTER ALAN ARTHUR

21st President

★

1881 to 1885

BORN: OCTOBER 5, 1829

BIRTHPLACE: FAIRFIELD, VT.

DIED: NOVEMBER 18, 1886

PARTY: REPUBLICAN

VICE PRESIDENT: NONE

FIRST LADY: ELLEN LEWIS HERNDON

CHILDREN: WILLIAM, CHESTER ALAN JR., ELLEN

NICKNAME: ELEGANT ARTHUR

OWNED EIGHTY PAIRS OF PANTS, WHICH HE CHANGED SEVERAL TIMES DAILY.

Americans hadn't thought much of James Garfield when he took office, and they thought even less of Chester Arthur when he became president following Garfield's death. Yet Garfield had surprised people with his about-face on the civil service issue, and Arthur would surprise them, too.

Arthur had been chosen as Garfield's running mate simply to appease Roscoe Conkling and the conservative Stalwarts. No one seriously believed that Arthur would, or should, become president.

Nevertheless, he had been an important cog in Conkling's political machine. As the collector of duties for the Port of New York, for example, he had forced his government employees to contribute money to Republican campaigns. Because of this practice, Pres. Rutherford Hayes had removed him from office in 1878.

Yet once he became president, Arthur began working for genuine civil service reform. His cronies soon came to Washington looking for jobs, but Arthur turned them away. "For the vice presidency, I am indebted to Mr. Conkling,"

EARPS WIN GUNFIGHT AT O.K. CORRAL

TOMBSTONE, Arizona Territory, October 26, 1881—The long-standing battle between the Earps and the Clantons for control of the town of Tombstone was settled today at the O.K. Corral.

The Earps killed Billy Clanton and Clanton allies Tom and Frank McLaury in a shootout there. Only Ike Clanton, leader of the Clanton gang, and Billy Claiborne escaped.

At stake was control of the rich silver trade, which has driven Tombstone's recent boom.

Town marshal Virgil Earp was backed up in the fight by his two brothers, Wyatt and Morgan, and also by Doc Holliday. Wyatt has been working as a gambler and guard at the Oriental Saloon. Holliday is also a gambler and gunman, who occasionally practices dentistry.

Virgil Earp insisted that he and his brothers were just enforcing the law. But townspeople, who believe that the gunfight was more likely murder, are planning to fire Earp and hire a new marshal to replace him.

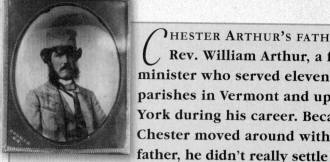

C HESTER ARTHUR'S FATHER was the Rev. William Arthur, a fiery Baptist minister who served eleven different parishes in Vermont and upstate New York during his career. Because Chester moved around with his father, he didn't really settle down until he entered Union College in 1845. As a student there, he took part in his fair share of pranks, once dumping the school bell into the Erie Canal.

THE EARLY YEARS

Soon after moving to New York City and becoming a lawyer in 1854, Arthur agreed to represent a black woman, Lizzie Jennings, who wanted to sue a streetcar company because she had been forced to leave one of its whites-only cars. Arthur eventually won the case, which ended racial segregation of public transportation in New York City.

★**HOT DOGS** German immigrant Anton Feuchtwanger made his living selling cooked sausages in St. Louis. At first, he served his sausages without wrappers. For his customers' convenience, however, he loaned them gloves to keep their fingers clean as they ate. The problem was that too many customers kept the gloves instead of returning them. In 1880, Feuchtwanger decided to solve this problem by asking his brother-in-law, a baker, to make special new buns that could hold the sausages. The result was the first hot dog.

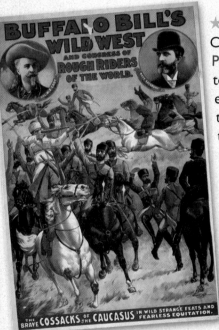

★**BUFFALO BILL** William Cody took a job as a rider for the Pony Express when he was just fourteen years old. He got his nickname eight years later, in 1868, when he took another job hunting buffalo to feed crews laying track for the Union Pacific Railroad. In just eight months, Cody killed 4,280 buffalo.

While serving as an army scout during the Indian Wars, Buffalo Bill began to realize the commercial possibilities of his frontier experience. In 1883, he organized the first of his hugely successful Wild West shows. These traveling entertainments featured real cowboys and Indians, as well as reenactments of a buffalo hunt, a stagecoach robbery, and a Pony Express ride. Cody's stars included sharpshooter Annie Oakley and the legendary Sioux chief Sitting Bull.

Arthur once said, "but for the presidency of the United States my debt is to the Almighty." In other words, there would be no payoffs.

In 1882, Arthur proved that he meant what he said by vetoing the Rivers and Harbors Act. This bill, which funded nineteen million dollars' worth of unnecessary construction projects, was an obvious example of "pork barrel" spending designed to benefit the districts of the most powerful congressmen. Although Arthur's veto was later overridden by Congress, he still won praise for attempting to stop the waste.

Arthur also vetoed a bill banning Chinese immigration for twenty years but did sign the compromise Chinese Exclusion Act of 1882, which halted immigration for ten years and kept Chinese already in the United States from becoming citizens.

This law placed the first significant restrictions on immigration to the United States. It also broke the Treaty of 1880 with China, which had reduced Chinese immigration but not banned it entirely. The Chinese Exclusion Act was renewed twice before being repealed in 1943.

CIVIL SERVICE REFORM

Later, in 1883, Arthur signed the most important legislation of his administration, the Pendleton Act, which permanently reformed the civil service. No longer would Americans believe that the civil service was filled only with politically connected people who did little or no work.

Strangely, it was President Garfield's assassination that made the Pendleton Act possible. Because Garfield's insane assassin, Charles Guiteau, had been seeking a government job at the time he shot the president, the public got the mistaken impression that Garfield's assassination was somehow linked to civil service corruption. Guiteau's

motives were altogether different, but voters nevertheless demanded immediate civil service reform, and to nearly everyone's surprise, Arthur enthusiastically took up the cause.

To begin with, the Pendleton Act created competitive examinations for government jobs. It also established the Civil Service Commission to oversee the new merit system and banned the practice of demanding campaign contributions from federal employees.

In reforming the civil service, however, the Pendleton Act also changed the way political parties were funded—not necessarily for the better. No longer able to rely on party-appointed civil servants for their money, political parties had to look elsewhere to pay for their campaigns.

Big businesses became the most frequent source of cash, and in return they expected favors. Huge companies such as John D. Rockefeller's Standard Oil and Andrew Carnegie's U.S. Steel had been looking eagerly for ways to influence lawmakers, and both major political parties were equally eager to accept the contributions.

ARTHUR'S CHANGE OF HEART

By 1884, many of Arthur's early critics had been won over by his handling of the presidency. But others couldn't understand his change of heart. Why, they wondered, did he keep turning his back on the politicians who had once been his allies in corruption?

The answer may have been a secret known only to Arthur and his doctors. Arthur had Bright's disease, an illness of the kidneys for which nineteenth-century medicine had no cure. Perhaps knowing that he would likely die soon gave Arthur the courage he needed to do the things that he believed to be right.

CAMPAIGN ★ 1884

THE DEMOCRATS HAD BEEN OUT OF POWER for twenty-eight years when they convened in 1884 to select a presidential candidate. Desperate for a win, the delegates chose Gov. Grover Cleveland of New York. Cleveland had made something of a name for himself by standing up to Tammany Hall, the corrupt political organization that controlled Democratic politics in New York City.

The Republicans picked James G. Blaine, who had served briefly as Garfield's secretary of state. Blaine had tried for the Republican nomination in 1876 and again in 1880 but had failed both times. At the convention, President Arthur put up some opposition, but his turnaround on civil service reform had angered many party regulars, especially his former Stalwart allies, without fully persuading reform-minded Republicans that he could be trusted.

The fall campaign turned on personal attacks. The Democrats talked up the Mulligan Letters, a series of documents that indicated Blaine had taken railroad bribes while serving in Congress. Blaine's cause was further hurt when he was observed having dinner with John Jacob Astor, Jay Gould, and other robber barons.

For their part, the Republicans unearthed the story that, ten years earlier, Cleveland had fathered a son out of wedlock. However, because the Democratic nominee immediately admitted the truth, most voters didn't hold it against him. To the Republican chant, "Ma, ma, where's my pa?" the Democrats responded, "Gone to the White House, ha, ha, ha!"

The election turned once again on New York, which Blaine lost by just a thousand votes. His close association with Protestants there cost him the support of New York's numerous Irish Catholic voters—and with it, the electoral votes he needed to beat Cleveland.

BORN: MARCH 18, 1837

BIRTHPLACE: CALDWELL, N.J.

DIED: JUNE 24, 1908

PARTY: DEMOCRAT

VICE PRESIDENT: THOMAS A. HENDRICKS

FIRST LADY: FRANCES FOLSOM

CHILDREN: RUTH, ESTHER, MARION, RICHARD, FRANCIS

NICKNAME: UNCLE JUMBO

THE FIRST DEMOCRAT ELECTED PRESIDENT AFTER THE CIVIL WAR.

1885

GROVER CLEVELAND
22nd President
★
1885 to 1889

By an extremely close vote, Grover Cleveland became the first Democratic president elected since the Civil War. But his tiny margin of victory wasn't his only handicap. He was also not well known around the country. Even in Washington, he was a stranger. His trip to the capital for his March 4, 1885, inauguration was only his second journey to the city, and the crowd that gathered at the Capitol to hear him speak was the largest he had ever seen.

A lesser person might have been overwhelmed by the presidency, but Grover Cleveland was a man of conviction, which gave him the strength he needed to endure. He had come to Washington to do a job, and he intended to see that job through. At first, he tried to do everything on his own. During his early months in office, for example, he worked without a secretary and even answered the White House telephone himself on occasion.

LABOR RIOT IN HAYMARKET SQUARE

CHICAGO, May 4, 1886— A workers' meeting held tonight in Haymarket Square turned into a riot after someone threw a bomb into a crowd of policemen, killing seven of them. The identity of the person who threw the bomb, which had a round metal casing, is still unknown.

The mass meeting had been called to protest yesterday's trouble at the McCormick Harvester Works, where police fired into a crowd of striking workers, killing four and wounding many more.

Tonight's Haymarket demonstration was organized in part by political radicals in the labor movement. "When you ask [your boss] to lessen your burdens, he sends his bloodhounds out to shoot you," one of the pamphlets announcing the meeting read. "To arms, we call you, to arms!"

Eight radicals have since been arrested for murder, although only one of them was actually present at tonight's meeting.

Moderate union leaders are worried that factory bosses will use popular hatred of these radicals, most of whom are foreign born, to undermine their fight for an eight-hour workday.

97

On the other hand, because of his hard work and attention to detail, Cleveland usually knew more about the issues of the day than any of his opponents. He always did his homework. Sometimes, however, he got so caught up in the specifics of an issue that he lost much of his perspective.

"HANDS-OFF" GOVERNMENT

Overall, the new president was rather blunt and hot-tempered. (Because of these traits, he made few friends in Washington and many enemies.) He also knew what he wanted, and that was a "hands-off" government. Cleveland believed that the people should support the government, and not the other way around.

In 1887, for example, when a severe drought hit Texas, causing devastating crop failures, Congress passed a bill to distribute free seed to farmers so that they could replant. Although the bill was extremely popular, Cleveland vetoed it, because he believed that people should be wary of government rather than looking to it for handouts.

THE INTERSTATE COMMERCE ACT

Because of this attitude, Cleveland played almost no role in the shaping of congressional legislation. He either signed bills, or he vetoed them. One of the most important bills he signed was the Interstate Commerce Act of 1887.

For many years, railroads had been able to charge passengers and shippers whatever they wanted. Often, these rates were outrageously high, and there could be favoritism as well. Most railroads used practices such as rebates to favor large corporations over smaller companies.

The Interstate Commerce Act was passed to make sure that all railroads charged "reasonable and just" rates.

G ROVER CLEVELAND WAS A BIG, STRONG BOY who loved fishing. In school, he was less than outstanding but worked hard and planned to go to college. Unfortunately, his father's death in 1853 forced the sixteen-year-old **THE EARLY YEARS** Cleveland to find a job instead. He worked for a year in New York City before being offered a full scholarship to college if he agreed to become a Presbyterian minister, as his father had been.

Although Cleveland yearned for a formal education, he turned down the offer and decided to head west. He got as far as Buffalo, where an uncle arranged for him to study law. He eventually entered politics. His remarkable success as a reform mayor in Buffalo led to his election as governor of New York State in 1882.

★ **A WHITE HOUSE MARRIAGE** Grover Cleveland became the first president married in the White House when he wed twenty-one-year-old Frances Folsom on June 2, 1886. Frances, the youngest first lady ever, was the daughter of the president's longtime friend and law partner Oscar Folsom. Cleveland, who was forty-nine at the time, had known Frances since her birth, but they didn't become romantically involved until she entered college.

The couple kept their engagement a secret for nearly a year, revealing it just five days before their wedding. John Philip Sousa and the Marine Band played at the ceremony, which was made the focus of much attention by the press. Although the couple took a five-day honeymoon, President Cleveland worked as usual on his wedding day. Shown here is a boxed piece of the wedding cake.

★ **COCA-COLA** An Atlanta druggist named John Pemberton invented Coca-Cola in 1886. At first, he promoted the beverage as a  health tonic, but it soon became popular as a soft drink. The name Coca-Cola was chosen by Pemberton's bookkeeper, Frank Robinson, who borrowed it from the syrup's active ingredients: coca leaf and kola nut extracts.

In 1891, Pemberton sold out to Asa G. Candler, who took the drink nationwide, building bottling plants in Dallas, Philadelphia, and Los Angeles. Under Candler's leadership, sales of Coca-Cola syrup rose from 9,000 gallons in 1890 to more than 370,000 gallons in 1900. Candler, who paid Pemberton $2,300 for Coca-Cola, sold out himself in 1919 for $25,000,000.

★THE AMERICAN FEDERATION OF LABOR

In 1886, Samuel Gompers organized the American Federation of Labor. The AFL was a new kind of union because its members were not workers but other unions. Until then, organizations such as the Knights of Labor had tried to win better working conditions through political action. But Gompers thought political reform was a waste of time. Instead, he believed any union's strength lay in its bargaining power with big business. A strong union could force a company to pay better wages and improve working conditions. The point of the AFL, one union official explained, was "not to assist men to lift themselves out of their class, as if they were ashamed of it,…but to raise the class itself in physical well-being and self-estimation."

★GERONIMO SURRENDERS

With the flight of Sitting Bull to Canada in 1877 and the murder of Crazy Horse that same year, Indian resistance to whites on the Great Plains all but ended. Only the Chiricahua Apaches of Arizona fought on under the leadership of the war chief Geronimo.

When Geronimo surrendered to Gen. Nelson Miles on September 4, 1886, it marked the third time that the Chiricahua had been captured by the U.S. Army. Twice before, he had escaped. This time, General Miles promised him that he would be able to return to his Arizona homeland after a temporary exile in Florida. But the government failed to keep this promise, and Geronimo never saw Arizona again.

The new Interstate Commerce Commission, created by the law to oversee the railroad industry, was the first regulatory agency ever established by Congress.

INDIAN AFFAIRS In 1881, Helen Hunt Jackson published *A Century of Dishonor*. This widely read book described the federal government's cruel treatment of Indians on the frontier, and it generated an enormous emotional response. Groups devoted to defending the rights of Indians soon formed all over the country.

The goal of these well-meaning groups was to help reservation Indians accept the ways of white people so they could become part of white society. At the instigation of several Indian rights groups, Congress even passed the Dawes Severalty Act of 1887, which granted citizenship to Indians willing to give up membership in their tribe. In exchange, the Indians would receive small plots of reservation land to own and homestead.

The reformers were sincere in their desire to help, but the Dawes Act was misguided because it failed to take into account the Indians' native culture. For centuries, tribes on the Great Plains had moved about freely, often sharing hunting grounds with neighboring bands. As a result, most Indians had no idea what the whites meant by private property and didn't believe that anyone could own the land. Those who received plots from the government often sold them for a small fraction of their worth. Thus, the Dawes Act generally did more harm than good.

PENSION BILLS Cleveland exercised his veto power most often when it came to bills that he considered raids on the Treasury. Chief among these were bills introduced by congressmen to provide special pensions for certain Union army veterans.

Cleveland agreed that the government was obligated to provide pensions for soldiers who had been injured in battle. But he worried that the prospect of easy pension money was leading to a great deal of fraud.

Corrupt lawyers often filed false claims on behalf of Union veterans who were perfectly healthy. Sometimes, the Pension Bureau accepted these claims without investigation. At other times, the bureau investigated and rejected them. But even then, an influential veteran could still persuade his congressman to introduce a private bill forcing the Pension Bureau to pay.

In this manner, pensions were given to deserters, criminals, and even men who had never fought in the army. To put an end to this cheating, Cleveland began reading each and every one of the private bills—there were hundreds—and he vetoed nearly all of them.

TARIFF REFORM Just before the end of his first term in office, Cleveland challenged Congress to reduce U.S. tariff rates. Ever since the Lincoln administration, when rates were raised to pay for the Civil War, tariffs had been extraordinarily high. After the war, the high rates had been kept in place to protect developing U.S. industries, but they had also pushed up prices and created a large federal surplus.

Congressmen were eager to spend the extra money on pork barrel projects in their home states, but Cleveland wouldn't allow it. Instead, he demanded that Congress lower the tariff rates.

Reaction to Cleveland's demand was strongly negative. Big business wanted to stay insulated from foreign competition, and labor leaders believed that high tariffs also kept workers' wages high. In fact, the reaction against Cleveland was so strong that it probably cost him the 1888 election.

CAMPAIGN ★ 1888

BY THE TIME THE REPUBLICANS met in June 1888 to nominate a presidential candidate, the party was united in its determination to unseat Grover Cleveland. James G. Blaine, the 1884 nominee, had even stepped aside so that the party could rally around a less controversial nominee.

After eight ballots, the delegates chose Benjamin Harrison, a former senator from Indiana and the grandson of Pres. William Henry Harrison. In addition to his well-known name, Harrison came from a state whose electoral votes were crucial to a Republican victory. His campaign slogan was "Grandfather's Hat Fits!"

Cleveland and Harrison were both rather dull men whose campaigns matched their personalities. Cleveland made only one public appearance, while Harrison, acting under the advice of his campaign manager, stayed home in Indianapolis, where he confined his remarks to prepared speeches before groups of people who had come to visit him.

The party platforms were also remarkably similar. Both favored lower taxes, a larger navy, and statehood for the western territories. The only significant difference had to do with tariff reform. Cleveland wanted lower rates, and the Republicans—who favored high, protective rates—used this issue to hurt him.

For the fourth time in a row, the election was very close. Cleveland won the popular vote by one hundred thousand ballots but lost the electoral vote, 233–168. Again, New York's thirty-six electoral votes, the most of any state, made the difference. Although Cleveland had been governor there, his enemies in Tammany Hall torpedoed his campaign in the state. Had Cleveland instead carried New York, he would have won reelection by seven electoral votes.

1889

BENJAMIN HARRISON

23rd President

★

1889 to 1893

BORN: AUGUST 20, 1833

BIRTHPLACE: NORTH BEND, OHIO

DIED: MARCH 13, 1901

PARTY: REPUBLICAN

VICE PRESIDENT: LEVI P. MORTON

FIRST LADY: CAROLINE LAVINIA SCOTT

CHILDREN: RUSSELL, MARY, ELIZABETH

NICKNAME: LITTLE BEN

THE FIRST PRESIDENT TO USE ELECTRICITY IN THE WHITE HOUSE.

U nlike Grover Cleveland, who could sometimes be pleasant and jovial, Benjamin Harrison was uncomfortable with people. He was very formal, and his personality lacked warmth. Some people called him a "human iceberg."

But Harrison shared a number of other traits with Cleveland, including an attention to detail and a strong work ethic. Harrison was also personally incorruptible, which was more than could be said for his campaign manager, Matt Quay.

After winning the 1888 election, President-elect Harrison declared that "Providence has given us the victory."

Upon learning of this remark, Quay laughed and said, "Think of the man! He ought to know that Providence hadn't a damn thing to do with it." It was likely, Quay continued, that Harrison "would never know how close a number of men were compelled to approach the gates of the penitentiary to make him president."

INDIANS MASSACRED AT WOUNDED KNEE

WOUNDED KNEE CREEK, South Dakota, December 29, 1890—The Seventh Cavalry today killed more than two hundred Sioux men, women, and children who only last night had surrendered to the regiment peacefully.

This morning, while the Sioux were being disarmed, a fight broke out over a young warrior's new rifle. A shot rang out, prompting the soldiers to fire wildly into the crowd.

The Indians' clubs and knives were no match for the machine guns of General Custer's former outfit. It has been suggested that the troopers' murderous ferocity can be traced back to the regiment's defeat at the battle of the Little Bighorn.

These Sioux were among the followers of Wovoka, a holy man whose Ghost Dance religion has recently inspired the revival of hope among the Plains tribes. According to Wovoka, performing the Ghost Dance will make warriors invulnerable to white men's bullets and bring Indian ancestors back from the dead.

1890

Whether Harrison knew it or not, Quay's handling of the campaign had left the Republican party with a large debt to big business that it would have to repay sooner or later.

THE SHERMAN ANTI-TRUST ACT

During the Gilded Age, large corporations had created near-monopolies in a number of important industries. In 1882, for example, John D. Rockefeller had formed the Standard Oil trust to corner the oil market legally.

In his inaugural address, Harrison warned that trusts such as Standard Oil needed to play by the rules of free trade or else face government discipline. When the trusts ignored his warning, Congress passed the first antitrust law in 1890.

The Sherman Anti-Trust Act, sponsored by Sen. John Sherman, made it a crime to limit trade by "combination in the form of a trust or otherwise." This meant that men such as Rockefeller could no longer control, or combine, several companies in order to monopolize a particular industry.

Lawyers found a number of ways around the law, however, that were soon upheld in court. "What looks like a stone wall to a layman is a triumphal arch to a corporation lawyer," political humorist Finley Peter Dunne proclaimed.

FOREIGN POLICY

Meanwhile, Navy Secretary Benjamin F. Tracy continued the huge shipbuilding program begun during the Cleveland administration. This modernization of the navy fit in well with Harrison's plan to expand U.S. influence in Latin America and the Pacific.

Harrison favored an aggressive foreign policy and helped arrange the first Pan-American Conference. Chaired by Secretary of State James G. Blaine, the

THE EARLY YEARS

BENJAMIN HARRISON WAS BORN at the North Bend, Ohio, home of Gen. William Henry Harrison. When he was seven years old, his grandfather was elected president. Benjamin's childhood was typical of a farm boy at that time. He fetched wood and water, fed the horses and cattle on the family's six-hundred-acre farm, hunted, fished, and swam.

In July 1862, after becoming a successful Republican lawyer in Indianapolis, Harrison went off to fight in the Civil War, joining the Seventieth Indiana Infantry as a second lieutenant. Rising eventually to the rank of brigadier general, he fought bravely in Kentucky, Tennessee, Alabama, and Georgia.

★**CARRY A. NATION** By 1890, alcoholism was becoming an increasingly severe social problem in the United States. Drunkenness was leading to the abuse of women and children as well as to absenteeism at work and frequent brawling in saloons. Women and church groups had for many years been working diligently to build an American temperance movement. Their goal was to ban the sale of liquor.

The most zealous of the new wave of temperance crusaders was Carry A. Nation, who believed that her name was literally her destiny. An imposing woman who stood six feet tall and weighed 175 pounds, Nation became famous for using a hatchet to wreck saloons in Kansas. She was jailed often but paid her fines using money raised from speaking tours and the sale of souvenir hatchets.

★**ELLIS ISLAND** During the 1890s, huge numbers of eastern and central European immigrants traveled by ship to the United States. Every day, thousands arrived in New York City. Overwhelmed port officials found themselves desperately in need of a place to hold all these people, many of them Jews and Italians, while their papers were being processed.

On January 1, 1892, the federal government finally opened a new processing station on Ellis Island in Upper New York Bay. Its windows looked out on the Statue of Liberty. For the next half century, the redbrick buildings of Ellis Island provided the first glimpse millions of immigrants got of their new home in the United States.

★OLD WHISKERS

President Harrison was an animal lover who always made sure that his grandchildren had plenty of pets. The Harrisons had dogs, horses, and even an opossum. Their favorite pet was a goat named Old Whiskers. One day, as Old Whiskers pulled Harrison's grandchildren

around the lawn in a cart, the White House gates were opened to let out the president's carriage. Seizing the opportunity, Old Whiskers dashed for freedom. He took off through the gates with the children still in tow. The president couldn't believe his eyes. Nor could the residents of Washington, who watched the president of the United States race down the street, waving his cane and chasing a goat.

★POPULISM

The populist movement of the 1890s had its origins in the farmers' alliances of the 1870s. One example was the Grange movement that took hold in both the South and the West. It was started in part to pass along agricultural knowledge and also to relieve the boredom of rural life. At first, the Grange merely sponsored lectures and social events, but it soon came to represent farmers' political views as well.

In February 1892, several labor and farmers' groups came together in St. Louis to form the People's party. Its members believed that big business had too much say in the way government was run. Wanting to reorganize things drastically, the populists called for public ownership of the railroads, an eight-hour workday, and a federal income tax.

conference expanded the U.S. presence in Latin America while reducing that of Great Britain. Harrison's specific goal was to control the narrow Isthmus of Panama, across which one day the United States might build a canal linking the Atlantic and Pacific Oceans.

Meanwhile in the Pacific, U.S. minister to Hawaii John L. Stevens landed troops to protect white business leaders who had recently rebelled against Queen Liliuokalani. After overthrowing her native government and setting up their own regime, the whites, mostly sugar growers, asked for the immediate annexation of Hawaii by the United States. State Department representatives negotiated a treaty of annexation during the president's final weeks in office, but it was still pending before the Senate when Harrison's term ended.

THE TREASURY SURPLUS

Another of the issues that Harrison faced at home was the huge Treasury surplus caused by high tariff rates. Republicans and Democrats both wanted to eliminate the surplus, but they disagreed as to how. The Democrats wanted to lower tariff rates and thereby take in less money. Harrison and the Republicans wanted to keep tariff rates high and spend the surplus.

The first large spending bill that the president signed was the Dependent and Disability Pensions Act of 1890. Harrison had been a general during the Civil War and had great sympathy for his fellow veterans. The Dependent and Disability Pensions Act showered money on them in the form of pensions for all Union veterans who were now unable to work for any reason at all. That is, their injuries did not have to be battle-related.

Meanwhile, new silver discoveries in Arizona and Nevada had created a large number of new boomtowns. The more

silver the miners dug up, however, the less valuable the metal became, because the market could only absorb so much silver. To keep its price high, miners lobbied the government to buy more silver by issuing more paper money. Farmers in the South and West supported this idea because it would lead to inflation, which would make their debts easier to pay off.

In the East, the bankers who controlled the government's monetary policy were horrified at the thought of unlimited silver coinage. But they needed the support of the South and West to pass a new tariff bill. So the two sides agreed to a compromise.

The Sherman Silver Purchase Act of 1890 committed the government to buy 4.5 million ounces of silver each month, or nearly the entire output of the western mines. About the same time, passage of the McKinley Tariff Act of 1890 completed the deal.

THE McKINLEY TARIFF

The McKinley Tariff was the Harrison administration's thank-you to big business for its support during the 1888 campaign. A highly protective measure, it raised tariff rates to 48 percent, their highest peacetime level ever.

But the bill, sponsored by future president William McKinley of Ohio, backfired. The point of the high tariff was to make foreign goods expensive, so that Americans would be more likely to buy domestic goods. But greedy manufacturers just raised their prices to match those of foreign goods.

Consumers were furious, and they turned their anger on the governing Republicans. A good many were voted out of office during the 1890 midterm elections, and two years later President Harrison was tossed out as well.

CAMPAIGN ★ 1892

ALTHOUGH BOTH MEN FACED OPPOSITION within their own parties, the election of 1892 turned out to be a rematch between Benjamin Harrison and Grover Cleveland. An early dump-Harrison movement had tried to build support for perennial Republican candidate James G. Blaine, but the president's backers still won renomination for him on the first ballot. Cleveland also won his party's nomination on the first ballot, despite vocal opposition from New York's Tammany Hall delegation and westerners who wanted free coinage of silver, which Cleveland strongly opposed.

The third candidate in the race was James B. Weaver, the nominee of the new People's party, which held its convention in Omaha. Weaver had run for president once before in 1880 as the choice of the short-lived Greenback party.

Again, the election turned on the tariff issue, but this time the resounding failure of the McKinley Tariff hurt the Republicans badly. Cleveland called attention to its upsetting effect on consumer prices and pointed out that he had favored a low tariff for years.

When the votes were counted, Cleveland won the popular vote by almost four hundred thousand, the biggest margin since Grant won reelection in 1872. In the Electoral College, he triumphed by an even wider margin. Even so, Weaver did remarkably well, becoming the first third-party candidate since 1860 to win a state. In fact, he carried four: Colorado, Idaho, Kansas, and Nevada.

GROVER CLEVELAND
24th President
★
1893 to 1897

BORN: MARCH 18, 1837

BIRTHPLACE: CALDWELL, N.J.

DIED: JUNE 24, 1908

PARTY: DEMOCRAT

VICE PRESIDENT: ADLAI E. STEVENSON

FIRST LADY: FRANCES FOLSOM

CHILDREN: RUTH, ESTHER, MARION, RICHARD, FRANCIS

NICKNAME: UNCLE JUMBO

THE BABY RUTH CANDY BAR WAS NAMED AFTER CLEVELAND'S DAUGHTER.

Grover Cleveland was the only president ever reelected after being voted out of office. He returned to the White House in 1893 determined to lower tariff rates. But before he could accomplish that, the Panic of 1893 hit, and the depression that followed lasted throughout his entire second term.

The financial panic began even before Cleveland took office. In February 1893, the Philadelphia & Reading Railroad went under. Soon, other railroads followed, until by 1896 one-quarter of the nation's lines were out of business.

With nearly one million workers, U.S. railroads had been the country's biggest employer, and financing railroads had been the biggest business on Wall Street. Now, the bankruptcies put hundreds of thousands of people out of work and brought

"SEPARATE BUT EQUAL" DOCTRINE UPHELD

WASHINGTON, May 18, 1896—The Supreme Court ruled today in the case of *Plessy v. Ferguson*. Its decision upheld Jim Crow laws in the South that require "separate but equal" facilities for black citizens.

The *Plessy* case challenged an 1890 Louisiana law requiring blacks and whites to travel in separate railroad cars. When Homer Plessy refused to leave a car designated for whites only, he was arrested.

Plessy's lawyers have argued that the Louisiana statute violates their client's rights, but the Court has now ruled that separate accommodations are not necessarily unequal.

The Court's decision notwithstanding, the intent of the Jim Crow laws has clearly been to support white supremacy in the South. These laws, first passed at the end of Reconstruction, have segregated southern schools, parks, theaters, restaurants, and even cemeteries, in addition to the railroads.

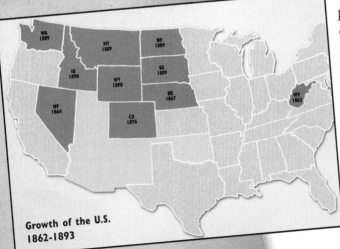

**Growth of the U.S.
1862-1893**

stock-trading activity on Wall Street abruptly to a halt.

Many people who lost their jobs also lost their homes and became wandering vagabonds. Cleveland genuinely wanted to help these people, but his belief in a "hands-off" government kept him from proposing any relief programs. Instead, he focused on keeping the economy steady until the storm of depression passed.

REPEAL OF THE SILVER PURCHASE ACT

The immediate crisis facing the government was the run on its gold reserves. Under the terms of the Sherman Silver Purchase Act, the government had to buy large amounts of western silver each year with paper money that could be exchanged for gold. When people began using this law as a way to trade silver for gold, the government's gold supply dropped sharply. By April 1893, the Treasury had less than one hundred million dollars in gold left.

Cleveland's first move was to call an emergency session of Congress to repeal the Sherman Silver Purchase Act. An angry fight then developed between conservatives, who favored the gold standard, and populists, who wanted free coinage of silver. Keeping the gold standard meant that U.S. currency would continue to be backed by gold alone, while free coinage of silver meant that money could be backed by either gold or silver, thereby increasing the supply.

Putting more dollars into circulation would necessarily force down the value of each one. Therefore, the prospect of inflation pleased southern and western farmers, who didn't have much cash. At the same time, it infuriated eastern bankers, who did.

The dispute created a deep division within the Democratic party between Cleveland's "goldbugs" and the populist

★ BREAKFAST CEREALS

The first flaked breakfast cereal was invented by Dr. John Harvey Kellogg while Kellogg was superintendent of the Battle Creek Sanitarium in Michigan. This health-care facility had been founded by Seventh-Day Adventists, who are vegetarians. Kellogg invented cornflakes in 1895 as a healthful substitute for animal foods.

Calling his new cereal Granose, Kellogg sold ten-ounce packages of the cornflakes for fifteen cents each. About the same time, C. W. Post, a patient at the sanitarium, saw commercial possibilities in the idea of ready-to-eat breakfast cereals. In 1897, he introduced Grape-Nuts. With each box of cereal, Post also included a copy of his pamphlet *The Road to Wellsville*.

A STEADY CUSTOMER

W. K. Kellogg

★ GIBSON GIRLS

Charles Dana Gibson was the highest-paid illustrator of his generation, and his turn-of-the-century drawings defined the American ideal of beauty. The women he drew looked pale, dreamy, and innocent. They typically wore full, upswept hair-styles, called pompadours, and had hour-glass figures. Their male companions were broad-shouldered and usually clean-shaven, which started a trend. Before the appearance of the Gibson man, mustaches and beards had been extremely fashionable.

★ COXEY'S ARMY

In response to the depression of the mid-1890s, Jacob Coxey of Ohio proposed a half-billion-dollar public works program to help the unemployed. To rally support for this idea, he decided to lead an "army" of unemployed workers to Washington. "We will send a petition to Washington with boots on," he said.

On March 25, 1894, Coxey began the march with one hundred people. He had hoped that a hundred thousand more might join him, but Coxey's Army numbered just five hundred when it reached the steps of the Capitol on April 30. Police immediately arrested Coxey for trespassing on the Capitol lawn, but his march did heighten public awareness of the problems being faced by unemployed people in the country.

★ **SECRET SURGERY** In 1893, President Cleveland's doctors discovered a cancerous tumor in his mouth. Believing that news of his illness might shock a nation already weakened by the Panic of 1893, Cleveland decided to have the cancer treated secretly. On July 1, he quietly boarded a friend's yacht, and while the boat sailed up New York's East River, a team of surgeons performed an hour-long operation. Working from inside Cleveland's mouth so as not to leave a visible scar, they removed part of the president's jaw and replaced it with a rubber substitute. The operation remained a secret until one of the doctors wrote a magazine article about it in 1917.

THE BIG TYPE WAR OF THE YELLOW KIDS.

★ **YELLOW JOURNALISM** In 1895, William Randolph Hearst bought the *New York Journal* and began a celebrated circulation war with Joseph Pulitzer's *New York World*. Their battle over who could sell the most copies changed the newspaper business forever. Hearst and Pulitzer both tried to attract readers by playing up sensational stories, especially those relating to a rebellion in Cuba. This kind of exaggerated, unnecessarily dramatic reporting came to be known as yellow journalism after a well-known *Journal* comic strip called "The Yellow Kid." The feverish reporting that Hearst and Pulitzer encouraged was in large part responsible for the Spanish-American War.

"silverites," who were led by William Jennings Bryan. This dynamic young congressman from Nebraska held Congress spellbound with electrifying tirades against the gold standard.

In the end, a coalition of Republicans and goldbug Democrats forced the repeal of the Sherman Silver Purchase Act. But even that didn't stop the gold drain—forcing Cleveland, now more desperate than before, to ask Wall Street for help.

At Cleveland's request, financier J. P. Morgan organized a group of New York bankers to come to the Treasury's aid. Their loan of sixty-two million dollars in gold halted the drain and stabilized the economy by restoring people's faith in the financial system. At the same time, Morgan and his friends made a lot of money on the deal, causing the populists to claim that the president had sold out to Wall Street.

LABOR UNREST Meanwhile, the nation's largest corporations used the depression as an excuse to lower workers' wages further. Because the workers' quality of life was already quite low, these additional cuts provoked some elements of the labor movement into aggression and violence.

After the Civil War, as U.S. manufacturing companies grew larger and more powerful, many forced their workers, especially their immigrant workers, to accept lower wages, longer hours, and more dangerous working conditions. For most people trapped in this life of misery, unionism provided their only hope.

The unions' principal weapon was the strike. During the late nineteenth century, however, most large companies responded to strikes by hiring thugs to beat up the striking workers. With the government (and therefore the police and army) also on their side, the company bosses usually won.

A famous example was the 1894 strike at the Pullman Palace Car Company, located just outside Chicago. When this railroad-car manufacturer cut its wages but refused to lower its company-owned housing rents as well, workers there appealed for help to the American Railway Union, founded by Eugene V. Debs only one year earlier.

Because Pullman refused to negotiate, Debs led 120,000 ARU members out on a peaceful, orderly strike that halted nearly all of the rail traffic into and out of Chicago. It seemed as though the workers would win, until Attorney General Richard Olney asked for and received a court order banning the strike. When Debs refused to obey the order, Olney sent in federal troops to end the strike and force the workers back to their jobs.

Olney's actions certainly ended the crisis, but they also sharply increased the tensions between business and labor. Organizations such as Samuel Gompers's American Federation of Labor later saw the 1894 crackdown as proof that business and government were conspiring to enslave the working class.

THE WILSON-GORMAN TARIFF

Meanwhile, President Cleveland was so preoccupied with the economic situation that he didn't get around to tariff reform until 1894. In that year, Rep. William L. Wilson of West Virginia sponsored a bill in the House that dramatically reduced tariff rates. But the bill was reworked in the Senate by Arthur Gorman of Maryland until it barely lowered them at all. Calling the result "party dishonor," the president refused to sign it. Having thus failed even to reduce tariff rates, Cleveland left office as one of the most unpopular presidents of all time.

CAMPAIGN ★ 1896

WILLIAM JENNINGS BRYAN WAS DETERMINED to include free coinage of silver in the 1896 Democratic party platform, and the convention speech that he gave on this topic, one of the most memorable in U.S. political history, also won him the nomination. "You shall not press down upon the brow of labor this crown of thorns; you shall not crucify mankind upon a cross of gold," Bryan said.

Meanwhile, the Republicans nominated William McKinley of Ohio on the first ballot. As a congressman, McKinley had sponsored the hated McKinley Tariff. Nevertheless, he had shown surprising strength at the 1892 Republican convention.

Both campaigns focused on the currency issue, which confused party loyalties. Unwilling to support either Bryan's prosilver policies or the high tariff rates advocated by McKinley, Cleveland and the goldbug Democrats backed their own candidate, John M. Palmer. Meanwhile, the populists threw in with Bryan, who had already adopted nearly all of their ideas.

The thirty-six-year-old Bryan crisscrossed the country, traveling eighteen thousand miles in three months, while McKinley stayed home and let his campaign manager, Mark Hanna, run the election. Bryan had tremendous popular support in the South and West, but the Republicans controlled the East, where the money was. Raising three million dollars from leading industrialists, Hanna was able to flood the country with Republican pamphlets written in different languages so that McKinley could attract immigrant voters. By comparison, Bryan raised only five hundred thousand dollars, mostly from the owners of silver mines.

Although Bryan's personal appeal was powerful, his target audience of farmers now made up less than half of the U.S. population. Buoyed by the growing power of urban manufacturing interests, McKinley won a decisive victory.

WILLIAM McKINLEY
25th President
★
1897 to 1901

William McKinley [signature]

BORN: JANUARY 29, 1843

BIRTHPLACE: NILES, OHIO

DIED: SEPTEMBER 14, 1901

PARTY: REPUBLICAN

VICE PRESIDENTS: GARRET A. HOBART, THEODORE ROOSEVELT

FIRST LADY: IDA SAXTON

CHILDREN: KATHERINE, IDA

NICKNAME: WOBBLY WILLIE

ALWAYS WORE A RED CARNATION IN HIS LAPEL FOR GOOD LUCK.

William McKinley had a notably warm and engaging personality. It was often said of him that a person could walk into his office angry and walk out with a smile.

It helped McKinley's popularity that, like Cleveland, he was a conservative, hands-off politician. Big business was given free rein during his term, and hugely powerful trusts were allowed to develop without much restraint.

McKinley's immediate problem upon taking office was a growing budget deficit. Because the Supreme Court had recently ruled that a proposed income tax was unconstitutional, the government's revenues still came primarily from tariffs on imported goods.

Tariff rates had been the hottest issue during the last three elections. When the Democrats were in power, they lowered the rates. With Republicans such as McKinley in office, the rates went up again. The Dingley Tariff, which replaced the

REMEMBER THE MAINE!

HAVANA, Cuba, February 15, 1898—The battleship *Maine* sank today in the harbor at Havana after an unexplained explosion punched a hole in its side. Two hundred and sixty sailors went down with the ship. Investigators have been unable to determine the cause of the blast. The Spanish have insisted that the explosion was an accident, but unsubstantiated reports in U.S. newspapers have blamed an underwater Spanish mine.

The *Maine* had been sent to the Spanish colony of Cuba in January as a show of force to discourage the seizure of U.S. property there. The Cubans have been fighting for their independence from Spain since 1895.

Given the current war fever in the United States, the sinking of the *Maine* will almost certainly lead to hostilities with Spain.

1898

1894 Wilson-Gorman Tariff, raised rates even higher than the protective McKinley Tariff had done in 1890.

At first, the public protested the Dingley Tariff, because it raised prices on consumer goods. But the protests didn't last long, as the country soon became distracted by events taking place in Spanish-held Cuba.

THE CUBAN REVOLT The depression in the United States caused by the Panic of 1893 had hurt Cuba's huge sugar industry badly. The Wilson-Gorman Tariff, which imposed a 40 percent duty on sugar, made matters even worse. By 1895, suffering and unemployment on the island moved the desperately poor Cubans to revolt against their Spanish colonial rulers.

The Spanish responded brutally, imprisoning the rebels in concentration camps where two hundred thousand people died of disease and starvation. Whipped into a frenzy by grisly and often exaggerated newspaper accounts of Spanish atrocities, Americans demanded that their government do something. But Grover Cleveland, who was still president, refused to interfere, and tensions continued to mount.

When McKinley became president, he tried to avoid a fight. As a veteran of the Civil War, he knew how bloody war could be. But the sinking of the *Maine* in the harbor at Havana made war inevitable.

The Spanish maintained that the explosion was an accident, and a U.S. investigation proved inconclusive. But "yellow" journalists kept insisting that the sinking of the *Maine* had been deliberate, and McKinley found it impossible to resist the public pressure for a declaration of war. On April 11, 1898, he sent a message to Congress urging the use of military force to pacify Cuba.

THE EARLY YEARS WILLIAM MCKINLEY WAS EIGHTEEN YEARS old when the Civil War began in April 1861. Two months later, he enlisted as a private and fought at Antietam, where he carried badly needed rations to the front. For his bravery under fire, he was promoted to second lieutenant. His new commanding officer was Col. Rutherford B. Hayes, the future president. Of McKinley, Hayes once wrote, "Young as he was, we soon found that in the business of a soldier…, young McKinley showed unusual and unsurpassed capacity." McKinley's political career began after the war when he helped Hayes win election as governor of Ohio in 1867.

★ **THE FIRST LADY** William McKinley met Ida Saxton in 1867 at a picnic in Canton, Ohio, where he had recently moved to set up a law practice. The future Mrs. McKinley was working as a cashier in her father's bank, an unusual job for a woman at the time. In fact, Ida McKinley was the first wife of a president to have worked in a profession other than teaching. Because the first lady suffered

from a form of epilepsy that caused occasional seizures, her husband insisted that she be seated beside him at all state dinners. This broke a White House tradition of seating the first lady at the opposite end of the table from the president.

★ **MOTION PICTURES** The first motion pictures were produced by Thomas Edison in 1894. He called them Kinetoscopes. People placed coins into machines and looked at these short films through peepholes. However, Edison's Kinetoscopes played to only one paying customer at a time, which limited their profitability.

A year later, the French brothers Auguste and Louis Lumière opened the world's first movie theater in Paris. Their Cinématographe was the first true motion picture projector. Unlike the Kinetoscope, it projected films onto a screen so that large audiences could view them. Four months after that, Edison's company purchased the rights to a rival projection system that it called the Vitascope.

★ THE KLONDIKE GOLD RUSH

Gold was first discovered along the Klondike Creek, a tributary of the Yukon River, in August 1896. But the remoteness of Canada's Yukon Territory and the onset of winter, which lasted from September until May, kept the news from the outside world.

Not until July 16, 1897, did word of the discovery finally reach the telegraph wires, beginning the wildest gold rush in North American history. Two days later, the first ship carrying Klondike gold—two tons of it—docked at San Francisco, adding to the excitement. As the forty-niners had during the California Gold Rush, tens of thousands of miners hurried to northern Canada and nearby Alaska to find their fortunes. The gold they mined expanded the money supply and helped to end the depression of the 1890s, muting populist calls for the free coinage of silver.

★ JAZZ

During the late 1890s, John Philip Sousa's Marine Band played the most popular music in the country. Sousa wrote highly patriotic marches such as "The Stars and Stripes Forever." In New Orleans, however, black musicians were developing a new kind of music. Adding complex ragtime rhythms to the brass band melodies favored by Sousa, they created a new style of music called jazz. Early jazz bands typically used marching band instruments such as trumpets, saxophones, trombones, and drums. Some groups also used pianos, bass fiddles, and guitars.

THE SPANISH-AMERICAN WAR

Secretary of State John Hay called the Spanish-American War a "splendid little war" because it was quick and relatively painless for the United States. Only a few hundred soldiers were killed in battle, although several thousand more died from tropical diseases.

The war began in earnest on April 30, 1898, when the U.S. Asiatic Squadron under Commo. George Dewey sailed into Manila Bay in the Philippines. The United States had long coveted this Spanish colony, and the next day Dewey easily defeated the outdated Spanish fleet in the harbor there.

A month later, seventeen thousand soldiers left Florida for Cuba. The First Volunteer Cavalry Regiment, nicknamed the Rough Riders, was led by Theodore Roosevelt, who had just resigned as assistant secretary of the navy.

The Rough Riders were generally untrained and disorganized, but the Spanish were even more hopeless. Caught between the Rough Riders and the powerful U.S. Navy, the Spanish agreed to surrender Cuba on August 12.

In the peace talks that followed, the Cubans were granted limited independence, but the United States took possession of Puerto Rico, Guam, and the Philippines. With the annexation of Hawaii that same year, the nation was now well on its way to becoming an imperial world power.

THE ANNEXATION OF HAWAII

Grover Cleveland had been so outraged by U.S. complicity in the overthrow of Queen Liliuokalani that, when he regained the presidency in 1893, he immediately threw out the Hawaiian annexation treaty that Benjamin Harrison had recently submitted to the Senate.

1900

Cleveland tried to restore native rule to the Hawaiian islands, but the provisional government run by the white planters held on firmly to its power. Then, when McKinley replaced Cleveland, U.S. policy changed again, and Hawaii was annexed in July 1898.

THE OPEN DOOR POLICY

One reason for all this U.S. interest in the Pacific was the new and potentially huge China trade. Because China was the most populous nation in Asia and still undeveloped, American businesses were eager to establish new markets there. But so were the western Europeans and also the Japanese.

Despite its enormous size, China was quite weak militarily. This caused Secretary of State John Hay to worry that the Europeans and Japanese would simply carve up the country into "spheres of influence," leaving little for the United States.

To prevent this, Hay developed the Open Door policy. In September 1899, he sent a series of notes to the European powers and Japan, asking them to agree to equal status for all nations trading with China.

Before the Open Door policy could be adopted, however, a group of nationalists rose up in the Chinese countryside and marched on the capital at Peking. These people were members of a secret society called the Righteous and Harmonious Fists. Westerners called them simply Boxers. Their goal was the removal of all foreigners from China.

In June 1900, the Chinese empress, who was sympathetic, ordered that all foreigners in China be killed. After the German minister was murdered, most of the remaining foreigners took refuge in the British embassy. The Boxer Rebellion ended when an international rescue force captured Peking on August 14.

CAMPAIGN ★ 1900

BY 1900, THE U.S. ECONOMY HAD TURNED around completely. The depression years of the mid-1890s had passed, thanks in part to the Klondike Gold Rush, and the country basked in its prosperity. Knowing a popular president when they saw one, the Republicans happily nominated William McKinley for a second term.

The only suspense at the Republican convention surrounded the choice of a new running mate for McKinley to replace Vice Pres. Garret Hobart, who had died. After McKinley announced that he would accept the will of the convention, Republican delegates chose Spanish-American War hero Theodore Roosevelt, then serving as governor of New York.

McKinley's opponent was once again William Jennings Bryan, the only Democratic leader with a truly national reputation. Although McKinley had beaten Bryan in 1896, the Nebraskan had retained control of his party and won renomination easily. Again, Bryan insisted that the Democrats include in their platform a free-silver plank, and again his uncompromising position drove away gold Democrats, whose support he badly needed.

During the election campaign that followed, Bryan denounced McKinley for turning the United States into an imperial power by keeping the Philippine Islands after the Spanish-American War. The Republicans responded that America was obliged to bring "civilization" to the nonwhite people who lived there.

Meanwhile, McKinley replayed his front-porch campaign of 1896, allowing the energetic Roosevelt to campaign in his stead. The Republican slogan, "Four Years More of the Full Dinner Pail," emphasized the country's prosperity and carried the party to victory.

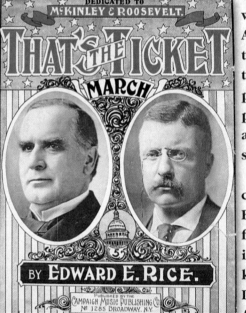

BORN: OCTOBER 27, 1858

BIRTHPLACE: NEW YORK, N.Y.

DIED: JANUARY 6, 1919

PARTY: REPUBLICAN

VICE PRESIDENT: CHARLES W. FAIRBANKS

FIRST LADY: EDITH KERMIT CAROW

CHILDREN: ALICE, THEODORE JR., KERMIT, ETHEL, ARCHIBALD, QUENTIN

NICKNAME: TR

THE FIRST PRESIDENT TO FLY IN AN AIRPLANE.

THEODORE ROOSEVELT

26th President

★

1901 to 1909

Theodore Roosevelt

Although still quite young when he unexpectedly became president, Theodore Roosevelt was nevertheless well prepared for his new job, being both well read and well traveled. In his spare time, he read books on every conceivable subject. Sometimes, he read as many as three books a day.

Yet Roosevelt was far from a shy, bookish intellectual. He loved exercise of all kinds, including horseback riding, hiking, swimming, hunting, and boxing. While he was governor of New York, he once wrestled the middleweight champion. As president, he kept in shape by boxing regularly with professional sparring partners. Every so often, he would invite political rivals to climb into the ring with him for a "friendly" round of boxing. This tough image served Roosevelt well. One of his first policy moves was also his most controversial.

ASSASSIN'S BULLET KILLS McKINLEY

VICE PRESIDENT ROOSEVELT SUCCEEDS HIM

BUFFALO, September 14, 1901—Pres. William McKinley died shortly after two o'clock this morning, eight days after he was shot by an unemployed millworker. McKinley's death surprised his doctors, who had thought the president would recover from the bullet wound in his abdomen.

Vice Pres. Theodore Roosevelt was sworn in today by U.S. District Court judge John R. Hazel. At forty-two, Roosevelt becomes the youngest president ever to take office. He had been vacationing at Lake Tear-of-the-Clouds in the Adirondack Mountains when a telegram reached him yesterday afternoon with news of McKinley's worsening condition.

Roosevelt traveled all night to reach a small town where he could catch a train for Buffalo. When he arrived at the station, he found another telegram waiting for him with the news that McKinley had died during the night.

McKinley was shot on September 6 by Leon Czolgosz, who had been waiting in line to shake the president's hand. A bandage over Czolgosz's right hand had concealed a revolver. According to Czolgosz, "I done my duty. I don't believe one man should have so much service and another man should have none."

LESLIE'S WEEKLY
McKINLEY EXTRA

New York, September 9, 1901

PRICE 10 CENTS

Soon after he took office, Roosevelt introduced "trust-busting."

TRUST-BUSTING Trusts are companies that work together to limit competition in a particular industry, such as tobacco or steel. The most famous trust in U.S. history was the Standard Oil Company, run by John D. Rockefeller Sr. The point of Rockefeller's trust was to fix the price of oil. Rockefeller understood that if he could control the supply of oil, he could set whatever price he wanted.

Turn-of-the-twentieth-century political leaders who defended the rights of working people against powerful business interests were known as Progressives. They opposed trusts because of the unfair practices that trusts used to drive smaller companies out of business. Progressives thought that breaking up the trusts would result in more competition and better prices for all.

In his first speech to Congress, President Roosevelt indicated his agreement that the most ruthless trusts needed to be reformed. But there was also a lot of political support for the trusts, especially within the president's own party.

THE NORTHERN SECURITIES CASE On March 10, 1902, Roosevelt brought suit under the Sherman Anti-Trust Act of 1890 against a railroad trust called the Northern Securities Company. The suit shocked many bankers on Wall Street, but it greatly pleased the public.

It helped Roosevelt that he understood Wall Street businessmen so well. In fact, he was practically one of them. His father had been a wealthy merchant who had served on many corporate boards of directors. As a result, President Roosevelt knew on a personal basis most of the important business leaders in the United States.

TEDDY ROOSEVELT WAS A SICKLY CHILD, suffering from asthma during much of his boyhood. This condition prevented him from attending school, and he often had to sleep sitting up in a chair so that coughing wouldn't keep him awake all night.

THE EARLY YEARS Many years later, in 1884, after the death of his first wife, Teddy moved out west to work as a rancher in the Dakota Territory. The two years that he spent there changed his life. He left New York with a thin, spindly body and returned with a thick neck and barrel chest.

Roosevelt later said that he never would have become president had it not been for his years in the Dakotas. Out west, where his wealth and connections meant little, he had to live with cowboys, gunslingers, drunks, and gamblers. The experience sharpened his wits and built up his character as well as his body. He married his second wife, Edith Carow, shortly after his return.

During the Spanish-American War, Roosevelt served with a volunteer cavalry regiment known as the **Rough Riders**. On July 1, he led a charge up San Juan Hill in Cuba. Press reports made him a national hero and helped him win election as governor of New York that same year.

★**THE TEDDY BEAR** In 1902, Roosevelt went hunting for bear in Mississippi, but the only one he found was a small black cub caught by the hunting dogs. TR refused to shoot the cub.

After hearing this story, Clifford Berryman drew a cartoon of the incident for the *Washington Post*. Two days later, Brooklyn toy maker Morris Michtom placed a copy of Berryman's cartoon in his store window next to a stuffed brown bear, which he called Teddy's Bear. The name, which stuck, was later shortened to teddy bear.

★ THE WRIGHT BROTHERS

Orville and Wilbur Wright operated a bicycle shop in Dayton, Ohio. They first began thinking about flying machines after reading newspaper articles about German experiments with gliders. They built their first glider in 1900.

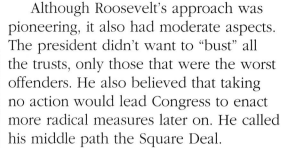

The Wrights' experiments with gliders taught them about flying machines. To build a powered airplane, they would have to develop a strong propeller and a lightweight engine, neither of which existed.

They called their first powered glider *Flyer I*. Orville made the first test flight on December 17, 1903, at Kitty Hawk, North Carolina. In the first sustained flight ever, *Flyer I* stayed aloft for twelve seconds, traveling 120 feet.

★ THE PANAMA CANAL

Both navigators and statesmen had long dreamed of a canal connecting the Atlantic and Pacific Oceans. Without a canal, ships traveling from New York City to San Francisco had to sail all the way around Cape Horn at the southern tip of South America. A canal across Central America would shorten the trip by seven thousand miles.

Construction of the canal began in 1904, but the work was delayed by tropical disease epidemics. A new plan developed by Chief Engineer John F. Stevens sped up construction, but a greater contribution was made by sanitary officer William C. Gorgas. It was Gorgas's work in reducing the number of yellow fever and malaria cases that made completion of the project possible. The fifty-mile-long canal opened to shipping on August 15, 1914.

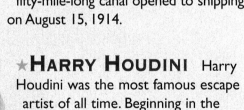

★ HARRY HOUDINI

Harry Houdini was the most famous escape artist of all time. Beginning in the early 1900s, he made an international reputation for himself as a magician. But he was most famous for his death-defying escapes. He would often be handcuffed, bound with ropes and chains, and placed inside a locked container, such as a trunk. Sometimes the container was even submerged in water. If Houdini didn't escape quickly, he would drown.

Although Roosevelt's approach was pioneering, it also had moderate aspects. The president didn't want to "bust" all the trusts, only those that were the worst offenders. He also believed that taking no action would lead Congress to enact more radical measures later on. He called his middle path the Square Deal.

Two years passed before the Northern Securities case reached the Supreme Court, where it would finally be decided. No one really knew how the justices would rule. In earlier cases involving the Sherman Anti-Trust Act, they had ruled in favor of big business. When the decision in the Northern Securities case finally came down, however, it was 5–4 against the trust.

The Court's decision was an important victory for Roosevelt's antitrust policy. The vote was especially close because one of the president's own appointees, Justice Oliver Wendell Holmes Jr., voted against the government. Upon hearing the news of Holmes's dissent, Roosevelt exclaimed, "I could carve a better judge out of a banana."

THE ANTHRACITE COAL STRIKE

The most serious domestic crisis of Roosevelt's first term in office began in May 1902, when anthracite coal miners in Pennsylvania went on strike for better wages and safer working conditions. (Anthracite is a hard coal that burns more cleanly than bituminous, or soft, coal.)

During the nineteenth century, U.S. presidents generally sided strongly with business owners against striking workers. But Roosevelt was a different sort of president. He sensed that times had changed and that Americans now wanted fairer treatment for workers.

One of Roosevelt's first moves was to send in federal troops—but not for the purpose of breaking up the strike. He said that the troops were being sent

to protect the mine owners' property. But they were really there to protect the striking miners from thugs hired by the mine owners.

Next, Roosevelt invited both sides to Washington, where he helped labor and management resolve their differences peacefully. The strikers won some concessions, and Roosevelt's popularity soared. More important, the success of his antitrust and prolabor policies made it clear that Roosevelt's government would protect the interests of the public against large, greedy corporations.

BIG STICK DIPLOMACY On the international stage, Roosevelt also benefited from his tough-guy image. His motto was "Speak softly and carry a big stick." As a result, his foreign policy was called Big Stick Diplomacy. The most noteworthy example of Roosevelt's approach to foreign affairs involved the Monroe Doctrine.

In 1823, Pres. James Monroe had warned European nations against further colonization in the Western Hemisphere. In 1904, Roosevelt added to the Monroe Doctrine what became known as the Roosevelt Corollary. (A corollary is a statement that logically follows from a previous statement.)

At the time, the government of the Dominican Republic was deeply in debt to several European nations—France and Italy, in particular. These countries were threatening to take over the Dominican government if the debt wasn't repaid promptly.

In a speech to Congress, Roosevelt repeated the essence of the Monroe Doctrine: The United States would not tolerate any European intervention in the Americas.

Then, the president went farther. In declaring the Roosevelt Corollary, he reserved for the United States the

CAMPAIGN ★ 1904

BY 1904, WHEN THE NEXT ELECTION came around, Teddy Roosevelt was thoroughly enjoying himself as president, and the public loved him, especially for his boundless enthusiasm and fun-loving family. But Roosevelt still had to convince the Republican party that he was the right man to nominate. After all, McKinley had been the 1900 nominee, and Roosevelt had become president only as a result of McKinley's assassination.

The older Republican leaders didn't like TR, whom they considered a dangerous upstart. These men would have preferred to nominate Mark Hanna, the political boss who had engineered McKinley's rise to the presidency. When Hanna died in February, however, the nomination went to Roosevelt.

Traditionally, the Republicans favored big business, while the Democrats supported more progressive candidates who advocated reform. Because Roosevelt was himself a Progressive, the Democrats weren't sure what to do. In the end, they nominated a conservative candidate, Judge Alton Parker of New York, hoping to capture disaffected Republican votes.

The result was one of the greatest landslides in American presidential history. Of course, Roosevelt had expected to win, but not by such an overwhelming margin. "My dear," he told his second wife, Edith, flashing one of his famous toothy smiles, "I am no longer a political accident."

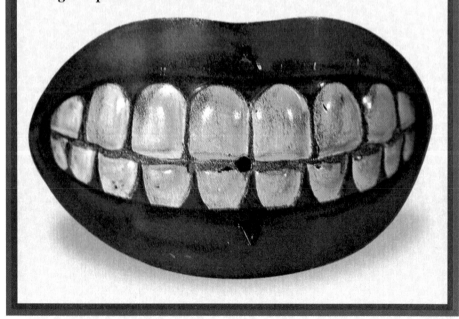

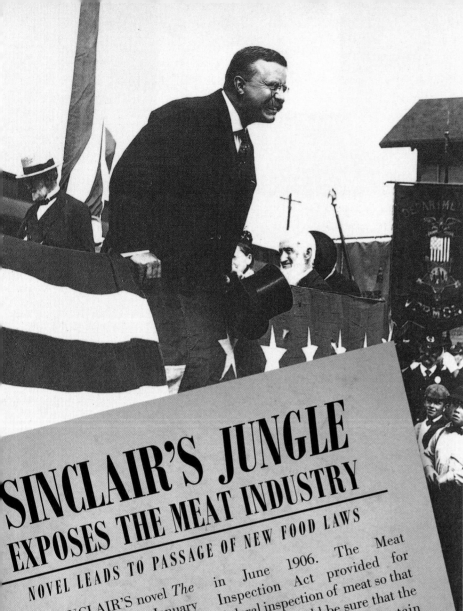

SINCLAIR'S JUNGLE EXPOSES THE MEAT INDUSTRY

NOVEL LEADS TO PASSAGE OF NEW FOOD LAWS

UPTON SINCLAIR'S novel *The Jungle* was published in January 1906. In telling the story of Jurgis Rudkus, a fictional Lithuanian immigrant working in a meat-packing factory, Sinclair exposed the corrupt and dangerous practices of the meat industry in the United States, especially in and around Chicago.

Throughout this period, a number of crusading journalists were busy investigating corruption in U.S. industry. But it was Sinclair's novel that turned public concern into outrage. Publication of *The Jungle* led President Roosevelt to call immediately for federal regulation of food and drugs.

Two bills were quickly passed by Congress and signed into law in June 1906. The Meat Inspection Act provided for federal inspection of meat so that consumers could be sure that the meat they ate met certain standards of freshness. Canned meats also had to be accurately labeled and dated.

The second bill, the Pure Food and Drug Act, established national standards to prevent businesses from adding harmful preservatives and other hazardous ingredients to food and drugs. Never before had the federal government regulated private business so closely.

right to intervene in the affairs of any Latin American country that proved incapable of governing itself.

The Roosevelt Corollary was highly controversial. Critics argued that it would lead to U.S. imperialism of the sort that Europeans still practiced in Asia and Africa. If that were the case, the countries of Latin America might become colonies of the United States.

Roosevelt's supporters, on the other hand, argued that the Roosevelt Corollary was simply common sense. The world was a dangerous place, and there was no nation better suited than the United States to police Latin America.

Whatever people thought, it was clear that Roosevelt was establishing American leadership in the world as no president had before.

THE PANAMA CANAL

One of the memorable achievements of Roosevelt's first term was the Panama Canal. Although the president was eager to begin work on the canal before his 1904 reelection campaign, he had one small problem: The canal zone still belonged to the nation of Colombia, and the Colombian government didn't want to sell.

In November 1903, however, revolution broke out in Panama. Roosevelt backed the rebels, and with U.S. help they won their independence. Afterward, the Panamanians gratefully sold the canal zone to Roosevelt on the same terms that the Colombians had rejected.

THE JUNGLE BY UPTON SINCLAIR

DOUBLEDAY, PAGE & Co. NEW YORK

1906

The next fall, Roosevelt's landslide victory in the 1904 presidential election gave him the popular mandate he needed to pursue his Progressive policies aggressively. A foreign crisis, however, soon captured his attention.

THE RUSSO-JAPANESE WAR The Russo-Japanese War began on February 8, 1904, when the Japanese army launched a surprise attack on Russian troops stationed at Port Arthur in Manchuria, once a part of China. (The Russians had recently broken a promise to withdraw their troops from Port Arthur.)

For months, President Roosevelt worked behind the scenes to stop the fighting. He proposed a number of cease-fire plans, but Russia and Japan couldn't agree on a formula for peace. Finally, on June 11, 1905, Roosevelt announced a breakthrough. The two warring nations had agreed to accept the U.S. president's latest plan for peace.

Formal talks began on August 9 in Portsmouth, New Hampshire. Three weeks later, the Russian and Japanese delegations agreed to a treaty ending the war. Roosevelt was thrilled, having used his skill and influence to achieve the peace. Russia and Japan gave Roosevelt ample credit for the Treaty of Portsmouth, and Britain, France, and Germany all joined in the applause for the president's accomplishment.

In 1906, Roosevelt became the first American to win a Nobel Prize when he received the prize for peace. (The Nobel Prizes are awarded annually in Sweden in such areas as science, medicine, and literature.)

Until Roosevelt's time, it was highly unusual for a U.S. president to be so active in world affairs. During the nineteenth century, presidents usually tried to stay out of European and Asian

★THE FIRST FAMILY

Journalists who covered TR said that life in the White House often resembled a circus. The president's two youngest sons, Archie and Quentin, caused most of the uproar. One of their favorite games was sliding down the White House's central staircase on metal trays. Once Quentin rode his pony, Algonquin, upstairs into Archie's bedroom to cheer up his brother, who was sick.

TR's oldest child, his daughter Alice, was called Princess Alice by the press. Like the rest of her family, she loved to shock people. She would smoke in public, which was considered very bad manners for a woman. She also defied the standards set for women of the day by going to racetracks and betting on horses. She would even show off her pet snake on occasion. Alice was very popular, however, and her name became a favorite one for babies.

★THE GREAT CONSERVATIONIST

Roosevelt had an especially strong love of nature. As a boy, he wanted to become a zoologist. He would later fill his Sagamore Hill home on New York's Long Island with trophies from his various hunting trips and safaris.

TR's love of nature drove him to be particularly active in the field of environmental conservation. In this work, he joined conservationists such as Californian John Muir, who argued that the United States should preserve its wilderness while that was still possible.

Congress had established the first national park, Yellowstone, in 1872, but little had happened since. Eighteen years later, however, Muir persuaded the federal government to create the Yosemite and Sequoia parks in California. Roosevelt (shown here with Muir at Yosemite in 1903) used his influence to preserve nearly two hundred million acres of public land, mostly in the Northwest and Alaska.

★THE MODEL T FORD

In October 1908, Henry Ford introduced the Model T. "I will build a car for the great multitude," he said. The first Model Ts sold for $850, a fortune at the time. But Ford kept his promise, developing the assembly-line process that made production of his cars much more efficient. This dramatically lowered both Ford's costs and the Model T's price.

By 1927, when the car was discontinued, the price had dropped to just three hundred dollars, making Model Ts easily affordable. In the meantime, Ford had sold more than fifteen million of them. In fact, half of the cars in the world were Model Ts.

★HOW THE OTHER HALF LIVES

During the 1880s, Jacob Riis began using a camera to document the terrible living conditions of poor immigrants to New York City. As a police reporter, he had plenty of access to urban tenement apartments. An immigrant himself, Riis crusaded for better conditions and in 1890 published his photos in *How the Other Half Lives*. This book awakened public opinion and did much to fuel the reforms of the Roosevelt, Taft, and Wilson administrations.

★MUCKRAKERS

Reform-minded journalists who wrote about corruption in big business during the early twentieth century were known as muckrakers. Important muckrakers included Upton Sinclair, Lincoln Steffens, and Ida Tarbell. Their articles rallied public support for Progressive causes, especially government reform. Ida Tarbell's work helped bring down the Standard Oil trust.

The word *muckraker* was coined by President Roosevelt, who borrowed it from *The Pilgrim's Progress* by English writer John Bunyan. Bunyan wrote about "the Man with the Muckrake… who could look no way but downward."

Roosevelt meant the name to be critical. He thought that muckrakers focused too much on what was wrong with modern life and ignored what was good about it. The name quickly took on a positive meaning, however, because of the useful work the muckrakers did.

disputes as much as possible. They were following George Washington's advice in his Farewell Address to remain free of foreign entanglements. But as the twentieth century began, the United States was becoming a world power.

During his second term in office, in particular, Roosevelt became increasingly worried about the possibility of a war in Europe. Powerful European nations such as Great Britain and Germany were already fighting each other indirectly in African colonial wars. The president feared that these conflicts might work their way back to Europe and eventually affect the United States. For this reason, he intervened in world affairs yet again.

Despite protests from Congress, Roosevelt sent American diplomats to a 1906 meeting held in Algeciras, Spain. The Algeciras Conference helped prevent war among Great Britain, France, and Germany over Morocco. U.S. participation in the talks emphasized the end of traditional American neutrality.

TAMING THE RAILROADS

Although Roosevelt paid more attention to foreign policy than any president before him, he still kept up a passionate interest in U.S. domestic affairs and worked hard to enact his Square Deal program.

The year 1906 was especially successful for Roosevelt. On May 18, after a long and difficult debate, the Senate passed the Hepburn Act, which gave the president the power to regulate the prices charged by railroads on routes that passed through more than one state. The law marked a new phase in federal efforts to regulate interstate commerce.

Progressives had long argued that the railroads, which were run by the wealthiest people in the country, charged unfairly high rates to move goods from one state to another. The Hepburn Act allowed the

president to use the Interstate Commerce Commission to adjust railroad rates for the benefit of consumers.

AN INDUSTRIAL NATION
The United States had changed vastly since the Civil War. Factories, not farms, now dominated the nation's economy. As a result, more and more Americans had to move to the great cities of the Northeast and Midwest to find work—where they were joined by millions of immigrants.

Working conditions in the cities were often terrible. Adults and children worked ten- and twelve-hour days for very little money. Meanwhile, the rich business owners got even richer.

Dirty smoke from the factories caused a great deal of pollution, and overcrowding made the quality of life in the cities even worse. Increasingly, people came to believe that the federal government should do something about these problems.

Roosevelt was the first national leader to adopt some Progressive solutions. Conservatives believed in laissez-faire economics. This French phrase refers to a hands-off approach to the economy. Progressives, however, believed that government had the right and duty to intervene in business affairs on behalf of the public.

THE PANIC OF 1907
Intervening, however, proved especially difficult when the economy was doing poorly. The Panic of 1907 began when a New York bank, the Knickerbocker Trust Company, failed in October 1907. Its collapse brought down a dozen more banks and some railroads as well. The president's critics blamed his Progressive policies for cutting corporate profits. He blamed bad business practices. Either way, a recovery began the following spring.

CAMPAIGN ★ 1908

THEODORE ROOSEVELT HAD MADE a big mistake. During the 1904 campaign, he had announced that "under no circumstances" would he run again for president in 1908. This was a mistake because, now that his term in the White House was up, he badly wanted to stay.

Roosevelt was just forty-nine years old, and he remained full of energy and ambition. But he also felt bound to keep his word. So he prepared to leave office.

As his successor, Roosevelt picked William Howard Taft, who had served in his cabinet as the secretary of war. TR's strong support ensured Taft the Republican nomination. Meanwhile, the horrendous loss suffered by conservative Democrat Alton Parker in 1904 had returned power to the party's populist wing, which succeeded in nominating William Jennings Bryan for the third time in the last four elections.

The issues that Bryan championed in 1896, in 1900, and again in 1908—women's suffrage, temperance, and an income tax—would all become law eventually. But the time apparently still wasn't right.

During the 1908 campaign, Bryan argued that Roosevelt's Progressive policies should be extended even further. He also promised to end government corruption and unfair business practices that continued to exist despite Roosevelt's reforms. Taft mostly promised to stay the course, and although Bryan was one of the best public speakers in American history, Taft was able to ride Roosevelt's popularity to victory.

BORN: SEPTEMBER 15, 1857

BIRTHPLACE: CINCINNATI, OHIO

DIED: MARCH 8, 1930

PARTY: REPUBLICAN

VICE PRESIDENT: JAMES S. SHERMAN

FIRST LADY: HELEN HERRON

CHILDREN: ROBERT, HELEN, CHARLES

NICKNAME: BIG BILL

THE FIRST PRESIDENT TO SERVE ON THE SUPREME COURT.

WILLIAM HOWARD
TAFT
27th President
★
1909 to 1913

People voted for William Howard Taft in the 1908 election because they believed that he would continue the popular policies of Theodore Roosevelt. Progressives expected Taft to enforce the federal antitrust laws and make sure that the country's natural environment was protected. They also wanted Taft to protect the many men, women, and children who worked in dangerous factory jobs.

Early in Taft's administration, however, Progressive support for the new president began to weaken. Part of the problem was that Roosevelt was a difficult man to follow, and Taft couldn't be another TR. Yet if he did something differently, he was criticized.

For instance, Taft began his term in office by appointing new cabinet members. Of course, this meant that some members of Roosevelt's last

TITANIC STRIKES ICEBERG
1,513 DIE AS LINER SINKS

OFF NEWFOUNDLAND, April 15, 1912—The British luxury liner *Titanic* hit an iceberg shortly before midnight last night. Less than three hours later, the enormous ship sank into the icy waters of the North Atlantic. More than fifteen hundred lives were lost. The *Titanic* was on its maiden, or first, voyage, bound for New York City.

Another passenger ship, the *Californian*, was less than twenty miles away from the sinking *Titanic*, but its radio operator was off duty at the time, so no one heard the *Titanic*'s calls for help. Not until ninety minutes after the *Titanic* went down did another ship, the *Carpathia*, arrive to help in the rescue.

The disaster is particularly shocking because the *Titanic*'s owners had bragged that the ship, the largest and most elegant in the world, was unsinkable.

Heroes of this ill-fated voyage include Isidor and Ida Straus, who gave up their spaces on a lifeboat so that younger passengers might live.

It is certain that the sinking of the *Titanic* will lead to the passage of new safety regulations for passenger ships. The *Titanic*'s lifeboats were able to hold only 1,178 of the 2,224 people aboard.

cabinet were not reappointed. Many newspaper editors interpreted this normal reshuffling as an abandonment of Roosevelt's policies, and their unsympathetic headlines charged that Taft was appointing corporate lawyers to defend the interests of big business.

The new president was by nature more conservative than Roosevelt, but these criticisms were still unfair. Not many people noticed, but more of Roosevelt's programs became law under Taft than under Roosevelt, whose administration had been much less efficient.

Taft's record on conservation, for example, was very good. In some ways, in fact, it was better than Roosevelt's had been. Taft was the first president to protect federal lands on which oil had been found. He also protected land that contained coal, which was even more widely used than oil at the time. Both of these decisions went against the interests of big business, which wanted to exploit those lands for profit.

Taft's trust-busting record was also impressive. During his four years in office, he oversaw twice as many prosecutions under the Sherman Anti-Trust Act as there had been during the seven years that Roosevelt had been president.

THE STANDARD OIL CASE The most famous antitrust case of the Taft years involved the Standard Oil Company. Roosevelt had ordered an investigation of Standard Oil's monopolistic practices before leaving office, but the case didn't reach the Supreme Court until Taft had become president. In May 1911, the Court found that the existence of the trust indeed violated the Sherman Anti-Trust Act, ordering that it be broken up because it unfairly restricted the oil trade.

Also during Taft's term, Congress passed the Sixteenth and Seventeenth

AS A BOY IN OHIO, Taft loved to play baseball. He was a good second baseman and could hit with power, but his extra weight made him a poor base runner. The weight helped him, however, when he refereed fights between his brothers.

After his graduation from Yale University and the University of Cincinnati College of Law, Taft used his father's political connections to get a job as an assistant county prosecutor. He became a state judge in 1887. Five years later, he was appointed to the federal court of appeals.

In 1900, President McKinley sent Taft to the Philippine Islands, which the United States had taken from Spain during the 1898 Spanish-American War. It was Taft's job to establish a new colonial government there.

★ THE AGE OF THE SKYSCRAPER

As the twentieth century began, so did the age of the skyscraper. The first skyscraper in the United States was the ten-story Home Insurance Company Building in Chicago, built in 1885.

Skyscrapers were inspiring feats of engineering, but they were also necessary. As more and more people moved to the cities, the need for space forced people to build up rather than out. There simply wasn't enough land left to build horizontally.

The new vertical architecture was made possible by two important developments. One was the introduction of safe passenger elevators. The other was the use of steel girders in construction. Because steel is both lighter and stronger than iron, it can support taller buildings. Most of the early skyscrapers were built in New York City and Chicago.

★ MODERN DANCE

Before Isadora Duncan, classical ballet was the only dance that most people considered to be art. As a child, however, Duncan had refused ballet lessons. Instead, she insisted on dancing more naturally, according to her own sense of movement and rhythm.

Duncan's innovative style initially held little appeal for Americans, so she moved to Europe at the age of twenty-one. Having very little money, she sailed to England on a cattle boat. Soon, however, she became a sensation. She scandalized Europe and filled concert halls, dancing barefoot while dressed as a woodland nymph out of Greek mythology.

★ PRESIDENTIAL FIRSTS

During Taft's four years in office, there were an unusual number of presidential firsts. For example, Taft bought the first cars for the White House. (To house them, he converted the White House stable into a garage.) Taft also started the presidential tradition of throwing out the first ball of the new baseball season.

In addition, weighing 332 pounds at his inauguration, Taft was the heaviest president. He was so large that he once got stuck in the White House bathtub. To prevent this from happening again, a bathtub large enough to hold four men was installed in its place.

★ HULL HOUSE

Jane Addams was one of the most well-known social reformers of her time. She became famous for her work at Hull House, which she founded in Chicago in 1889. Hull House was the first settlement house in the United States. Its purpose was to help immigrants "settle" successfully.

Hull House tried to bridge the gap between the rich and the poor by establishing a day nursery, a boardinghouse for working girls, and an employment service. Classes in cooking and sewing were also offered.

Addams played an important role in the 1912 election, during which she supported Theodore Roosevelt and his Bull Moose (Progressive) party.

Amendments, both of which were ratified in 1913. The Sixteenth Amendment made the income tax constitutional, and the Seventeenth Amendment provided for the direct election of senators. Previously, senators had been chosen by state legislatures instead of by the people.

DOLLAR DIPLOMACY

Taft's foreign policy was called Dollar Diplomacy because he relied on financial rather than military means to promote U.S. interests abroad. Taft's particular focus was Latin America.

He encouraged U.S. bankers to invest in Honduras and Haiti. In August 1912, however, he resorted to military force, sending marines to Nicaragua to crush a rebellion there that threatened to oust the business-friendly government.

If Taft had so many important achievements in office, why was he always being criticized? One reason was that he often seemed to be doing nothing—or, rather, playing golf. But this "inactivity" was itself deceptive: Usually, his golf partners were important business leaders.

Some newspapers complained that the president shouldn't be playing a rich man's sport with people who made unfair profits at the public's expense. Whether this was true or not didn't matter. People believed it.

But the most important reason for Taft's lack of popularity was that he was always being compared to Roosevelt. His temperament was not as appealing as TR's, and his huge size and slow manner made many people believe he wasn't in charge of his own government.

ROOSEVELT IN AFRICA

At the beginning of Taft's presidency, Roosevelt went on a well-publicized safari to Africa. He said that he wanted to hunt wild game animals. But he really wanted to give his friend Taft a

chance to make his own mark on the government.

Even in Africa, however, Roosevelt dominated the news. There were stories of his party being attacked by hippos, by a rhinoceros, and by an angry bull elephant. Each time, the newspapers reported how the former president rescued the group by bravely shooting the animals in question.

During his yearlong trip, Roosevelt shot three hundred animals, including eighteen rhinos, eight elephants, nine lions, and seven hippos. Many of these animals were later stuffed and sent to the Smithsonian Institution.

TAFT'S PUBLIC IMAGE — Taft couldn't compete with such stories. Next to accounts of TR's exploits, newspapers printed jokes that Taft's favorite sport was eating. During his first Thanksgiving at the White House, for example, the press made a fuss about the huge turkey sent by a constituent in Rhode Island and the fifty-pound mincemeat pie that came from New York.

Even worse, in 1910, a jealous Roosevelt suggested that his support for Taft might have been a mistake. This remark set off a storm of controversy and deeply hurt Taft, who had considered Roosevelt a close friend and mentor. Their relationship became strained, and Taft later said that the loss of his friendship with Roosevelt was one of the most painful events of his presidency.

For his part, Roosevelt believed that Taft had abandoned the Progressives. He had been angry when Taft rejected some of his cabinet appointees (after privately promising to keep them), but he was even more upset by Taft's support for conservatives within the Republican party.

CAMPAIGN ★ 1912

THE 1912 ELECTION WAS A MESS. The trouble began when Theodore Roosevelt decided that his choice of William Howard Taft as a successor had been a mistake. To correct this error, he decided to run against Taft himself.

Taft, of course, had no plans to step aside, so the two men competed for the Republican nomination. Roosevelt may have been the more popular among voters, but Taft had more influence with the leaders who controlled the party. As a result, he won the nomination.

Bitterly disappointed, Roosevelt decided to start his own political party. It was formally named the Progressive party, but most people simply called it the Bull Moose party. This nickname came from TR's often-quoted claim that he was as "strong as a bull moose."

The third candidate in the race was Democratic nominee Woodrow Wilson, who was not a particularly imposing figure. It took the Democrats forty-six ballots to nominate him, but he benefited significantly from the extreme chaos in the Republican camp.

The most important issue of the campaign was government reform, and Roosevelt became quite radical in his calls for change. He spoke often about the value of his tried-and-true Square Deal. Wilson called his own program the New Freedom.

The election was close, but Wilson won because of the votes that Taft took away from Roosevelt. Taft himself finished a distant, humiliating third. A decade later, however, Pres. Warren G. Harding appointed Taft to be chief justice of the Supreme Court.

BORN: DECEMBER 28, 1856

BIRTHPLACE: STAUNTON, VA.

DIED: FEBRUARY 3, 1924

PARTY: DEMOCRAT

VICE PRESIDENT: THOMAS R. MARSHALL

FIRST LADIES: ELLEN LOUISE AXSON,
EDITH BOLLING GALT

CHILDREN: MARGARET, JESSIE, ELEANOR

NICKNAME: PROFESSOR

THE FIRST PRESIDENT TO HOLD
A PRESS CONFERENCE.

1913

WOODROW WILSON

28th President
★
1913 to 1921

Woodrow Wilson

Woodrow Wilson set the tone for his presidency in his first inaugural address. In that speech, he outlined the issues facing the nation in terms of what was right and what was wrong. As the son of a Presbyterian minister, Wilson tended to view the job of chief executive as a moral responsibility.

He began his tenure with tremendous energy, and the first two years of his administration were extremely productive. During that time, Congress passed some of the most Progressive laws of the era, beginning with the Underwood Tariff.

During the 1912 campaign, Wilson had promised to lower tariff rates. Now, he followed through on that promise, calling Congress into special session in October 1913 to pass tariff reform.

WORLD WAR I IN EUROPE

U.S. STAYS OUT OF THE FIGHTING

WHEN WORLD WAR I began in August 1914, many Americans took sides. Because of their close ties to Britain and France, most southerners and easterners supported the Allies. The children of German immigrants in the Midwest, however, backed the Central Powers.

Even so, most Americans agreed that the United States should stay out of the fighting. They felt that becoming involved in a war an ocean away made little sense, because its outcome meant so little to American life.

Yet this policy of neutrality became harder to maintain once German submarines, called U-boats, began torpedoing American ships bound for England.

Public opinion turned strongly against the Germans in 1915, when a U-boat sank the British passenger liner *Lusitania*. Nearly twelve hundred people died, including 128 Americans. The Germans pointed out, however, that the *Lusitania* was carrying ammunition, so its voyage wasn't entirely innocent.

The Underwood Tariff cut the average rate from 41 to 27 percent, the lowest that tariff rates had been since the Civil War.

THE FIRST INCOME TAX

Of course, lower tariff rates meant less revenue for the government. So, to make up the difference, the new law also established the first national income tax. Americans making above three thousand dollars a year would have to pay 1 percent of their income to the government, with people making over twenty thousand dollars a year required to pay an additional amount as high as 6 percent.

The Supreme Court had once ruled that income taxes were unconstitutional, but ratification of the Sixteenth Amendment in February 1913 had changed the Constitution to make them legal. Even so, the new income tax was still highly controversial. Business groups fought against it, and many Americans resented paying it.

Another of Wilson's early achievements was the Federal Reserve Act of December 1913, which reorganized the nation's banking system.

THE FEDERAL RESERVE ACT

The U.S. banking system had been a source of conflict ever since the 1790 fight between Alexander Hamilton and Thomas Jefferson over the creation of the first national bank. Forty years later, Andrew Jackson and Nicholas Biddle clashed over the rechartering of the Second Bank.

Now, eighty years after that, a public shaken by the system's poor performance during the Panic of 1907 demanded substantial change. Wilson's Federal Reserve Act set up a new network of twelve regional banks, each of which reported to a national board of governors appointed by the president. The job of

THE EARLY YEARS

WOODROW WILSON'S EARLIEST MEMORY was as a four-year-old boy living in Georgia. He remembered a man telling him that Abraham Lincoln had won the presidency, so there would be war between the states.

As a white child living in the South, Wilson experienced Reconstruction as a period of great injustice. Although he later pursued academic and political careers in the North, he always considered himself a southerner. He believed that the South had been justified in seceding from the Union, and he also believed in the supremacy of the white race.

★ THE FIRST LADIES

A year and a half into his first term, Wilson's wife Ellen died. The president was so upset that he told an aide he hoped he would be assassinated. Ellen Wilson had been an active first lady, at one time lobbying Congress to pay for slum clearance in the District of Columbia.

About a year after Ellen died, the president became quietly engaged to a widow, Mrs. Edith Bolling Galt. When the press found out about the relationship and reported it, people criticized Wilson for deciding to remarry so soon after the death of his first wife. Because of the bad publicity, Wilson offered to end the engagement, but Mrs. Galt said that she would stand by him.

★ MARGARET SANGER

While working as a nurse in one of New York City's immigrant neighborhoods, Margaret Sanger saw firsthand the ways in which having too many babies kept poor families poor. The more children a family had, the more mouths it had to feed. Having witnessed the consequences, Sanger decided to devote her life to publicizing information about birth control.

At the time, her actions were illegal. The Comstock Act of 1873 had banned pamphlets about birth control because many people considered them obscene. Sanger ignored the law because she believed strongly in the right of every woman to plan the size of her family.

★ **JACK JOHNSON** Jack Johnson became the first black man to win the world heavyweight boxing championship when he knocked out Tommy Burns on December 26, 1908. While Johnson was champion, many white boxing fans cried out for a "great white hope" to defeat the confident, arrogant Johnson. They didn't believe that a black man should be champion. Johnson further outraged white America by twice marrying white women.

In his most famous fight—on July 4, 1910—Johnson beat thirty-five-year-old white former champion Jim Jeffries, who had been persuaded to come out of retirement to put Johnson "in his place." Johnson knocked out Jeffries in fifteen rounds.

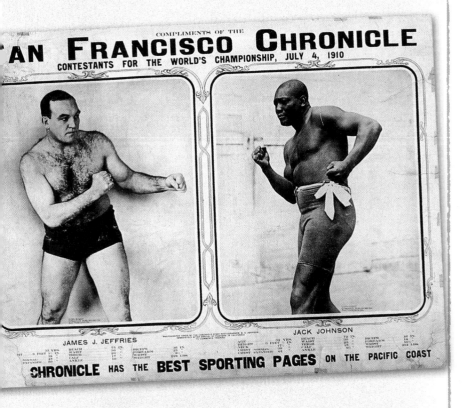

COMPLIMENTS OF THE

AN FRANCISCO CHRONICLE

CONTESTANTS FOR THE WORLD'S CHAMPIONSHIP, JULY 4, 1910

JAMES J. JEFFRIES   JACK JOHNSON

CHRONICLE HAS THE **BEST SPORTING PAGES** ON THE **PACIFIC COAST**

★ **THE ARMORY SHOW** Modern art developed in Europe around the turn of the twentieth century. As late as World War I, however, this new style of painting was almost unknown in America. Among the most influential modern artists were two Frenchmen, Paul Cézanne and Henri Matisse, and Pablo Picasso, a Spaniard living in France.

Modern art was first introduced to the United States in 1913 at an exhibition held at the Sixty-ninth Regiment Armory in New York City. The exhibition's most important works were in the cubist style. Cubist painters treated people and objects as though they were geometric shapes. Pres. Herbert Hoover's favorite cartoon of himself was one done in the cubist style.

this new board was to control the money supply, which is the amount of money available for investment.

During boom times, the board was supposed to raise interest rates, so that people wouldn't borrow and spend too much. During recessions, it was supposed to lower rates, so that people could get the credit that they needed.

Wilson's success in persuading Congress to enact these programs proved that he was a capable administrator. Very soon, however, he would have to prove that he was a capable war leader as well.

THE MEXICAN REVOLUTION The announcement of the Roosevelt Corollary to the Monroe Doctrine had strained relations between the United States and Latin America. Countries in Central and South America resented Theodore Roosevelt's claim that the United States could intervene in their affairs whenever it thought that Latin Americans weren't governing themselves properly.

When the Mexican Revolution broke out in 1910, officials in the Taft administration became worried that the fighting would spill over into Texas. In 1911, the violence subsided when dictator Porfirio Díaz was overthrown and Francisco Madero was elected president. But in February 1913, Madero was himself overthrown by Gen. Victoriano Huerta, who set up a military dictatorship. Although Huerta came to power with the backing of Taft's ambassador, Wilson later refused to recognize the Huerta "government of butchers" and instituted a policy of "watchful waiting."

Despite public pressure for an invasion of Mexico, Wilson resisted until April 1914, when an officer in Huerta's army arrested some U.S. sailors who had gone ashore in the port of Tampico. A superior officer quickly freed the sailors, but their

captain demanded a public apology as well, which the Mexicans refused.

Wilson used this incident as an excuse to increase the U.S. naval presence in Mexican waters. A few days later, he ordered some of those ships to seize the port of Veracruz in order to stop a German ship from delivering arms to Huerta's army. The resulting street fighting left 126 Mexicans dead.

In August 1914, the U.S.-supported forces of Venustiano Carranza captured Mexico City, forcing Huerta into exile. After Carranza took over, however, his Constitutionalist coalition split apart, and a new civil war began. Initially, Wilson considered backing Francisco "Pancho" Villa, who had risen up in northern Mexico. But international pressure later brought him back to Carranza. At this point, Villa, feeling betrayed, turned on the United States.

In March 1916, the worst U.S. fears came true when Villa crossed the border and attacked Columbus, New Mexico. He set fire to the town and killed twenty-four people. In response, Wilson sent Gen. John J. Pershing to capture the Mexican renegade. The chase, which took Pershing three hundred miles into Mexico, lasted until February 1917, when Wilson finally gave up. By that time, the United States was preparing to enter a much more important fight: the First World War.

U.S. NEUTRALITY

Wilson had dedicated much of his first term to preventing U.S. involvement in World War I. The Germans were making this difficult, however. The world was a much more interconnected place in the early twentieth century than it had ever been before, and even the vast Atlantic Ocean no longer protected the United States from European problems.

CAMPAIGN ★ 1916

WOODROW WILSON WON RENOMINATION easily at the Democratic national convention in St. Louis, where the party unveiled its campaign slogan for the fall: "He Kept Us Out of War." The Democrats judged correctly that U.S. neutrality with regard to World War I would be the biggest issue of the campaign, but their party platform also supported new health and safety standards for workers, a ban on child labor, and women's suffrage. The Republicans, who nominated Supreme Court justice Charles Evans Hughes, attacked Wilson for failing to protect American interests abroad. They believed that the United States should take a much tougher stance with Germany and at the same time build up its military. Hughes also supported a ban on child labor, benefits for workers who were injured on the job, and the right of women to vote.

Because a still-influential Theodore Roosevelt went even farther, urging U.S. entry into the European war, he backed the hawkish Republicans energetically, and other Progressives followed his lead.

As the election neared, some newspapers predicted that Hughes would win, and for three days after the balloting, the result remained in doubt. But a late vote count in California gave Wilson a narrow victory there and in the Electoral College as well—which Wilson won, 277–254. Had California gone Republican, Charles Evans Hughes would have been president.

Wilson at Versailles during the 1919 Paris peace talks.

In February 1915, the German government announced that it considered the waters around Great Britain to be a war zone. Therefore, all vessels found in those waters, including U.S. ships, would be subject to U-boat attack.

Wilson responded immediately, warning the Germans that attacks on neutral U.S. ships would force him to take military action. In response to this threat, Germany's military leadership backed down because it didn't want to bring America into the war.

ENTRY INTO WORLD WAR I

By the start of Wilson's second term in early 1917, however, the president found that he could no longer resist the strong pull toward war.

Wilson had long thought that a neutral United States could play an important role in ending the war in Europe and brokering a fair and sustainable peace. In a January 1917 speech before the Senate, he called on both the Allies and the Central Powers to accept "peace without victory." But Wilson's efforts at peacemaking, while respected, were generally ignored.

The United States moved much closer to war itself in January 1917, when Germany announced that it would resume unrestricted submarine warfare in the waters around Great Britain. This meant that, once again, U.S. neutrality would not be respected at sea. As a result, on February 3, Wilson broke off diplomatic relations with Germany.

WORLD WAR I ON THE HOME FRONT

BARUCH, HOOVER LEAD MOBILIZATION EFFORTS

THE UNITED STATES entered World War I in the late spring of 1917. But U.S. soldiers weren't ready to fight yet. Nor was the country mobilized for war.

To help manage the domestic side of the war effort, President Wilson recruited a number of important business leaders, many of whom worked full-time for the token salary of one dollar per year.

Wilson named Wall Street baron Bernard Baruch to head the new War Industries Board, which managed the output of American heavy industry. Wilson also appointed mining engineer Herbert Hoover as the nation's new food administrator.

Because Europeans had already been fighting the war for three years, food supplies in Europe were running dangerously low. To meet this need, Hoover worked tirelessly to increase food exports so that soldiers and civilians in Europe could be fed.

Food is Ammunition—
Don't waste it.

UNITED STATES FOOD ADMINISTRATION

129

1918

Most Americans were outraged by submarine warfare, which they considered particularly devious and cruel. Even so, the country was still not ready for war until March 1, when the decoded text of the Zimmermann Telegram was made public. This message from German foreign minister Arthur Zimmermann to his ambassador in Mexico had been intercepted by British intelligence agents. A copy was later provided to Wilson.

In the telegram, Zimmermann proposed an alliance between Germany and Mexico. Should the United States enter the war, he explained, Germany would help Mexico reconquer the "lost territories" of Texas, New Mexico, and Arizona.

Once the text of this message was released, public opinion turned sharply in favor of war. On April 2, Wilson asked Congress to declare war on Germany. In his speech, he said, "The world must be made safe for democracy."

During the rest of 1917, Wilson attended to the preparations for war. He recalled General Pershing from Mexico and ordered him to muster an American Expeditionary Force, which would be sent overseas to France and Belgium. He also looked toward the future, because he believed that arranging a lasting peace would be much more difficult than simply winning the war on the battlefield.

THE FOURTEEN POINTS On January 8, 1918, Wilson gave a speech outlining fourteen points upon which he believed peace should be made. These included arms reduction, free navigation of the seas, and self-determination for colonies.

The last point of the president's plan called for the formation of an ambitious League of Nations, which could avoid wars in the future by guaranteeing the rights and independence of all the world's nations.

★ **WHITE HOUSE SHEEP** First Lady Edith Wilson threw herself into the war effort. During her husband's second term, for example, she arranged for a flock of sheep to graze on the White House lawn and auctioned off their wool to raise money for the Red Cross.

Meanwhile, she spent many nights busy at her sewing machine, which she used to make surgical clothing for Red Cross doctors. She also promoted wartime rationing by observing gasless Sundays, meatless Mondays, and wheatless Tuesdays.

★ **PROHIBITION** During the nineteenth century, many social reformers objected to the high rate of alcohol consumption among American men. These temperance activists sought to remove the

temptation by passing "dry" laws that prohibited the manufacture and sale of strong drink.

Business leaders favored Prohibition because they thought it would reduce absenteeism at work. Religious groups also supported the idea because they believed that drinking was sinful. Progressive groups even argued that poverty, disease, and crime were largely due to alcoholism.

The 1916 election swept a large majority of "dry" candidates into office. As a result, the Eighteenth Amendment was soon passed and ratified by the states. This amendment, combined with the Volstead Act of 1919, began the Prohibition era in America.

★ **THE GREAT MIGRATION** The mass movement of southern blacks to northern cities began around 1910. During World War I, nearly half a million blacks left the rural South for urban centers such as New York City, Detroit, and Chicago. By 1940, almost two million blacks had taken part in the Great Migration, which changed the racial geography of America.

Southern blacks were drawn to the North because of all the good industrial jobs created by the wartime and postwar booms. Many of these jobs were on assembly lines that had been racially segregated until the need for workers forced their integration. "Prejudice vanishes when the almighty dollar is on the wrong side of the balance sheet," one black newspaper in Chicago explained.

★ CHARLIE CHAPLIN

English-born Charlie Chaplin was one of the earliest American movie stars. He began his film career in 1913 making brief film comedies, called shorts, for Mack Sennett's Keystone Company. Sennett was already famous for his slapstick Keystone Kops shorts.

While making his second film, *Kid Auto Races at Venice,* Chaplin developed his famous "tramp" character—or, as Chaplin called him, "the little fellow." Within two years, Chaplin's derby hat, cane, baggy pants, and small mustache became internationally known trademarks.

★ WOMEN'S SUFFRAGE

Women finally received the right to vote in August 1920, when the Nineteenth Amendment was ratified by the states. Until then, only women in a few western states had been permitted to cast ballots. The presidential election of 1920 was the first in which every female citizen in the United States could vote.

Women first began demanding the right to vote during the 1840s, but the women's suffrage movement didn't gain much momentum until after the Civil War. It succeeded during the late 1910s because of three factors: the contributions to the war effort made by women during World War I, the support of President Wilson, and the confrontational tactics of Alice Paul and others. For months, Paul's followers marched and picketed outside the White House. Sometimes they were arrested and jailed.

During the spring of 1918, before most of the U.S. troops had reached Europe, the Germans launched one last, desperate offensive. When that failed, so did the German war effort. By September 1918, there were more than a million American soldiers in Europe, shifting the balance of power considerably. Recognizing the inevitable, the Germans sent Wilson a note on the night of October 3–4, asking the president for a truce and peace talks based on the Fourteen Points that Wilson had outlined nine months earlier.

THE PARIS PEACE TALKS

Wilson was probably the most idealistic president in U.S. history. For years, his goal had been the creation of a world peace based on democratic principles. Now, he finally had his chance to bring that about. So he decided to lead the U.S. delegation to the peace talks himself.

On his way to Paris, where the talks were to be held, the president was greeted enthusiastically by Europeans, who considered him a hero because of his role in ending the war. In 1919, Wilson even won the Nobel Peace Prize.

But the leaders of Britain and France were much less impressed, and they fought Wilson on many points during their meetings at the Versailles palace. In the end, the Treaty of Versailles that the Germans were forced to sign placed many harsh burdens upon that defeated nation. It did, however, provide for the creation of a League of Nations.

Meanwhile, during the six months that Wilson spent abroad, his health began to fail him. He also began losing control of the U.S. government. When he finally returned home with his precious treaty in July 1919, the Senate was far from ready to ratify it.

From Wilson's point of view, the most important section in the Treaty of

1920

Versailles was the one establishing the League of Nations. But his opponents in the Senate wanted to eliminate this section, because they believed that the United States should stay out of world affairs. These senators, led by Henry Cabot Lodge, were called isolationists.

Lodge had the votes on his side, but Wilson was a stubborn man. Even with his health worsening and his patience exhausted, he refused to compromise.

WILSON'S STROKE Instead, in September 1919, Wilson began an ill-advised national speaking tour intended to rally public support for the treaty. He visited twenty-nine cities in three weeks but broke down physically in Pueblo, Colorado, on September 26. Soon, he suffered a stroke that paralyzed his entire left side. In time, the president recovered but never completely.

While Wilson recuperated, he continued to make the most important presidential decisions. But he allowed his second wife, Edith, to handle most of the details and to decide which matters were important enough to merit his attention. She reviewed all of his papers and ran the White House in his name. Meanwhile, Wilson never offered to step down, and no one confronted him about his condition.

During this period, the Senate voted in March 1920 to reject the Treaty of Versailles. The outcome of this vote had little effect on the fate of Germany, however, because the other Allies had already agreed to the treaty and were enforcing its terms.

The victors couldn't see this at the time, but the terrible financial strain that the treaty placed on Germany would soon lead to the rise of Adolf Hitler. Despite Wilson's efforts, the world had been made no safer for democracy.

CAMPAIGN ★ 1920

HAD WOODROW WILSON REMAINED HEALTHY, he might have run for a third term as president. Instead, he was forced to retire. But the election of 1920 still turned on his actions and policies.

To succeed Wilson, the Democrats nominated Ohio governor James M. Cox, who embraced the president's record. As Cox's running mate, the convention chose Franklin D. Roosevelt of New York, who had been Wilson's assistant secretary of the navy. (No doubt the Democratic leadership also felt that Roosevelt's famous last name would win the party a few extra votes.)

The deadlocked Republican convention nominated a compromise candidate, Sen. Warren G. Harding, also of Ohio. Harding's breakthrough came in Suite 404 of the Blackstone Hotel in Chicago, where the party bosses met secretly to work out a deal. At two o'clock in the morning, they called Harding to their "smoke-filled room" and asked him whether he had anything to hide. Harding thought for ten minutes and replied that he did not. The next day, he was nominated, and Massachusetts governor Calvin Coolidge became his running mate.

As Cox campaigned on Wilson's record, the Republicans railed against it. They charged that the president had been unprepared for World War I and attacked his cherished League of Nations.

Meanwhile, Cox urged Americans to work even harder for peace and Progressive reforms. He pointed to the still-unstable international situation and to the fact that one in six Americans was still illiterate. But a war-weary public was in no mood to meet his idealistic challenge. Instead, Americans embraced Harding's campaign slogan, which offered a "Return to Normalcy." The Republicans won in a landslide.

BORN: NOVEMBER 2, 1865

BIRTHPLACE: CORSICA, OHIO

DIED: AUGUST 2, 1923

PARTY: REPUBLICAN

VICE PRESIDENT: CALVIN COOLIDGE

FIRST LADY: FLORENCE KLING DE WOLFE

CHILDREN: NONE

NICKNAME: WOBBLY WARREN

THE FIRST PRESIDENT TO SPEAK OVER THE RADIO.

WARREN GAMALIEL HARDING

29th President

★

1921 to 1923

Warren G. Harding

Warren Harding thoroughly rejected Woodrow Wilson's idealism. During his "Return to Normalcy" campaign, Harding had avoided taking any position on the League of Nations. He had hoped that, by being vague, he could persuade both supporters and opponents of the League to vote for him. A month after taking office, however, he announced to Congress that he would not support U.S. membership in that organization.

Meanwhile, to bring the expanding executive branch under tighter control, Harding proposed a new government office, called the Bureau of the Budget. To run this office, he chose engineer and banker Charles G. Dawes.

In past years, each of the executive departments had managed its own budget. Now, the process would be unified and streamlined.

Harding also signed into law two new tariffs that replaced the Underwood Tariff of 1913 and raised rates to an average of 38 percent. Singled out for special protection were new

TEAPOT DOME SCANDAL

INTERIOR SECRETARY FALL CAUGHT IN CORRUPT DEAL

IN 1922, Interior Secretary Albert G. Fall made a secret deal with the Mammoth Oil Company, arranging for Mammoth to lease the government's Teapot Dome oil fields in Wyoming. The terms were very favorable to Mammoth. In exchange, company president Harry Sinclair paid Fall a bribe of three hundred thousand dollars.

Some people had suspicions when the lease was first signed, but the full story didn't come out until the release of a Senate report in October 1923. By that time, President Harding (who had appointed Fall) was dead, having passed away two months earlier.

Harding may have known before he died that his adminis-

tration was about to unravel, and this knowledge may have played a role in his own collapse. There was no evidence in the Senate report, however, that Harding ever profited personally from any of his friend's corrupt dealings.

Who Says a Watched Pot Never Boils?

industries that had grown up during World War I, especially the pharmaceutical and chemical industries.

In general, though, Harding found it difficult to be president. He had spent six years in the Senate but still found the complexities of legislation confusing. For example, the details of one tax reform bill eluded him completely. "I can't make a damn thing out of this tax problem," he admitted in one frustrated moment. "I listen to one side and they seem right, and then—God!—I talk to the other side and they seem just as right, and here I am where I started."

IMMIGRATION Harding responded to the national concern about continuing high levels of immigration by signing the Emergency Quota Act of 1921. This law established the first general quotas, or limits, on immigration in the nation's history.

The waves of immigration from eastern and southern Europe that took place just before World War I were the largest ever. Factory owners liked all the cheap labor that new immigrants provided, but many other Americans feared that poor Europeans would bring with them dangerous ideas about communism and socialism.

Workers who had come over during earlier waves of immigration also feared the loss of their jobs. In response, the Emergency Quota Act limited immigration from each country to 3 percent of the number of people from that country already in the United States in 1910.

On the issue of African-American civil rights, however, Harding was remarkably ahead of his time. In October 1921, he became the first president since the Civil War to deliver a speech in the South on behalf of equal rights for blacks.

Even so, Harding's biggest accomplishments came in foreign affairs.

THE EARLY YEARS WARREN HARDING GREW UP on a farm in Caledonia, Ohio, where his chores included milking the cows, tending to the horses, and painting the barns. In 1884, when he was not yet nineteen, he and two friends purchased an almost bankrupt newspaper in Marion, Ohio, for three hundred dollars. Before long, Harding became the sole owner of the *Marion Star*.

When Harding was twenty-five, he married Florence Kling De Wolfe, a thirty-year-old divorced woman with one son. Florence's father warned her not to marry Harding and at one point even threatened Harding's life. But the couple married anyway.

As it turned out, Florence Harding made an excellent circulation manager, and it was largely her work that built up the newspaper into a business profitable enough to launch her husband's political career.

★ **WOMEN'S WORK** The development of the typewriter opened up many new opportunities for women in the workplace. For female high school graduates, secretarial work provided an attractive alternative to traditional women's work, such as teaching and nursing. It was also far less backbreaking than farm or factory labor. Soon, huge "pools" of neat young women clattered away at manual typewriters in city offices nationwide. By 1930, there were eleven million women in the workforce, more than double the number in 1900.

★ THE ROARING TWENTIES

In a peculiar way, the outrageousness of the 1920s was caused by the restrictions of Prohibition. Because most people didn't take Prohibition seriously, the business at illegal speakeasies, or bars, was always good. And once people break a single law or social taboo, it's usually easier to break others.

The prosperity of the 1920s also contributed to the thrilling popular culture. Fashionable young women called flappers discarded their puffy prewar dresses in favor of short ones that clung tightly to their bodies. Dancing the nights away in speakeasies, they scandalized older Americans with their personal freedom. They were the first women to smoke cigarettes in public, and their favorite dance was the wild, flailing Charleston.

★ POKER

As a senator, Harding had voted for Prohibition. But as president, he secretly stocked the White House with illegal liquor. He liked to have some on hand for his poker games, which often ran late into the night. Harding especially enjoyed playing poker with members of his cabinet. Among the regulars were Secretary of War John Weeks, Attorney General Harry Daugherty, and Interior Secretary Albert Fall. Both Daugherty and Fall later became key figures in the Harding administration corruption scandals. During one unfortunate game, Harding gambled away a complete set of White House china.

★ NEGRO LEAGUES

During the 1920s and 1930s, blacks were not allowed to play major league baseball. Instead, they were forced to play in their own segregated leagues. The most famous of these was the Negro National League, founded in 1920.

Teams in the Negro leagues were often as popular as major league clubs in the same town. In Chicago, for example, the American Giants sometimes drew more fans than either the White Sox or the Cubs.

Perhaps the biggest Negro league star was the flamboyant pitcher Satchel Paige of the Kansas City Monarchs. Negro league games often had a carnival-like atmosphere, and sometimes Paige would dazzle fans by calling in his outfielders. He was that sure the opposing batter couldn't hit his famous fastball out of the infield.

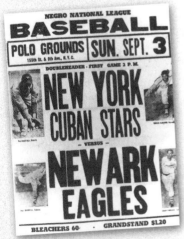

Because the victorious nations of World War I were already starting to maneuver for power, Harding convened an international conference on arms control. The Washington Conference for the Limitation of Armament was held in the nation's capital between November 1921 and February 1922.

The meeting ended with the United States, Great Britain, Japan, France, and Italy all agreeing to limit the size of their navies. The United States and Great Britain were granted the largest fleets, with the Japanese fleet capped at slightly more than half of their size. The French and Italian navies were limited to a little more than half the size of the Japanese fleet.

The conference also led to the Four Power Pact among the United States, Great Britain, Japan, and France. With this treaty, the four nations agreed to respect each other's territory in Asia. They also promised to resolve peacefully any disagreements among them.

TEAPOT DOME Despite these successes, by early 1923, Harding's presidency was in deep trouble. Rumors about corruption in his administration began circulating widely, and soon Sen. Thomas Walsh of Montana opened a formal investigation into them. It didn't take long for Walsh's committee to uncover evidence of what came to be known as the Teapot Dome scandal.

Harding's problem began with the people whom he had appointed to office. The only qualification most of them had was a longtime political friendship with the president. Usually, these men were more interested in private gain than public service. However, because Harding was rather weak-willed, he rarely refused a friend who asked for a job. Few voters doubted Harding's own integrity, but Walsh's investigation proved that many of his friends were crooks.

HARDING DIES IN OFFICE

PRESIDENT HARDING WAS TROUBLED by the growing charges of corruption in his administration. In late June 1923, just as Thomas Walsh's Senate investigation was getting under way, Harding set out on a nationwide speaking tour that he called the Voyage of Understanding. He wanted to explain his policies to the public and assure Americans that he was an honest man.

The long trip by railroad was unwise, however, because Harding was suffering from high blood pressure and heart trouble. His tiring schedule also weakened him. When he finally reached San Francisco at the end of July, he was exhausted and had to be carried from the train. On August 2, he died in his room at the Palace Hotel.

After Harding's death, some people claimed that his wife had poisoned him to spare him the indignity of impeachment. Others whispered that she killed him because he had been unfaithful to her. (Both as a senator and as president, Harding had kept mistresses and even fathered a child by one of them.) These rumors were fanned by the first lady's refusal to allow an autopsy. Nothing was ever proven, however, and historians today believe Harding died of natural causes.

CAMPAIGN ★ 1924

IN 1924, THE COUNTRY WAS PROSPEROUS and at peace. Under normal circumstances, these two conditions would have ensured the reelection of the party in power. But Republican leaders were worried. They weren't sure whether voters were going to hold the scandals of the Harding administration against them.

The party leaders were lucky that Calvin Coolidge happened to be Harding's vice president. In a very short time, Coolidge's direct, upright manner restored confidence in both the government and the presidency. As a reward, he was nominated unanimously at the first national convention ever broadcast over the radio.

On the other hand, the Democratic convention produced the longest deadlock in history.

For more than one hundred ballots, Californian William McAdoo, the choice of the rural South and West, battled New York governor Alfred E. Smith, who had the backing of the eastern cities. In the end, both men withdrew, and the nomination went to West Virginia lawyer John W. Davis on the 103rd ballot. Davis ran hard, but the Republicans' "Keep Cool with Coolidge" campaign proved unbeatable.

As the candidate of the **Progressive party**, maverick Republican senator Robert M. LaFollette mounted an unusually effective third-party challenge, winning 17 percent of the popular vote. But LaFollette's strength was spread much too thin, and the only state he carried on Election Day was his home state of Wisconsin.

CALVIN COOLIDGE
30th President
★
1923 to 1929

BORN: JULY 4, 1872

BIRTHPLACE: PLYMOUTH, VT.

DIED: JANUARY 5, 1933

PARTY: REPUBLICAN

VICE PRESIDENT: CHARLES G. DAWES

FIRST LADY: GRACE ANNA GOODHUE

CHILDREN: JOHN, CALVIN JR.

NICKNAME: SILENT CAL

HAD AN ELECTRIC HORSE INSTALLED IN HIS WHITE HOUSE BEDROOM.

LUCKY LINDY LANDS SAFELY IN PARIS

PARIS, May 21, 1927—Twenty-five-year-old airmail pilot Charles Lindbergh took off yesterday in his monoplane from Long Island, New York. Today, he landed at Le Bourget airfield outside Paris. During the intervening 33½ hours, Lindbergh became the first person to fly nonstop across the Atlantic Ocean.

The solo flight has made him an international sensation. It has also promoted public acceptance of the airplane as a means of transportation.

For his thirty-six-hundred-mile journey aboard the *Spirit of St. Louis*, Lindbergh took with him a few sandwiches, a quart of water, and also some letters of introduction.

Lindbergh grew up in Little Falls, Minnesota, and Washington, D.C., where his father was a congressman. Consumed by a passion for flying, he dropped out of college during his second year and instead enrolled in flying school. Lindbergh traveled around the country performing as a stunt pilot before becoming an airmail pilot in 1926.

Vice Pres. Calvin Coolidge was vacationing at his father's home in Plymouth Notch, Vermont, when President Harding died in San Francisco. The Coolidges didn't have a telephone, so a messenger had to be sent by car from a nearby town. It was after midnight when Coolidge was awakened with the news that the president was dead.

The shocked vice president knelt to say a prayer. Then he went downstairs to a sitting room, where he was sworn into office shortly before 3:00 A.M. His father, a justice of the peace, administered the oath at this informal ceremony. Afterward, Coolidge went back upstairs and back to sleep.

The new president had a big job ahead of him. Within months, the nation would be shaken again by news of the Teapot Dome scandal. Quickly, the phrase *Teapot Dome* became common shorthand for government bribery and corruption. It was Coolidge's task to restore faith in the government and faith in the governing Republican party.

1926

"Silent Cal" succeeded beyond anyone's expectations. His quiet style of leadership, in contrast to the wildness of the Roaring Twenties, became his greatest asset. He moved aggressively to root out corruption, and by remaining calm, he soon persuaded Americans that the government's problems were over. As a result, he became a much-celebrated symbol of integrity in office.

Throughout his term, people identified Calvin Coolidge with the values of old-fashioned America. The New England Puritan ethic that he lived by honored thrift, industry, dignity, morality, frugality, and faith. Coolidge's convictions stood out prominently because they contrasted so vividly with the excesses and extravagance of the time.

THE BUSINESS OF AMERICA

Coolidge understood that American prosperity was closely linked to the success of the country's business community. "The chief business of America is business," he often said. Therefore, almost everything he did was designed to benefit business. In many ways, Coolidge's sober conservatism made possible the conditions under which Americans could enjoy their lighthearted frolics.

In his March 1925 inaugural address, Coolidge proposed tax cuts. He argued that reducing the income tax burden on the wealthiest Americans would benefit everybody by increasing business activity. It was an appealing policy (at least to the wealthy), and it worked as long as the economy continued to grow.

The new tax laws that Coolidge shepherded through Congress were extremely favorable to business. They lowered income taxes and eliminated several other taxes that had been put in place to raise money during World War I. To a great extent, the prosperity of the 1920s resulted from these tax reforms.

THE EARLY YEARS

CALVIN COOLIDGE SPENT HIS CHILDHOOD in Plymouth, Vermont, where his father was a shopkeeper active in local politics. It was from his father that Calvin inherited both his New England thrift and his restrained manner. After college, he became a lawyer.

The event that made Coolidge nationally famous took place during his term as governor of Massachusetts. In September 1919, the police force in Boston went on strike, leading to a crime wave in that city. Coolidge sent in state troops and upheld the police commissioner's decision not to rehire the strikers.

When American Federation of Labor president Samuel Gompers appealed to the governor to reconsider his decision, Coolidge sent him a characteristically terse reply. The telegram was reprinted throughout the country. "There is no right to strike against the public safety by anybody, anywhere, anytime," Coolidge wrote.

★**SILENT CAL** President Coolidge was widely known as a man of few words. His nickname, Silent Cal, reflected his reserved nature. But Coolidge was also quite witty.

On one occasion at the White House, a dinner guest made a bet with a friend that she could get Coolidge to say more than two words. When she told the president about her bet, Coolidge paused for a moment. Then he said, "You lose."

★**RADIO** Beginning in the early 1920s, radio truly changed American life. The number of stations broadcasting programs exploded from thirty in 1922 to more than five hundred in 1923. A decade later, two-thirds of homes in the United States had radios, which was twice the number of homes with telephones.

At first, there wasn't much advertising on the radio, and commercials were just one way that radio stations financed their programming. During the 1930s, however, radio commercials gained acceptance and became the norm. Soap makers, for example, sponsored popular daytime dramas that became known as soap operas.

★ **WALT DISNEY** In 1928, little-known animators Walt Disney and Ub Iwerks produced the first animated cartoon with sound. Their short film, *Steamboat Willie,* starred a new character whom they called Mickey Mouse.

From the moment that he first appeared in movie theaters, people loved Mickey Mouse. This success persuaded Disney, who provided the voice for Mickey, that the public enjoyed watching cartoons featuring animals who talked and behaved as people did. To satisfy this popular demand, Disney soon created Donald Duck and the dogs Pluto and Goofy.

★ **HARLEM RENAISSANCE** After World War I, New York City's Harlem neighborhood became a center for the creative outpouring of many African Americans who had recently arrived as part of the Great Migration. During the Harlem Renaissance, older black writers, especially James Weldon Johnson, encouraged younger writers, artists, and musicians to create works of art that described the unique experience of being black in the United States. Authors such as Langston Hughes and Zora Neale Hurston were among the first to write with awareness and pride about the black experience.

★ **BABE RUTH** When the Boston Red Sox sold Babe Ruth to the New York Yankees in 1920 for $125,000, the price was both astronomical and a bargain. The Roaring Twenties was a golden age for sports, and no star shone more brightly than the Babe's. Ruth's popularity had such a powerful effect on ticket sales that sportswriters called the new Yankee Stadium "The House That Ruth Built."

Such astounding feats as the sixty home runs he hit during the 1927 season earned the Sultan of Swat unprecedented salaries. Before the 1930 season, he signed a contract for eighty thousand dollars a year. When asked how he felt about making more money than President Hoover, the Babe said, "I had a better year," referring to the 1929 stock market crash.

As Coolidge had predicted, the tax cuts encouraged rich people to invest more of their money in business. What the frugal president hadn't expected, however, was that so many people would begin taking foolish risks in the hope of receiving even higher returns. Such unrestrained speculation was later seen as the cause of the 1929 stock market crash.

AVIATION One of Coolidge's most successful initiatives was his promotion of commercial aviation. Ever since the sensational experiments of the Wright brothers at the turn of the century, the aviation industry had grown by great leaps, and now passenger aircraft were becoming available for the first time.

In May 1926, Congress passed the Air Commerce Act, which placed commercial aviation under government regulation so that the fledgling industry could be nurtured. The bill also approved the first two commercial airline routes, one north–south and the other east–west.

FARM POLICY Coolidge was also successful in defeating bills that he didn't like. Twice Congress passed the McNaury-Haugen farm bill, and twice the president vetoed it. Under its terms, the government would have been required to buy surplus crops from U.S. farmers at a fixed price and then sell them abroad, often at a loss. The purpose of this bill was to protect farmers from unstable crop prices.

Coolidge attacked the bill as contrary to the free-market economy that he championed. He argued that the government had no business fixing crop prices and that American farmers should make do with the laws of supply and demand. According to the president's economic philosophy, crops should cost what people were willing to pay for them.

At the time, Coolidge's vetoes seemed sensible to most Americans, but they contributed greatly to the suffering of farmers in the country and later played a role in deepening the Great Depression.

THE KELLOGG-BRIAND PACT In foreign affairs, Coolidge generally followed the Republican party's policy of isolationism. One exception, however, was the far-reaching international treaty negotiated by Secretary of State Frank Kellogg and French foreign minister Aristide Briand.

The Kellogg-Briand Pact of 1928 was the most ambitious peacemaking effort yet. The countries that joined the United States and France in signing it agreed not to use war as a means of national policy. Eventually, all but five of the world's nations signed the accord, and it was celebrated as the start of a new era in international relations.

As later became obvious, however, the Kellogg-Briand Pact didn't end war because its expectations were unrealistic and impractical. The international community had no means of enforcing the treaty or disciplining countries that broke it other than going to war itself. The treaty did nothing, for example, to slow the rise of Nazi Germany or any of the other factors that led to World War II. The pact was well intentioned but turned out to be a complete failure.

Even though the country was still prosperous when Coolidge's first full term came to an end in 1928, he nevertheless decided not to run for reelection. In a characteristically brief announcement, Coolidge said, "I do not choose to run for president in 1928." He gave no further explanation. Instead, he retired to write his autobiography, which was naturally a very short book.

CAMPAIGN ★ 1928

WHEN PRESIDENT COOLIDGE ANNOUNCED that he would not run for reelection in 1928, Secretary of Commerce Herbert Hoover became the Republican front-runner. Hoover's support—which came primarily from women, Progressives, and immigrants—was strong enough to win him the Republican nomination.

In his acceptance speech after the convention, Hoover said, "We shall soon, with the help of God, be in sight of the day when poverty will be banished from this nation."

As a candidate, Hoover was remarkably quiet and shy. In contrast, the Democratic nominee, New York governor Alfred E. Smith, was extremely colorful and witty. He was also the first Roman Catholic to be nominated for president by a major political party.

HOOVER LUCKY POCKET PIECE

Smith campaigned for religious tolerance, but he was largely unsuccessful. Republicans put out pamphlets, without Hoover's consent, claiming that Smith would be the servant of the pope in Rome. Unfortunately for Smith, many Protestants in the Midwest and West believed what they read.

In the northern and eastern cities, Smith attracted huge and enthusiastic crowds, but his appeal remained regional. Hoover ran a much more modest campaign that emphasized the prosperity of the Coolidge years. It was more than enough. In November, he carried forty of the forty-eight states.

★For President★
ALFRED E. SMITH
WM. T. WAGER 500 WILLIS AVE. BRONX N.Y. TEL. MELROSE 7592-5021

HERBERT CLARK HOOVER

31st President
★
1929 to 1933

BORN: AUGUST 10, 1874

BIRTHPLACE: WEST BRANCH, IOWA

DIED: OCTOBER 20, 1964

PARTY: REPUBLICAN

VICE PRESIDENT: CHARLES CURTIS

FIRST LADY: LOU HENRY

CHILDREN: HERBERT JR., ALLAN

NICKNAME: CHIEF

THE FIRST PRESIDENT TO HAVE AN ASTEROID NAMED FOR HIM.

At the beginning of his presidency, Herbert Hoover was seen as a new, modern leader who could run the U.S. government efficiently. Americans already knew of his accomplishments during World War I, when he managed the distribution of eighteen million tons of food to starving people in Europe. As a result, a new verb came into the language—to *hooverize,* meaning "to conserve food for the war effort."

Hoover was also a self-made millionaire, which made him seem the right person for the times. The country was prosperous and believed that Hoover could lead it to even greater economic heights. People were not jealous of his wealth, because they knew that he had been orphaned as a child and had worked hard to earn his money.

Early on in his presidency, Hoover announced his hope that Americans could create a "new day," fulfilling the country's potential, especially in the area of science.

STOCK MARKET CRASHES

BLACK TUESDAY ENDS BOOM YEARS

NEW YORK, October 29, 1929—Wall Street collapsed today, as prices on the New York Stock Exchange fell disastrously in heavy trading. In just a few hours, stock in the nation's companies lost ten billion dollars' worth of value. Stocks that had been selling for twenty, thirty, and forty dollars a share only a few weeks ago were dumped for pennies in the desperate rush to sell. The nosedive taken by the market last week was nothing compared to today's disaster.

The predictions recently made by prominent bankers that the worst was over turned out to be tragically wrong, as did President Hoover's claim that the country's economy was "on a sound and prosperous basis." Evidently, the panic had already set in.

Experts say that the leading cause of the crash is wild and unregulated stock speculation, financed by borrowing. As long as prices went up, everyone made money. But when prices started to fall a week ago, brokers called in their customers' debts.

Because these investors had all their money tied up in stocks, they had to sell in order to pay the brokers. These sales drove down the market even farther until a stampede developed.

1930

Then came the stock market crash. Hoover responded to the crisis with energy and determination. He met with business leaders and delivered speeches designed to restore confidence in the economy. In these ways, he was quite active—more so than any president before him when faced with an economic crisis. But his efforts weren't nearly enough to reverse the rapid economic decline.

THE GREAT DEPRESSION

The crash immediately bankrupted investors who had been borrowing money to speculate in the stock market. Its lasting effects, however, touched all Americans, whether they owned stocks or not. Five thousand banks went under, wiping out the savings of nine million ordinary people, and during the next three years, an average of one hundred thousand people a week lost their jobs.

It appears that President Hoover simply failed to understand how bad things were. In March 1930, for example, he announced that "the evidences indicate that the worst effects of the crash upon unemployment will have passed during the next sixty days." Instead, unemployment got even worse. People who were scared of losing their jobs, or had already lost them, stopped making unnecessary purchases. As a result, businesses suffered more. Then, as demand fell, more jobs were lost.

As people's savings ran out, they became unable to repay their debts, and many lost their homes. Farmers couldn't make a living, either, because crop prices were so low. By 1930, four million people were unemployed. By 1932, twelve million people were out of work. This meant that one in four Americans had lost his or her job.

During the worst years of the Great Depression, starving people lined up for free soup and bread in towns and cities

---

THE EARLY YEARS

HERBERT HOOVER WAS BORN in West Branch, Iowa, which made him the first president born west of the Mississippi River. After the death of his father when he was six, Herbert was sent to live with relatives.

For eight months, he lived with an uncle on the Osage Indian reservation in Oklahoma. There, he played with Osage children and learned how to hunt with a bow and arrow. When he was nine, his mother died, and he was sent to live permanently with another uncle in Oregon.

At Stanford University, Hoover studied geology. After his graduation, he got a job as a mining engineer with a company that sent him to Australia, Burma, and China. Hoover and his wife, Lou, learned Chinese so well that they often spoke the language in the White House to protect themselves against eavesdropping.

★**FLY FISHING** Hoover was a dedicated fly fisherman. Occasionally, on weekends, he liked to escape the worries of the presidency by taking fly fishing trips. He favored a stretch of the Rapidan River in Virginia that is now part of Shenandoah National Park.

★**AL CAPONE** Prohibition meant good business for organized crime. Making liquor illegal didn't end the demand for it, so bootleggers prospered, especially in Chicago. The biggest of the mob bosses there was Al "Scarface" Capone.

Capone ordered a great many killings. The most famous was the 1929 St. Valentine's Day Massacre. On February 14 of that year, members of Capone's gang disguised themselves as policemen and raided a garage run by rival gangster Bugs Moran. Capone's men lined the Moran gang up against a wall and machine-gunned them to death. Newspapers later dramatized the event, which became a symbol of the violence that engulfed Prohibition-era Chicago.

★ THE DUST BOWL

Depression life in Oklahoma was made much worse by a severe drought that hit the region in the early 1930s. Conditions there became so bad that sometimes huge dust storms completely blocked the sun.

Hoping for a better life in California, many "Okies" headed west to work as migrant fruit pickers. John Steinbeck's novel *The Grapes of Wrath* and the songs of Woody Guthrie describe the terrible disappointments these people found in California: low wages, brutal working conditions, and little hope.

★ THE MARX BROTHERS

Americans often sought emotional relief from the Great Depression in Hollywood movies. Watching a silly comedy usually helped people forget their troubles, at least for a time. The Marx Brothers kept many Americans laughing when they might otherwise have been crying.

There were originally five Marx Brothers: Groucho, Chico, Harpo, Gummo, and Zeppo. But Gummo left the act before the brothers began making movies in the late 1920s. In those movies, Groucho, Harpo, and Chico were the central characters. Their comedy was particularly popular because it poked fun at stuffy rich people from the point of view of poor, disadvantaged outsiders.

across the nation. Resorts became ghost towns, and passenger trains rolled along with empty cars because no one could afford the fares.

THE SMOOT-HAWLEY TARIFF
Congress's response was the Smoot-Hawley Tariff of 1930, which raised tariff rates to record levels. Hoover knew that the bill was dangerous, but he went along anyway, thinking that he had no other choice. The goal of the tariff was to increase sales of U.S. products by raising the cost of imported goods.

But the new rates quickly led to an international trade war, as other nations raised their tariffs as well. This drastically reduced sales of U.S. goods overseas and deepened the already tragic worldwide depression.

By 1931, most Americans had decided that the government should provide direct aid to the unemployed. Other nations, such as Great Britain, were already doing this, but Hoover refused to permit such payments.

The president wanted to help people who were suffering, but he was not willing to give up his commitment to individual responsibility. He worried that direct aid to people would make them dependent on the government and undermine their ability to earn a living.

HOOVERVILLES
As a result, many people came to blame Hoover personally for their suffering. Homeless families who lived in shacks made out of discarded lumber and cardboard called their shantytowns Hoovervilles. The newspapers that they often used to cover themselves for warmth became Hoover blankets, and the wild rabbits that they killed for food were Hoover hogs.

A short decade earlier, Hoover had been hailed as the Great Humanitarian for

his efforts to feed the starving people of Europe. Now, his reassurances that conditions for the starving people of America would improve were greeted with jeers. No one believed him anymore, and his campaign promises of 1928 came back to haunt him.

While running for president, Hoover had said, "We shall soon, with the help of God, be in sight of the day when poverty will be banished from this nation." Of course, things didn't work out that way.

Throughout his term, Hoover refused to allow direct aid to the unemployed. He did, however, propose creation of the Reconstruction Finance Corporation, which Congress approved in January 1932. This agency loaned two billion dollars to businesses, banks, and state governments to help them survive the Great Depression. Hoover believed the money would eventually trickle down to the people who needed it, but it was much too little and much too late.

THE BONUS MARCH In May 1932, World War I veterans organized the Bonus March on Washington, D.C. In 1924, Congress had awarded them pay bonuses in the form of insurance redeemable in 1945. Because of the depression, however, the veterans wanted the payments moved up. Many argued that they could not afford to live until 1945 unless the bonuses were paid immediately.

When Congress turned them down, some members of the Bonus Army went back home, but others remained at their camp near the Capitol. In July, Hoover finally lost his patience and ordered the U.S. Army to drive the Bonus Army away. The use of tear gas and fixed bayonets against the veterans and their families was widely criticized. Once again, Hoover seemed insensitive to the suffering caused by the depression.

CAMPAIGN ★ 1932

THE GREAT DEPRESSION DOMINATED the 1932 campaign. The Republicans renominated Herbert Hoover because discarding the president would have meant admitting that the depression had been the fault of his Republican administration.

The Democrats nominated Franklin D. Roosevelt, the innovative governor of New York. Although crippled by polio in 1921, Roosevelt had made a dramatic comeback. After his nomination, Roosevelt flew to Chicago, where he became the first presidential candidate to deliver an acceptance speech in person. Among his most wealthy and influential supporters was Joseph P. Kennedy, whose son John would later run for president himself.

Because Roosevelt was largely confined to a wheelchair, most people thought that he would run a quiet campaign. But he surprised nearly everyone with an energetic spin around the country during which he delivered more than fifty speeches.

Roosevelt promised to get the country back on its feet with public works projects and government aid to farmers. He called his program a "new deal for the forgotten man." It was no accident that FDR's New Deal sounded a lot like his distant cousin Teddy Roosevelt's popular Square Deal.

President Hoover insisted that Roosevelt's policies would not work and continued to warn against direct government aid. But the voters didn't believe that the country was going to pull out of the depression by itself, and they gave Roosevelt forty-two of the forty-eight states.

FRANKLIN DELANO
ROOSEVELT
32nd President
★
1933 to 1945

Franklin D Roosevelt

BORN: JANUARY 30, 1882

BIRTHPLACE: HYDE PARK, N.Y.

DIED: APRIL 12, 1945

PARTY: DEMOCRAT

VICE PRESIDENTS: JOHN N. GARNER, HENRY A. WALLACE, HARRY S. TRUMAN

FIRST LADY: ANNA ELEANOR ROOSEVELT

CHILDREN: ANNA, JAMES, FRANKLIN, ELLIOT, FRANKLIN DELANO JR., JOHN

NICKNAME: FDR

THE FIRST PRESIDENT TO APPEAR ON TELEVISION.

Like Abraham Lincoln, Franklin Roosevelt became president during a time of great national crisis. The Great Depression had closed banks around the country and cut industrial production in half. More than thirteen million people had been put out of work, and one-quarter of the nation's farmers had lost their land because banks had foreclosed on their loans.

With ordinary Americans lining up at free soup kitchens in order to avoid starvation, Roosevelt knew that something had to be done quickly. "Action and action now" was his March 1933 inaugural promise. Showing that he could be composed under pressure, Roosevelt tried to reassure people. "The only thing we have to fear is fear itself," he said.

Early on, FDR's cabinet appointments showed that he intended to make changes in the way government was run,

OWENS FOILS HITLER
SPRINTER WINS OLYMPIC GOLD

BERLIN, Germany, August 16, 1936—The Summer Olympics ended here today with the host nation, Nazi Germany, winning the most medals. But U.S. sprinter Jesse Owens captured headlines around the world with his four gold-medal performances.

Owens won the two sprint events and the long jump. He also ran the anchor leg for the winning American sprint relay team. He equaled or surpassed the previous Olympic record in each of these events.

German dictator Adolf Hitler had intended to use the Berlin Olympics to show the world how completely his country has recovered from World War I. He also hoped to use the games to prove his theories that the white people of northern Europe are by nature superior to other races.

The medals that Owens, an African American, won here have proven to the world that Hitler's theories are wrong.

choosing liberals who were not afraid to experiment with bold reforms. He even appointed the first female cabinet officer, Secretary of Labor Frances Perkins.

THE BANKING CRISIS The most immediate of the president's problems was the banking crisis. Because so many banks had already failed, the public was fast losing confidence in the nation's financial institutions. Worried depositors began lining up at banks to withdraw their money rather than lose it. These "runs" threatened the entire banking system. On March 4, the day that Roosevelt took office, nearly half of the states declared bank "holidays" to protect their remaining banks from being driven out of business by the runs.

Two days later, Roosevelt declared a national bank holiday, halting all banking operations in the United States. Three days after that, Congress, which he had called into special session, passed the Emergency Banking Act. This law endorsed the president's action and kept the banks closed until federal auditors could examine their books.

In his first "fireside chat," delivered on March 12, Roosevelt explained to the American people the government's new banking policy, which restored much of the public's faith in the system. By the end of March, more than twelve thousand banks with 90 percent of the nation's deposits had reopened. Meanwhile, the closing of the unsound banks had stopped the runs. This resolution of the crisis showed early on the type of leader that Roosevelt would be: energetic, determined, and unafraid to take risks.

The president then followed up with serious banking reform. In June 1933, he signed the Banking Act, which created the Federal Deposit Insurance Corporation to guarantee individual accounts up

THE EARLY YEARS

As a boy, Franklin Roosevelt led a sheltered life. The pampered child of a wealthy family, he wore dress-like outfits until he was five years old, and then his mother began dressing him in kilts. Not until he turned eight did he wear his first pair of pants or take his first unsupervised bath.

Following the career path of his fifth cousin Theodore Roosevelt, Franklin entered politics in 1910, winning election to the New York state senate. Three years later, Woodrow Wilson named him assistant secretary of the navy.

In 1921, after running for vice president on the losing 1920 Democratic ticket, Roosevelt contracted polio, a disease that paralyzed his legs. He had to wear braces and use a wheelchair for the rest of his life, which made him more sensitive to the troubles of other people. After seven years of difficult physical therapy, however, he made a remarkable political comeback, winning election as governor of New York State in 1928.

★**MARION POST WOLCOTT** In 1938, Marion Post Wolcott took a job as a photographer with the Farm Security Administration. This New Deal agency was hiring out-of-work photographers to compile a visual record of life in the United States. She and other FSA photographers, including Walker Evans and Dorothea Lange, traveled all over the country, documenting the lives of everyday people. Meanwhile, the Works Progress Administration put other unemployed artists to work. The Federal Writers Project published a series of state-by-state guidebooks, while the Federal Theater Project staged free dramatic performances, including a black version of *Macbeth* that played to more than 120,000 people.

★THE HINDENBURG

The German airship *Hindenburg* began regularly scheduled transatlantic passenger service in May 1936. The 830-foot-long, hydrogen-filled zeppelin was a source of great pride for the Nazis. It carried fifty passengers in private cabins at a cruising speed of seventy-eight miles per hour.

On May 6, 1937, as the *Hindenburg* was approaching its mooring station at Lakehurst, New Jersey, the airship mysteriously burst into flames. Thirty-six people died in the explosion, which ended the brief era of lighter-than-air transport. Coincidentally, Herbert Morrison's report of the disaster was the first coast-to-coast radio broadcast.

★FIRESIDE CHATS

Early in his first term as president, FDR began a series of informal radio speeches. He called them fireside chats. His purpose was to explain the government's New Deal policies directly to the people.

The fireside chats reassured a worried nation. Americans listening on the radio could hear the optimism and firmness in the president's mellow voice. Speaking from the White House, Roosevelt seemed to be talking to each member of the audience personally. As a result, people came to believe that he understood their problems as no president had before.

★HUEY LONG

One of the country's best-known and most controversial politicians during the Great Depression was Huey Long, the governor of Louisiana. Long won the support of poor whites by improving rural roads and expanding government services. He paid for these programs by taxing corporations and the rich.

Nicknamed the Kingfish, Long used folksiness to hide his ruthless manner. In 1931, he resigned as governor to enter the U.S. Senate. There, he developed the Share-Our-Wealth program, promising to make "every man a king." To his critics, Long was a demagogue, who charmed uneducated voters with simplistic plans and impractical promises. Long planned to run for president in 1936, but in September 1935, at the height of his influence, he was assassinated in the Louisiana state capitol by the son-in-law of a politician whose career he had ruined.

to five thousand dollars. As intended, the new law gave depositors confidence that even if a bank went under, they would not lose their money.

THE HUNDRED DAYS Overall, during his first hundred days in office, Roosevelt demonstrated a concern for suffering Americans that Hoover may have felt but never projected. He also revolutionized the federal government's approach to the crisis, pushing Congress to create and fund numerous new agencies whose sole purpose was to offer relief. "Only a foolish optimist can deny the dark realities of the moment," Roosevelt said.

Between March and May 1933, Roosevelt sent stacks of New Deal legislation to Capitol Hill—where an obedient and heavily Democratic Congress, desperate for recovery, approved nearly all of the president's requests. Most of these were spending bills, because the New Deal's basic assumption was that massive government spending could "prime the pump" and get the economy moving again.

THE CIVILIAN CONSERVATION CORPS Unlike Hoover, Roosevelt believed that it was the federal government's responsibility to address the problems of the needy. The first New Deal program to help the unemployed was the Civilian Conservation Corps (CCC), which gave jobs to men between the ages of eighteen and twenty-five.

Recruited in the cities, these young men were put to work in rural camps built by the War Department. (The CCC camps were also run like army camps.) Workers made thirty dollars a month planting trees, building dams, and doing other jobs that helped conserve the environment. Twenty-two dollars of their salary was sent home each month to their families.

1936

Between 1933 and 1941, nearly three million Americans spent some time living and working in CCC camps.

In addition to jobs, the federal government also began giving out money. The Federal Emergency Relief Administration (FERA), created in May 1933, offered the first unemployment relief program. Led by Harry Hopkins, the FERA initially made cash payments directly to the unemployed. Then, because Hopkins believed that jobs were even more important, the FERA began providing those as well.

AGRICULTURAL PROGRAMS

Roosevelt also had the crisis in agriculture to resolve. Even before the Great Depression, farmers had been suffering from low crop prices, which fell even farther after the 1929 stock market crash. In April 1933, the *New York World-Telegram* wrote that "actual revolution already exists in the farm belt." In Iowa, farmers violently resisted when banks called in overdue mortgages, threatening to throw families out of their homes, and rioting in several counties forced the governor to declare martial law there.

The Agricultural Adjustment Act of May 1933 attempted to raise crop prices by cutting farm production. It authorized the government to pay farmers for taking land out of cultivation. This seemed a cruel thing to do while millions of Americans were starving in the cities, but Secretary of Agriculture Henry A. Wallace argued that farmers could not make a living any other way. "Agriculture cannot succeed in a capitalist society as a philanthropic enterprise," he said.

Another bold, original New Deal program was the Tennessee Valley Authority (TVA), which Congress created to build and run dams in seven southeastern states.

CAMPAIGN ★ 1936

NO ONE DOUBTED THAT FRANKLIN ROOSEVELT would be nominated for a second term. In his acceptance speech at the Democratic convention, the president said, "There is a mysterious cycle in human events. To some generations much is given. Of other generations much is expected. This generation of Americans has a rendezvous with destiny."

The Democrats used the New Deal to portray themselves as the party of ordinary people. Farmers, workers, and the unemployed were all firmly behind Roosevelt, as were blacks, who abandoned the party of Lincoln for the first time since the Civil War. Meanwhile, most Americans viewed Republicans as the party of wealthy conservatives.

Roosevelt's Republican opponent, Kansas governor Alfred M. Landon, campaigned against the New Deal, which he said was undermining American individualism and self-sufficiency. He also accused the Roosevelt administration of massive waste and inefficiency in its relief programs. FDR ignored these attacks and reminded voters that the Great Depression had started during a Republican administration.

While Landon wanted the federal government to stay out of business affairs, Roosevelt believed that it had a responsibility to protect workers by regulating the economy. Roosevelt's economic activism gave the Democrats a huge advantage.

DRIVE AHEAD WITH ROOSEVELT

A curious poll conducted by the *Literary Digest,* using names taken at random from telephone books, predicted that Landon would win in a landslide. Of course, the poll was wrong. It didn't take into account the fact that, during the Great Depression, most Americans were too poor to afford telephones. Those who did have phones, therefore, were more likely to be well-to-do Republicans who planned on voting for Landon. Instead of winning the election in a landslide, the Kansas governor lost by more than ten million votes in one of the worst defeats ever suffered by the presidential nominee of a major party.

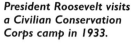

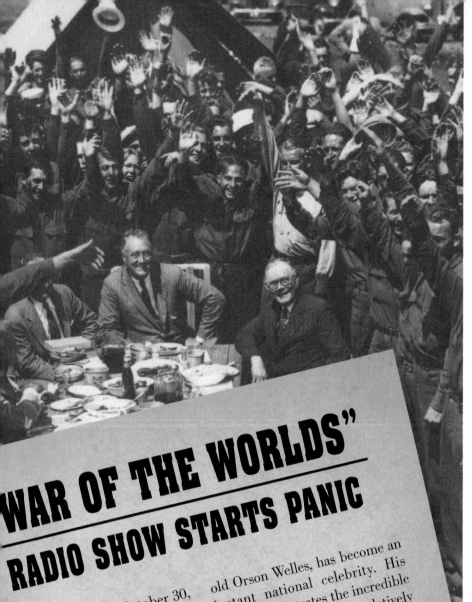

President Roosevelt visits a Civilian Conservation Corps camp in 1933.

Many of the TVA's four hundred thousand customers were rural farmers who had never before had access to electric power. Furthermore, besides generating and selling electricity, the TVA carried out reforestation and flood control projects as well.

THE NATIONAL RECOVERY ADMINISTRATION

Of all the New Deal programs, however, the cornerstone was the National Industrial Recovery Act of June 1933. This law established the National Recovery Administration (NRA), which worked with business groups and trade associations to create "codes of fair competition" for their industries. It was believed that these codes would provide a practical basis for regulating the marketplace.

Roosevelt agreed to suspend the nation's antitrust laws so that prices and production quotas could be fixed. In exchange, however, he demanded a number of concessions for workers, especially higher wages.

Eventually, 746 different NRA codes were developed, but they proved to be unwieldy and inefficient. Even worse, their complexity persuaded many conservative business leaders that the entire New Deal was terribly impractical. Factory owners also objected to Section 7(a) of the NRA law, which guaranteed workers the right to bargain collectively. This meant that unions could negotiate a single contract to cover everyone working in a factory.

WAR OF THE WORLDS" RADIO SHOW STARTS PANIC

NEW YORK CITY, October 30, 1938—A radio program broadcast on the CBS network tonight is causing a nationwide panic. The Mercury Theater of the Air's *War of the Worlds* radio play about a Martian invasion is causing thousands of people to flee their homes despite repeated announcements that the broadcast is only a dramatization.

The show features simulated news reports about a Martian landing at Grover's Mill, New Jersey. On a single block in nearby Newark, more than twenty families ran out into the street with wet towels over their faces because they believed the realistic reports of a gas raid.

The creator of this Halloween media hoax, twenty-three-year-old Orson Welles, has become an instant national celebrity. His work demonstrates the incredible power of radio, still a relatively new medium of communication.

SOCIAL SECURITY

One of the most lasting of Roosevelt's innovations was the Social Security Act of August 1935. This law provided for payments to people who were old, unemployed, sick, or disabled.

About the same time, Congress also passed the National Labor Relations Act (or Wagner Act), which made it illegal for employers to interfere with union organizing, and the Revenue Act of 1935 (or Wealth Tax), which raised individual income tax rates as high as 75 percent for people earning more than five million dollars a year.

What little political opposition there was to the early New Deal ended in November 1934, when the results of the midterm congressional elections added even more clout to what were already strong Democratic majorities in the House and Senate. In the House, Democrats won 319 of the 435 seats, while in the Senate, the party now controlled 69 of the 96 seats.

SUPREME COURT OPPOSITION

The only effective brake on President Roosevelt's ambitions during those years came from the Supreme Court, which struck down more than a few of his initiatives during 1935 and 1936. For example, the Court ruled that the NRA codes, the Agricultural Adjustment Act, and congressional acts relating to railroad retirement, the coal industry, farm mortgages, and cities that went bankrupt were all unconstitutional.

Although the specifics of these decisions varied, the justices generally agreed that the president had seized too much power that rightfully belonged to the states and Congress.

Meanwhile, heeding complaints that his New Deal agencies were disorganized, Roosevelt proposed a reorganization that

★THE FIRST LADY

Shy and insecure as a young woman, Eleanor Roosevelt later blossomed into the most active and admired of first ladies. She was also the first wife of a president to make public statements on current political issues.

Because both of her parents died while she was still in her teens, Eleanor grew up in an exclusive girls' boarding school in London. When she returned to New York as an adult, she took a job performing social work in the city's slums. That same year, she met Franklin Roosevelt, her fifth cousin once removed. Once their courtship began, Eleanor helped open Franklin's eyes to the terrible conditions endured by people who lived in the poor neighborhoods where she worked. Her uncle Theodore Roosevelt gave the bride away at their 1905 wedding.

After thirty-nine-year-old FDR contracted polio in 1921, Eleanor encouraged him to fight the disease and return to politics. Meanwhile, she attended political meetings on his behalf and became active in human rights organizations. In 1939, she resigned from the Daughters of the American Revolution to protest their refusal to let black singer Marian Anderson perform at Washington's Constitution Hall. After her husband's death, Pres. Harry Truman made Mrs. Roosevelt a member of the first U.S. delegation to the United Nations.

★AMELIA EARHART

Like Charles Lindbergh before her, Amelia Earhart performed such remarkable feats as a pilot and adventurer that she became a national hero. Earhart was the first woman to equal Lindbergh's solo transatlantic flight, and she was also the first person to fly solo from Hawaii to California, an even greater distance.

During the 1930s, she used her fame to promote two cherished causes: commercial aviation and women's rights. In 1937, she attempted to fly around the world with navigator Fred Noonan. Their twin-engine Lockheed Electra disappeared on July 2 during the most dangerous leg of the trip, from New Guinea to tiny Howland Island in the middle of the Pacific Ocean. Their fate remains a mystery.

★ THE ABRAHAM LINCOLN BATTALION

In 1936, a civil war began in Spain between the Nationalist rebels and the Republicans who had been elected to govern the country. Fascist Italy and Nazi Germany sent troops and tanks to support the Nationalists, while the Republicans turned to the Soviet Union for help. Although the U.S. government decided not to become involved, many Americans supported the Republican cause on a personal basis.

Soviet officials organized the International Brigades, made up of idealistic young volunteers eager to fight for democracy and freedom in Spain. One of these brigades included the Abraham Lincoln Battalion, at first made up entirely of Americans. Nearly three thousand young men, mostly students without any military training, served in the battalion. Republican sympathizer Ernest Hemingway set his popular 1940 novel *For Whom the Bell Tolls* during the Spanish Civil War, which the Nationalists won in 1939.

★ NYLON

During the 1930s, DuPont chemist Wallace H. Carothers developed the first artificial fiber, later named nylon. In 1938, the first nylon toothbrushes were put on sale. Two years later, the first women's stockings made from this "miracle fabric" appeared in department stores across the country.

Nylon stockings quickly became the rage, helping to define a new 1940s fashion. The first nylons had dark seams running up the back of each leg. Like silk stockings, they were held up by garters. When the government began rationing nylon during World War II—to the horror of American women—a black market quickly developed. Meanwhile, women who couldn't get nylons began decorating their legs with black lines that looked like stocking seams.

Congress passed as the Emergency Relief Appropriations Act of April 1935. This law consolidated most of the existing New Deal relief programs, including the FERA, into a new agency, the Works Progress Administration (WPA), which former FERA head Harry Hopkins was immediately named to run. During the next eight years, the WPA developed and funded public works projects that created jobs for over eight million people.

PACKING THE SUPREME COURT

By the time that Roosevelt began his second term in 1937, government spending had brought about a limited recovery. But the president was frustrated by his less-than-complete success, and he was especially angry with the Supreme Court, whose aging justices had blocked many of Roosevelt's unorthodox initiatives for being constitutionally questionable.

To bypass this roadblock, Roosevelt proposed in February 1937 a plan to re-organize the Supreme Court. Specifically, he wanted to appoint a new justice for each justice currently over seventy years of age. Because six of the justices were already older than seventy, enactment of this plan would have allowed Roosevelt to appoint six additional justices, bringing the total number to fifteen.

Most Americans agreed that something ought to be done to prevent the Court from continually blocking the president's reforms, but few people liked the reorganization plan. Publicly, Roosevelt claimed that he was merely trying to reduce the workloads of the aging justices. But most people realized that he was really attempting to control the Court by creating a new majority that would favor the New Deal.

The Senate eventually rejected the plan, but in the meantime, the justices got the message. While the bill was still

under consideration, a previously conservative justice began voting with the Court's liberal bloc. This switch made the difference in two important 5–4 rulings supporting minimum wage laws and the Social Security Act.

AMERICA IN ISOLATION The many difficulties at home made it especially easy for Americans to ignore threatening events abroad. For example, during the 1930s, Germany, Italy, and Japan all became increasingly aggressive. Germany took back land that it had lost during World War I, while Italy invaded Ethiopia and Japan conquered Manchuria on the Chinese mainland. The U.S. response in each case was essentially to ignore what had happened. Isolationists at home believed that the Atlantic and Pacific Oceans were enough to insulate the nation from other countries' wars.

In keeping with this isolationist attitude, Congress enacted a series of neutrality acts, beginning in August 1935, which prevented Americans from selling arms to nations at war. After World War I, many people had come to believe that arms dealers had secretly conspired to start that war because wars were good for businesses. It was thought, therefore, that banning arms sales would stop the fighting.

Unfortunately, this policy benefited the aggressor nations, which had been stockpiling weapons for years, at the expense of their victims, who were often unprepared for invasion. During the Spanish Civil War, for example, U.S. neutrality laws prevented Americans from helping the Republican side, while the Nationalists received huge amounts of military aid from fellow fascists in Italy and Germany.

In his famous "quarantine" speech of October 5, 1937, President Roosevelt demanded that freedom-loving nations

CAMPAIGN ★ 1940

DURING THE SUMMER OF 1940, FDR kept his reelection plans secret. Not even the delegates to the Democratic convention knew what he intended. When Postmaster General James Farley, a trusted political ally, asked FDR's permission to launch his own campaign, the president told him to go ahead. Farley thought that Roosevelt had decided to retire, but Roosevelt was really working behind the scenes to have the convention draft him.

Never before had a president run for a third term, and Roosevelt was worried that the voters might think him arrogant. By having the convention draft him, which it did, FDR could pretend that a third term had been forced on him by the will of the people.

To oppose Roosevelt, the Republicans nominated Indiana businessman Wendell L. Willkie, who ran a power company. Willkie had been a Democrat as late as 1932, when he contributed $150 to Roosevelt's first campaign. But he later became a Republican after breaking with the president over the Tennessee Valley Authority, which competed with Willkie's own company.

Unlike FDR's first two campaigns, which had been dominated by economic issues, the 1940 race focused on the war in Europe and the prospect of an unprecedented third term for Roosevelt. Both candidates pledged to keep the country out of the war, but those who wanted the United States to take a stronger stand against Hitler tended to favor Roosevelt.

Because Willkie basically agreed with Roosevelt on economic matters, he attacked the president instead for defying the tradition of stepping down after two terms. Given the dangerous international situation, this wasn't much of a reason to vote for Willkie, and the country decided to stick with a proven, trusted leader. Although three-quarters of the nation's newspapers endorsed Willkie, FDR's strong support in the cities and among the working class carried him to victory.

President Roosevelt in a wartime discussion with Winston Churchill.

of the world spurn aggressor nations. Ninety percent of the world's nations wanted peace, he said. The remaining 10 percent needed to be controlled as though they were a disease.

"We are determined to keep out of war," the president said, but the world's interdependence "makes it impossible for any nation completely to isolate itself from economic and political upheavals in the rest of the world, especially when such upheavals appear to be spreading and not declining."

Roosevelt's speech created an uproar among isolationists, who feared that he was inching America closer to war. In response, FDR backed away from this strong public position but remained privately determined to resist aggression as best he could.

THE GOOD NEIGHBOR POLICY

Throughout his first two terms in office, Roosevelt worked hard to improve U.S. relations with Latin America. In his first inaugural address, he said that he wanted to "dedicate this nation to the policy of the good neighbor."

For many decades, of course, the United States had been a difficult neighbor. As recently as the 1920s, Presidents Harding and Coolidge had sent U.S. troops into Panama, the Dominican Republic, and Honduras. When violence followed the withdrawal of U.S. troops from Nicaragua in 1925, Coolidge didn't hesitate to send them back in order to meet our "moral responsibility" there.

Roosevelt now promised to put an end to such interference. At the Montevideo Conference of American States in

JAPANESE ATTACK PEARL HARBOR!

SURPRISE AIR RAID SINKS PACIFIC FLEET

PEARL HARBOR, Hawaii, December 7, 1941—At five minutes before eight this morning, Japanese dive-bombers and torpedo planes launched a surprise attack on the U.S. naval base at Pearl Harbor.

Eight battleships were crippled at their moorings. Meanwhile, at a nearby army air base, half of the fighter planes were destroyed while they sat on the tarmac. In all, more than twenty-three hundred U.S. servicemen were killed during the raid.

The Japanese can now proceed with their plans for the conquest of East Asia unhindered by the U.S. Pacific Fleet, which has been seriously damaged.

President Roosevelt is expected to ask for a declaration of war when he appears before a joint session of Congress tomorrow.

December 1933, Secretary of State Cordell Hull voted in favor of a declaration that "no state has the right to intervene in the internal or external affairs of another." Having thus resolved the issue in a friendly manner, the Roosevelt administration was later able to count on Latin American governments when it needed their help in the fight against Hitler.

PREPARATIONS FOR WAR World War II began in September 1939, when Nazi Germany invaded Poland. This caused Britain and France, which were allies of Poland, to declare war on Germany. Although the current neutrality law prevented the Roosevelt administration from taking sides in the conflict, the president made it more than clear which side he favored. "Even a neutral cannot be asked to close his mind or his conscience," the president said.

Throughout 1940, with Great Britain in danger of collapse, Americans debated what to do. Isolationists organized the America First Committee to publicize their view that the country should mind its own business. At committee rallies, prominent isolationists, such as Charles Lindbergh, warned that the United States would suffer terribly if it became drawn into the war. But Roosevelt quite clearly saw the threat that Hitler posed, and after the fall of France in June 1940, he did everything he could within the law to save the British.

On September 3, 1940, for example, he sent fifty surplus destroyers to Great Britain in exchange for the use of naval bases in Newfoundland and Bermuda. The British desperately needed these destroyers to fight the German U-boats that were sinking many British (and some American) ships in the North Atlantic.

Later, in a December 1940 fireside chat, Roosevelt again declared his support

★**JAPANESE INTERNMENT CAMPS** During the months after Pearl Harbor, many Californians began focusing their

anger on the 127,000 Japanese Americans living in the United States, mostly on the West Coast. Rumors spread quickly that Japanese Americans were planning to sabotage military bases. In February 1942, President Roosevelt ordered all Japanese Americans, whether they were citizens or not, removed from the West Coast to internment

camps as far away as Arkansas. This policy was urged on him in part by people who proceeded to buy up—at bargain prices—the rich farmland that relocated Japanese families were forced to sell. No similar efforts were made to curb the freedoms of German or Italian Americans, however.

★**FALA** One of the most famous White House pets was FDR's dog Fala. This little black Scottie went everywhere with the president. When Roosevelt and British prime minister Churchill met at sea to sign the Atlantic Charter in 1941, Fala was there at his master's feet. Later, on a presidential voyage to Hawaii in 1944, sailors aboard the cruiser *Baltimore* lured Fala belowdecks to pluck tufts of his hair for souvenirs.

★ THE HOME FRONT

After its entry into World War II, the United States mobilized to fight on three fronts: in Asia, in Europe, and at home. Between 1941 and 1945, fifteen million men—and for the first time, nearly two hundred thousand women—served in the armed forces. At home, however, the men who joined the military left behind important jobs on the nation's assembly lines that had to be filled. A government campaign featuring a character called Rosie the Riveter encouraged women to do their part for the war effort. The enthusiastic response allowed factories in crucial war-related industries to keep up production both day and night.

★ THE MANHATTAN PROJECT

In August 1939, Albert Einstein, the most famous scientist in the world, wrote a letter to President Roosevelt on behalf of colleagues who had recently fled Nazi Germany. In this secret letter, Einstein warned the president that the Germans were already working on an atomic bomb, and he advised the U.S. government to do likewise.

Although a little slowly at first, Roosevelt eventually devoted two billion dollars to atomic research. The code name given the bomb program was the Manhattan Project, because most of the early work took place at Columbia University in Manhattan.

On July 16, 1945, the first atomic bomb was detonated near Alamogordo in the New Mexican desert. The blast produced a flash of light that could be seen as far as 180 miles away. It also vaporized the bomb tower and turned desert sand to glass for four hundred yards around.

★ THE GEODESIC DOME

R. Buckminster Fuller was a visionary architect and engineer who devoted his life to conserving the natural resources of the planet he called Spaceship Earth. During the 1940s, he developed the geodesic dome. Fuller's revolutionary geometric design was uniquely balanced so that gravity didn't limit its size. People could build geodesic domes as large as they wanted.

Fuller's domes offered many possibilities for the future. Because their strength actually increased with their size, geodesic domes could be built to enclose entire cities or to protect people living underwater or on other planets. One of the most famous geodesic domes would be built to house the U.S. pavilion at the 1967 World's Fair in Montreal.

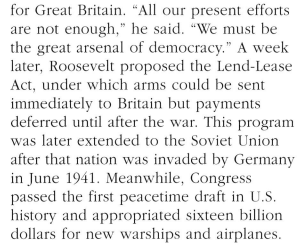

for Great Britain. "All our present efforts are not enough," he said. "We must be the great arsenal of democracy." A week later, Roosevelt proposed the Lend-Lease Act, under which arms could be sent immediately to Britain but payments deferred until after the war. This program was later extended to the Soviet Union after that nation was invaded by Germany in June 1941. Meanwhile, Congress passed the first peacetime draft in U.S. history and appropriated sixteen billion dollars for new warships and airplanes.

In August 1941, Roosevelt met with British prime minister Winston Churchill aboard a battleship anchored off Newfoundland. The meeting marked the beginning of an exceptionally close relationship between the two men. Together, they drew up the Atlantic Charter, which defined their common war aims. Chief among these aims was the right of every people to choose their own form of government.

"DR. WIN THE WAR" The United States finally entered World War II after the Japanese bombed Pearl Harbor in December 1941. Tensions between the United States and Japan had been building since the Japanese invasion of China in July 1937. Then, in September 1940, Japan joined Axis powers Germany and Italy in signing the Tripartite Pact, which stated that war against one meant war against all.

With characteristic energy and determination, Roosevelt set about retooling the country's economy for war. In his own words, "Dr. Win the War" was replacing "Dr. New Deal." Soon, nearly every person and resource in the country was playing some part in the war effort. Meanwhile, the new Office of Price Administration was beginning to ration strategically important commodities, such as rubber, gasoline, and even sugar.

After the Allied invasion of North Africa in November 1942, Roosevelt met with Churchill at Casablanca in Morocco. In November 1943, the two leaders met again, this time with Soviet premier Joseph Stalin at Teheran in Iran.

At Teheran, Roosevelt and Churchill assured Stalin that they would invade German-occupied France the following summer. Yet Stalin was less than pleased because he had already been waiting a year for this promised second front in Europe. Meanwhile, the German army had been focusing its troop strength on the Russian front in the East, where the Soviets were taking heavy losses.

D DAY Gen. Dwight D. Eisenhower, the top Allied commander in Europe, decided that the invasion of France would take place in Normandy on June 6, 1944, code-named D day. The success of this invasion, the largest amphibious operation in history, gave the Allies a foothold in Europe, which they kept expanding until France was liberated and Germany itself threatened.

When the Big Three met for the last time in February 1945 at Yalta in the Soviet Union, the end of the war was definitely in sight. By this time, however, Roosevelt's health was failing.

At Yalta, Stalin forced the president to agree to the creation of Communist governments in Eastern Europe. Many historians have since used Roosevelt's poor health to explain his concessions. But others have pointed out that Roosevelt had little choice. To have fought Stalin at Yalta would have meant little unless the U.S. Army was willing to fight the Soviets in Eastern Europe as well.

On April 12, 1945, as the Allies converged on Berlin, Roosevelt died. Less than a month later, on May 7, the Germans formally surrendered, ending the war in Europe.

CAMPAIGN ★ 1944

AFTER TWELVE DIFFICULT YEARS in the White House, Roosevelt's health was clearly failing. The Democratic party was certain to nominate him for a fourth term, but a few top party leaders understood that Roosevelt would probably die in office and that his running mate would therefore become president. Because most of these men disliked Vice Pres. Henry A. Wallace, whom they considered a socialist, Wallace was replaced at the convention with Sen. Harry Truman of Missouri.

The Republican candidate, New York governor Thomas E. Dewey, had been the front-runner for the 1940 nomination before Wendell Willkie took it away from him. This time, Dewey won on the first ballot with 1,056 of the 1,057 votes. (The other vote went to Gen. Douglas MacArthur.)

During the 1930s, Dewey had made a name for himself fighting organized crime as the district attorney in New York City. As governor, he had battled corruption in the state's police department and improved conditions in its mental health facilities.

With World War II still under way, Dewey refused to criticize Roosevelt's foreign policy. He did, however, make Roosevelt's health an issue, attacking "the tired old men" in Washington who had been running the country for so many years. In response, FDR's doctor announced publicly that the president was in excellent health. Roosevelt also campaigned in bad weather to prove that he was fit enough to lead.

Meanwhile, the Democrats argued that Dewey, who had no foreign policy experience, was not qualified to become president during wartime. Their slogan, "Don't Change Horses Midstream," supported this criticism and summed up Roosevelt's appeal. In November, FDR won again, but this time by a narrower margin than in any of his previous victories.

Born: May 8, 1884

BORN: MAY 8, 1884

BIRTHPLACE: LAMAR, MO.

DIED: DECEMBER 26, 1972

PARTY: DEMOCRAT

VICE PRESIDENT: ALBEN W. BARKLEY

FIRST LADY: ELIZABETH (BESS) VIRGINIA WALLACE

CHILDREN: MARGARET

NICKNAME: MAN FROM INDEPENDENCE

THE FIRST PRESIDENT TO TRAVEL UNDERWATER IN A MODERN SUBMARINE.

1945

HARRY S. TRUMAN

33rd President
★
1945 to 1953

Harry Truman

On April 12, 1945, just five weeks into his vice presidency, Harry S. Truman was suddenly called to the White House. He met Eleanor Roosevelt in her study. The first lady put her arm around Truman's shoulder and said, "Harry, the president is dead."

Truman's first thoughts were for FDR's widow. "Is there anything I can do for you?" he asked Mrs. Roosevelt. She shook her head and replied, "Is there anything we can do for you? For you are the one in trouble now."

Franklin Roosevelt had been running the country for more than twelve years when he died. For Truman—or anyone else—to succeed him would not be easy, especially during wartime.

ATOMIC BOMB DROPPED ON HIROSHIMA

HIROSHIMA, Japan, August 6, 1945—The first atomic bomb ever used in warfare was dropped today on the Japanese city of Hiroshima. Of the 344,000 people living there, approximately one hundred thousand were killed instantly. Another hundred thousand died later from burns and radiation poisoning.

The ten-foot-long bomb, code-named Little Boy, was carried by the *Enola Gay*. This B-29 bomber dropped Little Boy from an altitude of thirty-two thousand feet. The bomb exploded two thousand feet above the ground, leveling more than four square miles of the city. Waves of flame engulfed the rest of Hiroshima, and the river flooded, trapping wounded people too weak to move.

President Truman justified the massive civilian casualties by pointing to the hundreds of thousands of U.S. servicemen who might have died during an invasion of Japan.

Roosevelt had brought the country through the Great Depression and won World War II in Europe. But Japan still had to be defeated, and Communism already seemed to be threatening the stability of the postwar world.

THE POTSDAM CONFERENCE Truman began at an even greater disadvantage because Roosevelt had never included him in policy meetings. Therefore, Truman wasn't even briefed on the atomic bomb project until after he became president. As a result, he had to learn many things in a hurry. His first important test came in July 1945, when he traveled to Germany to meet with British prime minister Winston Churchill and Soviet premier Joseph Stalin.

At their conference, held in the Berlin suburb of Potsdam, the three leaders agreed to divide postwar Germany into four zones of occupation, each controlled by an Allied power (their three nations plus France). The zones roughly corresponded to Allied troop positions at the end of the war—except with regard to Berlin. Although the German capital fell entirely within the Soviet zone, it was nonetheless divided into four sectors, one for each Allied power.

THE ATOMIC BOMB On July 16, the day before the Potsdam conference began, American scientists conducted the first atomic bomb test near Alamogordo, New Mexico. The British were aware of the test because they had helped with the research, but the Soviets had been told nothing of the Manhattan Project. After learning of the test's success, Truman decided to tell Stalin about the new U.S. superweapon.

Ten days later, the Allied leadership at Potsdam decided to send an ultimatum to the Japanese: "The alternative to surren-

THE EARLY YEARS

Harry Truman had to wear thick glasses during his childhood in Independence, Missouri—and because the glasses were expensive, his mother wouldn't allow him to play contact sports. Other boys sometimes teased him for taking piano lessons instead.

"I was kind of a sissy," Truman later recalled. After serving in World War I, he opened a men's clothing store in Kansas City. The business failed in 1922, but that same year, with the backing of local political boss Thomas J. Pendergast, Truman won election to the top job in Jackson County. In 1934, also with help from Pendergast, he won a seat in the U.S. Senate.

Although Truman was sometimes called "the senator from Pendergast," most Washington insiders considered him a capable and honest public servant. The Pendergast machine was no doubt corrupt, but Truman said that Pendergast never asked him to do anything dishonest because "he knew I wouldn't do it."

★ THE GI BILL OF RIGHTS

The GI Bill of Rights was the name that soldiers gave to the Servicemen's Readjustment Act of 1944. Congress passed this bill to provide benefits for GIs fighting in World War II. It established a system of veterans' hospitals to offer free medical care. It also set aside funds for GIs in the form of low-interest mortgages, small-business loans, and college scholarships. The money that the GI Bill provided for tuition and living expenses allowed nearly eight million veterans to attend colleges and trade schools after the war. In this way, the GI Bill played an important part in retraining soldiers for jobs in the peacetime economy.

★ THE BUCK STOPS HERE

Harry Truman had a particularly feisty personality. "If you can't stand the heat, get out of the kitchen," he liked to say. He occasionally lost his temper in public and was known to use vulgar language at times. But Truman's scrappiness gave him the self-confidence he needed to make difficult decisions. A sign on his desk read, "The Buck Stops Here." This meant that he never "passed the buck," or made someone else take responsibility for a decision.

★ **THE UNITED NATIONS** The United Nations was created at the end of World War II. Its purpose was to prevent wars, promote human rights, and aid economic development throughout the world. Delegates from fifty nations attended the conference in San Francisco at which the UN Charter was drafted and then signed in June 1945.

Twenty-five years and one world war earlier, the U.S. Senate had debated the League of Nations Covenant to the Treaty of Versailles for eight months before rejecting it. This time around, the United States became the first country to join the new international organization. After just six days of debate in July 1945, the Senate ratified the UN Charter by a vote of 89–2.

JACKIE ROBINSON

third base BROOKLYN DODGERS

★ **JACKIE ROBINSON** On April 15, 1947, twenty-eight-year-old Jackie Robinson became the first black to play in a major league baseball game. Until Robinson broke the color barrier, African Americans were forced to play in segregated Negro leagues.

All through Robinson's rookie year with the Brooklyn Dodgers, fans and players taunted the second baseman, calling him "nigger" and "jungle boy." But the dignified and courageous Robinson never retaliated. He just played as well as he could. That year, he was named the National League's Rookie of the Year. Two years later, he won the league's Most Valuable Player award.

der is prompt and utter destruction." But the Japanese, unaware of the atomic bomb, saw no reason to surrender.

Japan's defiance compelled Truman to make one of the most terrifying decisions ever forced on a president: whether or not to use an atomic bomb on a city. If he did use the bomb, hundreds of thousands of Japanese civilians would die. If he didn't use the bomb, hundreds of thousands of American soldiers might also die during the planned invasion of Japan. Although Truman feared the consequences of unleashing the new weapon, he decided that his primary responsibility was to safeguard the lives of U.S. servicemen.

When the August 6 attack on Hiroshima failed to produce an immediate Japanese surrender, Truman ordered a second bomb dropped on Nagasaki. On August 10, Japan sued for peace. As one war ended, however, another began.

THE COLD WAR Stalin had made it clear at Yalta that he would accept nothing less than secure postwar borders for the Soviet Union. This meant there would have to be Soviet-dominated Communist governments in Eastern Europe. Stalin feared that the Germans would recover quickly, as they had after World War I, and he wanted a buffer zone.

Truman and Churchill, however, feared the Germans now much less than the Soviets, and they were particularly concerned about Stalin's imposition of Communism on Eastern Europe. In a March 1946 speech delivered in Fulton, Missouri, Churchill declared that an "iron curtain" was falling across Europe. On one side were the democrats of the West; on the other, the Communists of the East.

The struggle between these competing political philosophies became known as the Cold War. Although the United States

1948

and the Soviet Union never fought each other directly, they used surrogates, notably the Koreans and the Vietnamese, to fight their battles for them.

THE TRUMAN DOCTRINE

The first important conflict of the Cold War took place in the Mediterranean, where Communist rebels threatened to overthrow elected governments in Greece and Turkey. Many experts pointed out that these governments often treated their people harshly, but Truman didn't really care. He believed that their strong anticommunism was more important, because he wanted to check the spread of Soviet influence wherever he could.

He outlined his policy for the containment of Communism in a speech he delivered to Congress on March 12, 1947. Justifying his four-hundred-million-dollar aid request for Greece and Turkey, Truman argued that the United States must help every nation facing a Communist threat. This policy later became known as the Truman Doctrine.

THE MARSHALL PLAN

Meanwhile, Secretary of State George C. Marshall tackled the rebuilding of war-ravaged Europe. Four hundred thousand U.S. soldiers had died in World War II, but almost none of the fighting had taken place on American soil. Central Europe was not so fortunate. Nearly six years of tank battles and Allied bombing had reduced its industrial cities to rubble. (This destruction was in addition to the deaths of some seven million Germans, about the same number of Poles, and more than twenty million Soviets.)

Three months after the president's Truman Doctrine speech, Marshall unveiled his plan to rebuild Europe. The only way to save the exhausted

CAMPAIGN ★ 1948

BEFORE THE 1948 CAMPAIGN, most political professionals wrote Truman off as a caretaker president. Liberals within the Democratic party, including FDR's sons, tried to persuade retired general Dwight Eisenhower to run for president as a Democrat, but Eisenhower refused. Things got worse for Truman at the convention, where Mayor Hubert H. Humphrey of Minneapolis led a successful fight to include a strong civil rights plank in the party platform. Thirty-five southern delegates walked out in protest.

After the convention, a group of southern Democrats met in Birmingham, Alabama, to form the States' Rights (or Dixiecrat) party and nominate South Carolina governor Strom Thurmond for president. Meanwhile, the liberal Roosevelt wing of the party, upset with Truman's tough stand against the Soviet Union, put up Henry Wallace as the candidate of the Progressive party. Wallace promoted peace with the Soviets and criticized the Marshall Plan as an insidious attempt by U.S. corporations to take over Europe.

Abandoned by so many members of his own party, Truman wasn't given much of a chance to beat Thomas Dewey, again the Republican nominee. But while Dewey sat back and waited for victory, Truman fought hard. During a thirty-thousand-mile "whistle-stop" train campaign, he made three hundred speeches to six million people. His gutsy  manner and blunt attacks on the "do-nothing Eightieth Congress" roused the country. "Give 'em hell, Harry," one man yelled at a rally in Seattle.

Yet all the polls and even the early returns indicated that he would lose. On Election Day, the early edition of the *Chicago Tribune* ran the headline DEWEY DEFEATS TRUMAN. Later, the president posed with this headline after upset victories in California and Ohio clinched his election.

FOR PRESIDENT

nations of Western Europe from Communism, Marshall believed, was to get their economies rolling again. For this, they would need lots of U.S. dollars.

Between 1948 and 1952, Congress appropriated thirteen billion dollars for the Marshall Plan. Half of this money went to Britain, France, and West Germany, which was created in 1949 out of the merger of the British, French, and American zones of occupation.

Marshall offered to include the Soviets in his reconstruction program. "Our policy is directed not against any country or doctrine, but against hunger, poverty, desperation, and chaos," he said. But Stalin, ever suspicious, turned down the offer.

THE BERLIN AIRLIFT

Soon, the Soviet Union decided to test the West's resolve in Berlin. In order to get the British, French, and Americans to leave, the Soviets decided to blockade West Berlin, beginning in April 1948.

Responding quickly and decisively, Truman ordered the airlifting of goods to the besieged city. Using a constant shuttle of cargo planes, the United States and Great Britain were able to keep West Berlin supplied with food, coal, and other necessities. The blockade ended in May 1949, when the Soviets reopened roads leading into and out of the city.

The Berlin airlift made clear the need for a united front in Western Europe. This need was met by the North Atlantic Treaty

COMMUNISTS INVADE SOUTH KOREA

NEW YORK, June 25, 1950— The Communist government of North Korea launched a full-scale military invasion of South Korea today, as North Korean troops crossed the Thirty-eighth Parallel border in force.

In an emergency meeting this afternoon, the UN Security Council voted 9–0 to hold North Korea accountable for the attack. The resolution is a prelude to sending UN troops to Korea. U.S. soldiers are expected to make up more than three-quarters of the combat troops used in this UN "police action."

As a permanent member of the Security Council, the Soviet Union could have vetoed the resolution, but the Soviet leadership continues to boycott Security Council meetings. The boycott began when the other council members refused to recognize the Communist People's Republic as the rightful government of China.

Organization (NATO), created in April 1949. Truman's active support for NATO finally put an end to the isolationism that had directed U.S. foreign policy since the time of George Washington.

The president had hoped that his use of the atomic bomb in 1945 would scare other nations, especially the Soviet Union, into maintaining the peace. But the testing of a Soviet bomb in August 1949 forced him to change his thinking. Now he concluded that peace depended on a stable "balance of terror" between the two superpowers.

THE FAIR DEAL With regard to domestic issues, Truman had an easier time, at least initially. Of all the nations that fought in World War II, only the United States came out of the war better off economically. After years of rationing, Americans were eager to spend the money they had saved on large purchases such as cars, houses, and home appliances.

Truman's biggest problem was how to handle the massive demobilization of troops. At the end of World War II, there were twelve million men and women serving in the armed forces. Within a year, nine million would be discharged.

The president's economic advisers worried that discharged soldiers would have a difficult time finding new jobs now that many of their old jobs had been taken over by women and blacks. "Rosie the Riveter isn't going back to emptying slop jars," one union leader said. "Times have changed. People have become accustomed to…new ways of being treated."

Two trends did ease the job crunch, however. On the one hand, many women began leaving the workforce to become housewives and mothers. On the other, the nation's postwar spending spree created enough new jobs, especially in

★ **THE FIRST FAMILY** Truman first met Bess Wallace in Sunday school. "I had only one sweetheart from the time I was six," he said later. But Harry and Bess didn't start dating until 1913, when they were both nearly thirty years old, and they didn't marry until 1919. In 1924, their only child, Margaret, was born. She was outgoing, like her mother.

During her father's presidency, Margaret Truman tried to launch a singing career. She made her debut before a national radio audience in March 1947. In 1950, the *Washington Post* music critic wrote that she "cannot sing with anything approaching professional finish." After reading this review, the president sent the critic an angry letter: "I have just read your lousy review….You sound like a frustrated old man who never made a success….I never met you, but if I do you'll need a new nose."

★ **LEVITTOWN** The return of soldiers to civilian life caused a severe housing shortage during the years immediately following World War II. To relieve this problem, the construction firm of Levitt and Sons built a planned community on New York's Long Island that soon provided a model for suburban development all over the country.

The secret of Levittown's success was its construction methods. Using prefabricated materials and assembly-line techniques, Levitt's construction crews were able to put up as many as thirty identical houses a day. The homes may have lacked individuality, but they were remarkably affordable, selling for as little as seven thousand dollars each. With a GI Bill mortgage, a veteran could buy a house in Levittown for sixty-five dollars a month, with no money down.

★THE COMPUTER AGE

Besides atomic energy, scientists made other important discoveries during World War II. At the University of Pennsylvania, J. Presper Eckert (above) and John W. Mauchly began the computer age when they built the first all-electronic digital computer. They called the machine an electronic numerical integrator and calculator—or ENIAC, for short.

The first computers, including ENIAC, used vacuum tubes to relay information. Because these tubes took up so much space, ENIAC covered fifteen hundred square feet and weighed thirty tons. The invention of the transistor in 1948 allowed scientists to do away with vacuum tubes and shrink the size of computers substantially. A transistorized ENIAC would have fit inside a refrigerator.

★THE BABY BOOM

During World War II, many families put off having children until the war was over. After 1945, there seemed little reason to wait, and so the Baby Boom began. It lasted until about 1960.

Because of its extraordinary size, the interests and concerns of the Baby Boom generation have always had a powerful effect on American society.

The book that most parents used to raise Baby Boomers was *Baby and Child Care* by Dr. Benjamin Spock. This 1946 manual sold twenty-four million copies—more than any other book in history, except the plays of William Shakespeare and the Bible. It emphasized flexibility instead of the rigid discipline favored by earlier generations.

manufacturing and home building, to keep unemployment low.

With his Fair Deal program, President Truman tried to adapt Franklin Roosevelt's depression-era policies to the new realities of postwar prosperity. Truman's top priorities were a national health care system and a civil rights bill. Yet both of these initiatives were defeated by Republican majorities in the new Eightieth Congress, elected in 1946.

Instead, much to the president's displeasure, the Eightieth Congress overrode his veto and enacted the Taft-Hartley Act of June 1947, which rolled back many of the legal gains that unions had made since passage of the National Labor Relations Act in July 1935.

After his surprise reelection, Truman reintroduced his Fair Deal program, this time before a much more receptive Democratic Congress. He succeeded in raising the minimum wage from forty to seventy-five cents an hour and won passage of the National Housing Act, which funded slum clearance and low-income housing.

With regard to civil rights, Truman had already used an executive order in July 1948 to end racial segregation in the armed forces. But the united opposition of southern Democrats in Congress prevented him from making any further progress on this issue.

WHO LOST CHINA

The "loss" of China to Communism in 1949 had hurt the Truman administration badly. Although U.S. government experts had expected Mao Tse-tung's Red Army to beat the hopelessly corrupt Nationalist forces of Chiang Kai-shek, ordinary Americans were not prepared for this outcome. Afterward, they began to ask, "Who lost China?" Congressional Republicans blamed Truman's new secretary of state, Dean

Acheson, whom they said was "soft on Communism."

THE KOREAN WAR In the midst of this debate, Communist North Korea invaded anticommunist South Korea in June 1950. Truman quickly sent in U.S. troops. Although the North Koreans had penetrated deeply into South Korea, Gen. Douglas MacArthur's brilliant landing behind enemy lines at Inchon turned the war around. By October, United Nations forces under MacArthur's command had recrossed the border into North Korea and were advancing quickly on the Yalu River, which separated North Korea from China.

As MacArthur approached the Yalu River, Chinese officials warned the United States that they would not "sit back with folded hands." But MacArthur dismissed these warnings almost casually. With his air force controlling the skies above Korea, the general was sure that he could handle the Chinese if they foolishly decided to enter the war.

MacArthur, of course, was wrong. On November 26, Chinese soldiers streamed across the Yalu, inflicting heavy casualties and chasing the UN forces all the way back across the South Korean border. MacArthur's command eventually regrouped, but the best he could now achieve was a stalemate.

He began asking Truman for permission to carry the war into China. When Truman refused, MacArthur took his case to the public. This was more than any commander in chief could tolerate from a subordinate, so Truman relieved MacArthur of command in April 1951.

Three months later, peace talks began, but no treaty was signed until after Truman left office. Meanwhile, despite occasional cease-fires, the fighting continued.

CAMPAIGN ★ 1952

PEOPLE HAD BEEN TRYING TO PERSUADE World War II hero Dwight D. Eisenhower to run for president ever since the German surrender in May 1945. There was a problem, however: Eisenhower didn't belong to a political party. The Democrats courted him in 1948, but it turned out that the general's views were more in keeping with those of the Republican party.

The Republican platform in 1952 called for a strong national defense and criticized the Democrats for "appeasement of Communism at home and abroad." This approach played to Eisenhower's strength as a symbol of U.S. military might. "Let's face it. The only excuse for Ike's candidacy is that he's the man best qualified to deal with Stalin," one Republican strategist said. At Thomas E. Dewey's suggestion, Eisenhower picked anticommunist crusader Richard M. Nixon of California as his running mate.

Eisenhower's Democratic opponent was Illinois governor Adlai E. Stevenson, grandson of Grover Cleveland's second vice president. Stevenson was both well educated and well spoken, although many voters dismissed him as an "egghead," or too intellectual.

For the most part, Eisenhower's campaign proceeded smoothly. The one rough spot came when *The New York Times* reported that Nixon had used campaign contributions to create a "slush" fund, out of which he had paid some of his personal expenses. With Eisenhower threatening to drop him from the ticket, Nixon went on national television to explain himself. In his famous September 23 "Checkers" speech, he denied the report but did admit to receiving one gift, a cocker spaniel named Checkers. "Regardless of what they say about it," Nixon declared, "we're going to keep it." Eisenhower locked up the election a few weeks later, when he declared that, if elected, he would go to Korea personally to get the stalled peace talks moving again.

DWIGHT DAVID EISENHOWER
34th President
★
1953 to 1961

BORN: OCTOBER 14, 1890

BIRTHPLACE: DENISON, TEX.

DIED: MARCH 28, 1969

PARTY: REPUBLICAN

VICE PRESIDENT: RICHARD M. NIXON

FIRST LADY: MARIE (MAMIE) GENEVA DOUD

CHILDREN: DOUD, JOHN

NICKNAME: IKE

HAD A PUTTING GREEN INSTALLED ON THE WHITE HOUSE LAWN.

As the supreme Allied commander in Europe during World War II, Dwight D. Eisenhower developed a reputation for smooth, effective leadership. Later, during his two terms as president, he ran the country in much the same way he had run the army—that is, he delegated members of his staff to create and direct national policy under his supervision.

Unlike feisty Harry Truman, Eisenhower always seemed to be relaxed. As a result, his years in the White House are remembered as serene, prosperous, and bland. Of course, the country was neither as serene nor as prosperous as Eisenhower's mood made it appear.

Philosophically, the president believed that the government should

SENATOR MCCARTHY WARNS OF COMMUNISTS IN GOVERNMENT

WHEELING, West Virginia, February 9, 1950—Speaking before a Republican women's club, Sen. Joseph R. McCarthy of Wisconsin shocked his audience tonight when he declared that Communists are secretly working in important positions throughout the federal government.

The senator repeatedly waved a piece of paper that he claimed was a list of 205 "card-carrying Communists" currently working in the State Department. He has not yet revealed any of their names, nor has he provided any evidence to back up his sensational charges.

McCarthy's attack comes only a month after former State Depart-

ment official Alger Hiss was found guilty of lying about his Communist past. For the crime of perjury, or lying under oath, Hiss was given a ten-thousand-dollar fine and five years in jail.

Time magazine editor Whittaker Chambers, himself an admitted Soviet agent, accused Hiss of spying for the Soviet Union in testimony before the House Un-American Activities Committee. Hiss still maintains his innocence.

1954

remain as small as possible. This attitude led him to criticize both the New Deal and the Fair Deal for ignoring traditional American individualism. Above all, however, Eisenhower was a moderate who followed "that straight road down the middle" and didn't make sharp turns.

THE KOREAN WAR ENDS

In December 1952, the president-elect kept his campaign promise and traveled to Korea, where he tried to revive the stalled Korean War peace talks. He threatened to extend the war into China, as Douglas MacArthur had wanted, and even warned that he might use small-scale atomic weapons. Whether or not this drumbeating helped is hard to say. In any case, the talks dragged on for another seven months before an armistice was finally signed.

By the time this "limited" war in Korea ended in July 1953, the United States had spent fifty-four billion dollars. To avoid paying such a high price in the future, Eisenhower and Secretary of State John Foster Dulles developed the policy of "massive retaliation." In their view, the Soviet Union would not attack the United States, or any of its allies, as long as the leaders in the Kremlin believed that the United States would respond with nuclear devastation.

Because nuclear weapons seemed to offer "more bang for a buck" than conventional weapons, Eisenhower ordered severe cutbacks in army ground troops and instead invested in nuclear warheads. He also spent money on the missiles and bombers needed to deliver these weapons. But the savings turned out to be illusory, as the cost of ever more sophisticated hardware kept defense spending high.

Meanwhile, the country remained obsessed with reckless charges that Communists at home were subverting

DWIGHT EISENHOWER GREW UP in Abilene, Kansas, as the third of six sons born into a rather poor family. Other boys often teased him for wearing tattered clothing and his mother's hand-me-down shoes. Young Dwight hoped that one day he might become a railroad engineer. Instead, he passed the West Point entrance examination, which earned him both a free education and an army career.

THE EARLY YEARS

After his graduation from the academy, Eisenhower became a tank commander. Although he requested an overseas assignment during World War I, he was ordered to spend the war stateside as a training instructor. In 1932, he joined the staff of Douglas MacArthur and helped disperse the Bonus Army. During World War II, he led the invasions of North Africa, Sicily, and Italy before becoming the supreme Allied commander in Europe in December 1943.

★**THE ROSENBERG CASE**   In July 1950, federal agents arrested Julius and Ethel Rosenberg and charged them with transmitting top-secret information to the Soviet Union. The Rosenbergs

were apparently part of an atomic-bomb spy ring that included Ethel's brother, who testified against them at their trial. The couple claimed that they were innocent, but anticommunist hysteria was everywhere at the time, and Julius's active membership in the Communist party hurt their case badly. Eventually, they were sentenced to death, and despite a number of international protests, they were executed in June 1953.

★ HAIL! HAIL! ROCK 'N' ROLL!

Memphis record producer Sam Phillips often boasted that, with "a white boy who could sing black," he could make a million dollars. On July 6, 1954, that boy recorded his first song for Phillips's Sun Records. Nineteen-year-old Elvis Presley sang in the rhythm-and-blues style that teenagers loved. The black musicians who had created rhythm-and-blues couldn't get their records played on many radio stations in the segregated South. But Elvis was different, because his white skin made him acceptable. Many parents condemned Presley for the sexy way he shook his hips. They even tried to ban his records. But the campaigns against him and his rock 'n' roll music only made teenagers want more.

★ PRESIDENTIAL RECREATION

Golf was President Eisenhower's favorite sport, and his strong interest in the game encouraged a nationwide trend. On sunny days, he could often be found on the White House lawn practicing his chip shots. He usually scored in the eighties.

Eisenhower was also an accomplished cook. His best dishes were vegetable soup, charcoal-grilled steak, and cornmeal pancakes. He and his wife, Mamie, often hosted barbecues for their friends on the White House roof.

★ THE MONTGOMERY BUS BOYCOTT

On December 1, 1955, in Montgomery, Alabama, a tired seamstress named Rosa Parks was told to give up her seat on a city bus so that a white man could sit down. When Parks refused, she was arrested, because it was illegal in Montgomery for a black person to sit down on a bus while a white person stood. To protest Parks's arrest, local black ministers, led by twenty-six-year-old Martin Luther King Jr., organized a boycott of the bus system. For more than a year, African Americans in Montgomery walked, used car pools, and even rode horses rather than ride the segregated buses. The boycott ended in December 1956, when a Supreme Court decision forced the city to stop segregating bus passengers.

the federal government. President Truman had been forced to institute a loyalty program in 1947, and now the witch hunt continued under Eisenhower. According to Truman's own attorney general, J. Howard McGrath, Communists were "everywhere—in factories, offices, butcher shops, on street corners, in private business—and each carries with him the germs of death for society."

Wisconsin senator Joseph R. McCarthy quickly became famous for his crusade against Communists in the State Department, which he claimed was full of them. McCarthy cleverly spoke in half-truths and insinuations that could be neither proved nor disproved. Most of what he offered as evidence were stories that government employees had attended meetings of the Communist party during the 1930s, when Communism was still considered respectable.

Although McCarthy never proved any of his outrageous accusations, Eisenhower and others in positions of power refrained from criticizing him because they feared his wrath. Many were also afraid that attacking McCarthy would make them look suspicious.

People accused by Senator McCarthy, especially writers and actors, were often prevented from working, because their employers desperately wanted to appear loyal. The practice of "blacklisting," or not hiring people because they were suspected of being Communists, ruined the careers of many innocent people.

THE ARMY-McCARTHY HEARINGS McCarthy's arrogance finally caught up with him in 1954. That summer, he chaired a series of nationally televised hearings relating to alleged Communists in the armed forces. A lawyer for the army named Joseph Welch finally challenged the senator publicly after McCarthy tried to smear one of Welch's

young legal assistants. "You have done enough," Welch curtly told McCarthy. "Have you no sense of decency, sir, at long last?"

Welch's very public rebuke broke McCarthy's spell over Washington, and in December 1954, the Senate voted to reprimand McCarthy for "conduct unbecoming a member." Since then, the term *McCarthyism* has come to mean "persecution based on unproven and often unfair accusations."

FOREIGN POLICY Generally, Eisenhower delegated conduct of the nation's foreign policy to John Foster Dulles. The secretary of state's long experience in foreign affairs, dating back to the Wilson administration, made it difficult for others in the White House to challenge him.

Dulles's viewpoint, which Eisenhower accepted, was that nations were either friends of the United States or friends of the Soviet Union. No nation, in Dulles's mind, could be both.

For five years, the Truman administration had pursued a foreign policy of containment. Now Dulles wanted a bolder policy of "liberation," so that people living in "captive nations" could be freed. When actually given the opportunity to liberate people, however, the secretary of state backed down. For example, when the East Germans in 1953 and later the Hungarians in 1956 tried to free themselves from Soviet domination, the United States did nothing to stop Red Army tanks from crushing those rebellions.

Therefore, as a practical matter, the Eisenhower administration continued to practice containment. In Southeast Asia, for example, Dulles advised his boss to help South Vietnam win its struggle against Communist North Vietnam.

Eisenhower worried about what would happen in the world should

CAMPAIGN ★ 1956

THE REPUBLICANS' GREATEST CONCERN during the 1956 campaign was Dwight Eisenhower's health. A year earlier, the president had suffered what his doctors called a "moderate" heart attack, and earlier in 1956, he had undergone serious intestinal surgery. Although Ike was already back at his desk following two months of rest, some voters doubted his ability to serve four more years.

As for the Democrats, Adlai Stevenson decided to set aside the thumping he had received four years earlier,

and again he ran for president. During the primaries, he was opposed by Tennessee senator Estes Kefauver, who had become nationally famous for fighting government corruption. In the end, Stevenson was renominated on the first ballot, and afterward he excited the convention by allowing the delegates to choose his running mate. Massachusetts senator John F. Kennedy made a strong pitch, but this time Kefauver got the nod.

There weren't many campaign issues. Eisenhower had ended the Korean War, as promised, and he had stood up to the Soviet Union. At home, the president's record was also good. Employment was up, and people felt prosperous. The only issue that the Democrats could use was Eisenhower's health, and yet they hesitated to bring this up for fear of offending voters.

As a result, Eisenhower and Nixon were reelected easily, winning two million more votes and two more states than they had in 1952. Yet the president's popularity didn't extend to other Republican candidates. Both the House and the Senate remained Democratic. It was the first time since Zachary Taylor won in 1848 that a victorious presidential candidate had failed to carry a single house of Congress for his party.

SOVIETS LAUNCH FIRST SATELLITE

BAIKONUR, Soviet Union, October 4, 1957—The Soviet Union began the space race today when it launched the first human-made object into orbit. The 184-pound satellite is called *Sputnik*, which means "fellow traveler" in Russian.

Sputnik is a steel sphere containing a radio transmitter and batteries to power the transmitter. Four aerials are attached to its outside casing.

Sputnik's orbit carries it over the Baikonur launch facility every ninety minutes or so. Soviet scientists have been able to track *Sputnik*'s progress by monitoring the bleep-bleep-bleep of its radio transmitter.

The rocket that sent *Sputnik* into orbit was powered by the same engine that the Soviet Union uses for its new intercontinental ballistic missiles, or ICBMs.

The successful launch of *Sputnik* has been a severe blow to American prestige. Many U.S. government officials privately consider the Soviet lead in space to be a sign of potential U.S. military weakness.

South Vietnam fall to the Communists. "You have a row of dominoes set up," he said, "and you knock over the first one, and what will happen to the last one is the certainty that it will go over very quickly."

In political terms, this "domino theory" suggested that the fall of one nation to Communism would lead to the fall of others. Eventually, if the chain reaction wasn't stopped in time, all the "dominoes" would fall, even the United States.

THE WARREN COURT

Meanwhile, the Supreme Court was grabbing headlines. When Eisenhower named California governor Earl Warren to be the new chief justice in September 1953, he thought that he was making an uncontroversial, middle-of-the-road appointment. Instead, Warren led a revolution on the Court, particularly in the area of civil rights law.

In May 1954, for example, the Court unanimously reversed *Plessy v. Ferguson*, the 1896 case that had upheld the legality of "separate but equal" treatment for blacks. In deciding *Brown v. Board of Education*, Warren wrote that segregating white and black students in public schools was unequal and therefore unconstitutional.

"To separate [black children] from others of similar age and qualifications solely on the basis of their race generates a feeling of inferiority...that may affect their hearts and minds in a way never to be undone," the chief justice wrote. "We conclude

169

that in the field of public education the doctrine of 'separate but equal' has no place." Later, Eisenhower said that appointing Warren was "the biggest damn fool mistake I ever made."

THE CIVIL RIGHTS MOVEMENT In part because of the *Brown* decision, the civil rights movement gained great momentum during the Eisenhower years, when Martin Luther King Jr. rose out of Montgomery, Alabama, to become the movement's most eloquent spokesperson. The Montgomery bus boycott that King led galvanized the black community and drew national attention to the fight for equal rights.

Personally, Eisenhower objected to racial segregation, but he also believed that trying to force integration on the South would be politically disastrous. When he finally sent troops into Little Rock to ensure the admission of black students into Central High School there, he did so only because the Arkansas governor was challenging federal authority, not because he believed that integrating public schools was desirable at that time.

SPUTNIK With public attention so closely focused on Little Rock during the fall of 1957, it came as a shock to most Americans when the Soviet Union announced the successful October 4 launch of *Sputnik,* the first human-made object ever placed in orbit around the earth.

Angry and fearful because the Soviet Union had beaten the United States into space, Congress passed the National Defense Education Act in September 1958. Its goal was to develop new scientific talent through the funding of school laboratory construction and college scholarships for promising students. Before receiving any money, however,

★THE FIRST LADY

Dwight and Mamie Eisenhower were married in 1916, when Dwight was still an army lieutenant. During their marriage, Mamie was a dutiful army wife. She adjusted quickly to life on military bases and moved twenty-eight times with her husband as he changed duty assignments.

As first lady during the 1950s, Mamie Eisenhower did what most American women of the 1950s did. She tried to be a good wife and mother—or, in her case, grandmother. Being the wife of the president, however, required more from her than from most housewives. She had to plan state dinners and supervise the White House domestic staff. But she also valued her privacy and made few public appearances.

★THE LITTLE ROCK NINE

After the Supreme Court's ruling in *Brown v. Board of Education,* most school districts in the border states stopped operating separate schools for blacks. In the Deep South, however, school systems refused to change, and in September 1957, Little Rock, Arkansas, became the focus of southern resistance when Gov. Orval Faubus used the National Guard to prevent nine black students from attending all-white Central High. Later, when a federal judge ordered

Faubus to admit the students, he did. But he refused to protect the teenagers from the angry white mob outside the school. Faubus's actions forced President Eisenhower to send in federal troops. It was the first time since Reconstruction that federal troops had been used to defend the rights of blacks.

★THE COMICS CODE

Comic books became big business during the Eisenhower years. More than a billion were sold annually. During the mid-1950s, however, parents began to complain about violence, gore, and sexuality in horror comics. In 1954, in order to avoid legal action, comic book publishers created the Comics Code to clean up the industry and ban offensive stories.

William Gaines and Harvey Kurtzman were two of the most successful creators of horror comics. To beat the new code, they began printing their comic book, *Mad,* on glossy paper. The glossy paper technically turned *Mad* into a magazine, so the Comics Code didn't apply. *Mad* soon became famous for making fun of everything held sacred by most Americans.

FEAR OF THE BOMB Once the Soviet Union exploded an atomic bomb in 1949, the world was suddenly faced with the possibility of nuclear war. In the United States, where the Cold War was peaking, civil defense officials tried, often foolishly, to prepare people for nuclear attack.

Elementary school students were taught to "duck and cover" if they saw a bright flash, signaling the explosion of an atomic bomb. Meanwhile, parents invested in expensive underground bomb shelters to protect their families from the deadly radioactive fallout of an atomic explosion.

★**THE BEAT GENERATION** The Eisenhower years are remembered for their conformity, meaning that people liked to do much the same things as everybody else. But there were some people who rebelled against the safe routine of suburban life. The Beats were a group of writers, performers, and hangers-on who lived mostly in New York City's Greenwich Village and San Francisco's North Beach neighborhoods. They wore black clothing (especially turtlenecks), grew beards (usually goatees), and stayed up late at night in coffeehouses like this one listening to music (always jazz).

The most famous Beat writers were Allen Ginsberg and Jack Kerouac. Ginsberg wrote "Howl" and other works that turned poetry on its head. Kerouac wrote the novel *On the Road* during a three-week burst in 1951 on a single roll of printer's paper. The book celebrated a life of adventure unburdened by possessions and family ties.

the students had to sign a loyalty oath swearing that they were not sympathetic to Communism. Many refused the money on principle rather than sign the oath.

THE KITCHEN DEBATE In an attempt to "thaw" the Cold War, Eisenhower and Soviet premier Nikita Khrushchev agreed to a series of cultural exchanges. In July 1959, Vice Pres. Richard Nixon visited Moscow to open a U.S. exhibition there. He encountered Khrushchev at a model kitchen display, where the pair engaged in a loud, spontaneous debate as to whether communism or capitalism was the better economic system. The press called this the Kitchen Debate.

Two months later, Khrushchev made a goodwill visit to the United States. He was disappointed when security concerns prevented him from visiting Disneyland, but he had useful conversations with Eisenhower. The two leaders met at Camp David, the presidential retreat named after Eisenhower's grandson. Afterward, they agreed to continue working together in "the spirit of Camp David" and made plans for a meeting in Paris the following May.

THE U-2 INCIDENT Less than two weeks before the Paris summit, however, the Soviet Union shot down a U.S. spy plane deep within Soviet airspace. At first, the State Department issued denials, but Eisenhower later admitted that U-2 planes had been making secret high-altitude flights over Soviet territory for years. He said he would end the flights but refused to apologize for them. In response, Khrushchev canceled the Paris summit and Eisenhower's upcoming trip to Moscow.

In addition to angering Khrushchev, the early State Department denials also caused many Americans to question for

1960

the first time the truthfulness of their government. "Up until now it has been possible to say to the world that what came out of the Kremlin was deceitful and untrustworthy but that people could depend on what they were told by the government of the United States," the *Wall Street Journal* wrote. "Now the world may not be so sure that this country is any different."

REVOLUTION IN CUBA

In the meantime, an even more threatening situation was developing closer to home. On New Year's Day 1959, Cuban revolutionary Fidel Castro toppled the corrupt dictatorship of Fulgencio Batista. Although Batista had been cruel to his people, he nevertheless enjoyed American support because of his favorable treatment of U.S. business and gambling interests.

At first, Castro sought an alliance with the United States, but then he seized foreign property, much of it belonging to U.S. corporations. He claimed that this was the only way he could free Cuba from the imperialism that had imprisoned it for centuries. When Eisenhower retaliated by halting trade with Cuba, Castro turned to the enemy of his enemy, the Soviet Union.

Just before leaving office, President Eisenhower delivered a memorable farewell address in the style of George Washington's. In the speech, he warned Americans to be wary of a growing "military-industrial complex."

The former general called attention to the network of close relationships that had been developing in recent years between the Pentagon and its contractors, pointing out that this combination might one day exert too much influence over policy. Later, as the country became more involved in the war in Vietnam, Eisenhower's words sounded wiser and even more prophetic.

CAMPAIGN ★ 1960

WHEN DEMOCRAT JOHN F. KENNEDY BEGAN his 1960 campaign for president, the experts agreed that the young senator from Massachusetts didn't have a chance. Because Eisenhower had been a popular president, most insiders assumed that Vice Pres. Richard M. Nixon would win the election easily.

Also, Democrats worried that Kennedy's Catholic religion would hurt him, as it had Al Smith in 1928.

Kennedy's early victory in the West Virginia primary, however, proved that he could win votes in a heavily Protestant state.

Kennedy and Nixon had similar political ideas. Both believed in a strong military, both were ardently anticommunist, and both promised to support welfare programs for the poor. Throughout the summer, the race stayed close.

Then, on September 26, Kennedy and Nixon met in the first of four debates. Although there had been presidential debates before, none had been televised nationally. Because the two candidates were so close in the polls, most people believed that the debates would decide the winner of the election.

Over one hundred million Americans tuned in to watch the two candidates. Both men spoke

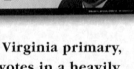

well, but Vice President Nixon, who had recently been in the hospital, looked pale and uncomfortable, while Senator Kennedy appeared tan and in charge. When Kennedy narrowly won the election six weeks later, many people believed that it was due to his much more presidential appearance during the debates.

BORN: MAY 29, 1917

BIRTHPLACE: BROOKLINE, MASS.

DIED: NOVEMBER 22, 1963

PARTY: DEMOCRAT

VICE PRESIDENT: LYNDON B. JOHNSON

FIRST LADY: JACQUELINE LEE BOUVIER

CHILDREN: CAROLINE, JOHN JR., PATRICK

NICKNAME: JFK

THE FIRST BOY SCOUT PRESIDENT.

1961

JOHN FITZGERALD KENNEDY

35th President

★

1961 to 1963

John F. Kennedy

The youngest man ever elected president, John F. Kennedy is best remembered for the hope that he gave the nation. In 1961, the United States was threatened by racial injustice at home and Cold War abroad. In his inaugural address, the new president admitted these problems but also spoke optimistically of a new generation of Americans ready to solve them.

In one of the most quoted speeches ever, Kennedy set forth the goals of his New Frontier program. He promised to work for freedom around the world but also asked Americans to give something of themselves. "Ask not what your country can do for you," he said. "Ask what you can do for your country."

MISSILES IN CUBA!

WASHINGTON, October 22, 1962—President Kennedy gave a speech on national television tonight in which he showed spy-plane photographs of Soviet nuclear missiles being installed on Cuba.

After condemning the Soviet Union for lying about the missiles, the president announced a naval blockade of Cuba, beginning immediately and continuing until the missiles are removed. The blockade is intended to prevent Soviet ships carrying missile parts from reaching the island.

Kennedy made it clear that the presence of nuclear missiles on Cuba, so close to the U.S. shore, is unacceptable.

Before the speech, high-level sources close to the president said that Kennedy was also considering bombing the missile bases. The president was concerned, however, that such an action would lead to a harsh Soviet military response and perhaps nuclear war.

MRBM FIELD LAUNCH SITE
SAN CRISTOBAL NO 2
14 OCTOBER 1962

1962

THE COLD WAR

Kennedy's major foreign policy concern was the Cold War with the Soviet Union. All over the world, he watched vigilantly for signs of Soviet expansionism.

When Eisenhower left office, he told Kennedy that the Central Intelligence Agency (CIA) was secretly training Cuban exiles to overthrow Fidel Castro. Since Castro's successful 1959 revolution, Cuba had become increasingly friendly with the Soviet Union. The idea of having a Soviet ally so close to the Florida shore made most Americans, including the president, nervous. So Kennedy allowed the secret training to continue.

On April 17, 1961, fourteen hundred Cuban exiles landed at the Bay of Pigs. Their mission was to lead a popular revolt against Castro, but few Cubans joined them and promised U.S. air support never came. As a result, the invasion was a disaster, and President Kennedy was forced to take the blame for a major blunder at the very start of his administration.

Then, in August 1961, the Soviet-backed government of East Germany built a wall separating East Berlin from West Berlin. The United States protested, but because the wall was built entirely on the East Berlin side, it was allowed to stand.

THE CUBAN MISSILE CRISIS

Kennedy had an even more serious confrontation with the Soviet Union in October 1962, when he discovered that the Soviets were building nuclear missile bases on Cuba. The president ordered navy ships to surround the island and dared the Soviets to run the blockade.

Kennedy's gamble paid off when Soviet premier Nikita Khrushchev agreed to remove the missiles in exchange for a U.S. promise not to invade Cuba. The

THE EARLY YEARS

*J*OHN F. KENNEDY WAS THE SECOND of nine children born to Joseph P. Kennedy, a wealthy Irish-Catholic businessman from Boston. Joseph Kennedy was so rich that he gave each of his children one million dollars.

As a child, John (or Jack, as the family called him) was frail and sickly. He looked up to his older brother, Joe, whom their father predicted would one day become president. But Joe was killed during World War II, after which Jack had to bear the burden of his father's ambitions.

Jack also served in the war and was nearly killed when a Japanese destroyer rammed into his gunboat, *PT-109*. But he survived the crash and won a medal for saving his crew. After the war, Jack began a career in politics, as did his brothers Bobby and Teddy.

★THE FIRST FAMILY

As first lady, Jacqueline Kennedy set fashion trends across the United States. Her hairdo and pillbox hats inspired thousands of women to copy the Jackie Look. The young Kennedy children, Caroline and John Jr., also kept the nation charmed.

John Jr. (known as John-John) was often photographed hiding underneath his father's desk in the Oval Office during important meetings. His sister, Caroline, loved animals. One of her pets was a goodwill gift from the Soviet Union—a puppy named Pushinka, whose mother was the first dog to travel in space. Another was her horse, Macaroni.

★SPACE RACE

In a speech made soon after his inauguration, Kennedy vowed that the United States would land a man on the moon by the end of the decade. To achieve this goal, he launched a five-billion-dollar space program.

Space was yet another arena in which the United States and the Soviet Union competed with each other. At first, the Soviets held the lead. In April 1961, cosmonaut Yuri Gagarin became the first human to orbit the planet. Three weeks later, however, a Project Mercury rocket sent U.S. astronaut Alan Shepard into space.

★ POPULAR MUSIC

Life in America during the Kennedy years was sometimes silly, sometimes troubled, but most often hopeful. During the early 1960s, the songs of the Great Dance Craze replaced those sung by the leather-jacketed rebels of the Eisenhower years. Chubby Checker had number-one hits with "The Twist" and "Pony Time." In New York City's Greenwich Village, however, folksingers such as Bob Dylan (left) and Joan Baez sang political protest songs.

★ PEACE CORPS

President Kennedy created the Peace Corps in March 1961 so that Americans could help the people of developing countries directly. Doctors, teachers, scientists, and other volunteers built hospitals, started schools, and improved farming methods all over the world. Many recent college graduates were inspired to join the Peace Corps by a growing concern for the world beyond the United States.

★ CIVIL RIGHTS

During the early 1960s, the civil rights movement surged ahead in its struggle for equality. In February 1960, the first sit-in to protest racial discrimination was held at a Woolworth's lunch counter in Greensboro, North Carolina. Two years later, despite a campus riot, James Meredith became the first black student to enroll at the University of Mississippi.

The movement probably reached its height during the August 1963 March on Washington, when Martin Luther King Jr. delivered his famous "I Have a Dream" speech in front of 250,000 people at the Lincoln Memorial.

Cuban Missile Crisis was the closest that the world has ever come to nuclear war.

Meanwhile, in Vietnam, the United States moved deeper into a different sort of war. Under Kennedy, the number of U.S. military advisers there rose from a few hundred to more than ten thousand.

Historians still argue about what Kennedy would have done in Vietnam had he lived. Some claim that he was planning to pull out all of the advisers. Others say that he would have sent more troops, just as Lyndon Johnson did.

CIVIL RIGHTS At home, Kennedy reluctantly heeded the black community's growing demand for civil rights. Although he personally favored equal rights for all, he wanted to move slowly so as not to offend segregationist Democrats in the South. Yet activists such as Martin Luther King Jr. were tired of waiting, and they forced Kennedy to act.

In May 1961, for example, thirteen black and white Freedom Riders boarded a Greyhound bus in Washington, D.C., headed for the Deep South. Their purpose was to protest racial segregation in public transportation. At nearly every stop, they were attacked and beaten. Because what they were doing was legal, Kennedy was eventually forced to protect them.

ASSASSINATION IN DALLAS Almost everyone who was alive at the time remembers what he or she was doing when news of Kennedy's assassination in Dallas was announced. The event still haunts people, because it symbolizes the end of hope and the beginning of violence.

President Kennedy once described himself as "an idealist without illusions." As a national leader, he was particularly successful touching the idealism of others, especially young people. When he was killed, however, their faith in the future was shattered.

ALTHOUGH JOHN F. KENNEDY won the election of 1960 by the slimmest of margins, he went on to become a popular president. On November 22, 1963, about a thousand days into his presidency, Kennedy flew to Dallas to deliver a speech.

He and Jackie were greeted by huge cheering crowds all the way from the airport. As their open car entered Dealey Plaza, however, a number of shots were fired at Kennedy from the Texas School Book Depository building. Two hit the president, one in the throat and the other in the back of the head. Kennedy died at nearby Parkland Hospital about half an hour later.

That afternoon, U.S. District Court judge Sarah T. Hughes administered the oath of office to Vice Pres. Lyndon Johnson aboard *Air Force One*, the president's airplane. Later, Lee Harvey Oswald was arrested for Kennedy's murder.

Johnson quickly appointed a group of respected government officials, led by Supreme Court chief justice Earl Warren, to investigate the assassination. Ten months later, the Warren Commission issued a report concluding that Oswald had acted alone in shooting the president.

In the years since the September 1964 release of the Warren Commission report, many people have argued that more than one assassin was involved. The truth may never be known, because two days after his arrest Oswald was shot in the basement of the Dallas County Jail by Jack Ruby, a nightclub owner allegedly connected to organized crime.

CAMPAIGN ★ 1964

HAD JOHN KENNEDY LIVED, he surely would have run for reelection in 1964. With Kennedy gone, however, the top spot on the Democratic ticket belonged to Lyndon Johnson, who was nominated by acclamation at the Democratic national convention in Atlantic City. Johnson's slogan was "All the Way with LBJ."

To oppose LBJ, the Republicans picked Sen. Barry Goldwater, an extremely conservative Arizonan, whose policies frightened many Americans. Goldwater proposed deep cuts in social programs and a large increase in defense spending so that he could drive the Communists out of South Vietnam. Goldwater also opposed civil rights laws and wanted to make Social Security payments voluntary, which alarmed senior citizens.

However, it was Goldwater's statements about nuclear war that hurt him the most. People worried that he might actually start one. Goldwater's "In Your Heart, You Know He's Right" slogan was satirized as "In Your Heart, You Know He Might." The Johnson campaign played on these fears with a television commercial that implied Goldwater would use atomic bombs if elected.

Johnson's strong stand on civil rights hurt him in the South, but nearly everywhere else, Americans voted for LBJ in overwhelming numbers, and he won a resounding victory.

LYNDON BAINES JOHNSON

36th President
★
1963 to 1969

BORN: AUGUST 27, 1908

BIRTHPLACE: STONEWALL, TEX.

DIED: JANUARY 22, 1973

PARTY: DEMOCRAT

VICE PRESIDENT: HUBERT H. HUMPHREY

FIRST LADY: CLAUDIA ALTA (LADY BIRD) TAYLOR

CHILDREN: LYNDA BIRD, LUCI BAINES

NICKNAME: LBJ

THE FIRST PRESIDENT SWORN IN BY A WOMAN.

Lyndon B. Johnson had been in office just two months when he delivered his first State of the Union address. The country was still in shock over the assassination of its young president, but Johnson knew that there was work to be done.

"Unfortunately, many Americans live on the outskirts of hope, some because of their poverty and some because of their color," the new president said. To relieve this despair, Johnson proposed an unconditional "war on poverty."

As he proved often during his presidency, Lyndon Johnson was a shrewd politician who knew how to get things done. By August 1964, with some expert arm-twisting, he had persuaded Congress to approve ten new antipoverty programs with a total funding of one billion dollars.

These included the Job Corps for disadvantaged teenagers and Head Start for preschool children.

RIOTS RAVAGE WATTS

LOS ANGELES, August 16, 1965—The rioting in the Watts section of Los Angeles finally ended today after six days of burning, looting, and death. Thirty-four people have been killed, and nearly four thousand arrested. It took a combined force of fifteen thousand police officers and National Guardsmen to restore order in this overwhelmingly black neighborhood.

The rioting began on August 11, after a patrolman arrested a black motorist for reckless driving. When the officer drew his gun, angry residents attacked him.

"Martin Luther King ain't my leader," one Watts youth said as he prepared to set fire to a building.

"The so-called Negro leaders have no contact with us. They don't know us; they don't know how we feel or what we want any more than you do, Mr. White Man."

The damage, covering five hundred square blocks, is estimated at upward of forty million dollars. Two hundred businesses have been destroyed, many owned by whites.

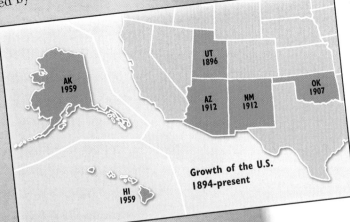

Growth of the U.S. 1894–present

1966

To help African Americans, Johnson pushed through the Civil Rights Act of 1964, which made it illegal for employers to discriminate on the basis of race. The new law also outlawed segregation in public places, such as hotels and restaurants, ending Jim Crow forever.

Meanwhile, the Federal Bureau of Investigation continued its six-week-long manhunt for three missing civil rights workers. Andrew Goodman, Michael Schwerner, and James Chaney had been taking part in the Mississippi Summer Project, whose goal was the organization of an integrated political party to challenge the all-white state Democratic party. On August 4, the brutalized bodies of Goodman, Schwerner, and Chaney were found buried in an earthen dam.

At the end of 1964's Freedom Summer, most of the young white volunteers went back to school, where many organized protests. The most compelling of these took place at the University of California's Berkeley campus, where the Free Speech Movement defended the rights of students to distribute political pamphlets. The Free Speech Movement also showed that students were no longer satisfied with the world as their parents had run it.

THE VOTING RIGHTS ACT Of all the laws passed during his presidency, Lyndon Johnson was probably most proud of the Voting Rights Act of 1965, which outlawed literacy tests and other unfair practices used to keep blacks from registering to vote. The new law thus made huge voter registration drives possible, and with more blacks registered, black candidates won more elections.

Prominent black mayors were elected in Cleveland, Ohio, and Gary, Indiana. Meanwhile, in 1966, Edward Brooke of Massachusetts became the first black elected to the Senate since 1881.

THE EARLY YEARS SAM EALY JOHNSON JR. was an educated man and a Texas state legislator, but he lost all of his money in 1906, when the great San Francisco earthquake destroyed a shipment of cotton in which he had invested. By the time his son Lyndon was born two years later, the family was suffering. Once Lyndon was old enough, he worked as a shoeshine boy and trapped animals to earn extra money.

From an early age, Lyndon enjoyed listening to his father talk about politics. Later, he would often repeat his father's advice to him: "If you can't come into a roomful of people and tell right away who is for you and who is against you, you have no business in politics."

For two years after college, Johnson taught public speaking but quit in 1931 to work for one of Texas's Democratic congressmen. In 1937, he ran for the House himself, winning in a crowded field with just 27 percent of the vote. In 1948, he won a controversial Senate race by just eighty-seven votes out of nearly one million cast.

★**BEATLEMANIA** In the months following the Kennedy assassination, grief-stricken Americans yearned desperately for something to relieve their gloom. In February 1964, relief arrived from England. That month, the Beatles made their first U.S. appearance on the CBS Sunday-night variety show hosted by Ed Sullivan. The ratings for Sullivan's show set records, and the Beatles soon had six songs in the Top Ten. Teenagers all over the country responded to the Fab Four's bouncy music, cute Liverpool accents, and mop-top hairstyles. Boys started growing their hair long, and girls rushed out to buy "mod" miniskirts popularized by British designer Mary Quant. The British Invasion that followed the Beatles included such bands as the Rolling Stones, the Animals, and the Who.

Starring in their first full-length, hilarious, action-packed film! The BEATLES A Hard Day's Night UNITED ARTISTS

★MALCOLM X

Malcolm Little spent World War II selling drugs in Harlem and Boston. In 1946, the twenty-one-year-old hustler was arrested for burglary. In prison, he joined the Nation of Islam, a black Muslim group whose members believed that white people were devils. Malcolm changed his name to Malcolm X because *Little* was a name some white master had given his slave ancestors.

During the early 1960s, Malcolm's fiery civil rights speeches made him famous. Unlike Martin Luther King Jr., who emphasized nonviolent methods, Malcolm preached violence as a reasonable response to violence. In 1964, however, Malcolm broke with the Nation of Islam and became a traditional Muslim, devoting himself to peace. While giving a speech in February 1965, he was shot and killed by four members of the Nation of Islam.

★HIM AND HER

When LBJ moved into the White House, he brought a pair of beagles with him. Their names were Him and Her. The dogs soon became almost as popular as the president. In June 1964, they appeared on the cover of *Life* magazine.

The dogs were also a source of controversy. When Johnson was photographed picking them up by their ears, dog lovers around the country demanded both an explanation and an apology. LBJ refused. "It's good for them," the president said.

★THE MY LAI MASSACRE

Every night, the television networks showed footage of the war in Vietnam, and every night, Americans had to decide what to make of the brutality they were being shown. Even so, the most horrifying events were usually kept off the airwaves. In March 1968, for example, troops under Lt. William Calley massacred 347 unarmed civilians in the Vietnamese farming village of My Lai. The killings were kept secret for more than a year. In April 1971, a military court sentenced Calley to life in prison, but he was freed after forty months. As his commander pointed out, singling out Calley was unfair. "Every unit of brigade size has its My Lai hidden someplace," he said. Guerrilla warfare made it difficult to recognize the enemy, and frightened soldiers often fired first and asked questions later.

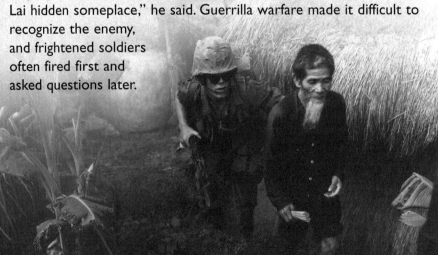

A year later, President Johnson nominated Thurgood Marshall to the Supreme Court. In 1954, Marshall had argued the landmark *Brown v. Board of Education* case before the Court. Now, he became the first black justice to sit on it.

THE GREAT SOCIETY After Lyndon Johnson's landslide victory in the 1964 election, the Great Society became the theme of his domestic program. Johnson developed Medicaid and Medicare to help poor people and the elderly pay their medical bills. He also won passage of the first significant environmental and consumer laws, which set standards for air and water quality as well as auto safety.

Some of the Great Society initiatives were early successes, adding momentum to LBJ's War on Poverty. But there was another war under way that wasn't going nearly so well. Already, the Vietnam War was turning costly, and as the fighting escalated, Johnson urged an increasingly reluctant Congress to fund both "guns and butter." Of course, even the prosperous United States couldn't afford both.

THE TONKIN GULF RESOLUTION In early August 1964, the president announced that the destroyer *Maddox* had been attacked by North Vietnamese patrol boats in international waters while patrolling the Tonkin Gulf off the coast of Vietnam. The North Vietnamese claimed that the *Maddox* had been protecting South Vietnamese raiders.

The president immediately sent Congress a resolution granting him nearly unlimited authority to use U.S. military force in Vietnam. White House staff had prepared the resolution well in advance, hoping for just such an opportunity. The Tonkin Gulf Resolution passed unanimously in the House, and

only two votes were cast against it in the Senate—by Wayne Morse of Oregon and Ernest Gruening of Alaska.

In a televised speech, Johnson told the nation, "We seek no wider war." But seven months later, he sent the first combat troops to Vietnam. Only thirty-five hundred marines landed at Da Nang in March 1965, but within two years, there would be four hundred thousand more.

THE TET OFFENSIVE Johnson's military advisers kept promising that a U.S. victory was "just around the corner." But their assurances meant little after January 30, 1968, when the North Vietnamese and their Vietcong allies launched a surprise attack on major cities in the South. One Vietcong unit even reached the grounds of the American embassy in Saigon. The assault was called the Tet Offensive, because it began during a cease-fire to celebrate Tet, the Vietnamese New Year.

Although U.S. troops counterattacked successfully, the Communists had made their point. Until the Tet Offensive, it was possible for Americans to believe the U.S. Army might actually be winning the war. After Tet, it was obvious that victory was either impossible or a long way off. As a result, many moderates, feeling betrayed, joined the growing antiwar movement.

In March 1968, Minnesota senator Eugene McCarthy, running as a peace candidate, nearly upset President Johnson in the New Hampshire Democratic primary. Johnson's slim, seven-point victory forced him to rethink running for a second full term.

On March 31, he announced on national television a temporary halt to the bombing of North Vietnam, so that peace talks could begin. At the end of his speech, almost as an afterthought, he revealed that he would not seek another term as president.

CAMPAIGN ★ 1968

LYNDON JOHNSON'S DECISION NOT TO RUN for reelection changed everything. Quickly, Vice Pres. Hubert Humphrey declared his candidacy, as did New York senator Robert F. Kennedy, brother of the late president. In fact, Kennedy had already decided to run as a peace candidate based on Eugene McCarthy's strong showing in the New Hampshire primary.

Humphrey's biggest problem was Vietnam. The war was unpopular, and the continued bombing of North Vietnam made it difficult for him to distance himself from Johnson's failed policies. Meanwhile, Kennedy gained momentum, winning the June 5 California primary. That same night, however, he was assassinated by Palestinian immigrant Sirhan Sirhan.

Kennedy's death assured Humphrey of the nomination, but it also deeply divided the party. At the Democratic convention in Chicago, thousands of antiwar activists demonstrated outside, while rampaging police officers beat journalists and protesters alike. Later, an independent commission called the chaos a "police riot."

Republican nominee Richard Nixon merely watched as the Democrats self-destructed. Discussing issues only vaguely, the former vice president talked mostly of the need for more law and order and of his own "secret plan" to end the war in Vietnam.

Finally, Alabama governor George Wallace mounted a third-party challenge based on victory in Vietnam and an end to school busing as a means of achieving racial integration.

Nixon opened up an early lead, but Humphrey made a strong comeback, especially after Johnson halted the bombing of North Vietnam on October 31. In the end, Nixon won the election by less than 1 percent of the popular vote. Wallace got forty-six electoral votes from the Deep South, yet these weren't enough to stop Nixon.

1969

BORN: JANUARY 9, 1913

BIRTHPLACE: YORBA LINDA, CALIF.

DIED: APRIL 22, 1994

PARTY: REPUBLICAN

VICE PRESIDENTS: SPIRO T. AGNEW, GERALD R. FORD

FIRST LADY: THELMA CATHERINE (PAT) RYAN

CHILDREN: PATRICIA, JULIE

NICKNAME: TRICKY DICK

THE FIRST PRESIDENT TO RESIGN HIS OFFICE.

RICHARD MILHOUS
NIXON
37th President
★
1969 to 1974

Richard Nixon

During the late 1960s, protests against the government grew in both size and vigor. Ten years earlier, Americans had feared nuclear war with a Communist superpower halfway around the world. Now, they worried about riots at home.

The assassination of Martin Luther King Jr. in April 1968 shattered the nonviolent civil rights movement. Afterward, like Humpty Dumpty, its pieces couldn't be put back together again. Some people continued King's work, but others joined militant groups like the Black Panthers, who demanded "black power." The antiwar movement also became more combative.

Pres. Richard M. Nixon ignored these protests because he believed that he had the support of the "silent majority" of Americans. However, no matter how hard Nixon tried, he simply couldn't avoid the war in Vietnam. During the 1968 campaign, he had boasted of a "secret plan" to end

ASTRONAUTS WALK ON THE MOON

SEA OF TRANQUILITY, July 21, 1969—The United States won the space race today when *Apollo 11* astronaut Neil Armstrong became the first human to walk on the moon. "That's one small step for man, one giant leap for mankind," Armstrong said as he climbed down from the lunar module *Eagle*.

Watching on television, millions of people around the world saw the moon landing last night and the moon walk early this morning. The former redeemed the late president John F. Kennedy's pledge to land a man on the moon by the end of the decade.

During the moon walk, Armstrong and fellow astronaut Edwin "Buzz" Aldrin planted a U.S. flag, set up three experiments, and collected rock samples. They also spoke briefly with President Nixon.

The *Apollo 11* crew is expected to bring back data of enormous scientific value. However, the astronauts will be quarantined upon their return to ensure that no lunar disease has returned with them.

1970

the conflict, but the peace talks that President Johnson had started were going nowhere. The delegates couldn't even agree on what shape their conference table should be.

VIETNAMIZATION Nixon's secret plan turned out to be Vietnamization. The idea was to replace U.S. combat troops with South Vietnamese soldiers. Kennedy and Johnson had also thought this would be a good idea, but both had eventually concluded that the South Vietnamese were incapable of fighting their own war. Nixon went ahead with the plan anyway, because it was the only way he could think of to withdraw U.S. troops and still keep the war going.

To make up for the resulting decline in combat strength, Nixon stepped up the bombing of North Vietnam. As a result, more American bomb tonnage was dropped on North Vietnam than on Germany, Italy, and Japan during all of World War II. The president also ordered the secret bombing of nearby Cambodia, where the Vietcong had supply bases.

NIXON IN CHINA Meanwhile, as he tried to bring about "peace with honor" in Vietnam, Nixon worked on the greatest foreign policy coup of his career. All his life, he had fought Communism, and his hostility toward Communists was quite well known.

That's why Nixon's August 1971 announcement that he would visit the People's Republic of China stunned the world. Arranged by aide Henry Kissinger, the trip took place in February 1972 and included a meeting between Nixon and Mao Tse-tung. Diplomatic relations were not yet restored, but the president's trip ensured that they soon would be.

THE EARLY YEARS RICHARD NIXON WAS BORN in a house that his father built, and every morning before school, he helped his father fetch produce from nearby Los Angeles to sell at the family's market in Whittier, California. As a student, Frank Nixon's second son was bright, serious, and quiet.

The adult Richard Nixon worked as a lawyer until 1946, when he won election to Congress. There, he made a name for himself as an anticommunist with his dogged cross-examination of alleged Soviet spy Alger Hiss.

In 1950, Nixon ran for the Senate against Helen Gahagan Douglas. Referring to Douglas as the Pink Lady, Nixon distributed "pink sheets" that showed how Douglas's voting record allegedly served Communist aims. Because of this political trick, a Southern California newspaper nicknamed the new senator Tricky Dick.

★THE ENEMIES LIST Historians have sometimes called Nixon paranoid, meaning that he often thought people were out to get him. As proof, they point to the list of enemies that the president ordered his staff to keep. This list included not only political opponents, but also journalists, businessmen, athletes, and movie stars. Names on the Enemies List included Bill Cosby, Jane Fonda, and quarterback Joe Namath. Nixon ordered FBI director J. Edgar Hoover to collect damaging information on some of these people using illegal wiretaps. After the Watergate hearings revealed the existence of the Enemies List, Nixon claimed that the wiretaps were justified because of "national security concerns."

★EARTH DAY On April 22, 1970, a number of environmental groups organized the first Earth Day. The environmental movement and its goals were still new to most people. So "teach-ins" were held on college campuses around the nation to focus public attention on such ecological issues as air, land, and water pollution. Since 1970, Earth Day activities have included beach and park cleanups, as well as tree plantings.

★ WOODSTOCK NATION

During the late 1960s, many college-age Baby Boomers developed their own distinctive styles of dress and music, as well as new ways of speaking and behaving. They called their new way of living a counterculture. Referring to themselves as freaks and hippies, they gathered together at rural communes and in city neighborhoods such as San Francisco's Haight-Ashbury.

One of the most memorable countercultural events was the Woodstock Music and Art Fair held in upstate New York in August 1969. More than three hundred thousand people showed up to listen to Jimi Hendrix, the Jefferson Airplane, and many other performers. Because of the massive crowd and the lack of proper food, medical care, and sanitation, the concert site was declared a disaster area. But the show went on.

★ THE BLACK PANTHERS

Bobby Seale and Huey P. Newton (left) founded the Black Panther Party for Self-Defense in Oakland, California, in 1966. The group's original purpose was to patrol black neighborhoods and protect residents there from police brutality. Soon, the organization set up chapters in other cities, notably Chicago, and became much more political. Chief spokesperson Eldridge Cleaver encouraged blacks to buy guns, because the Panthers believed that an armed showdown between blacks and whites was inevitable. Trouble between the police and the Panthers led to a number of shoot-outs. Newton, the Panthers' minister of defense, was later convicted of killing a policeman during one of these gun battles.

DÉTENTE

Having opened the door to China, long considered an enemy of the United States, Nixon was now able to play on the strained relations between the People's Republic and the Soviet Union. Although both countries were run by Communist governments, neither trusted the other. Nixon hoped that by forging ties with China, he could weaken Soviet power and influence, which remained the United States' greatest concern.

Nixon referred to his foreign policy as détente, which means "a relaxing of tensions," and not long after his return from China, he followed up that success with another remarkable trip. This time, he was going to Moscow.

Nixon had visited Moscow once before, in 1959, when he and Nikita Khrushchev had met in the Kitchen Debate. The highlight of his May 1972 trip, however, was the signing of a nuclear arms control treaty. The agreement was known as the SALT accord, because it had been negotiated during the Strategic Arms Limitation Talks.

PEACE WITH HONOR

Nixon's foreign policy triumphs proved that détente could work. They also boosted his 1972 reelection campaign, as did Henry Kissinger's announcement in October 1972, just two weeks before the election, that peace was "at hand" in Vietnam. The "breakthrough" proposal that Kissinger and North Vietnamese negotiator Le Duc Tho worked out during secret meetings in Paris called for an immediate cease-fire followed by a general election in South Vietnam.

After the U.S. election, however, the agreement hit a snag when each side accused the other of bargaining in bad faith. To bring the North Vietnamese back to the table, Nixon ordered the

1972

heaviest bombing of the war. During the "Christmas bombing" of December 1972, more than two hundred B-52s flew missions around the clock over North Vietnam.

A formal peace agreement was finally signed on January 27, 1973. The South Vietnamese government retained control of Saigon, while the Vietcong remained in place in the countryside. The United States agreed to remove all of its combat troops within sixty days in return for the release of prisoners of war. Publicly, Nixon claimed that he had achieved "peace with honor," but Kissinger predicted privately that South Vietnam wouldn't last eighteen months. What Kissinger didn't know was that the Nixon administration wouldn't last much longer.

THE WATERGATE BREAK-IN On June 17, 1972, police arrested five men caught breaking into Democratic National Committee headquarters in Washington. One of the men arrested at the Watergate office building was James McCord, a former FBI agent now working for the Committee to Reelect the President. When asked about the break-in, President Nixon denied any knowledge, insisting that no one at the White House knew anything of this "bizarre incident." The cover-up had begun.

At first, the scandal seemed limited to Nixon's reelection committee. But in October 1972, *Washington Post* news reporters Bob Woodward and Carl Bernstein began writing stories that suggested the break-in had been part of a much larger "dirty tricks" campaign.

Woodward and Bernstein's allegations were soon confirmed by McCord in a letter he wrote to federal district court judge John J. Sirica, who was hearing the Watergate burglary case.

CAMPAIGN ★ 1972

TWO IMPORTANT CHANGES IN THE WAY that delegates were selected made the 1972 Democratic convention a world apart from the violent 1968 event. First, the party's rules were changed to include more women and minority delegates. Then, in 1971, the Twenty-sixth Amendment lowered the voting age to eighteen. These changes, along with the ongoing Vietnam War, made it possible for a liberal candidate like Sen. George McGovern of South Dakota to win the party's nomination. McGovern promised to withdraw U.S. troops from Vietnam immediately.

Alabama governor George Wallace had challenged McGovern during the primaries, earning surprising wins in Maryland and Michigan, where he was particularly popular with blue-collar workers who felt that the Democrats had conceded too much power to minority groups. Wallace's campaign was cut short, however, when a gunman shot him at a rally. He survived but remained paralyzed below the waist.

Although the Watergate burglary had already taken place, no one paid much attention to it, allowing Richard Nixon and Spiro Agnew to win easy renominations at the Republican convention.

What bothered voters more was the news that McGovern's running mate, Sen. Thomas Eagleton of Missouri, had once undergone electric shock therapy for depression. McGovern stood by Eagleton for a time but then bowed to public pressure and replaced him with former Peace Corps director Sargent Shriver.

McGovern accused Nixon of being the most corrupt president in U.S. history, but few people believed him. Instead, they listened to Henry Kissinger announce that peace was "at hand" in Vietnam. On Election Day, Nixon's margin of victory was nearly twenty million votes.

FOUR STUDENTS KILLED AT KENT STATE

KENT, Ohio, May 4, 1970— National Guardsmen fired into an antiwar demonstration at Kent State University today, killing four students. The guardsmen were using live ammunition, rather than the rubber bullets typically used for crowd control.

The noon demonstration, attended by one thousand students, was held to protest the invasion of Cambodia announced last week by President Nixon. The president's action led many students to believe that he was widening the war in Vietnam, instead of ending it as he had promised.

The National Guard was called to the campus yesterday after a demonstration on May 2 turned into a riot. That night, students burned an army-related building

to the ground. This afternoon's demonstration also spun out of control when students began chanting at the armed soldiers, "Pigs off campus! We don't want your war!"

Students have held protests against the war in Vietnam since the early 1960s. But antiwar efforts have become much more vigorous ever since the Tet Offensive caused many Americans to reconsider whether the government has been telling them the truth.

Asking for leniency, McCord admitted that officials had lied under oath. Later, he named former attorney general John Mitchell as "the overall boss."

In February 1973, the Senate created a special committee to look into "any illegal, improper, or unethical activities" that might have occurred during the 1972 campaign. During this committee's televised hearings, Sen. Howard Baker of Tennessee asked nearly every witness, "What did the president know, and when did he know it?"

On July 16, 1973, presidential assistant Alexander Butterfield revealed in passing that President Nixon had been secretly recording Oval Office conversations. The Senate committee then subpoenaed, or legally demanded, the tapes, as did Watergate special prosecutor Archibald Cox. When Nixon refused to turn them over, arguing that executive privilege allowed him to keep the conversations private, Cox decided to fight him in the federal courts.

VICE PRESIDENT FORD One factor that delayed Nixon's impeachment was the reality that, if forced from office, he would be succeeded by Vice Pres. Spiro T. Agnew, whom Democrats despised even more than Nixon himself. Agnew was best known for his attacks on intellectuals (as "an effete corps of impudent snobs") and reporters (as "nattering nabobs of negativism"). Most Democrats considered the prospect of an Agnew presidency simply horrifying.

On October 10, 1973, however, Agnew was forced to resign the vice presidency after pleading no

STOP THE WAR NOW

contest to charges of accepting bribes while governor of Maryland. Two days later, Nixon nominated Michigan congressman Gerald Ford to replace him.

Meanwhile, the tapes case, *U.S. v. Nixon,* had reached the Court of Appeals, which ordered the president to turn over the tapes.

On Saturday, October 20, 1973, Nixon tried to quash Cox's original subpoena by ordering Attorney General Elliot Richardson to fire the special prosecutor. Rather than carry out this order, Richardson resigned. So did his deputy, William Ruckelshaus. Eventually, Solicitor General Robert H. Bork fired Cox and closed the office of the Watergate special prosecutor.

The public response to Nixon's "Saturday night massacre" was overwhelmingly negative. Three days later, Rep. Peter Rodino announced that the House Judiciary Committee, which he chaired, would begin impeachment hearings.

RESIGNATION Throughout the winter and spring of 1974, subpoenas for White House tapes continued to be issued, and Nixon continued to fight them. At one point, he released a few recordings and provided edited transcripts of others, but the House committee kept pressing for the actual recordings of the most sensitive conversations. Finally, on July 24, 1974, the Supreme Court ruled unanimously that Nixon had to turn over all the tapes. Three days later, the Judiciary Committee approved the first of three articles of impeachment against him.

On August 5, the president released transcripts of three June 23, 1972, conversations that proved he both knew about and directed the cover-up. On August 8, speaking on national television, he announced his resignation. The embattled president blamed a loss of congressional support. He confessed nothing.

★ WOMEN'S LIBERATION

The women's liberation movement of the late 1960s emerged from the civil rights and anti-war movements of that time. While taking part in these other crusades, young women came to realize that men rarely treated them as equals. They were often expected to make coffee instead of speeches and policy. Soon, these women banded together to demand equal treatment. Important women's issues included day care for the children of working mothers and equal pay for equal work. Men who believed that a woman's proper place was in the home were ridiculed as "male chauvinist pigs."

★ ROE V. WADE AND ABORTION

During the late 1960s, abortion became an important political issue in America, especially among members of the women's liberation movement. "Pro-life" advocates believed that an unborn fetus had the right to live and that it was wrong to interfere with a pregnancy. "Pro-choice" supporters believed that it was a woman's right to choose whether or not to have a baby. Because abortions were illegal then and had to be performed secretly, women often risked their lives in order to end their pregnancies. In January 1973, however, the Supreme Court ruled in *Roe v. Wade* that every woman had a legal right to an abortion during the first three months of her pregnancy. Although the women's movement praised this decision, the ruling was widely criticized. Religious groups called it immoral, and conservative scholars said it showed bad legal reasoning by the Court.

★ THE FIRST FAMILY

Richard Nixon first met Pat Ryan in 1938 at auditions for a local play in Whittier, California. Nixon proposed that first night. "I thought he was nuts," the future Mrs. Nixon remembered. She turned him down but continued to date him. Two years later, she finally gave in. In the meantime, Nixon had become so devoted to her that he sometimes drove her to meet other men for dates because she didn't have a car.

The Nixons and their daughters were an unusually close family. In 1968, Julie Nixon married David Eisenhower, grandson of the former president. Three years later, her sister, Tricia, married Edward Cox in a Rose Garden ceremony. Throughout the Watergate ordeal, the president's family stood by him and urged him not to resign.

BORN: JULY 14, 1913

BIRTHPLACE: OMAHA, NEB.

DIED: DECEMBER 26, 2006

PARTY: REPUBLICAN

VICE PRESIDENT: NELSON A. ROCKEFELLER

FIRST LADY: ELIZABETH ANNE (BETTY) BLOOMER WARREN

CHILDREN: MICHAEL, JOHN, STEVEN, SUSAN

NICKNAME: MR. NICE GUY

HIS DAUGHTER, SUSAN, HELD HER SENIOR PROM AT THE WHITE HOUSE.

GERALD RUDOLPH FORD
38th President
★
1974 to 1977

Gerald R. Ford

Gerald Ford was sworn in as president on August 9, 1974, just minutes after Richard Nixon's resignation took effect. "Our long national nightmare is over," Ford said after the ceremony.

Ford had been a football star at the University of Michigan. Later, as a congressman from that state, he developed a reputation in Washington as a fair and decent man. For twenty-five years in the House of Representatives, he spoke out for Middle American values. Yet, despite these athletic and political accomplishments, he was often teased for being mentally slow and physically awkward. A common joke was that Ford couldn't walk and chew gum at the same time.

Exactly one month after taking office, President Ford moved to pardon Richard Nixon for any crimes that Nixon might have committed while in office. It was Ford's belief that the country needed to be spared the spectacle of a former president standing trial.

THE WAR IS OVER
COMMUNISTS CAPTURE SOUTH VIETNAM

SAIGON, Vietnam, April 30, 1975—The Vietnam War ended today, when Gen. Duong Van Minh surrendered the South Vietnamese capital of Saigon to a force of North Vietnamese and Vietcong soldiers.

The cease-fire agreement of January 1973—which had guaranteed the United States, in President Nixon's words, "peace with honor"—lasted less than a year. By 1974, the war had restarted. In March 1975, the "strategic retreat" ordered by South Vietnamese president Nguyen Van Thieu quickly turned into a rout.

Sensing on April 18 that the end of the war was near, Secretary of State Henry Kissinger ordered all U.S.

citizens to leave South Vietnam immediately.

Operation Frequent Wind, which ended today when the U.S. embassy was overrun, has been the largest helicopter evacuation in history. Nearly seven thousand people, including fourteen hundred Americans, have been airlifted to U.S. ships waiting offshore.

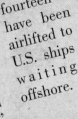

1976

Some critics suggested that a deal had been made, while others pointed out that Nixon had been pardoned while Vietnam draft resisters had not been.

Ford's pardon of Nixon contributed to the low expectations that Americans had for him. He was the first president to serve without being elected president or vice president. Consequently, people tended to view him more as a caretaker than as a leader.

THE ARAB OIL EMBARGO

Although the Vietnam War was finally over, its enormous cost had a lasting effect on the U.S. economy. As a result, under Ford, the nation began to experience the worst inflation and unemployment rates since the Great Depression.

Aggravating the decline was an oil embargo that ended the era of cheap energy in the United States. In October 1973, Israel and its Arab neighbors had fought the Yom Kippur War. Afterward, Arab oil-producing nations decided to punish the United States for helping Israel by cutting off U.S. oil imports. Within a year, gasoline prices jumped 70 percent.

Ford's most publicized solution to the country's economic woes was the Whip Inflation Now campaign. Buttons were printed up with the initials *WIN* and citizens' committees were formed, but the program went nowhere. Ford later admitted that the idea was "probably too gimmicky."

The campaigns launched by his wife, Betty, were generally much more successful. As first lady, she became an outspoken advocate of women's rights, supporting both liberalized abortion laws and the Equal Rights Amendment. After developing breast cancer, she talked about her condition publicly so that other women could learn about the importance of early detection.

CAMPAIGN ★ 1976

KNOWING THAT NIXON'S DISGRACE would make it difficult for the Republican party to retain the White House in 1976, more than a dozen Democrats entered the race for president. The first was former Georgia governor (and peanut farmer) Jimmy Carter, who announced his candidacy in December 1974. At first, Carter didn't even show up on the national public opinion polls. People often said, "Jimmy who?" But early primary victories in Iowa and New Hampshire made him the front-runner, and by the start of the Democratic convention in July, he had more than enough votes to win the nomination on the first ballot.

Carter had a pleasant, informal personality and a big, toothy smile. He talked a lot about restoring people's faith in government, and the fact that he was a Washington outsider helped him persuade voters that his election could make a difference.

Although Gerald Ford had been president now for more than a year, it still wasn't certain that he would win the Republican nomination. Former California governor Ronald Reagan ran strongly against him in the primaries, and Ford barely held Reagan off, taking the nomination with 1,187 votes to Reagan's 1,070.

Early polls showed Carter leading Ford by more than thirty percentage points. During the fall, however, the president narrowed the gap, and by the time of the debates in early October, the election seemed too close to call. However, Ford probably lost the race during the second debate, when he blundered in mistakenly saying that Poland was free of Soviet domination.

The November election attracted one of the lowest turnouts of the century. But turnout among African Americans was high, and their loyal support for the Democratic candidate made the difference in a very tight race. Carter's victory made him the first president elected from the Deep South since Zachary Taylor in 1848.

BORN: OCTOBER 1, 1924

BIRTHPLACE: PLAINS, GA.

PARTY: DEMOCRAT

VICE PRESIDENT: WALTER F. MONDALE

FIRST LADY: ELEANOR ROSALYNN SMITH

CHILDREN: JOHN, JAMES EARL III, JEFFREY, AMY

NICKNAME: HOT

THE FIRST PRESIDENT BORN IN A HOSPITAL.

JIMMY CARTER

39th President

★

1977 to 1981

Jimmy Carter (signature)

*J*immy Carter came to Washington determined to change the way that government worked. His informal public style helped him accomplish that task. After promising in his inaugural address that he would return control of government to the people, he and First Lady Rosalynn Carter walked hand in hand from the Capitol to the White House rather than ride in the traditional limousine.

Later, when Carter traveled, he often carried his own luggage and sometimes stayed in the homes of ordinary Americans. He even signed his name Jimmy Carter instead of James Earl Carter Jr., his formal name.

Gerald Ford's Whip Inflation Now campaign had focused public attention on the rising U.S. inflation rate, which was 6 percent when Carter took office. In other words, prices were increasing at an average rate of 6 percent each year. Because salaries weren't growing nearly as fast, people's standard of

EGYPT AND ISRAEL SIGN CAMP DAVID PEACE ACCORDS

CAMP DAVID, September 17, 1978—Pres. Anwar el-Sadat of Egypt and Prime Minister Menachem Begin of Israel signed two unprecedented peace documents today after nearly two weeks of private negotiations at the presidential retreat here.

One of the Camp David accords outlines a proposed peace treaty between Egypt and Israel. The other is a framework for peace in the Middle East. Begin and Sadat have both applauded President Carter for the role he has played as host and mediator.

Before this, the last major advance in the peace process came in November 1977, when Sadat traveled to Jerusalem to address the Israeli parliament.

The Egyptian president's trip was condemned by other Arab leaders, who still refuse to recognize Israel's right to exist.

Later, when peace talks between the two nations broke down, Carter invited Sadat and Begin to Camp David.

Israel and Egypt have been in a formal state of war since the founding of the Jewish state in 1948. The Camp David accords are expected to bring peace soon.

living was slipping. Under Carter, inflation got much worse, doubling to 12 percent.

THE ENERGY CRISIS
Carter's biggest obstacle in solving the country's economic problems was the energy crisis. Throughout his term, oil prices kept going up. In 1979 alone, the Organization of Petroleum-Exporting Countries (OPEC) was able to raise the price of oil from fourteen to more than twenty-eight dollars a barrel, leading to shortages of gasoline. When lines at some pumps reached a mile and a half long, most states introduced gasoline rationing.

The gas shortage was a disaster for U.S. automakers. With prices soaring, people began buying smaller, more fuel-efficient Japanese cars rather than the "gas guzzlers" still being made by U.S. companies. As many as three hundred thousand autoworkers lost their jobs, and more would have been fired if Congress hadn't approved more than a billion dollars in loan guarantees for Chrysler.

To reduce American dependence on foreign oil, Carter proposed an energy bill that included strict conservation rules as well as funds for the development of new energy sources. For eighteen months, the president struggled with Congress before it finally passed a watered-down version of the bill in November 1978.

During this time, Carter's status as a Washington outsider began to hurt him. Democrats had majorities in both houses of Congress, but Carter didn't work well with them and rarely got his way.

HUMAN RIGHTS
The basis of Carter's foreign policy was the issue of human rights. The president believed that it was immoral for the United States to support governments that abused their citizens—even if those

THE EARLY YEARS
*J*IMMY CARTER GREW UP NEAR PLAINS, GEORGIA, where his father owned a peanut warehouse. Although the Carters were better off than most families, their home had neither electricity nor running water. Jimmy's nickname as a boy was Hot, short for Hot Shot.

After his graduation from the naval academy in 1946, Carter studied nuclear physics and served aboard one of the country's first nuclear submarines. He planned to make a career for himself in the navy, but when his father died in 1953, Carter returned to Plains to manage the family's peanut business. Soon, he entered local politics, helping to ease the conflicts and tensions brought about by the Supreme Court's decision in the *Brown* case. In 1962, he was elected to the Georgia state senate. Eight years later, he was elected governor.

★**PROPOSITION 13** Fed up with their tax bills, which skyrocketed during the 1970s, Howard Jarvis and Paul Gann began circulating a petition in California that demanded limitations on local property taxes. Jarvis and Gann collected more than one million signatures, or twice the number they needed to put their proposal on the ballot. In 1978, California voters approved their plan, known as Proposition 13, by a two-to-one margin. The result was a nearly 60 percent cut in property taxes. But this meant that government services had to be cut deeply as well, which proved painful to some.

★**THE FIRST FAMILY** Jimmy Carter projected a down-home style to show that he was a man of the people. He dressed casually, often in sweaters. He also preferred to stay in ordinary people's homes when he traveled, instead of in hotels. His youngest child, Amy, was nine years old when the Carters moved into the White House. She attended public school in Washington and often brought friends home to play in her tree house on the White House grounds. Her dog was named Grits, and her cat Misty Malarky Ying Yang.

★ NO NUKES

During the late 1970s, some Americans began opposing the construction of nuclear power plants. At first, their protests were small and local. In May 1977, however, fifteen hundred demonstrators were arrested when they tried to stop construction of the Seabrook nuclear plant in New Hampshire. Then, in March 1979, an accident at the Three Mile Island plant outside Harrisburg, Pennsylvania, awakened the public to the possible dangers of nuclear power.

In May 1979, sixty-five thousand people gathered in Washington to protest nuclear power. In September of that same year, more than two hundred thousand people attended a No Nukes rally and concert in New York City. These protests halted plans to build a number of new facilities and led to improved safety at those nuclear plants that continued to operate.

★ THE ERA

Passage of the Equal Rights Amendment, known as the ERA, was one of the chief goals of the women's liberation movement during the 1970s. The ERA stated that "Equality of rights under the law shall not be denied or abridged...on account of sex."

Women's groups saw it as a way to include women's rights in the Constitution. Critics claimed that the ERA was unnecessary because women already had equal rights.

The ERA passed both houses of Congress and was sent to the states for ratification in 1972. During the next six years, thirty-five of the required thirty-eight states had approved the amendment, but the number stuck there. The ERA's leading opponent, Phyllis Schlafly, claimed that the new law threatened women's traditional family role. Schlafly finally won the battle in June 1982 when the time allowed by Congress for ratification expired.

governments also opposed Communism. Proving that he meant what he said, he cut off all U.S. aid to brutal dictatorships in Argentina, Ethiopia, and Uruguay.

The United States also withdrew its support from longtime ally Anastasio Somoza Debayle in Nicaragua. This sped up Somoza's decline, and in July 1979, his tyrannical regime was overthrown. At this point, Carter offered to resume U.S. aid to Nicaragua, despite the Communist sympathies of its new Sandinista government.

Carter's policy in Nicaragua followed an earlier success in Central America. In September 1977, he had signed an agreement with Panamanian leader Omar Torrijos Herrera regarding the future of the Panama Canal. The new treaty called for the United States to return the Canal Zone to Panama by the end of 1999.

Conservative Republicans, notably Ronald Reagan, opposed the treaty because they claimed it was a giveaway. Carter lobbied hard for its ratification, however, and won a narrow victory in the Senate after months of debate. The final 68–32 tally was just one vote more than the required two-thirds.

SALT II With regard to the Soviet Union, Carter continued Nixon's policy of détente as well as the Strategic Arms Limitation Talks. In early 1979, these talks produced another treaty, which Carter and Soviet premier Leonid Brezhnev signed in June.

In late 1979, however, before SALT II could be ratified, the Soviet Union invaded Afghanistan, beginning an ill-conceived war to defend that country's shaky Communist government against rebelling Islamic fundamentalists. The fighting reminded many Americans of the disastrous U.S. effort in Vietnam. Carter responded by cutting off U.S. grain sales to the Soviet Union and

leading a sixty-four-nation boycott of the 1980 Moscow Summer Olympics.

Carter's successes in foreign affairs, however, including his triumph at Camp David, were soon overshadowed by the hostage crisis that eventually destroyed his presidency.

THE HOSTAGE CRISIS On November 4, 1979, a mob of Islamic students attacked the U.S. embassy in Iran and took its staff hostage. Earlier that year, an Islamic revolution had toppled the U.S.-backed government of Iranian shah Mohammad Reza Pahlavi. The student radicals in the embassy wanted the shah returned to Iran, so that he could be put on trial for the crimes of his government. Their plan was to exchange the American hostages for the shah, who was then receiving cancer treatments in New York City.

President Carter did not approve of the torture that the shah had used to control Iran, but neither was he willing to submit to terrorism. Instead, he tried to free the hostages through diplomatic efforts, all of which failed.

In the meantime, as months passed, public pressure on the president grew. Finally, when nothing else seemed to work, Carter approved a military rescue plan. Unfortunately, the April 1980 mission failed when helicopter problems forced the commander to abort. Even worse, eight soldiers died when one of the helicopters crashed into a transport plane. Secretary of State Cyrus Vance, who had opposed the raid from the start, resigned in protest, and the president's public image suffered badly.

It wasn't until January 19, 1981, his last full day in office, that Carter finally negotiated the hostages' release, ending 444 days of captivity.

CAMPAIGN ★ 1980

IN HIS CAMPAIGN FOR REELECTION, **Jimmy Carter was in trouble from the start. Inflation was eating away at the value of money, and soaring interest rates were making borrowing expensive. Meanwhile, the Iranian hostage crisis dragged on. All this made Carter's presidency seem to be a failure. He even had to face a primary challenge from Sen. Edward Kennedy of Massachusetts.**

The liberal wing of the Democratic party rallied to the youngest of the Kennedy brothers, but an incident from his past doomed his candidacy. In 1969, Kennedy had driven off a bridge in Chappaquiddick, Massachusetts. Even though a female passenger had died in the accident, Kennedy didn't report it right away. Criminal charges were never filed, but many people questioned Kennedy's conduct. As a result, Carter beat him in the primaries, but the struggle weakened the president and disrupted the party.

Ronald Reagan, who nearly beat Gerald Ford in 1976, won the Republican nomination easily. His strongest challenger, George Bush, withdrew before the convention. At first, fearing that his extreme conservatism might scare away voters, Reagan tried to work out a vice-presidency deal with Ford. When that fell through, he settled on Bush as his running mate. Another of Reagan's Republican challengers, Rep. John Anderson of Illinois, dropped out of the primary race early to run a third-party campaign. He combined Reagan's conservative economic philosophy with Carter's commitment to social welfare. Both he and Carter attacked Reagan for his many frightening statements, especially about getting tough with the Soviet Union, but none of the criticisms stuck. Voters watching him on television saw not a dangerous warmonger but a strong leader, and he won in a landslide. The defining moment of the campaign came during the single televised debate when Reagan looked into the camera and asked, "Are you better off than you were four years ago?"

BORN: FEBRUARY 6, 1911

BIRTHPLACE: TAMPICO, ILL.

DIED: JUNE 5, 2004

PARTY: REPUBLICAN

VICE PRESIDENT: GEORGE H. W. BUSH

FIRST LADY: NANCY DAVIS

CHILDREN: MAUREEN, MICHAEL,
PATRICIA, RONALD

NICKNAME: DUTCH

THE FIRST PRESIDENT TO HAVE BEEN DIVORCED.

RONALD WILSON REAGAN

40th President

★

1981 to 1989

Ronald Reagan

A t sixty-nine years of age, Ronald Reagan was the oldest person ever elected president. But he worked hard to remain youthful. A veteran movie actor, he also liked to play the tough guy. This image had always been important to him. Now, it became central to the way that he governed.

Reagan owed much of his enormous personal appeal to the way he made people feel about their country. His speeches and television appearances encouraged Americans to believe that the nation's social and economic ills could be solved easily and painlessly, if only everyone pulled together.

The president, who was uncomfortable with details, liked to speak in folksy generalities like "a rising tide lifts all ships." He meant that good times for some Americans would bring good times for all.

Reagan always presented himself as a man of deep conviction and principle. For example, even after he was shot,

DRIFTER SHOOTS PRESIDENT

REAGAN SURVIVES ASSASSINATION ATTEMPT

WASHINGTON, March 30, 1981—President Reagan was shot in the chest today outside the Washington Hilton Hotel, where he had just delivered a speech. The president was rushed to a nearby hospital, where an emergency surgical team was standing by.

"I forgot to duck," Reagan joked as the doctors prepared him for surgery to remove the bullet lodged in his left lung. Despite the seventy-year-old president's age, doctors say that he appears to be making a remarkable recovery.

Also injured in the attack were a policeman, a secret service agent, and presidential press secretary James Brady, who suffered permanent brain damage from a bullet wound to the head. Reagan's would-be assassin, twenty-five-year-old John W. Hinckley Jr., appears not to have any political motivation. Instead, Hinckley claims that he tried to kill the president as a love offering to actress Jodie Foster, whom he has never met.

he remained firmly opposed to gun control laws.

By keeping his focus on the big picture, he was able to avoid most of the mistakes that new presidents tend to make. He was also aware that presidents with too many proposals usually get nothing done, so he concentrated on just a few ideas. Because he had won election in a landslide, Congress enacted these ideas without a fight.

In Reagan's view, all government spending (with the possible exception of defense spending) was wasteful. "Government is not the solution to our problems," he said in his inaugural address; "government is the problem."

Uniting Republicans and conservative Democrats into a new coalition, Reagan was able to lower taxes, raise defense spending, and cut deeply into such social programs as food stamps and unemployment benefits. Social spending, he argued, was better managed by the states in any case.

In other areas as well, the Reagan administration reversed liberal policies that had been supported by every president since Franklin Roosevelt. Environmentalists, for example, were outraged when the Environmental Protection Agency cut the endangered species list in half and the Interior Department moved to open up federal lands for private developers.

REAGANOMICS When Reagan took office, the inflation rate was over 13 percent, and economic growth was slow. But the new president had a plan for fixing these problems based on supply-side economics. According to supply-side theory, increasing the amount of money in people's hands would increase both investment and demand, making the economy stronger.

THE EARLY YEARS

THE SON OF A SHOE SALESMAN, Ronald Reagan grew up in Dixon, Illinois, where he collected butterflies and bird eggs and watched cowboy movies at the local theater.

In high school, he was elected student body president and acted in school plays. At Eureka College, his grades were more often Cs than As. Afterward, he looked for work as a radio announcer.

In 1937, Reagan moved to Hollywood, signing an acting contract with the Warner Brothers studio. A year later, he met actress Jane Wyman during the filming of *Brother Rat*. They were married in 1940 but divorced eight years later while Reagan was president of the Screen Actors Guild. In 1952, he married another actress, Nancy Davis.

Reagan began his political career as a New Deal Democrat, but his views gradually changed. He joined a Democrats-for-Eisenhower group in 1952 and the Republican party ten years later. In 1966, he won the governor's race in California by nearly twenty percentage points. Reagan soon gained national attention for reforming California's welfare system, balancing its budget, and ordering gas attacks on antiwar demonstrators.

★**SANDRA DAY O'CONNOR** During his presidential campaigns, Ronald Reagan promised to reverse the direction of the Supreme Court by appointing conservatives to replace liberal justices as they retired. The decision he most wanted the Court to reverse was *Roe v. Wade* (1973), which had legalized abortion. In 1981, he made his first appointment to the Court, choosing Arizona judge Sandra Day O'Connor. She became the first woman ever to serve on the Supreme Court. Although Justice O'Connor generally sided with the new conservative majority, she refused to support a complete reversal of *Roe v. Wade*.

★ THE GREAT COMMUNICATOR

Ronald Reagan was the first professional movie actor to become president. In *Knute Rockne—All American* (1940), he popularized the phrase "Win one for the Gipper," and in *Bedtime for Bonzo* (1951), he played a college professor trying to raise a chimpanzee as a child.

Early in his career, Reagan had worked as a radio sportscaster. In those days, the briefest descriptions of out-of-town baseball games were telegraphed to radio stations, where the announcers had to make up the details. Later Reagan became a spokesman for General Electric. Because of his ability and experience in front of a microphone, White House reporters called him the Great Communicator. Better than any other president, Reagan used carefully planned television appearances to promote his policies.

★ MICHAEL JACKSON

People magazine once called Michael Jackson the most famous man in the world. His 1983 album *Thriller* set new records, selling more than forty million copies and winning an unprecedented eight Grammy awards. His dancing also captivated the public. While performing his "moonwalk" routine, Jackson appeared to be walking forward as he actually moved backward. The single, sequined glove that he wore on his right hand started a fashion craze all over the world.

★ PERSONAL COMPUTERS

Early computers were huge, expensive, and complicated to use. Only large businesses could afford them. Around 1980, however, companies such as IBM and Apple developed personal computers, or PCs, that ordinary people could use and afford. Apple was founded in a California garage in 1976 by two college dropouts in their twenties. Their Apple II computer, introduced in 1977, used a regular television set as a monitor and stored data on audiocassettes. It also sold for just $1,298. IBM introduced its first PC in 1981.

To begin this beneficial chain of events, Reagan proposed a major tax cut for the rich because they were the people most likely to invest and spend. He assured the public that, soon enough, the benefits of tax cutting would "trickle down" to everyone else. During the 1980 campaign, candidate George Bush had ridiculed the plan as "voodoo economics," but now, as vice president, he supported the president loyally.

As enacted by Congress, the Reagan income tax cut lowered individual rates by 25 percent over three years. As a result, rich people were indeed left with more of their money, but most didn't invest it. Instead, they spent it.

Very little prosperity trickled down to the middle class, and even less to the poor. Meanwhile, the country as a whole moved deeper into the worst economic recession since World War II.

During this recession, high interest rates and a drop in world oil prices combined to lower inflation to 2 percent. But unemployment soared, rising to nearly 11 percent by November 1982, as a record number of people filed for bankruptcy. Many lost their family farms.

BUDGET DEFICITS At the same time, as many economists had warned, the annual federal budget deficits spiked. The Reagan tax cut reduced revenues, and though billions were saved by cutting social programs, these savings were offset by even larger increases in the defense budget.

The president repeatedly called on Congress to pass a constitutional amendment requiring a balanced budget, but he never submitted a balanced budget himself. Instead, during Reagan's eight years in the White House, the national debt more than doubled, and interest payments on that debt became the third-largest federal spending item.

1984

THE EVIL EMPIRE With regard to foreign policy, Reagan's thinking reminded many of the Cold War mentality of the 1950s. The president believed that the free, democratic United States was engaged in mortal combat with the Soviet Union, which he called "the focus of evil in the modern world."

In a nationally televised March 1983 speech, he proposed that the United States build a space-based missile defense system that would use satellites to shoot down incoming nuclear missiles. The price tag for Reagan's Strategic Defense Initiative was in the trillions of dollars, so it became immediately controversial on Capitol Hill.

The program was nicknamed Star Wars because it reminded people of special effects they had seen in science-fiction films. After Reagan's speech, some scientists pointed out that the missile shield, as the president had described it, couldn't be built. But Reagan insisted on going ahead with his plan, believing that the surest and safest way to beat the Soviets in the arms race was to outspend them.

NICARAGUA In Central America, the president fought another type of Cold War. During his first term, he sent large amounts of economic and military aid to the anticommunist government in El Salvador, despite evidence that official "death squads" were murdering that government's political enemies.

During his second term, Reagan focused his attention on Nicaragua. After the 1979 revolution there, the remnants of the Somoza dictatorship took the name Contras, which means "against" in Spanish, and began a guerrilla war against the new Sandinista government from bases in Honduras.

CAMPAIGN ★ 1984

FEW AMERICANS BELIEVED THAT President Reagan would lose his reelection bid in 1984. The recent recession had bottomed out, and new hirings had cut unemployment in half. Also, the country was at peace.

The early Democratic front-runner was former vice president Walter Mondale. His most significant challengers were Sen. Gary Hart of Colorado and the Rev. Jesse Jackson of Chicago. Hart stressed "new ideas" and attacked Mondale for his close ties to Democratic special-interest groups. Jackson was the first African American to run a major national campaign for president. He worked to organize a "rainbow coalition" that would speak for poor and otherwise disadvantaged minority voters.

Mondale proved to be unstoppable, however, and at the Democratic national convention in July, he unveiled two major surprises. First, he declared that he would raise people's taxes to bring soaring budget deficits under control. "Mr. Reagan will raise taxes, and so will I," Mondale said. "He won't tell you. I just did." Mondale also announced that he had chosen Rep. Geraldine Ferraro of New York to be his running mate. Ferraro thus became the first woman to run on a major-party ticket.

Reagan hit Mondale hard on taxes, promising to raise them only as a last resort. He also pointed out that most Americans were better off than they had been four years earlier. More generally, his friendliness and good humor had wide appeal, as did his vision of national progress and strength. "It's morning in America," his TV ads began.

Mondale criticized Reagan's economic policies for benefiting the rich at the expense of the poor and middle class. But he stopped short of condemning Reagan personally, because he worried that such attacks might offend voters. This strategy, not surprisingly, helped Reagan win an even more impressive victory than he had in 1980.

FERRARO 19 84 FOR VICE PRESIDENT

President Reagan speaks in West Berlin in June 1987.

1985

Immediately after taking office in January 1981, the Reagan administration cut off aid to the Sandinistas and instead began supporting the Contras, whom Reagan called "freedom fighters." By 1983, the Contras had blossomed into a trained army of some seventy-five hundred soldiers.

Meanwhile, the CIA secretly mined Nicaraguan harbors and gave lessons in political assassination to Contra gunmen. When Congress found out about these programs, it reacted with passage of the Boland Amendment, which banned future military aid to the Contras. To bypass this law, White House officials assigned Lt. Col. Oliver North of the National Security Council to help the Contras quietly raise money from private sources.

TERRORISM During the 1980 campaign, Ronald Reagan repeatedly attacked Jimmy Carter for his handling of the Iranian hostage crisis. Reagan promised Americans that, as president, he would never negotiate with terrorists. But once more hostages were taken, he found that promise difficult to keep. This time, the kidnappers were Lebanese Muslims with ties to Iran.

SPACE SHUTTLE EXPLODES
SEVEN ABOARD CHALLENGER DIE IN CRASH

KENNEDY SPACE CENTER, Florida, January 28, 1986—The space shuttle *Challenger* exploded seventy-three seconds after liftoff this morning, killing all seven members of its crew.

Low temperatures preceding the launch have been blamed for the disaster. Last night was unusually cold, and this morning there were icicles on the launch tower.

It is believed that the cold caused a seal in the shuttle's booster rockets to fail. Once the seal failed, the shuttle was immediately engulfed in a fireball.

The *Challenger* crew included Christa McAuliffe, chosen from among eleven thousand applicants to become the first teacher in space. McAuliffe had prepared several lessons on space science

that she planned to broadcast directly from the orbiting shuttle to U.S. classrooms.

Because of McAuliffe's participation in the mission, millions of schoolchildren were watching the launch on television when the *Challenger* exploded.

1986

During the 1980s, Lebanon was beset by a civil war between Christians and Muslims that the United States had been trying to settle for years. Marines had already been sent to Beirut, the Lebanese capital, for peacekeeping duty. In October 1983, a van filled with explosives rammed into their barracks. The ensuing blast collapsed the building, burying hundreds of soldiers in the rubble and killing 241 of them.

Nor were terrorist attacks against American targets limited to Lebanon. In October 1985, several Palestinians hijacked the Italian cruise ship *Achille Lauro*, shooting a disabled American in a wheelchair and throwing his body over-board. In April 1986, an explosion at a West Berlin nightclub killed one U.S. serviceman and injured sixty others.

Concluding that Libya had been responsible for the nightclub bombing, the president retaliated with an air raid. A squadron of F-111 bombers attacked Libya on April 15, striking military targets as well as the living quarters of leader Muammar Qaddafi and his family.

THE GORBACHEV ERA

Meanwhile, in March 1985, an extraordinary new leader came to power in the Soviet Union. Mikhail Gorbachev, then fifty-three, was open-minded enough to realize that his country could not afford to match the massive U.S. arms buildup. He also understood that the Soviet economy would continue to lag behind unless Soviet society was itself reformed.

The two fundamental principles of Gorbachev's new program were *glasnost*, meaning "openness," and *perestroika*, meaning "restructuring." Under *glasnost*, censorship was eased so that people could express their ideas more freely. Meanwhile, *perestroika* attempted to revitalize the Communist economic

★ **THE FIRST LADY** Nancy Reagan was one of the most controversial first ladies ever. Because she had helped her husband build his political career, many people wondered how much influence she had over him. The president obviously adored her, and White House staffers feared displeasing her.

Mrs. Reagan was criticized early in her husband's first term when she spent nearly a million dollars redecorating the White House. Later, she was attacked for accepting free gowns from famous designers. Her expensive tastes in furniture and clothing seemed out of place at a time when social programs to aid the poor were being cut sharply. During President Reagan's second term, the first lady improved her image by devoting her energies to the "Just Say No" campaign against drug use.

★ **WALL STREET GREED** The deal-making on Wall Street was remarkably fast-paced during the Reagan years. The highest of the highfliers was Michael Milken, who invented the "junk" bond. Milken's junk bonds used high interest rates to lure people into making risky investments. The money that these people invested was used to buy companies worth more than the amount put up in cash. Therefore, the deals were called leveraged buy-outs, or LBOs. In 1987, Milken made an estimated $550 million. Three years later, however, after many of the deals went wrong, he pled guilty to insider trading and went to jail.

★ C. EVERETT KOOP

One of the most curious figures of the Reagan administration was C. Everett Koop. The president picked Koop for the post of surgeon general because he thought that the pediatrician shared his conservative values. Pro-choice groups opposed Dr. Koop's nomination for the same reason. They felt that Koop would let his personal feelings against abortion influence his judgment. But Koop's critics greatly underestimated his devotion to public service. Often during his eight years in office, the surgeon general enraged conservatives by choosing public health over politics. Koop's most controversial moment came in October 1986, when his report on the AIDS epidemic recommended that AIDS education begin in elementary schools as early as the third grade.

★ THE MORAL MAJORITY

President Reagan wanted to outlaw abortion and bring prayer back into the public schools. He spoke about these issues often but made little progress on them.

Another public figure with a great deal to say about conservative social issues was Baptist minister Jerry Falwell (shown here with Reagan in 1983). As leader of the Moral Majority, an ultraconservative religious group that he founded in 1979, Falwell was one of several television evangelists who had far-reaching influence during the 1980s. Televangelism raised hundreds of millions of dollars but came crashing down in 1987, when Jim Bakker was exposed for cheating his followers out of $150 million.

★ LIVE AID

In 1984, Bob Geldof produced a record featuring fellow British rock stars singing "Do They Know It's Christmas?" Proceeds from this song were donated to famine relief efforts in Ethiopia. A similar project, "We Are the World," raised money in the United States. During the summer of 1985, Geldof organized a benefit concert that would take place simultaneously in London and Philadelphia. The July 13 event, called Live Aid, was broadcast via satellite to 152 countries around the world. Performers included U2, Sting, Paul McCartney, and Madonna. The seventeen-hour show raised more than seventy million dollars for famine relief.

system with a bit of capitalist private enterprise.

Although U.S.-Soviet relations had been tense throughout Reagan's first term, Gorbachev's willingness to make peace helped wind down the Cold War. In December 1987, for example, he and Reagan signed the Intermediate-Range Nuclear Forces agreement. For the first time, the two superpowers agreed to reduce the number of nuclear warheads in their respective arsenals by destroying an entire class of weapons.

THE IRANIAN ARMS SALE

In 1980, the Persian Gulf nations of Iran and Iraq began fighting an eight-year-long border war. The Iranians desperately needed arms, because President Reagan had pressured U.S. allies into not selling them any. At the same time, members of his own national security staff were secretly negotiating the sale of U.S. arms to so-called moderates in Iran. In exchange, the moderates were supposed to arrange the release of U.S. hostages in Lebanon.

Using a group of private arms dealers as middlemen, National Security Council staff sold the arms to Iran at hugely inflated prices. Three hostages were later released, but soon three more were taken. In the meantime, the sale was kept hidden from Congress and the public.

Halfway around the world, the administration's policy with regard to Nicaragua was also stuck. Reagan was especially frustrated by the Boland Amendment, because the success of the Contras was important to him. Finally, a workaround was proposed: Use some of the lavish profits from the Iranian arms sale to buy more weapons for the Contras.

The arms sale and the diversion of funds to the Contras both took place at the highest levels of government amid great secrecy. When congressional

committees questioned members of the president's staff during hearings, the witnesses either gave misleading answers or lied. Not until November 1986 was news of the arms sale finally published in a small Beirut magazine.

THE IRAN-CONTRA SCANDAL The first investigation into the scandal was conducted by Edwin Meese, who had just become attorney general. Meese's Senate confirmation hearings had taken more than a year because there had been many serious charges to investigate. A special prosecutor later concluded that Meese had probably broken the law a number of times but that there was too little evidence to prosecute him.

Perhaps intentionally to protect his colleagues, Meese badly bungled his probe of the Iran-Contra affair. While Meese's aides conducted interviews in one room, Oliver North and his boss, National Security Advisor John Poindexter, shredded crucial documents in another. Poindexter later admitted that he destroyed Reagan's signed authorization for the Iranian arms sale to save the president embarrassment. Other officials tried to protect Reagan by lying under oath about the order in which events took place.

During the lengthy congressional investigations and criminal trials that followed, Reagan administration officials portrayed the president as a passive chief executive, detached from details and overly willing to delegate authority. The president himself claimed not to have known what was going on. This seems doubtful, but many people believed it, because it seemed in keeping with Reagan's inclination to leave work early and his tendency to become confused when talking about the specifics of his own policies.

CAMPAIGN ★ 1988

WITH PRESIDENT REAGAN RETIRING, the primary races in both parties were wide open. Vice Pres. George Bush finished an embarrassing third among Republicans in Iowa but came back strong in New Hampshire and never looked back.

The Democratic campaign began even more wildly, when Colorado senator Gary Hart was forced out by a sex scandal. Massachusetts governor Michael Dukakis became the new front-runner, and with each primary he added to his lead. One by one, his rivals dropped out, except for Jesse Jackson. The Rainbow Coalition leader stayed in the race until the convention. His goal was the vice-presidential nomination, but Dukakis disagreed with some of his ultraliberal positions and instead picked conservative senator Lloyd Bentsen of Texas.

Bush's acceptance speech at the Republican convention called for an end to the greed of the 1980s. He said that he wanted to lead a "kinder and gentler nation." However, when public opinion polls showed that he was twenty points down, Bush ignored his own words and went on the offensive. His campaign was one of the most negative in history.

Avoiding serious but complicated issues, Bush attacked Dukakis for vetoing a bill that would have required schoolchildren to recite the Pledge of Allegiance. So while Dukakis explained his health insurance plan, Bush visited a flag factory. About the only thing that Bush said regarding his own policies was, "Read my lips: No new taxes!"

As Bush turned the word *liberal* into an insult, Dukakis's lead in the polls disappeared. Even more to the point, the vice president's promise to carry on the Reagan Revolution propelled him to victory. Bush thus became the first sitting vice president to be elected president since Martin Van Buren in 1836.

BORN: JUNE 12, 1924

BIRTHPLACE: MILTON, MASS.

PARTY: REPUBLICAN

VICE PRESIDENT: J. DANFORTH QUAYLE

FIRST LADY: BARBARA PIERCE

CHILDREN: GEORGE, ROBIN, JOHN, NEIL, MARVIN, DOROTHY

NICKNAME: POPPY

THE FIRST PRESIDENT TO REFUSE PUBLICLY TO EAT BROCCOLI.

GEORGE HERBERT WALKER
BUSH
41st President
★
1989 to 1993

Ronald Reagan may have fought the deciding battle of the Cold War, but the forty-year struggle between the United States and the Soviet Union ended during George Bush's presidency. First, in December 1988, Soviet leader Mikhail Gorbachev declared in a speech to the United Nations that the Cold War was over. Then, he followed up those words with some remarkable actions.

In addition to undertaking reforms at home, Gorbachev reduced the presence of Soviet troops in Eastern Europe and later removed them altogether. For the first time since World War II, East Germans, Hungarians, Czechs, and others were permitted to run their own governments. The world was no longer dominated by two superpowers challenging each other with nuclear weapons. Instead, in Bush's words, there was a "new world order."

While monitoring events in Europe, Bush also became involved in Panama.

UNITED NATIONS HOLDS
EARTH SUMMIT

RIO DE JANEIRO, Brazil, June 14, 1992—The United Nations Earth Summit ended today as representatives of 153 nations signed treaties designed to reverse disturbing trends in the global environment.

These agreements concern such issues as global warming and biodiversity. Global warming involves the greenhouse effect, which is the increase in global temperature caused by industrial chemicals trapped in the atmosphere.

Biodiversity refers to the incredible variety of plant and animal life on the planet. Environmental scientists have warned that the continuing destruction of South American rain forests threatens many species that live there.

Environmental protection has become a particularly prominent issue in U.S. politics since March 24, 1989, when the oil tanker *Exxon Valdez* struck a reef off the Alaskan coast. The accident spilled ten million barrels of oil into Prince William Sound. The oil spill, the worst in the nation's history, killed thousands of birds, otters, fish, seals, and other animals.

1990

This strategically located Central American country was ruled in 1989 by dictator Manuel Noriega. Under the Reagan administration, the CIA had allowed Noriega to smuggle drugs because he gave the United States important intelligence information. As Noriega's anti-American speeches became more pronounced, however, President Bush found it difficult to ignore his illegal drug-trafficking activities.

At first, Bush imposed economic sanctions and encouraged Noriega's rivals to overthrow him. When neither of these tactics worked, the president ordered military action. Twelve thousand U.S. soldiers invaded Panama in December 1989. Noriega was captured and flown to Florida to stand trial on drug charges. Most Latin American countries publicly condemned the raid but privately expressed satisfaction with the result.

THE PERSIAN GULF WAR A year later, Bush again considered military action. On August 2, 1990, Iraqi troops invaded the Persian Gulf nation of Kuwait. Although only a tiny country, Kuwait possessed about 10 percent of the world's oil reserves. If Iraqi dictator Saddam Hussein someday conquered neighboring Saudi Arabia as well, he would control nearly half of the world's oil.

Following the lead of President Bush, the UN Security Council voted to impose economic sanctions and gave member nations permission to enforce them with military means. Even the Soviet Union, Saddam Hussein's biggest arms supplier, stopped selling weapons to Iraq.

Six days after the invasion, Bush began sending U.S. troops to defend Saudi Arabia. Eventually, more than half a million American soldiers took part in Operation Desert Shield. Meanwhile, the president and Secretary of State James

THE EARLY YEARS GEORGE BUSH'S FATHER was a Wall Street banker and later a U.S. senator from Connecticut. Prescott Bush taught his children that people of wealth and privilege should give something back to their country.

On his eighteenth birthday in June 1942, George put off attending Yale University so that he could enlist in the navy. A year later, he earned his wings as the youngest navy pilot. During World War II, Bush flew fifty-eight combat missions against the Japanese and won the Distinguished Flying Cross.

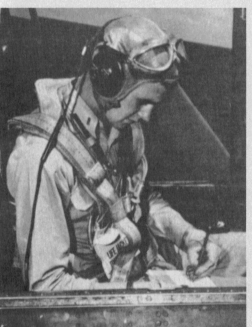

After the war, he turned down a job with his father's Wall Street firm and instead moved to Texas, where he entered the oil business and became a millionaire. In 1966, running as a moderate Republican, he won election to the House of Representatives from Houston. Four years later, at the request of President Nixon, he ran for the Senate from Texas. After he lost that race, Nixon named Bush U.S. ambassador to the United Nations. Later, Bush served President Ford as the official U.S. representative to China and as director of the CIA.

★**THE FIRST LADY** Seventeen-year-old Barbara Pierce met her future husband at a Christmas dance in 1942. He was the first boy that she ever kissed. George Bush later named his bomber *Barbara* after her. As first lady, Mrs. Bush immediately distanced herself from Nancy Reagan by becoming involved in charitable causes. She founded an organization to help illiterate adults learn how to read and also spoke out for the homeless. It was often said that Barbara Bush was more popular than the president. One reason might have been the best-selling *Millie's Book* that she wrote from the point of view of the Bush family dog.

★ NELSON MANDELA

African National Congress leader Nelson Mandela was sent to prison in 1964 for planning to sabotage the white South African government. Mandela wanted to overthrow the South African system of apartheid. In South Africa, blacks could

not vote, and whites got favored treatment in every situation. During the 1980s, the United States and other nations used economic sanctions, such as the halting of trade, to push the white minority government into sharing power with the black majority. Although Mandela served many years at hard labor, his spirit remained unbroken. He was finally freed in February 1990 by President F. W. de Klerk, who wanted Mandela to help him negotiate a peaceful end to apartheid.

★ HIP-HOP

Like most trends in popular music, including rock 'n' roll, hip-hop originated in the black community. Its popularity spread quickly after MTV, the cable music television network, began airing *Yo! MTV Raps* in 1989. That show brought hip-hop music, fashion, and dance styles into the mainstream. Soon baggy pants, baseball caps, gold jewelry, and hooded sweatshirts were being worn all over the country by young people who wanted to look cool. Although a handful of white performers jumped onto the hip-hop bandwagon, the music never lost its black urban roots.

★ MAGIC JOHNSON AND AIDS

On November 7, 1991, basketball star Earvin "Magic" Johnson told a packed news conference that he was retiring from the Los Angeles Lakers

because he had become infected with the virus that causes AIDS. Magic's announcement stunned the world. Many people had refused to believe that such a skilled and popular athlete could get AIDS. For that reason, Johnson said he planned to devote the rest of his life to educating teenagers about

how people become infected with AIDS. George Bush quickly appointed Johnson to the presidential AIDS commission, but Johnson resigned from that post in September 1992 after criticizing Bush for not providing the commission with enough support.

Baker worked to persuade other countries to join an international coalition against Iraq. Great Britain, France, Egypt, and Syria all provided troops, while other nations sent planes and ships.

OPERATION DESERT STORM In November 1990, the Security Council set a deadline of January 15, 1991, for the complete withdrawal of Iraqi troops from Kuwait. If the Iraqis did not obey, UN member nations could use force to compel an Iraqi pullout. On January 12, Congress voted to give the president the authority to wage war against Iraq. Seven hours after the deadline passed, Bush began Operation Desert Storm.

During the next six weeks, coalition bombers flew more than a hundred thousand sorties, devastating the Iraqi military. Then, on February 23, the ground assault began. Within one hundred hours, troops under Gen. Norman Schwarzkopf had overrun the Iraqi army, liberating Kuwait.

After the war, Bush enjoyed enormous popularity. The United States had won an important military victory as part of a worldwide coalition effort. This was the new world order that Bush had been talking about. Furthermore, the president had proven that he could handle himself well in an international crisis. But a crisis at home—that was another matter.

From the start of Bush's term, critics had complained that he had no goals for the country. During the election of 1988, he had promised to be the Education President and the Environmental President. Americans waited patiently for proposals on these issues, but few came. What came instead was a banking scandal, followed by an economic recession.

During the 1980s, speculation in the financial markets grew as the Reagan administration relaxed federal oversight of the nation's savings and loan industry.

That oversight had been put in place during the 1930s to protect depositors in the wake of the banking crisis.

THE SAVINGS AND LOAN SCANDAL

Many savings and loan owners used this new freedom to make risky loans. Others simply cheated their depositors. One of the worst offenders, Charles Keating, made large campaign contributions to five senators in exchange for their help in warding off the few bank examiners still on the federal payroll.

By the time that the savings and loan scandal broke in 1989, hundreds of billions of dollars in government-insured deposits had been stolen. U.S. taxpayers ended up repaying the money, and only a few of the guilty went to jail.

In early 1990, the news got even worse. Most indicators of economic activity began to show a decline, and unemployment rose sharply, soon reaching a three-year high. At first, the president blamed what Federal Reserve chairman Alan Greenspan called "a meaningful downturn" on the rise in oil prices during the Persian Gulf War. But most Americans believed that the real problem was the out-of-control federal budget deficit.

Bush had vowed to cut the deficit, but it was only getting worse. Finally, congressional Democrats offered him a deal: They would agree to further cuts in social spending if he agreed to raise certain taxes. Bush's problem was that his best-remembered campaign promise was, "Read my lips: No new taxes!"

Quietly, in late June 1990, Bush announced in a brief written statement that he was willing to compromise on the tax issue. Much later, after conservative Republicans broke with him over this reversal, Bush called the tax hikes "a mistake."

CAMPAIGN ★ 1992

IN EARLY 1991, AT THE END of the Persian Gulf War, George Bush was hugely popular. His 89 percent public approval rating seemed to guarantee him reelection, but the expanding recession soon weakened people's confidence in his leadership.

Although Democrat Bill Clinton experienced some dramatic ups and downs during the primary season, he was nevertheless nominated on the first ballot. The forty-six-year-old Arkansas governor claimed that he was a "new kind of Democrat," liberal on social issues yet conservative on economic ones. His theme was "change." But his campaign was dogged for months by two controversial accusations. One was that, while married, he had carried on a twelve-year affair with another woman. The other was that he had misled his draft board in order to avoid the Vietnam War. Although Clinton denied these charges, it sometimes seemed as though they might sink him.

A New Voice for a New America

★ CLINTON-GORE '92 ★

Meanwhile, voters began to sense that Bush's many years in Washington had left him out of touch with the lives of ordinary people. When Ross Perot entered the race as an independent candidate, the self-made billionaire focused attention on the federal budget deficit. Lecturing the public with charts and graphs, he explained that he would run the government in the same successful way that he had run his own business. Some voters saw Perot as capable and others saw him as eccentric, but all became interested in the deficit issue.

Perot received 19 percent of the popular vote, Bush took 38 percent, and Clinton won 43 percent. With Perot's votes, Bush would have won in a landslide. Instead, Clinton won the election, and though he received fewer than half of the ballots cast, 62 percent of the electorate did vote for change.

PEROT for President

BORN: AUGUST 19, 1946

BIRTHPLACE: HOPE, ARK.

PARTY: DEMOCRAT

VICE PRESIDENT: ALBERT A. GORE JR.

FIRST LADY: HILLARY RODHAM

CHILDREN: CHELSEA

NICKNAME: BUBBA

THE FIRST PRESIDENT TO HAVE BEEN A RHODES SCHOLAR.

WILLIAM JEFFERSON
CLINTON
42nd President
★
1993 to 2001

Bill Clinton

ARREST MADE
IN WORLD TRADE CENTER BOMBING

NEW YORK, March 4, 1993—The FBI made the first arrest today in the World Trade Center bombing case. Agents captured Mohammed Salameh in Jersey City, New Jersey, when he attempted to collect his rental deposit on the van used in the bombing.

Salameh had told the rental company that the van had been stolen. The FBI found Salameh by tracing the vehicle using an identification number found on a piece of twisted metal at the bomb site. Salameh is a member of a Jersey City mosque attended by radical Islamic fundamentalists.

Just last week, Lower Manhattan was thrown into turmoil when a huge explosion rocked the twin towers of the World Trade Center. The February 26 blast, the worst terrorist attack to date on U.S. soil, was caused by a van loaded with explosives. The van had been parked in a public garage beneath the 110-story buildings.

Five people were killed by the explosion and at least one thousand injured. The bomb left a crater in the garage seven stories deep.

As the first Baby Boomer president, Bill Clinton was often influenced by the values that he adopted during the 1960s. For example, he chose Al Gore as his running mate because he shared Gore's concern for the environment. Yet in his first inaugural address, Clinton showed that he understood traditional values as well. "It is time to break the bad habit of expecting something for nothing," he said. In other words, the "change" for which he had campaigned would require sacrifice.

Many Americans, even those who had voted against Clinton, hoped that his election would end the gridlock that had taken hold in Washington. For the first time in twelve years, both the White House and Congress would be controlled by the same party. Change didn't come easily, however, and early stumbles by the Clinton team didn't help. For example, the president's first nominee for attorney general, Zoe Baird, was forced to withdraw after admitting that she and her husband had failed to pay social security tax for their two

household employees. Still, Clinton remained committed to appointing a female attorney general, and his second choice, Florida prosecutor Janet Reno, won Senate confirmation easily.

TRADE AGREEMENTS During his first two years in office, the president had some difficulties with the Democrats in Congress, but he did win two important trade battles. In November 1993, the House approved the North American Free Trade Agreement (NAFTA), which created a free-trade zone linking the United States, Mexico, and Canada. A year later, Congress ratified the General Agreement on Tariffs and Trade (GATT).

With regard to health care, however, Bill and Hillary Clinton were much less successful. A White House task force led by the first lady proposed reforms that would have covered all Americans and guaranteed them a minimum package of benefits. But doctors, hospitals, and insurance companies fought the plan, and many congressmen criticized it for being too expensive. Some moderate senators proposed compromises, but these were also rejected, and the gridlock on health care continued.

THE 1994 ELECTIONS The president's party often loses seats during midterm congressional elections, but the 1994 results were especially disastrous for the Democrats. Republicans won control of both the House and the Senate for the first time since 1955. Even Tom Foley lost his seat, becoming the first Speaker of the House since 1862 to be voted out of office.

"Republicans did a good job of defining us [the Democrats] as the party of government," President Clinton said after the election, "and that [was] not a good place to be."

BILL CLINTON'S FATHER DIED in a car accident before he was born. When Bill was seven, his mother, Virginia, remarried. Her new husband, Roger Clinton, was a car dealer and an alcoholic who sometimes beat his wife. At fourteen, Bill confronted his step-

THE EARLY YEARS

father. "Daddy, if you're not able to stand up, I'll help you," he said, "but you must stand up to hear what I have to say. Don't ever, ever, lay your hand on my mother again."

In 1963, as part of a trip sponsored by the American Legion, Bill visited Washington, D.C., where he met Pres. John F. Kennedy. From that moment, he knew that he wanted a career in politics. In 1978, at age thirty-two, he was elected to lead Arkansas, becoming the youngest governor in the country. At the end of his first term, he was voted out of office for raising the state gasoline tax to pay for highway improvements. But he accepted this defeat as a lesson in humility and regained the governorship in 1982.

★**THE FIRST LADY** Hillary Rodham met Bill Clinton at Yale Law School, where they were both students during the early 1970s. She introduced herself to him after she noticed him staring at her in class. In 1974, she set aside plans for her own career in politics and moved to Arkansas to marry him. In Little Rock, Mrs. Clinton worked full-time as a lawyer and became active in children's issues. "If you elect Bill, you get me," she often said during the 1992 campaign. Soon after taking office, President Clinton appointed the first lady to head an important task force on health care.

Although both Clintons have supported public education, they sent their daughter, Chelsea, to a private school. Once when Chelsea needed permission to take some medicine, she told school officials to call her father, the president. Her mother, she said, was too busy.

★**SPACE** Although the *Challenger* disaster began a period of hard times for the U.S. space program, the National Aeronautics and Space Administration (NASA) rebounded strongly in 1996. In August of that year, NASA announced that it might have discovered evidence that life once existed on the planet Mars. The possible proof was a potato-sized meteorite found near the South Pole in 1986. Using a powerful microscope, NASA scientists had discovered features on the rock that looked like fossilized bacteria. A month later, the space shuttle *Atlantis* brought Shannon Lucid back to earth following a 188-day stay aboard the Russian space station Mir. Lucid's mission broke endurance records both for an American astronaut and for a woman.

★**OKLAHOMA CITY BOMBING** Shortly after 9:00 A.M. on April 19, 1995, a bomb hidden in a rental van exploded outside the Murrah Federal Building in Oklahoma City, Oklahoma. The force of the blast collapsed most of the building, killing 168 people. At the time, the Oklahoma City bombing was the worst terrorist attack ever committed on U.S. soil.

At first, because of the parallels between the Oklahoma City and World Trade Center bombings, many people assumed that the terrorists were foreigners, perhaps even Islamic fundamentalists. As it turned out, FBI agents traced the bomb to two Americans, Timothy McVeigh and Terry Nichols. Both men belonged to the militia movement, whose members stockpiled guns and other weapons because they believed that the U.S. government was planning to take away their constitutional rights.

★**THE INTERNET** The Internet is the infrastructure along which digital information travels. Although its origins date back to a Defense Department system of the late 1960s, the general public didn't begin "surfing the Net" in large numbers until the mid-1990s. To take advantage of this new traffic, many organizations, including the White House, set up Web sites for people to visit electronically using their personal computers.

When it came to governing, however, the new Republican majority in the 104th Congress ran into trouble. In particular, new House Speaker Newt Gingrich learned that running the government was much more difficult than attacking it.

CONTRACT WITH AMERICA Most of the new Republican congressmen had backed the Contract with America, Gingrich's list of campaign promises that had included a new line-item veto for the president and an end to unfunded federal mandates (laws that required states to carry out programs but included no funds to pay for them). The Contract with America also promised swift passage of a balanced-budget amendment and legal reforms to reduce the number of lawsuits.

The first two of these measures were enacted during the first hundred days of the new Congress. But the last two, along with many other aspects of the Contract with America, stalled in the Senate, where Republicans were much less radical than in the House.

Meanwhile, the battle between Congress and the president over the budget continued for nearly a year, reaching its climax during the fall of 1995. In late October, the House and Senate passed a bill that would have cut taxes and balanced the budget by 2002. To do so, health, education, and environmental spending would have been cut deeply.

Objecting to this strategy, Clinton vetoed the bill. He offered a compromise, but the Republicans turned him down. With no budget law in place, the government began to run out of money.

GOVERNMENT SHUTDOWNS In mid-November, the budget impasse forced a partial shutdown of the federal government. Offices were closed, and eight hundred thousand workers were sent home.

The shutdown lasted six days. Finally, when President Clinton accepted the Republican goal of balancing the budget within seven years, the House and Senate approved stopgap spending bills.

Even so, the president and Congress continued to disagree over just how to balance the budget, and in mid-December, Congress forced another government shutdown. It lasted three weeks.

This time, however, the Republicans miscalculated, and a frustrated public turned against them. Voters who had once encouraged the Republicans to dismantle the federal government now praised President Clinton for defending from a reckless Congress popular programs such as Medicare.

THE WAR IN BOSNIA In the arena of foreign policy, Clinton also encountered some difficult and risky situations. In the former Yugoslavia, for example, Serbs, Croats, and Bosnian Muslims were fighting the bloodiest war in Europe since World War II. The Serbs wanted to carve out of the independent state of Bosnia an ethnically pure Serbian homeland. During four years of fighting, 250,000 people had died.

In November 1995, with the budget crisis swirling around him, President Clinton brought the warring factions together at an air force base in Dayton, Ohio. After three weeks of tense and bitter negotiations, the three parties finally agreed on a peace plan.

In his most daring foreign policy move yet, President Clinton agreed to send twenty thousand troops to Bosnia to help guarantee the peace. These soldiers policed Bosnia as part of a ninety-thousand-soldier United Nations Implementation Force (IFOR). The Dayton peace plan, which preserved

CAMPAIGN ★ 1996

ALTHOUGH PRESIDENT CLINTON'S POPULARITY dropped during his first two years in office, it rose again in the aftermath of the government shutdowns. Polls confirmed that the same voters who threw out the Democrats in 1994 didn't like the way the Republicans were acting, either.

To take advantage of the Republicans' move to the political right, the president moved deliberately into the political center. In August 1996, he staged a series of White House bill signings that emphasized his moderate policies. The bills that he signed raised the minimum wage, expanded access to health insurance, and overhauled the welfare system. The president signed the welfare reform bill despite strong opposition from liberals within his own administration. They believed that the new law would dangerously weaken the social safety net that had been set up for poor people.

To run against Clinton, the Republicans nominated Senate Majority Leader Bob Dole of Kansas. In his convention acceptance speech, the seventy-three-year-old Dole, a World War II veteran, talked about building a "bridge to the past," to the years immediately following World War II, when Americans felt confident and prosperous. Making use of the same imagery, Clinton spoke in his own acceptance speech of building a bridge to the future.

In the end, as is usually the case, the election turned on how voters felt about the economy. Several character issues dogged Clinton, especially his involvement in a troubled Arkansas land deal known as Whitewater. But the generally good economic news buoyed his campaign and carried him to a decisive victory.

96 USA

ENCORE!

DOLE ★ KEMP

ECONOMIC BOOM SETS RECORD

WASHINGTON, February 1, 2000—The economic expansion that began in March 1991 became the longest in U.S. history today when it reached 107 consecutive months of growth. Over that time, there has been an uninterrupted rise in the nation's gross domestic product (the value of goods and services produced). The previous record was set during the 1960s.

In an interview today, President Clinton credited such factors as freer trade, rapid advances in technology, and the Federal Reserve's skillful handling of interest rates and inflation. Federal Reserve chairman Alan Greenspan, first appointed in 1988, is the individual most often linked to the current prosperity.

One consequence of the boom is that fights over how to cut the budget deficit have been replaced by fights over how to spend the new budget surplus. Congressional Republicans have proposed large tax cuts, but President Clinton has vetoed them, arguing that they would threaten important government programs.

GROSS DOMESTIC PRODUCT 1991–2000

12000	
10000	
8000	
6000	
4000	
2000	
0	1991 1992 1993 1994 1995 1996 1997 1998 1999 2000

IN BILLIONS OF DOLLARS

the unity of Bosnia, called for limited disarmament to be followed by free elections. These elections were held peacefully in September 1996.

However, Serbian president Slobodan Milosevic continued to act aggressively elsewhere in the Balkans. Frustrated in Bosnia, he turned his attention to Kosovo, a province in southern Serbia where nine out of ten residents were ethnic Albanians. (That is, their families had come to Kosovo from neighboring Albania.) In late 1997, what had been political and economic discrimination escalated into violence, as Christian Serb security forces began "cleansing" Kosovo of its many Muslim Albanian citizens.

THE BOMBING OF KOSOVO The Serbian violence became so brutal that in October 1998, NATO issued an ultimatum to Milosevic, threatening air strikes unless he immediately withdrew the rampaging Serbian forces from Kosovo. Milosevic responded by recalling just enough troops to delay the bombing. Negotiations continued for several more months until NATO issued another ultimatum.

This time, neither side backed down, and in March 1999, NATO began an eleven-week aerial offensive, the first NATO military operation ever mounted against a sovereign country.

As is nearly always the case, the decision to use force posed risks, both at home and abroad. Clinton knew, for example, that the American public's reluctant support for the air war would vanish overnight if it became necessary to use ground troops. (Ground wars always produce much higher casualties.)

Furthermore, by personally identifying himself with the task of freeing Kosovo, the president risked losing the public's confidence should the NATO effort fail.

RELATIONS WITH RUSSIA

Clinton also had to worry about the Russians, who were longtime allies of the Serbs and who strongly opposed NATO's strong-arm tactics. At the time, Russia was experiencing a difficult transition from Communism to multiparty democracy, and its military forces were in decline. Nevertheless, the possibility remained that Russia would intercede militarily on Serbia's behalf, if only to boost its own sinking national morale and divert attention from its economic problems.

Since the end of the Cold War, the United States had done its best to promote political and free-market reforms within the former Soviet Union. This policy had relied on economic aid as well as strong support for Boris Yeltsin during the hotly contested 1996 Russian presidential campaign.

Because of Yeltsin's close personal ties to President Clinton, the State Department was able to enlist Yeltsin's help in pressuring Milosevic to concede. On June 9, the war in Kosovo ended when a battered Serbia agreed to withdraw its troops. Meanwhile, a United Nations peacekeeping force entered the province to govern in Serbia's place. Although Milosevic still clung to power for more than a year, the massive fraud he engineered during the September 2000 Serbian elections led to a civil revolt that chased him from office within two weeks.

CLINTON'S PERSONAL DIPLOMACY

The president's fondness for personal diplomacy also helped him make headway in two of the world's perennial trouble spots: Northern Ireland and the Middle East. He helped forge the April 1998 Good Friday peace accords, which created a new power-sharing arrangement in Northern

★THE TOBACCO SETTLEMENT

During the late 1990s, a number of states filed lawsuits against cigarette makers to recover money that they had spent under Medicaid treating smoking-related illnesses. These lawsuits were backed by emerging evidence that

He has his daddy's eyes and his momma's lungs.

Secondhand Smoke Kills.

seemed to support charges that cigarette companies had deceived the public about the health risks of smoking. In November 1998, the four largest U.S. tobacco companies agreed to the biggest civil settlement ever, a $206 billion deal that called for a twenty-five-year payout beginning in 2000, restrictions on cigarette advertising, and an industry-funded campaign to reduce teen smoking. Although the parties originally intended the money to be used for public health programs, state governments instead spent most of it on other priorities ranging from education and tax cuts to new roads and prisons. Meanwhile, the Centers for Disease Control continued to report that cigarette smoking remained the leading preventable cause of death in the United States.

★THE HUMAN GENOME PROJECT

At a White House ceremony on June 26, 2000, the leaders of two massive research efforts, one run by the public U.S. Human Genome Project and the other by privately funded Celera Genomics, announced the

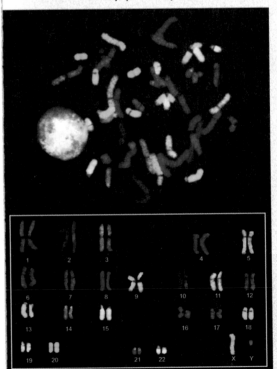

creation of a "working draft" of the genetic sequences that make up human DNA. This "road map" is expected to revolutionize the practice of medicine by allowing scientists to create new diagnostic tests and treatments for a variety of illnesses. However, the availability of this information also raises important ethical, legal, and social questions. For example, unless a person's privacy is protected, employers and insurance companies may be able to use genetic information to discriminate against people who have genetic predispositions with regard to certain diseases.

★ **COLUMBINE** During the 1990s, the rising level of school violence became one of the most important local issues in the United States. The school year 1999–2000 was the first in seven years without a fatal mass shooting in a U.S. public school. The worst of these incidents took place at Columbine High School in Littleton, Colorado, on April 20, 1999. That day, two students armed with semiautomatic rifles and explosives murdered twelve students and a teacher before killing themselves.

★ **Y2K** Until the late 1990s, computer memory was in short supply. So computer programmers used a shortcut when writing software that contained dates. Instead of using all four digits of a year, such as 1993, they used only the last two digits, or 93.

As the year 2000 approached, programmers realized that this shortcut would no longer work, because computers would think that 00 meant 1900 rather than 2000. During the years leading up to 2000, both the government and the private sector spent billions of dollars on efforts to avoid a Year 2000, or Y2K, crisis. A few people moved to the countryside because they feared that widespread computer shutdowns would lead to riots in the cities. This was an extreme reaction, but most people made sure that they had fresh batteries in their flashlights in case problems with utility company computers caused the power to go out. In the end, the transition went surprisingly smoothly.

★ **FRANKENFOOD** As the skills of genetic engineers improved during the 1990s, many began working on new foodstuffs that might ease malnutrition around the world. One of these was a rice that scientists modified genetically to contain beta-carotene, a source of vitamin A. However, despite the potential benefits of this rice to poor people in Asia (whose diets depend on rice), opponents argued that genetic modification was too risky, because combining genes from different species threatened the health of the planet's gene pool. For this reason, they referred to genetically modified foods as Frankenfood, after the fictional monster created by Dr. Frankenstein. Meanwhile, similar concerns about mass-produced food led to a boom in organic farming. Organic farmers (such as the one shown above) avoid chemical fertilizers and pesticides. Instead, they use traditional techniques such as composting and crop rotation to renew their soils and discourage destructive insects.

Ireland. He also involved himself deeply in ongoing talks between Israel and the Palestinians over implementation of the 1993 Oslo peace plan, a negotiating breakthrough that had already produced limited Palestinian self-rule in the Gaza Strip and on the West Bank.

At Maryland's Wye Conference Center in October 1998 and at Camp David in July 2000, Clinton spent days at a time with the Israeli prime minister (first Benjamin Netanyahu, later Ehud Barak) and Palestinian leader Yasir Arafat, trying to work out the stubborn details of a "land for peace" deal. On both occasions progress was made, yet many issues, such as the future of Jerusalem and the fate of Jewish settlements on the West Bank, still separated the two sides, and the talks collapsed.

BUDGET SURPLUS President Clinton was able to commit so much time and energy to making peace around the world because at home the U.S. economy was booming. An indication of the good times was the persistent rise of stock prices. In March 1999, for example, the Dow Jones Industrial Average topped ten thousand points—a figure with great psychological, if not economic, significance. At the same time, low unemployment, low inflation, and high productivity—along with earlier government belt tightening—eliminated the troublesome budget deficits.

In February 1998, Clinton proposed the first balanced budget since 1969, and a year later, the government was running a surplus. That is, its income from taxes and fees exceeded the amount it spent on programs and interest payments on the national debt.

In fact, the only issue the president seemed to be having touble with was the Whitewater investigation. Begun soon after his inauguration, it continued until

2000

the end of his second term. Many of his allies attacked Independent Counsel Kenneth Starr for needlessly prolonging the inquiry. The first lady even insisted on national television that her husband was being victimized by "a vast right-wing conspiracy." Nevertheless, Starr's probe did result in jail time for two of the Clintons' partners in that failed Arkansas land deal.

IMPEACHMENT As Starr's investigation dragged on, new charges emerged. The most explosive of these was that the president had lied under oath to conceal an intimate relationship he had had with a young White House staff member.

For months after the story broke in January 1998, Clinton denied the affair. On August 17, however, accumulating evidence forced him to admit that he had been misleading people.

He apologized, but few Americans were satisfied because they believed that his apology was insincere and intended only to break the gathering momentum for impeachment. Much of the problem was Clinton's continuing insistence that his testimony, although misleading, had been "legally correct."

After the November 1998 midterm elections, Starr presented his evidence to the Republican-controlled House, which on December 19 approved two of four articles of impeachment. Both related specifically to Clinton's attempt to conceal his extramarital affair.

Meanwhile, despite the widespread belief that the president had lied, voters continued to give him high approval ratings. These no doubt influenced the Senate's decision two months later to acquit him. But there was something that the president did lose, if not his job: He lost the moral authority that usually comes with the Oval Office.

CAMPAIGN ★ 2000

WITH BILL CLINTON RETIRING after two terms, Vice Pres. Al Gore began the 2000 presidential campaign as the most likely candidate to succeed him. The reason was that, with prosperity at home and peace abroad, voters usually stick with the incumbent party.

Meanwhile, the Republican faithful rallied around Texas governor George W. Bush, son of the former president, who raised nearly forty million dollars before the primaries even began. Although this early money made him seem invincible, he had to withstand a tough challenge from Arizona senator John McCain, a longtime advocate of campaign finance reform. McCain beat Bush in the first Republican primary, held in New Hampshire, but Bush soon derailed McCain's underfinanced campaign with a strong showing in the March cluster of primaries known as Super Tuesday.

During the general election campaign, both Gore and Bush followed Clinton's 1996 tactic of hugging the political center. This caused some progressive Democrats to leave Gore and instead support Green party nominee Ralph Nader. However, opinion polls showed that most voters were looking for steadiness rather than big, new ideas.

Gore's public stiffness helped the amiable Bush take an early lead, but the momentum shifted when the vice president unexpectedly chose Connecticut senator Joseph Lieberman as his running mate. Lieberman thus became the first Jew to run on a major party's presidential ticket, and his strong religious convictions undercut the Republicans' faith-based attacks on Gore.

The campaign seesawed back and forth until Election Day—and even afterward, with the balloting in several states just too close to call. Charges of fraud and incompetence followed, adding to the confusion. One thing was certain, however: Had Gore received the bulk of the Democratic votes cast for Nader, he would have been elected president.

BORN: JULY 6, 1946

BIRTHPLACE: NEW HAVEN, CT.

PARTY: REPUBLICAN

VICE PRESIDENT: RICHARD B. CHENEY

FIRST LADY: LAURA WELCH

CHILDREN: BARBARA, JENNA

NICKNAME: DUBYA

THE FIRST PRESIDENT TO HAVE FATHERED TWINS.

GEORGE WALKER BUSH

43rd President
★
2001 to 2009

RULING IN BUSH V. GORE
COURT DECIDES ELECTION

WASHINGTON, December 12, 2000—At ten o'clock tonight, the Supreme Court issued a ruling that made Republican candidate George W. Bush the winner in the 2000 presidential election. The controversial decision came just two hours before the deadline for state certification of presidential electors.

The justices, by a vote of 5–4, overturned a Florida Supreme Court decision permitting the recount by hand of ballots in several disputed Florida counties.

With its decision in *Bush v. Gore*, the Court stopped this recount and gave the state to

Bush, who was leading at the time by 537 votes out of nearly 6 million cast. Whichever candidate won Florida's electoral votes would have become the next president.

Instead of taking the White House, Democrat Al Gore became the fourth candidate in history to win the popular vote but not the presidency.

The 2000 presidential election was one of the closest and most controversial in U.S. history. In the end, the winner had to be decided by the Supreme Court. As a result, when George W. Bush took office in January 2001, he became president of a deeply divided nation.

As a candidate, Bush had routinely described himself as a "compassionate conservative" who could "bring people together." Now he had the chance to do just that. In his inaugural address, he vowed to lift the country above partisan politics, and he said that he would establish a new era of "civility" in government. As president, however, he relied primarily on a small circle of close advisers—a style of governance that made people with differing views often feel excluded.

From the start of his presidency, Bush governed with a strong sense of moral certainty that pleased Americans who shared his deep religious faith. Aligning his policies with the goals of powerful Christian groups, he limited the federal funding of stem cell research (because stem cells are derived

213

from human embryos); offered federal money to faith-based social programs; and appointed highly controversial, socially conservative judges to the federal bench.

UNILATERALISM These policies were unpopular with liberals, who became even more upset when Bush and Vice President Dick Cheney reversed decades of multilateralism in U.S. foreign policy. (Multilateralism means acting in alliance with other nations, as opposed to unilateralism, or acting alone.) In March 2001, Bush rejected the 1997 Kyoto treaty on global warming because he said that it would hurt the U.S. economy. In May 2002, he withdrew the United States from another multilateral treaty, signed by President Clinton in 2000, that established the International Criminal Court.

An equally dramatic reversal came in the nation's tax policy. Under President Clinton, Congress had shifted the tax burden significantly from the bottom 80 percent to the top 1 percent of the population. In February 2001, two weeks after taking office, President Bush proposed "spending" the large budget surplus that Clinton's economic policies had generated on a ten-year, $1.6 trillion tax cut. Of this amount, 43 percent would go to the richest 1 percent of Americans. The money belonged to the American taxpayers, Bush said, and they should get to keep it. Congress eventually approved a $1.35 trillion tax cut.

THE 9/11 ATTACKS In September 2001, the world changed. About eight o'clock in the morning on September 11, nineteen men belonging to the Islamic terrorist group al-Qaeda seized control of four airborne passenger jets. At 8:46 A.M., one of those planes crashed into the North Tower of the World Trade Center in New York City.

THE EARLY YEARS GEORGE WALKER BUSH WAS BORN in New Haven, Connecticut, where his father, future president George Herbert Walker Bush, was attending Yale University after his discharge from the navy. When young George was two years old, the family moved to western Texas, where the elder Bush had accepted a job in the oil business. George W. attended elementary and junior high school in Midland before being sent back east to the elite Phillips Academy in Andover, Massachusetts. Later, he attended Yale, like his father, and Harvard Business School.

At Yale and afterward, Bush was known less for his good work habits—he did just enough to get by—than for his partying. His playboy behavior continued well into his thirties. During the mid-1980s, however, he joined a men's Bible study group and became a born-again Christian. His heavy drinking had been a strain on his marriage, but under pressure from his wife and with the help of his new faith, he gave up alcohol shortly after his fortieth birthday.

★**THE FIRST LADY** Schoolteacher and librarian Laura Welch first met George W. Bush at a summer 1977 barbecue in Midland, Texas, hosted by mutual friends. Although they had both gone to the same junior high school and lived in the same Houston apartment complex, neither recalled the other. Their first date included a round of miniature golf. Three months later, they were married. They skipped their honeymoon, however, because Mr. Bush was in the middle of a race for Congress (which he lost).

A shy person by nature, Mrs. Bush found it difficult at first to make campaign appearances. Her first attempt—a short speech she gave on the courthouse steps in Muleshoe, Texas—ended abruptly when she couldn't think of what to say. By the 2000 campaign, however, "she had come a long way," according to one newspaper columnist. She spoke effectively not only about her husband but also about her favorite causes, which included early education and literacy.

★ HARRY POTTER

At midnight on July 21, 2007, U.S. bookstores began selling *Harry Potter and the Deathly Hallows*, the seventh and final title in the popular fantasy series written by British author J. K. Rowling. During the book's first twenty-four hours on sale, it sold 8.3 million copies in the United States, making it the fastest selling book in U.S. publishing history. Overall, Rowling's Harry Potter novels have sold more than four hundred million copies in sixty-five languages worldwide.

The series chronicles the adventures of Harry, a young orphan forced to live with his dreary aunt and uncle, who are Muggles—that is, people without a drop of magic in them. Harry's life changes, however, on his eleventh birthday, when he is invited to attend the Hogwarts School of Witchcraft and Wizardry. At Hogwarts, Harry learns how to use magic and becomes part of the Wizarding world.

A divorced single mother, Rowling wrote the first book in the series, *Harry Potter and the Sorcerer's Stone* (1997), while living in Edinburgh, Scotland, on public assistance. She composed the text sitting at a table in a local café while her infant daughter napped at her side.

★ CORPORATE SCANDALS

During economic boom times such as the 1990s, greedy corporate executives sometimes cut corners, not always legally, to earn more money. As long as the boom continues, hardly anyone pays attention to the lawbreaking and poor ethics. But when the downturn comes and investors look for reasons to explain their losses, past misdeeds usually come to light.

Some newsmagazines called 2002 "the year of the corporate scandal" because that year many well-known companies were accused of financial wrongdoing. The first and biggest scandal involved energy trader Enron, the nation's seventh-largest company. In order to keep Enron's stock price high, company executives illegally hid seven billion dollars in debt. When the company's true economic situation became known, the stock price plummeted. This primarily hurt Enron's rank-and-file employees, whose retirement savings were heavily invested in Enron stock.

Soon, another plane hit the South Tower, and a third was flown into the Pentagon outside Washington, D.C. The fourth jet never reached its target, probably the White House or the Capitol. Learning from cell phone conversations what had already happened, passengers on board that plane stormed the cockpit and forced the jet to crash in rural Pennsylvania, killing everyone aboard. Altogether, three thousand people died in the 9/11 attacks.

THE WAR ON TERRORISM

Not since the Japanese bombing of Pearl Harbor in December 1941 had the nation received such a shocking blow. At first, President Bush reacted hesitantly. But then, as he came to believe that the attacks gave his presidency a purpose, he responded with growing strength and confidence. Specifically, he promised to lead the nation in a "war on terrorism" that would "rid the world of the evildoers."

This theme of good versus evil became central to Bush's policies and left little room for differences of opinion. "Every nation in every region now has a decision to make," the president said. "Either you are with us, or you are with the terrorists."

The first battlefield in the war on terrorism was Afghanistan. Because the Taliban government there had been sheltering Osama bin Laden and other al-Qaeda leaders, President Bush's plan to depose the Taliban received a great deal of international support. Beginning on the night of October 7, 2001, U.S. and British bombers began attacking targets inside Afghanistan. Soon, the forces of the rebel Northern Alliance, aided by troops from a large coalition of nations, removed the Taliban from power and established a new pro-Western government.

HOMELAND SECURITY

At home, President Bush began reorganizing his administration around the war on terrorism. He supported the creation of a new Department of Homeland Security, which brought together 170,000 workers from twenty-two different agencies. This rearrangement of the federal government was the most far-reaching since the 1940s. President Bush also backed the October 2001 USA PATRIOT Act, which granted sweeping new powers to law-enforcement agencies at the expense of some civil liberties. For example, the act expanded the federal government's ability to intercept e-mails, search financial and other records, and detain people.

About the same time, the president secretly authorized the National Security Agency (NSA) to begin eavesdropping on the telephone conversations of suspected terrorists without obtaining the necessary court warrants. When the *New York Times* revealed this program in December 2005, most experts described it as illegal. But instead of thoroughly investigating what Bush had done, members of Congress passed a new law authorizing a similar program.

Meanwhile, the Bush administration made plans to invade Iraq. Throughout 2002, Bush, Vice President Cheney, and National Security Advisor Condoleezza Rice repeatedly declared that Iraq was a threat to the United States. Iraq's dictator, Saddam Hussein, had weapons of mass destruction, they said, and he also had strong ties to al-Qaeda.

Many of America's closest European and Asian allies—including France, Germany, and China—disagreed. Since the end of the 1991 Persian Gulf War, UN inspectors had been searching for evidence that Iraq possessed biological, chemical, or nuclear weapons. No

CAMPAIGN ★ 2004

IN THE AFTERMATH of the 9/11 attacks, President Bush's approval ratings soared to as high as 89 percent of those polled. By early 2004, however, his popularity had fallen dramatically. The growing violence in Iraq had led many Americans to question Bush's decision to go to war, and his two justifications—Iraq's possession of weapons of mass destruction and its links to al-Qaeda—had both been discredited. In addition, an April 2004 prisoner-abuse scandal made the Bush administration look even worse.

The early leader among the nine Democrats challenging Bush was former Vermont governor Howard Dean, who had opposed the war in Iraq from the start. Dean rallied his party by championing its traditional liberal values. "I represent the Democratic wing of the Democratic party," Dean said, referring to what he considered the overly centrist attitudes of his fellow candidates.

Yet once the primaries began, Democratic voters abandoned their flirtation with Dean and voted instead for Massachusetts senator John F. Kerry, a Vietnam War hero whose chief asset was that, as a centrist, he was considered "electable."

Kerry and his running mate, North Carolina senator John Edwards, waged a tough campaign against Bush. They called his conduct of the war in Iraq "incompetent" and charged that his administration had damaged the economy by cutting the taxes of wealthy Americans and running up huge budget deficits, including a record $477 billion deficit in 2004.

Nevertheless, many voters still thought the nation's security was at risk, and they didn't trust Kerry as commander in chief. That difference, along with high turnout among conservative Christian voters, gave Bush a narrow victory.

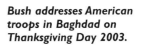

Bush addresses American troops in Baghdad on Thanksgiving Day 2003.

KATRINA HITS NEW ORLEANS

NEW ORLEANS, Louisiana, August 31, 2005—Two days after Hurricane Katrina passed over the Gulf Coast, New Orleans is a shambles. After flying over the city, President Bush announced a massive federal mobilization but said that recovery "will take years."

Katrina's high winds ripped away much of the roof of the Louisiana Superdome, where an estimated thirty thousand people have taken shelter from rising floodwaters.

The storm surge generated by Katrina has overwhelmed the city's protective system of levees. Numerous breaches in canal walls have caused more than 80 percent of the city to flood.

In some areas, such as the Lower Ninth Ward, floodwaters reached fifteen feet. Many poor residents, unable to evacuate the city, climbed onto rooftops to avoid drowning. They were later rescued by the Coast Guard. Others were not so fortunate. When asked about the likely hurricane death toll, Mayor Ray Nagin said, "Minimum, hundreds. Most likely, thousands."

evidence of these weapons was ever found, nor was any evidence found of a relationship between Saddam Hussein and al-Qaeda.

THE BUSH DOCTRINE Nevertheless, President Bush decided to move ahead, establishing a policy of preemptive war. According to this highly controversial policy, known as the Bush Doctrine, the United States could attack a country that it considered a threat to its national security, even if that country hadn't yet attacked the United States.

The Bush doctrine made it seem to other nations that there were few limits to U.S. unilateralism, and important American allies refused to go along with the president. Nevertheless, he asked Congress in October 2002 to authorize the use of military force in Iraq. By large margins in both houses, Congress approved the president's request.

THE INVASION OF IRAQ On March 19, 2003, the United States went to war with Iraq. Aided by the British, U.S. troops captured the Iraqi capital of Baghdad and scattered Saddam Hussein's army in about six weeks. On May 1, President Bush declared victory in Iraq using the phrase MISSION ACCOMPLISHED.

But the fighting didn't end. Instead, it got worse. During the next five years, Iraqi resistance fighters, known as insurgents, staged ambushes and car bombings that killed more than four thousand American soldiers. The death toll among Iraqi civilians was about twenty times higher.

2006

During 2004 and 2005, the president's handling of the war in Iraq came under increasing attack. One reason, of course, was the failure of his military strategy. More generally, Americans began to realize that the Bush administration hadn't thought through what to do with Iraq once Saddam Hussein was removed from power.

Despite warnings from several army generals, Secretary of Defense Donald Rumsfeld failed to deploy enough U.S. troops to establish law and order in Iraq. Furthermore, the civilian officials who were appointed to govern occupied Iraq knew little about the region and even less about how to defeat an insurgency. Finally, many corrupt American and Iraqi companies stole billions of dollars in reconstruction funds. Often, the work that these companies performed was below standard. At other times, the work wasn't performed at all.

THE PRISONERS AT GUANTÁNAMO

As part of the war on terrorism, President Bush used his power as commander in chief to imprison hundreds of people at Guantánamo Bay, Cuba. Although the Bush administration claimed that these people were terrorists, few were ever charged with a crime or allowed to defend themselves in court. Meanwhile, they were held for years and interrogated using methods, approved by President Bush, that many people considered to be torture.

The Bush administration argued that because the Guantánamo prisoners were being held at a naval base on Cuban soil, they were outside the jurisdiction of American judges. In June 2004, the Supreme Court disagreed, ruling that all prisoners being held at Guantánamo Bay had to be given access to U.S. courts. The Bush administration refused to heed

★ ALTERNATIVE ENERGY

Americans get most of their energy from fossil fuels, especially oil. When George Bush (who once ran an oil company) became president in January 2001, a barrel of oil cost $28. By July 2008, however, oil prices had shot up to $147 a barrel. Because gasoline is made from oil, gas prices also spiked, rising from $1.47 to $4.11 per gallon during the same period. One reason was growing worldwide demand. Another reason was political instability in the oil-rich Middle East caused by the Iraq War.

Although high prices made it difficult for many Americans to pay their fuel bills, there was a positive side to the problem. Americans became interested again in alternative energies, such as wind and solar power, which had been largely ignored since the energy crisis of the 1970s. Rising fossil fuel costs made these alternative technologies much more attractive, and investment in them took off again. Americans also began reducing their energy consumption, buying small hybrid cars and turning down their furnaces and air conditioners.

★ PRESIDENTIAL PILOT

The young George Bush learned how to fly a plane between 1968 and 1973 while serving in the Texas Air National Guard. He logged more than three hundred flight hours, most of them in F-102A fighter jets. In 1970, Bush's commanding officer recommended him for promotion, calling him "a top-notch fighter interceptor pilot" and "a natural leader."

In May 2003, to mark what he called an end to "major combat operations in Iraq," President Bush delivered a nationally televised speech from the flight deck of the aircraft carrier *Abraham Lincoln* off the coast of California. Memorably, Bush arrived on the carrier in a U.S. Navy S-3B jet. He made the flight from the mainland sitting in the copilot's seat and even took a turn at the controls.

★ **THE STEROIDS ERA** In 2001, thirty-seven-year-old Barry Bonds set a major league record, hitting seventy-three home runs in a single season. Six years later, the San Francisco Giants slugger broke another celebrated record, hitting the 756th home run of his career to surpass Hank Aaron's mark of 755. By then, however, Bonds had become deeply embroiled in a scandal involving the use of performance-enhancing drugs.

In 2005, Bonds's trainer, Greg Anderson, pleaded guilty to illegally distributing steroids, leading to speculation that Bonds had taken them. Sportswriters pointed out how unusual it was for the statistics of a player in his late thirties to improve in the dramatic way that Bonds's had. Bonds denied any involvement, but in November 2007 he was indicted for perjury after telling a federal grand jury that he had never knowingly taken steroids.

The years between the late 1980s and the early 2000s are often referred to as the steroids era in baseball. In March 2006, Commissioner Allan H. "Bud" Selig appointed George Mitchell to investigate the use of performance-enhancing drugs in the sport. In December 2007, the former Senate majority leader released his report. It identified many well-known players as drug users and criticized baseball management for failing to respond effectively to the problem.

★ **SOCIAL NETWORKING** Just like the interstate highway system, which links cities together, Internet sites such as MySpace and Facebook link people together. These social networking sites allow users to create profiles of themselves, which they can link to profiles created by their friends. In this way, people can find out whom their friends know and get to know these people as well. Using social networking, people can make new friends, learn about new jobs, and even find future husbands and wives. During the mid-2000s, the use of social networking sites grew at an incredible pace. Facebook, for example, which three Harvard University students began in their dorm room in February 2004, reached fifty million users in October 2007.

this decision and instead pressured Congress into passing a military tribunal law. The Supreme Court found this law unconstitutional as well. Even so, the Bush administration left office still refusing to grant the Guantánamo prisoners any legal rights.

THE MIDTERM ELECTIONS By 2006, the war in Iraq had become so unpopular that the Democratic party made opposition to the war the focus of its midterm congressional campaign. Most Democratic candidates promised to end the war quickly and bring the troops home. Supporting this goal, the voters abandoned President Bush's Republican party and gave the Democrats control of both houses of Congress.

With the violence in Iraq spiraling out of control and public pressure for a troop withdrawal building, President Bush realized that he would have to change strategies. But rather than bring the troops home, he decided to send more troops to Iraq.

THE TROOP SURGE President Bush called his new policy a "troop surge." He reasoned that deploying five additional brigades to Iraq would reduce the violence, thereby allowing the Iraqis to reach the political settlement that everyone agreed was necessary for a lasting peace. Although the Democrats in Congress had argued during the 2006 campaign for exactly the opposite strategy, they didn't take any practical steps to stop the surge, such as introducing legislation to limit its funding.

In the end, the results of the surge were mixed. Because violence in Iraq declined substantially, most people considered the surge a success. But the purpose of the surge had been to resolve Iraq's political problems, and

this didn't happen, leaving the future of the country uncertain.

While continuing to be faulted for mishandling the Iraq War, President Bush was also strongly criticized during his second term for the way he ran the federal government. The poor performance of the Federal Emergency Management Agency (FEMA) during the 2005 Hurricane Katrina crisis called attention to some of the people he had appointed to high-paying federal jobs. For example, Michael Brown, whom the president had appointed to run FEMA, lacked relevant job experience.

The Bush administration was also accused of hiring and firing government employees based not on their qualifications and job performance but on their political views. Such a practice violated federal law.

THE U.S. ATTORNEYS SCANDAL In December 2006, Attorney General Alberto Gonzales fired nine U.S. Attorneys. A congressional investigation later determined that these U.S. Attorneys, whose job it was to prosecute federal crimes, had been dismissed because the president's political advisers didn't think they were partisan enough.

Although strongly defended by President Bush, Gonzales and several other Justice Department officials were eventually forced to resign. Later, in September 2008, Gonzales's successor, Attorney General Michael B. Mukasey, appointed a special prosecutor to look into whether criminal charges should be brought in the case.

CAMPAIGN ★ 2008

THE REPUBLICAN CANDIDATES IN 2008 had to be careful what they said. If they praised President Bush, who was broadly unpopular, they risked angering moderate voters. However, if they criticized the president, they risked losing the support of conservative Christian voters who still liked President Bush and turned out heavily in the primaries. In the end, Arizona senator John McCain won the Republican nomination because his support for the surge in Iraq showed his loyalty to Bush, while his reputation as a party maverick gave him the necessary distance.

On the Democratic side, the contest between New York senator Hillary Rodham Clinton and Illinois senator Barack Obama looked as though it might go all the way to the convention. The former first lady enjoyed the support of party insiders, but Obama had a wide appeal that turned out to be decisive. Relying on his grassroots support, Obama competed strongly in all fifty states, narrowly losing most of the large states to Clinton but winning enough delegates in the small states to eke out the nomination. His campaign theme was CHANGE WE CAN BELIEVE IN.

McCain began the general election campaign by emphasizing his leadership. When that strategy failed, he tried to wrest the "change" theme from Obama. He surprised everyone by picking a Washington outsider, Alaska governor Sarah Palin, as his running mate. McCain promised that he and Palin would reform the federal government. But Obama responded that the Republican party had been in charge for the past eight years and couldn't be counted on to change anything.

The dominant issue turned out to be the economy. In September, several prominent banks failed, setting off a severe financial crisis. Because most voters blamed the crisis on the Republicans, it caused the momentum of the campaign to shift strongly in Obama's direction.

BORN: AUGUST 4, 1961

BIRTHPLACE: HONOLULU, HAWAII

PARTY: DEMOCRAT

VICE PRESIDENT: JOSEPH R. BIDEN JR.

FIRST LADY: MICHELLE ROBINSON

CHILDREN: MALIA, SASHA

NICKNAME: BARRY

THE FIRST AFRICAN AMERICAN
PRESIDENT.

BARACK OBAMA

44th President
★
2009 to 2013

When Barack Obama began running for president, he must have thought that his greatest challenge would be ending the war in Iraq, which he opposed. Instead, even before he took office, he found himself facing an economic crisis that dominated all other issues.

The bailout passed by Congress only a month before Obama's election was the largest ever in U.S. financial history. At first, outgoing treasury secretary Henry Paulson couldn't decide what to do with the seven hundred billion dollars. Initially, he wanted to use it to relieve banks of bad mortgages, but soon he changed his mind. Instead, he used two hundred fifty billion to buy stock in the nation's largest banks. Paulson wanted to improve their financial position and encourage them to start lending again.

Acting with the same steadiness that characterized his presidential campaign, President-elect Obama quickly made it clear that he didn't want Paulson writing a "blank check" to "Wall Street" while "Main Street" was suffering so badly.

BAILOUT APPROVED
Stock Crash Moves House to Act

WASHINGTON, October 3, 2008—By a vote of 263–171, the House of Representatives passed a bill today appropriating seven hundred billion dollars to bail out the nation's troubled financial services industry.

The vote came four days after the House narrowly defeated a similar plan, 228–205. Before the first vote, public opinion had been running strongly against the bailout. However, the reaction of the stock market to the defeat of the plan changed many people's minds.

On the day that the House defeated the first bailout bill, the Dow Jones Industrial Average, a key stock market measure, dropped 777 points, its biggest single-day loss ever.

The current financial crisis, the most serious since the Great Depression, began in the home mortgage market. In recent years, mortgage companies have unwisely (and sometimes fraudulently) given out home loans to people who can't afford them. The banks that now hold these loans have lost a great deal of money, leading to a severe tightening of credit and a loss of confidence in the financial markets.

221

PRESIDENTIAL ELECTION RESULTS

PRESIDENT / VICE PRESIDENT	TERM	CANDIDATES	POPULAR VOTE	ELEC. VOTE
1789		George Washington		69
		John Adams		34
George Washington	1789–1797	John Jay		9
John Adams	1789–1797	Others		26
		(NOT VOTED)		8
1792		George Washington (Federalist)		132
		John Adams (Federalist)		77
		George Clinton (Dem.-Rep.)		50
		Others		5
		(NOT VOTED)		6
1796		John Adams (Federalist)		71
		Thomas Jefferson (Dem.-Rep.)		68
John Adams	1797–1801	Thomas Pinckney (Federalist)		59
Thomas Jefferson	1797–1801	Aaron Burr (Dem.-Rep.)		30
		Others		48
1800		Thomas Jefferson (Dem.-Rep.)		73
		Aaron Burr (Dem.-Rep.)		73
Thomas Jefferson	1801–1809	John Adams (Federalist)		65
Aaron Burr	1801–1805	Charles C. Pinckney (Federalist)		64
		John Jay (Federalist)		1
1804		Thomas Jefferson (Dem.-Rep.)		162
		Charles C. Pinckney (Federalist)		14
George Clinton	1805–1809			
1808		James Madison (Dem.-Rep.)		122
		Charles C. Pinckney (Federalist)		47
James Madison	1809–1817	George Clinton (Independent)		6
George Clinton	1809–1812	(NOT VOTED)		1
1812		James Madison (Dem.-Rep.)		128
		DeWitt Clinton (Fusion)		89
		(NOT VOTED)		1
Elbridge Gerry	1813–1814			

PRESIDENT / VICE PRESIDENT	TERM	CANDIDATES	POPULAR VOTE	ELEC. VOTE
1816		James Monroe (Dem.-Rep.)		183
		Rufus King (Federalist)		34
James Monroe	1817–1825	(NOT VOTED)		4
Daniel D. Tompkins	1817–1825			
1820		James Monroe (Dem.-Rep.)		231
		John Quincy Adams (Independent)		1
		(NOT VOTED)		3
1824		Andrew Jackson	151,271	99
		John Quincy Adams	113,122	84
John Quincy Adams	1825–1829	William H. Crawford	40,856	41
John C. Calhoun	1825–1829	Henry Clay	47,531	37
1828		Andrew Jackson (Democrat)	642,553	178
		John Quincy Adams (Nat. Rep.)	500,897	83
Andrew Jackson	1829–1837			
John C. Calhoun	1829–1832			
1832		Andrew Jackson (Democrat)	701,780	219
		Henry Clay (Nat. Rep.)	484,205	49
		John Floyd (Independent)		11
		William Wirt (Anti-Mason)	100,715	7
Martin Van Buren	1833–1837	(NOT VOTED)		2
1836		Martin Van Buren (Democrat)	764,176	170
		William Henry Harrison (Whig)	550,816	73
Martin Van Buren	1837–1841	Hugh L. White (Whig)	146,107	26
Richard M. Johnson	1837–1841	Daniel Webster (Whig)	41,201	14
		Willie P. Mangum (Independent)		11
1840		William Henry Harrison (Whig)	1,275,390	234
		Martin Van Buren (Democrat)	1,128,854	60
William Henry Harrison	1841			
John Tyler	1841			

PRESIDENT / VICE PRESIDENT	TERM	CANDIDATES	POPULAR VOTE	ELEC. VOTE
John Tyler	1841–1845	Succeeded to the presidency on the death of William Henry Harrison.		
1844		James Knox Polk (Democrat)	1,339,494	170
James K. Polk	1845–1849	Henry Clay (Whig)	1,300,004	105
George M. Dallas	1845–1849	James G. Birney (Liberty)	62,103	
1848		Zachary Taylor (Whig)	1,361,393	163
Zachary Taylor	1849–1850	Lewis Cass (Democrat)	1,223,460	127
Millard Fillmore	1849–1850	Martin Van Buren (Free Soil)	291,501	
Millard Fillmore	1850–1853	Succeeded to the presidency on the death of Zachary Taylor.		
1852		Franklin Pierce (Democrat)	1,607,510	254
Franklin Pierce	1853–1857	Winfield Scott (Whig)	1,386,942	42
William R. King	1853	John P. Hale (Free Soil)	155,210	
1856		James Buchanan (Democrat)	1,836,072	174
James Buchanan	1857–1861	John C. Frémont (Republican)	1,342,345	114
John C. Breckinridge	1857–1861	Millard Fillmore (American)	873,053	8
1860		Abraham Lincoln (Republican)	1,865,908	180
Abraham Lincoln	1861–1865	John C. Breckinridge (Southern Dem.)	848,019	72
Hannibal Hamlin	1861–1865	John Bell (Constitutional Union)	590,901	39
		Stephen A. Douglas (Democrat)	1,380,202	12
1864		Abraham Lincoln (Republican)	2,218,388	212
		George B. McClellan (Democrat)	1,812,807	21
		(NOT VOTED)		1
Andrew Johnson	1865			
Andrew Johnson	1865–1869	Succeeded to the presidency on the assassination of Abraham Lincoln.		

PRESIDENT / VICE PRESIDENT	TERM	CANDIDATES	POPULAR VOTE	ELEC. VOTE
1868		Ulysses S. Grant (Republican)	3,013,650	214
Ulysses S. Grant	1869–1877	Horatio Seymour (Democrat)	2,708,744	80
Schuyler Colfax	1869–1873			
1872		Ulysses S. Grant (Republican)	3,598,235	286
		Horace Greeley (Democrat)	2,834,761	66
Henry Wilson	1873–1875			
1876		Rutherford B. Hayes (Republican)	4,034,311	185
Rutherford B. Hayes	1877–1881	Samuel J. Tilden (Democrat)	4,288,546	184
William A. Wheeler	1877–1881			
1880		James A. Garfield (Republican)	4,446,158	214
James A. Garfield	1881	Winfield S. Hancock (Democrat)	4,444,260	155
Chester A. Arthur	1881	James B. Weaver (Greenback Labor)	305,997	
Chester A. Arthur	1881–1885	Succeeded to the presidency on the assassination of James A. Garfield.		
1884		Grover Cleveland (Democrat)	4,874,621	219
Grover Cleveland	1885–1889	James G. Blaine (Republican)	4,848,936	182
Thomas A. Hendricks	1885			
1888		Benjamin Harrison (Republican)	5,443,892	233
Benjamin Harrison	1889–1893	Grover Cleveland (Democrat)	5,534,488	168
Levi P. Morton	1889–1893	Clinton B. Fisk (Prohibition)	249,819	
1892		Grover Cleveland (Democrat)	5,551,883	277
		Benjamin Harrison (Republican)	5,179,244	145
Grover Cleveland	1893–1897	James B. Weaver (People's)	1,024,280	22
Adlai E. Stevenson	1893–1897	John Bidwell (Prohibition)	270,770	
1896		William McKinley (Republican)	7,108,480	271
		William J. Bryan (Democrat/People's)	6,511,495	176
William McKinley	1897–1901			
Garret A. Hobart	1897–1899			

Left column

PRESIDENT / VICE PRESIDENT	TERM	CANDIDATES	POPULAR VOTE	ELEC. VOTE
1900		William McKinley (Republican)	7,218,039	292
		William J. Bryan (Democrat)	6,358,345	155
Theodore Roosevelt	1901			
Theodore Roosevelt	1901–1907	Succeeded to the presidency on the assassination of William McKinley.		
1904		Theodore Roosevelt (Republican)	7,626,593	336
		Alton B. Parker (Democrat)	5,082,898	140
Charles W. Fairbanks	1905–1909	Eugene V. Debs (Socialist)	402,489	
1908		William H. Taft (Republican)	7,676,258	321
William H. Taft	1909–1913	William J. Bryan (Democrat)	6,406,801	162
James S. Sherman	1909–1912	Eugene V. Debs (Socialist)	420,380	
1912		Woodrow Wilson (Democrat)	6,293,152	435
		Theodore Roosevelt (Progressive)	4,119,207	88
Woodrow Wilson	1913–1921	William H. Taft (Republican)	3,486,333	8
Thomas R. Marshall	1913–1921	Eugene V. Debs (Socialist)	900,369	
1916		Woodrow Wilson (Democrat)	9,126,300	277
		Charles E. Hughes (Republican)	8,546,789	254
		Allan L. Benson (Socialist)	589,924	
1920		Warren G. Harding (Republican)	16,153,115	404
Warren G. Harding	1921–1923	James M. Cox (Democrat)	9,133,092	127
Calvin Coolidge	1921–1923	Eugene V. Debs (Socialist)	915,490	
Calvin Coolidge	1923–1929	Succeeded to the presidency on the death of Warren G. Harding.		
1924		Calvin Coolidge (Republican)	15,719,921	382
		John W. Davis (Democrat)	8,386,704	136
Charles G. Dawes	1925–1929	Robert M. La Follette (Progressive)	4,832,532	13

Right column

PRESIDENT / VICE PRESIDENT	TERM	CANDIDATES	POPULAR VOTE	ELEC. VOTE
1928		Herbert C. Hoover (Republican)	21,437,277	4
Herbert C. Hoover	1929–1933	Alfred E. Smith (Democrat)	15,007,698	
Charles Curtis	1929–1933			
1932		Franklin D. Roosevelt (Democrat)	22,829,501	4
Franklin D. Roosevelt	1933–1945	Herbert C. Hoover (Republican)	15,760,684	
John Nance Garner	1933–1941	Norman M. Thomas (Socialist)	884,649	
1936		Franklin D. Roosevelt (Democrat)	27,757,333	5
		Alfred M. Landon (Republican)	16,684,231	
		William Lemke (Union)	892,267	
1940		Franklin D. Roosevelt (Democrat)	27,313,041	
		Wendell L. Willkie (Republican)	22,348,480	
Henry A. Wallace	1941–1945			
1944		Franklin D. Roosevelt (Democrat)	25,612,610	
		Thomas E. Dewey (Republican)	22,017,617	
Harry S. Truman	1945			
Harry S. Truman	1945–1953	Succeeded to the presidency on the death of Franklin Roosevelt.		
1948		Harry S. Truman (Democrat)	24,179,345	
		Thomas E. Dewey (Republican)	21,991,291	
		J. Strom Thurmond (States' Rights)	1,176,125	
Alben W. Barkley	1949–1953	Henry A. Wallace (Progressive)	1,157,326	
1952		Dwight D. Eisenhower (Republican)	33,936,234	
Dwight D. Eisenhower	1953–1961	Adlai E. Stevenson (Democrat)	27,314,992	
Richard M. Nixon	1953–1961			
1956		Dwight D. Eisenhower (Republican)	35,590,472	
		Adlai E. Stevenson (Democrat)	26,022,752	
		Walter B. Jones (Independent)		

PRESIDENT VICE PRESIDENT	TERM	CANDIDATES	POPULAR VOTE	ELEC. VOTE
1960 John F. Kennedy Lyndon B. Johnson	1961–1963 1961–1963	John F. Kennedy (Democrat) Richard M. Nixon (Republican) Harry F. Byrd (Independent)	34,226,731 34,108,157	303 219 15
Lyndon B. Johnson	1963–1969	Succeeded to the presidency on the assassination of John F. Kennedy.		
1964 Hubert H. Humphrey 1965–1969		Lyndon B. Johnson (Democrat) Barry M. Goldwater (Republican)	43,129,566 27,178,188	486 52
1968 Richard M. Nixon Spiro T. Agnew	1969–1974 1969–1973	Richard M. Nixon (Republican) Hubert H. Humphrey (Democrat) George C. Wallace (American Indep.)	31,785,480 31,275,166 9,906,473	301 191 46
1972 Gerald R. Ford	1973–1974	Richard M. Nixon (Republican) George S. McGovern (Democrat) John Hospers (Libertarian)	47,169,911 29,170,383 3,673	520 17 1
Gerald R. Ford Nelson A. Rockefeller	1974–1977 1974–1977	Succeeded to the presidency on the resignation of Richard M. Nixon.		
1976 James E. Carter Jr. Walter F. Mondale	1977–1981 1977–1981	James E. Carter Jr. (Democrat) Gerald R. Ford (Republican) Ronald W. Reagan (Independent)	40,830,763 39,147,793	297 240 1
1980 Ronald W. Reagan George H. W. Bush	1981–1989 1981–1989	Ronald W. Reagan (Republican) James E. Carter Jr. (Democrat) John B. Anderson (Independent)	43,904,153 35,483,883 5,720,060	489 49

PRESIDENT VICE PRESIDENT	TERM	CANDIDATES	POPULAR VOTE	ELEC. VOTE
1984		Ronald W. Reagan (Republican) Walter F. Mondale (Democrat)	54,455,075 37,577,185	525 13
1988 George H. W. Bush J. Danforth Quayle	1989–1993 1989–1993	George H. W. Bush (Republican) Michael S. Dukakis (Democrat) Lloyd M. Bentsen Jr. (Independent)	48,886,097 41,809,074	426 111 1
1992 William J. Clinton Albert A. Gore Jr.	1993–2001 1993–2001	William J. Clinton (Democrat) George H. W. Bush (Republican) H. Ross Perot (Independent)	44,909,326 39,103,882 19,741,657	370 168
1996		William J. Clinton (Democrat) Robert J. Dole (Republican) H. Ross Perot (Reform)	47,402,357 39,198,755 8,085,402	379 159
2000 George W. Bush Richard B. Cheney	2001–2009 2001–2009	George W. Bush (Republican) Albert A. Gore Jr. (Democrat) Ralph Nader (Green) (NOT VOTED)	50,456,141 50,996,039 2,882,807	271 266 1
2004		George W. Bush (Republican) John F. Kerry (Democrat) Ralph Nader (Independent) John Edwards (Independent)	59,459,765 55,949,407 400,706	286 251 1
2008 Barack Obama Joseph R. Biden Jr.	2009–2013 2009–2013	Barack Obama (Democrat) John McCain (Republican) Ralph Nader (Independent) (NOT YET DECIDED)	65,939,668 57,727,778 685,487	364 162 12

(as of November 11, 2008)

A HISTORY OF THE WHITE HOUSE

★ This is the oldest known photograph of the White House. It was taken by John Plumbe Jr. sometime around 1846.

*I*n March 1791, Pres. George Washington personally selected some land on the Potomac River between Virginia and Maryland for the site of the nation's new capital. A year later, as plans for the District of Columbia took shape, Washington announced a national competition to design a house for the president. It would be one of the most important buildings constructed in the District of Columbia before the government moved there in 1800.

Washington organized the contest at the suggestion of his secretary of state, Thomas Jefferson, who was an accomplished amateur architect. Jefferson himself submitted a design anonymously, but it wasn't the one chosen. Instead, the Board of Federal Commissioners selected the design submitted by James Hoban. Hoban's winning design resembled an English country house. (The other entries were mostly enlarged courthouses or awkward mansions.)

Washington's interest in the house was so great that after Hoban's victory was announced on July 17, 1792, the president began meeting regularly with him to discuss and revise the plans. Although Washington and Hoban continued to make changes until late 1793, work on the house moved ahead quickly.

★ This is the design for the president's house submitted anonymously by Thomas Jefferson.

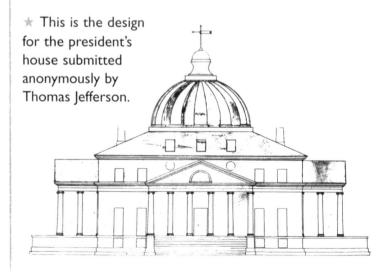

ORIGINAL DESIGN FOR THE WHITE HOUSE, BY JAMES HOBAN, 1792.
From the collection of Mr. Glenn Brown, F. A. I. A.

★ Hoban's original plans called for a mansion four times as large as the one that was built. Even so, the new house, which measured 168 feet east to west and 85 feet north to south, was larger than any house built in the United States until the 1870s.

Ships hauled sandstone for the walls up the Potomac River from the Aquia Creek quarry, which also supplied stone for the new U.S. Capitol. Construction work on the president's house began each year in mid-April and continued until mid-October, when the weather became too cold for the mortar (used between the stones) to set properly.

Ironically, the house's greatest patron, George Washington, was the only president never to live in it. When Washington left office in March 1797, the building was still just a stone shell. Another full year passed before the exterior walls received their first coat of whitewash.

The recipe for this famous paint included salt, ground rice, glue, and lime. Almost immediately, people began calling the building the "white house," but the nickname didn't appear in print until November 1810, and it wasn't until 1901 that Pres. Theodore Roosevelt officially changed its name from the Executive Mansion to the White House.

JUNE 1800 *Pres. John Adams visits Washington, D.C., to inspect the public buildings under construction. He complains that the work is proceeding too slowly and won't be finished before the government's arrival on November 1.*

After touring the partially completed president's house, Adams ordered that the nude figures carved into the mantelpieces be removed and replaced with carvings of fruit and flowers. He also ordered the installation of a bell system to summon servants. Without one, he would have had to station a servant in each room, as was the custom in large houses at the time.

In November 1800, the president arrived to find that, as he had suspected, his new house was still under construction. It smelled of plaster and wallpaper paste (made from flour and beer). Its mahogany floors were not yet finished, and the grand staircase on the north front of the house had not yet been built. Instead, wooden planks were being used to span the gap from the doorway to the crude gravel road that led up to the house.

★ Until the house's laundry yard was completed, Abigail Adams had her servants hang the first family's laundry in the unfinished East Room.

AUGUST 24
1814

After learning of the British victory at Bladensburg, First Lady Dolley Madison flees the Executive Mansion around 3:30 P.M. with the Declaration of Independence, the national seal, and her pet parrot. The invading British troops reach Washington, D.C., about 7:30 P.M.

After burning the Capitol, Rear Adm. George Cockburn and Maj. Gen. Robert Ross entered the president's house, where they found the dining room table set (the Madisons had been expecting forty guests for dinner) and food already prepared in the kitchen. In President Madison's dressing room on the second floor, the battle-stained officers paused long enough to wash up and change into some of Madison's clean underwear. Orders were then given to burn the house.

★ After the War of 1812, Pres. James Madison ordered the public buildings in Washington, including the Executive Mansion, rebuilt exactly as they had been before the British burned them.

MARCH–MAY
1833

Running water is installed in the Executive Mansion.

When the president's house was first built, it did not have running water. Instead, the water needed for drinking, cooking, and bathing was carried into the house by servants, who fetched it in buckets from two wells. These wells were located in the breezeways between the house and each of its wings. James Hoban first proposed the idea of piping running water into the Executive Mansion in 1816, but Hoban's idea was rejected as too complicated. Finally, in 1831, during the presidency of Andrew Jackson, the Committee on Public Buildings purchased a nearby spring that could be used as a source for running water, but two more years passed before work on the project actually began.

The system, as designed by Robert Leckie, was remarkably simple. Water from the spring ran downhill through iron pipes into a sand-lined fountain outside the president's house. The motion of this fountain kept the water

from stagnating. From the fountain, more iron pipes carried the water into the house. All that was needed to power the system was an attendant, who used a hand pump to create the necessary water pressure in the pipes.

Although few American homes then had running water, President Jackson was not overly impressed with the new arrangement. During the 1830s, Americans, including Jackson, still considered running water more of a luxury than a necessity, and Leckie's system was installed at the Executive Mansion more for reasons of fire safety than for the personal convenience it offered.

★ Although more than a few luxuries were added to the Executive Mansion during Andrew Jackson's administration, Old Hickory worked hard to maintain his image as a man of the people. For instance, as part of a Washington's Birthday celebration in 1837, he invited the public to the president's house to consume a huge fourteen-hundred-pound cheese that he had been given as a gift by supporters in upstate New York. In less than two hours, the cheese was gone, but the house smelled of it for several years afterward.

1840

Pres. Martin Van Buren orders construction of a centralized hot-air heating system for the Executive Mansion. This system replaces the many wood- and coal-burning fireplaces that have previously heated the house.

Unlike Andrew Jackson, Martin Van Buren made no secret of his desire for the comforts that came with urban life. His wealthy friends in New York City, for example, all had central heating in their homes, so Van Buren wanted it, too. In fact, thoughts of their comfort made his life in the drafty, chilly president's house nearly unbearable.

To bring the Executive Mansion up to date, Van Buren had workers install a large coal furnace in the basement. This furnace was then tied into a network of plaster-lined ducts that ran upstairs through the floor and walls. It produced hot air that warmed all the state rooms on the first floor. Unfortunately, the air didn't reach the second-floor family rooms, which were still heated by fireplaces.

The system was operated by a fireman, who continually fed coal into the furnace. During the winter months, he was on duty twenty-four hours a day, but he did get the summer months off.

1848

Gaslight comes to the Executive Mansion during the Polk administration.

In 1847, Congress hired the Baltimore Gas Company to build a gas plant on the Capitol grounds so that the Capitol could be lit by gaslight. Gaslight was cheaper than candles and oil lamps and also safer, because gas lamps didn't tip over and start fires. Soon, the plan was expanded to include

the Executive Mansion. Coal gas from the Capitol plant was piped along Pennsylvania Avenue to the president's house, feeding streetlights along the way.

Before gaslight, the Executive Mansion was lit primarily by oil lamps that burned foul-smelling lard (made from animal and vegetable fats). Candles were also used, but they were expensive and so usually reserved for special occasions.

Most of the formal rooms in the Executive Mansion had chandeliers that were lowered on pulleys when servants needed to light them or change their candles. In 1848, pipes and burners were attached to these chandeliers, converting them to gaslight. First Lady Sarah Polk preferred candlelight, however, and so she refused to allow the chandelier in the Blue Room to be converted. At first, people made fun of her for this, but all the teasing stopped on the night of the first gaslit state reception. No one had thought to warn the Capitol plant to stay open late. So when the gas company shut down as usual around nine o'clock, all the lights in the Executive Mansion went out—except the chandelier in the Blue Room, beneath which Mrs. Polk stood in her usual spot, bathed in candlelight.

| MAY 10 **1879** | *The National Telephone Company installs the first telephone in the president's house, mounted on a wall in the telegraph room.* |

One problem that Pres. Rutherford B. Hayes had with his new telephone was that there was almost no one to call. Because telephones were so new in 1879, very few people had one. For example, Treasury Secretary John Sherman was the only cabinet member with telephone service.

Nine months later, another invention arrived at the Executive Mansion. It was the typewriter. This machine, unlike the telephone, had an immediate impact on the way the president's staff worked. In fact, it soon revolutionized the way that the Hayes administration took care of its business. Before Hayes's purchase of the Fairbanks & Company Improved Number Two Typewriter, his clerks, who specialized in fancy penmanship, had to write out each piece of presidential correspondence. Using this new machine, however, they could type out letters quickly and get a lot more done.

★ After Pres. James Garfield's death in September 1881, the Executive Mansion was draped in black.

| JULY **1881** | *During an emergency, the Executive Mansion is outfitted with the first primitive air-conditioning.* |

After the shooting of James Garfield on July 2, 1881, well-wishers deluged the president with a variety of gifts, ranging from flowers and cards to food and clothing. Garfield's doctors, however, were particularly interested in two machines offered by their inventors. These devices were designed to cool the room in which the badly wounded president lay, suffering in Washington's humid summer heat.

Both machines used ice to cool air, which was then piped into the president's sickroom. The problem with the first machine was that

it moved the cool air too slowly through its pipes. The other machine used an innovative electric blower to move its cool air much more quickly, but the icy draft it produced made the sickroom too damp.

On the night of Friday, July 9, army doctor J. J. Woodward called Prof. Simon Newcomb to the Executive Mansion. Woodward wanted Newcomb, a scientist who worked for the navy, to analyze the two machines and come up with a solution to the dampness problem. Newcomb quickly developed a third, much larger machine that used several tons of ice but kept the dampness to a minimum. Working around the clock, he built the new air conditioner with the help of R. S. Jennings, inventor of the electric-blower machine, and John Wesley Powell, director of the U.S. Geological Survey. On Monday morning, Newcomb turned the system on, and it worked.

SEPTEMBER 1881

Pres. Chester Arthur begins the most extensive work on the Executive Mansion since it was rebuilt after the 1814 fire.

Chester Arthur, a New Yorker with elegant tastes, considered the president's house worse than shabby and below the standard of even a third-rate Manhattan hotel. During a tour of the Executive Mansion a few weeks after Garfield's death, he announced, "I will not live in a house like this." He insisted that the public rooms be completely redecorated before he moved in.

From late October 1881 until early December, Arthur personally supervised this redecoration. He inspected the work nightly and regularly made changes and additions. Then, shortly after moving into the Executive Mansion on December 7, he let it be known that he considered the work, which had cost thirty thousand dollars, only temporary.

In early 1882, he asked Congress for more money to demolish and rebuild the Executive Mansion. When preservationists blocked this plan, Arthur instead settled for another eighty thousand dollars' worth of renovations.

To perform this work, Arthur hired the most fashionable designer in New York City, Louis Comfort Tiffany, son of the famous jeweler. During the early summer of 1882, Arthur moved out of the president's house so that Tiffany's men could work freely. Castoff furnishings, which included Andrew Jackson's

★ Tiffany's work, completed for the most part by October 1882, included a dramatic stained-glass screen that was not finished until early 1883.

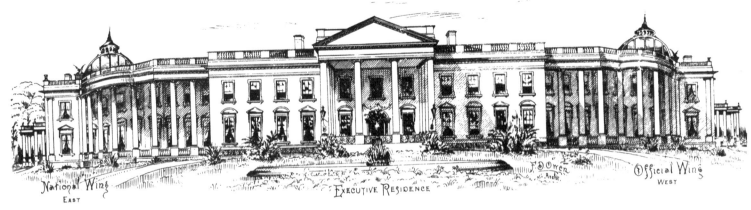

★ Mrs. Harrison's 1891 plan called for new east and west wings to be joined to the Executive Mansion by semicircular colonnades. These wings were never built.

desk and James Polk's dining room chairs, were carted off in twenty-four wagonloads and sold at auction. By the time Tiffany finished his work, the Executive Mansion was indeed the showplace that Arthur had wanted. "History remembers only a few things about [Chester Arthur]," wrote White House historian William Seale, but "one is that he had taste."

1891

Workmen cut into the walls of the Executive Mansion to wire the house for electricity.

In January 1891, Sen. Leland Stanford of California introduced a bill that called for a major reconstruction and expansion of the Executive Mansion. The plans for this work had been personally developed by First Lady Caroline Harrison. For many years, presidents and their wives had complained about the lack of space in the president's house, which had not increased in size since the time of Jefferson.

Mrs. Harrison's bold plan was turned down in March. But a few months later, she took charge of an extensive redecoration made possible by the installation of electricity in the Executive Mansion.

As a first step, workmen scraped and washed away almost all of the finish work that Tiffany had applied at President Arthur's direction. They scrubbed the walls and ceilings until the original plaster showed through. Then, electricians from the Edison General Company of New York made gouges in the walls deep enough to hold the new wiring. After the wires were installed, the walls were replastered, and the redecorating began.

Normally, the new electrical wires would have been pushed through the existing gas pipes, but President Harrison did not have much faith in the new technology. He wanted the gas lights kept as a backup system in case the electricity failed. In fact, throughout their stay in the Executive Mansion, the Harrisons refused to operate the electrical switches for fear of being shocked. Instead, servants turned the lights on and off for them.

APRIL 15 1902

First Lady Edith Roosevelt asks New York architect Charles F. McKim to provide a quick and easy solution to the problem of overcrowding in the White House. McKim tells Mrs. Roosevelt that a complete renovation will be necessary to keep the president living there.

Like many other New Yorkers, the Roosevelts considered Washington a second-rate city. Once it became obvious that the White House needed repairs, they called in Charles McKim, a founding partner of McKim, Mead & White, one of New York City's leading architectural firms. In hiring McKim, Roosevelt bypassed the Army Corps of Engineers, which normally had control over any construction undertaken at the White House.

The most pressing problem was space. The state dining room didn't seat nearly enough people, and eight rooms upstairs were not enough for the Roosevelts and their large family. On June 28, 1902, Congress appropriated $475,445 for McKim's work, which the president insisted be finished by December 1.

One of McKim's most important changes was to move the offices of the president's staff out of the White House and into another building on the grounds, known then as the Temporary Executive Offices. Removing these offices from the second floor nearly doubled the amount of living space available there. McKim's goal, which he largely achieved, was to preserve the historic White House while making it workable for a modern president.

★ This photograph shows the Oval Office under construction in 1909. The Executive Office Building in which the president works is today more commonly known as the West Wing.

MAY 1909

Needing even more office space, Pres. William Howard Taft approves plans for an addition to the Executive Office Building. These plans include the first Oval Office.

When Charles McKim built the Temporary Executive Offices on the west side of the White House in 1902, he expected the building to be just that—temporary. However, with President Roosevelt's ever-increasing need for space, the building stayed. In fact, by the time of Taft's inauguration in 1909, Congress had appropriated forty thousand more dollars to enlarge the building. McKim had moved only staff offices out of the White House, but now the president's office would be moved as well.

Taft, who had a strong personal interest in architecture, decided not to build a second floor and instead chose to extend the building southward. According to plans drawn up by Nathan C. Wyeth, the president's new office would be oval in shape, like the Blue Room in the White House. Taft first occupied the new Oval Office in October 1909.

1913

With the help of landscape architect George Burnap, First Lady Ellen Wilson designs a rose garden for the area between the White House and the West Wing.

Even in Princeton, New Jersey, a town famous for its beautiful gardens, the plantings designed by Ellen Wilson stood out. After Mrs. Wilson moved into the White House in 1913, she surveyed the southwest garden from her dressing room window. Edith Roosevelt had planted it as a colonial garden, full of old-fashioned multicolored flowers. But that sort of arrangement didn't appeal to Mrs. Wilson, whose taste was more formal. "Come and look, children," she said, pointing out the window. "It will be our rose garden."

★ This photo shows the White House on the night of December 7, 1941, after the Japanese attack on Pearl Harbor. On December 14, several government departments presented President Roosevelt with a report on how to protect the White House from enemy air attacks. The suggestions rejected by Roosevelt included camouflaging the White House, painting its windows black, and setting up machine guns on the roof. However, FDR did agree to build a bomb shelter underneath the new East Wing.

MARCH 14
1933

The New York Daily News *announces a campaign to raise money for a swimming pool at the White House. The pool will be built for Pres. Franklin Roosevelt, whose paralysis (caused by polio) is sometimes eased by exercise in a pool. Most of the donors are schoolchildren, who pool their pennies to make twenty-five- and fifty-cent contributions.*

The White House pool, built indoors in the arcade between the main house and the West Wing, was designed by Lorenzo S. Winslow, and Roosevelt liked the work so much that he later made Winslow the official White House architect. Because FDR loved building and remodeling, he and Winslow worked together on many more projects during the next twelve years, including a new East Wing built in 1942. Roosevelt and Winslow also took on numerous small projects. For example, they opened up the chimney in the diplomatic reception room so that FDR would no longer have to hold his fireside chats in front of a fake fireplace.

MAY 10
1948

Congress approves fifty thousand dollars for a structural survey of the White House, where many walls have large cracks. Just how badly the house has deteriorated becomes clear a few months later when the leg of a piano falls through the floor of Margaret Truman's sitting room.

The moment he learned of the accident involving his daughter's piano was the time when Harry Truman decided to rebuild the White House. Not surprisingly, the structural

★ Perhaps because he felt guilty about demolishing the inside of the White House, Truman refused to let construction crews touch the exterior stone walls. As a result, the crews had to take apart a bulldozer piece by piece, pass it through an opening in one wall, and reassemble it before they could dig the new basement.

survey found that much of the building's framework was unsound. The repeated drilling into Hoban's beams for gas pipes, plumbing, and electrical wires had cut some of them completely in half.

The gutting of the White House began on December 7, 1949. Truman's plan was to raze everything except the stone walls and rebuild the interior from the ground up. As a result, all that remains today of the original White House are the same walls that survived the 1814 fire. The Trumans did not move back into the rebuilt White House until March 27, 1952.

....

Half a century later, the White House remains the house that Truman rebuilt. Nearly a dozen families have lived there since the Trumans left in 1953, but none has made significant alterations.

The only noteworthy change has been the historical redecoration work begun by Mamie Eisenhower during the late 1950s and greatly expanded by Jacqueline Kennedy in 1961. These first ladies championed the idea of filling the White House with antiques from various periods in the history of the building. On February 14, 1962, Mrs. Kennedy led forty-seven million viewers on a televised tour of the White House, pointing out many of the newly acquired furnishings. It is generally agreed that her stewardship restored to the White House the sense of history that had been lost following the Truman-era reconstruction.

But the White House will surely not remain the way it is today. It will change again and adapt as new circumstances and tastes demand. Just as Teddy Roosevelt's need for a larger staff forced construction of the West Wing a century ago, some new necessity will undoubtedly force more changes. One thing will remain constant, however, and that is the White House's role as a stable, enduring symbol of the presidency.

★ The White House today.

INDEX

INDEX

INDEX

INDEX

INDEX

INDEX